MACHINE LEARNING FOR BIOMEDICAL APPLICATIONS

MACHINE LEARNING FOR BIOMEDICAL APPLICATIONS

With Scikit-Learn and PyTorch

MARIA DEPREZ
King's College London
London, United Kingdom

EMMA C. ROBINSON
King's College London
London, United Kingdom

ACADEMIC PRESS
An imprint of Elsevier

Academic Press is an imprint of Elsevier
125 London Wall, London EC2Y 5AS, United Kingdom
525 B Street, Suite 1650, San Diego, CA 92101, United States
50 Hampshire Street, 5th Floor, Cambridge, MA 02139, United States
The Boulevard, Langford Lane, Kidlington, Oxford OX5 1GB, United Kingdom

Copyright © 2024 Elsevier Ltd. All rights reserved.

MATLAB® is a trademark of The MathWorks, Inc. and is used with permission.
The MathWorks does not warrant the accuracy of the text or exercises in this book.
This book's use or discussion of MATLAB® software or related products does not constitute endorsement or sponsorship by The MathWorks of a particular pedagogical approach or particular use of the MATLAB® software.

No part of this publication may be reproduced or transmitted in any form or by any means, electronic or mechanical, including photocopying, recording, or any information storage and retrieval system, without permission in writing from the publisher. Details on how to seek permission, further information about the Publisher's permissions policies and our arrangements with organizations such as the Copyright Clearance Center and the Copyright Licensing Agency, can be found at our website: www.elsevier.com/permissions.

This book and the individual contributions contained in it are protected under copyright by the Publisher (other than as may be noted herein).

Notices

Knowledge and best practice in this field are constantly changing. As new research and experience broaden our understanding, changes in research methods, professional practices, or medical treatment may become necessary.

Practitioners and researchers must always rely on their own experience and knowledge in evaluating and using any information, methods, compounds, or experiments described herein. In using such information or methods they should be mindful of their own safety and the safety of others, including parties for whom they have a professional responsibility.

To the fullest extent of the law, neither the Publisher nor the authors, contributors, or editors, assume any liability for any injury and/or damage to persons or property as a matter of products liability, negligence or otherwise, or from any use or operation of any methods, products, instructions, or ideas contained in the material herein.

ISBN: 978-0-12-822904-0

For information on all Academic Press publications
visit our website at https://www.elsevier.com/books-and-journals

Publisher: Mara Conner
Acquisitions Editor: Tim Pitts
Editorial Project Manager: Maria Elaine D. Desamero
Production Project Manager: Anitha Sivaraj
Cover Designer: Vicky Pearson

Typeset by VTeX

Contents

Preface

Machine learning in today's world

Machine learning is the process of **teaching machines to learn patterns from data**. Machine learning-powered tools have transformed many industries and are increasingly impacting our daily lives. Machine learning underpins facial recognition technologies, online streaming, marketing and retail recommendation systems, spam filtering, Google's Text-to-Speech, finance applications including fraud detection, and autonomous driving vehicles.

Machine learning has considerable potential as **a power for good in the healthcare and biomedical field**. It can support and improve diagnosis, prognosis, and treatment planning. This is important since today's healthcare systems are facing increasing patient numbers and volumes of data. Complex pattern matching from diverse sources of data, including tissue and blood samples, clinical records, genetics, and imaging data has the potential to improve diagnosis, and even help us to understand a disease and its biological mechanisms, potentially leading to new and better treatments. For example, from MRI brain scans, machine learning can automatically predict whether a baby is preterm [18], detect lesions [31] and recognize signs of Alzheimer disease [1]. It can also identify heart failure from cardiac MRI [36], help correct breathing patterns in abdominal MRI to enable better visualization of abdominal organs [8] and diagnose cancer from histological images [14,48].

The aims of this book

As we observe the ever increasing impact of machine learning in healthcare and biomedicine, we feel that it is important to offer accessible machine learning teaching material for students interested in the biomedical field and even for biomedical experts who want to gain skills in machine learning. We aim to provide a step-by-step guided approach with just the right mix of theory and practical skills, starting with basic coding skills and leading to confident implementation of state-of-the-art deep learning at the end of the book.

Our choice to spend a considerable amount of time on classical machine learning rather than starting immediately with deep learning stems from our aim to design an effective pedagogical approach that will build understanding, knowledge and practical skills based on thorough foundations. This way, we aim to make the state-of-the art deep learning accessible even to a reader with a limited background in mathematics and computing. For example, did you know that classical logistic regression covered in Chap. 4 is a special case of the neural network classifier with a single artificial neuron? Or did you know that ensembles (Chap. 7) of deep neural networks provide not only state-of-the-art segmentation performance [24], but also alert us when the model provided an unreliable result [27]? In addition to that there are still many problems for which simpler classical machine learning models provide more efficient and reliable solutions. Nevertheless, you will also build solid skills in deep learning, and after reading this book, you will be able to choose the best approach to solve your biomedical problem.

We have selected Python, Scikit-learn [34] and Pytorch [33] for implementation of the machine learning techniques presented in this book. These practical machine learning tools are by far the most popular in both academia and industry and should be a part of the skill set of every aspiring data scientist or deep learning practitioner. We hope you enjoy reading this book and building your machine learning skills with us!

Learning objectives

On completion of this book the reader will have gained:

- a thorough grounding in the fundamental principles of machine learning and its role in biomedical data analysis;
- an in-depth theoretical understanding of a variety of machine learning techniques to ensure confident selection of suitable solutions to real-world biomedical problems;
- applied data-science skills to implement new solutions including
  - training in Python, Scikit-learn and PyTorch API
  - model selection, evaluation and troubleshooting
  - best practice implementation and generalization to new data;
- the ability to integrate theory with practice by applying machine learning techniques to authentic biomedical problems.

How to use this book

The book can be used for self study, or as a companion for a standard undergraduate or postgraduate course in machine learning. Each chapter provides theoretical insights and principles illustrated with biomedical examples implemented in Python, Scikit-learn or PyTorch. We also provide implementations from scratch for several important concepts to reinforce and deepen the understanding of the machine learning techniques. Each section of the book ends with a set of theoretical revision questions and practical exercises.

Each chapter is accompanied by interactive Python Notebooks, available from github.com/MachineLearningBiomedicalApplications/notebooks. The notebooks provide the practical tutorials, activities and skeleton code for the practical exercises given at the end of each section. Solved notebooks are also available.

The book consists of 11 chapters. The first two chapters, aimed at complete beginners, explain basic programming and machine learning concepts and provide a practical Python and Scikit-learn tutorial. Chapters 3–8 focus on in-depth description of essential machine learning techniques, including popular Support Vector Machines and Random Forests. The last three chapters introduce the state-of-the-art deep learning concepts, and provide Pytorch tutorial alongside the theoretical understanding. These final chapters are aimed at more advanced reader confident in programming and classical machine learning. We recommend the readers interested primarily in deep learning to work through the first four chapters to acquire basic machine learning knowledge (perhaps skipping kernel trick and support vector classifier) and then move straight to Chapter 9 on Deep Learning Basics. The detailed content of the individual chapters is listed below:

- *Chapter 1—Programming in Python*: This chapter provides a Python tutorial for beginners, including Python packages Numpy for linear algebra, Matplotlib for plotting and Pandas for data handling. We also introduce the reader to Python Notebooks and provide instructions for installation of the Anaconda software package.
- *Chapter 2—Machine learning basics*: We introduce basic machine learning concepts, provide Scikit-learn tutorial and teach the reader how to train and evaluate machine learning models.
- *Chapter 3—Regression*: We introduce the mathematical foundations of multivariate linear, nonlinear and penalized regression. We also demonstrate the problem of overfitting with an example of predicting the age of a baby from brain volumes extracted from MRI scans. We introduce the kernel trick. The chapter covers Ridge, Lasso and Kernel Ridge regression techniques.
- *Chapter 4—Classification*: This chapter provides the mathematical foundations of linear and nonlinear classification. We focus on two popular classifiers, Logistic Regression and the Support Vector Classifier. We introduce the kernel trick for classification. We demonstrate these concepts with an example of predicting heart failure using the features extracted from cardiac MRI, ultrasound and ECG.
- *Chapter 5—Dimensionality reduction*: We introduce linear and nonlinear dimensionality reduction methods, including Principal Component Analysis, Independent Component Analysis, and Laplacian Eigenmaps. We show how we can prevent overfitting in prediction of the age of a baby from volumes of brain structures by reducing features using PCA.
- *Chapter 6—Clustering*: In this chapter we describe key clustering algorithms for linear and nonlinear problems. The techniques covered include K-means, Gaussian Mixture Model and Spectral Clustering. We demonstrate these techniques on the segmentation of brain tissues in MRI and clustering of whole MRI images of term and preterm babies.

- *Chapter 7—Ensemble learning*: In this chapter we introduce Decision Trees. We explain concepts of bagging, boosting and bootstrapping. We introduce Random Forests and Adaboost.
- *Chapter 8—Feature selection and extraction*: In this chapter we describe key techniques to extract salient features from biomedical signals and images. We will then show how to select the best features for training machine learning models.
- *Chapter 9—Deep learning basics*: We introduce the basic building blocks of Neural Networks, including the Artificial Neuron and Single-layer Perceptron. We cover activation functions, loss functions for regression and classification, and training of single-layer neural network models. We provide a Pytorch tutorial and implement neural network regression and classification examples in Pytorch.
- *Chapter 10—Fully connected neural networks*: We describe how multiple linear layers and nonlinear activation functions are combined to create a Multilayer Perceptron, which is the simplest example of a Deep Neural Network. We cover training of Neural Networks using backpropagation. We show a complete Pytorch deep-learning solution for a real-world biomedical problem to predict age of the baby from structural brain connectivity.
- *Chapter 11—Convolutional neural networks*: In this chapter we describe a more advanced deep learning architecture, the Convolutional Neural Network. We show how to predict prematurity of a baby directly from the MRI images. Finally, we present an example of segmentation of neonatal brain MRI into anatomical regions using U-Net architecture, while demonstrating how to handle large datasets in PyTorch.

Prerequisites

This book provides self-contained material that will take a beginner in machine learning from learning the basic Python commands, through understanding of classical machine learning techniques and implementing them in Scikit-learn, all the way towards the state-of-the-art deep learning in PyTorch. However, the knowledge of basic programming principles in any programming language, as well as the basic linear algebra, calculus and probability theory, will allow the reader to fully absorb the materials in this book and gain in-depth understanding and confidence. For readers with no programming background we recommend to complement this book with one of the popular online courses or books on Python for beginners.

Acknowledgments

We would like to thank the following people for their contribution to the development of this book:

- Our colleagues at King's College London: Dr. Andrew King for recommending us for writing this book and providing cardiac MRI datasets; Prof. Julia Schnabel who codesigned with us the machine learning module on which this book is based; Dr. Esther Puyol Anton, Dr. James Clough, Dr. Irina Grigorescu, Dr. Thomas Varsavsky, Dr. Cher Bass and Dr. Abdulah Fawaz for contributing practical machine learning examples.
- Developing Human Connective Project for providing the neonatal brain MRI dataset and segmentations.
- Our Biomedical Engineering and Healthcare Technologies students at King's College London who have taken our machine learning modules over the past few years and provided us with valuable feedback.
- The publishers, Elsevier: Tim Pitts for prompting us to write this book, Rachel Pomery and Maria Elaine D. Desamero for managing the process, and for their patience when we had to delay writing due to the coronavirus pandemic.
- Our families for patience and support while we wrote this book.

CHAPTER 1

Programming in Python

The purpose of this chapter is to introduce the key features of Python coding that are needed to follow the content of this book. While MATLAB® remains the language of choice for most biomedical engineers, we insist on training in Python because it is increasingly the dominant language of data science and machine learning. As well as being arguably better resourced and supported for such problems, Python is open-source, and forms the backbone of Pytorch and Tensorflow, the most commonly used deep learning libraries. This chapter assumes basic knowledge of coding, and focuses predominantly on core Python functionality and syntax. However, many of the most powerful features of Python involve importing external libraries. Here, we introduce NumPy [32], a package that provides support for multidimensional array manipulation and linear algebra. Further details of other important packages (such as Scikit Learn [34] for machine learning) will be covered in subsequent chapters.

1.1. Getting started

Python is what is referred to as a high-level, interpreted language. This means that it has been designed to be easy to read and use, and that, like MATLAB [30], it is possible to type directly into a Python console and run code immediately without having to compile it.

1.1.1 Install

Arguably the easiest way to get up and running with Python is to install the Anaconda package.[1] This performs a comprehensive installation of all the scientific and data science libraries required by this book, packaged together with multiple coding environments, including console and web-based solutions. Clear instructions on how to download and install for your operating system are available on the Anaconda website.[2]

1.1.2 Coding in an IDE

The best place to start coding Python is through using an Integrated Development environment (or IDE). These enable (line-by-line) running of code in the console, the running and developing of Python scripts in the editor, quality checking of variables in the variable explorer, debugging and plotting. There are many excellent, open-source

[1] https://www.anaconda.com/.

[2] https://docs.anaconda.com/anaconda/install/.

Machine Learning for Biomedical Applications
https://doi.org/10.1016/B978-0-12-822904-0.00006-6
Copyright © 2024 Elsevier Ltd.
All rights reserved.

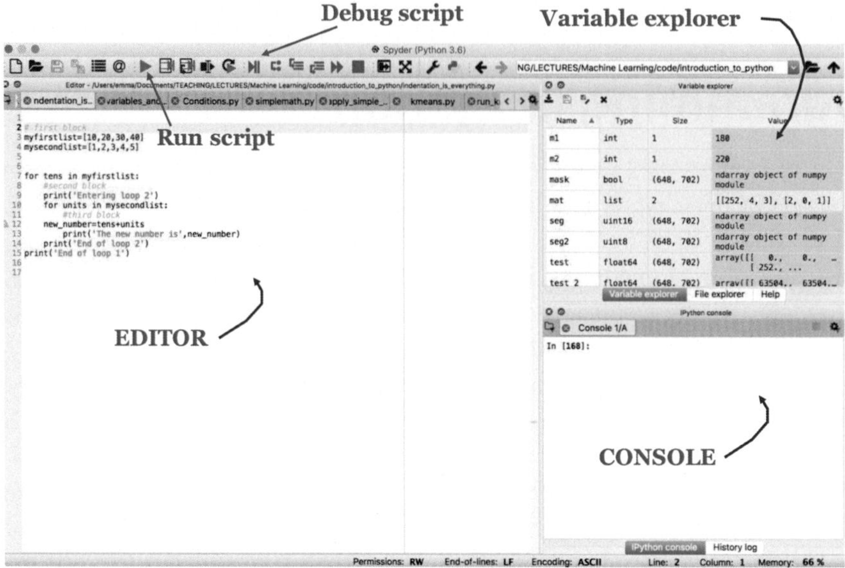

Figure 1.1 The Spyder IDE.

IDEs available, but for this book we recommend Spyder[3] because this closely resembles the MATLAB console. Spyder can be accessed for free with Anaconda, either through the Anaconda navigator, or (Linux or macOS) terminal, by typing the application name. An example of what to expect from this IDE is shown in Fig. 1.1.

1.1.3 Coding in a web browser

Jupyter[4] notebooks and Google Colab[5] present alternatives to IDEs, supporting code to be run in interactive web-based environments. Neither system is exclusive to Python, but regardless offer the ability to run Python from a browser, which runs a Python kernel in the background. Both systems offer the considerable advantage of being able to interleave code with text (see Fig. 1.2). The main difference is that Jupyter notebooks run code on the local CPU, whereas Colab notebooks are run in the cloud, offering limited GPU support for free (something that may become important for the deep learning chapters). Note that Jupyter notebooks come installed with Anaconda, whereas Colab is accessed through a Google account. For those with no access to Google, alternative cloud services include Kaggle Notebooks[6] and gradient by Paperspace.[7]

[3] https://www.spyder-ide.org/.
[4] https://jupyter.org/.
[5] https://colab.research.google.com/.
[6] https://www.kaggle.com/kernels.
[7] https://gradient.paperspace.com/notebooks.

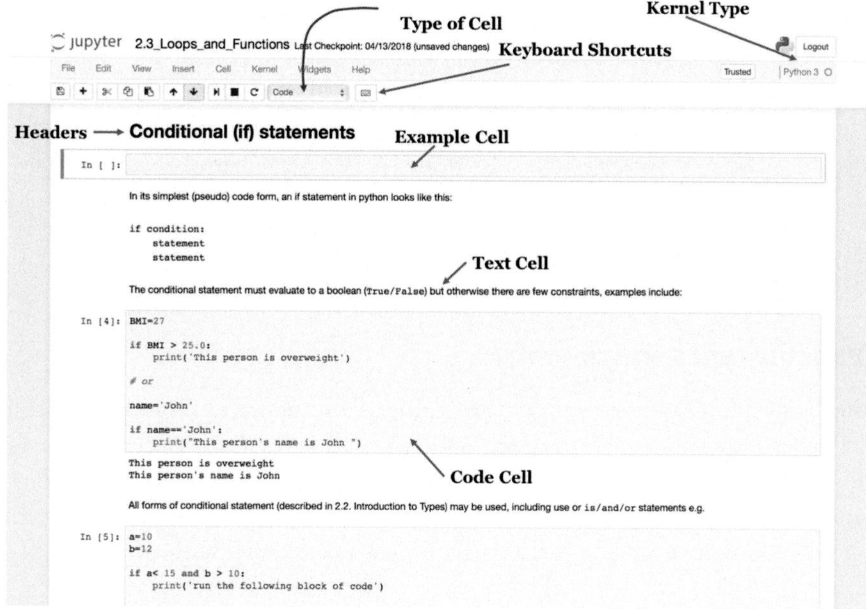

Figure 1.2 The Jupyter notebook environment.

1.1.4 Writing your first Python program

The simplicity of Python is never better demonstrated than through the well-known 'Hello World' example. Specifically, to print 'Hello World' in Python all you need is the print function:

```
print("Hello World")
```

This can be entered into a console and run directly, or saved in a `hello_word.py` file for running from an editor or command line. By contrast, performing the same action in C++, requires several more lines of code, and importing standard libraries:

```
# include <iostream>
using namespace std;


int main()
{
    cout << "Hello, World!";
    return 0;
}
```

More fundamentally, C++ code will not run until it has been compiled.

1.1.5 Commenting

Finally, before moving onto discussions of specific Python syntax, the final thing to emphasize is the importance of commenting on code so that others can better read and use it. In Python comments are indicated by the `#`:

```
# this is a code comment
```

These will appear throughout this book and the supporting notebooks to guide you through the code.

1.2. Variable types and operators

In Python, as with all programming, data typing is an important concept. Variables of different types have different properties, and each has its own set of functions, which do different things. In this section we will cover simple data types (numbers, strings and Booleans), as well as more complex data structures (lists, tuples and dictionaries). At the same time we look at a range of arithmetic (+, −, ÷, ×) and Boolean (`and`, `or`, `not`) operators.

1.2.1 Simple variable types

Numeric

The first group of variables we consider is numeric data types. Python supports three types of numbers: integers (or whole numbers), floats (decimal numbers) and complex numbers. An example of assigning a variable an integer value is:

```
myint = 5
```

Examples of float declarations are:

```
myfloat1=12.1
# casting an integer type as float
myfloat2=float(myint)
```

To then verify what type a variable has, you can use the function `type` (e.g., `type(myint)`. Complex numbers will not be used in this course.

Strings

Character strings are defined either with a single quote or a double quotes:

```
string1="a string"
string2='another string'
string2="Emma's string"
```

where, if you need a apostrophe inside, you must use double quotes on the outside.

Format strings

In some cases we will use printed statements with formatted output using the `str.format` method for strings. Using this formulation, it is possible to cast different data types within the string, whilst also truncating the precision of floats, for example

```
print('var 1: {1}, var 2 {0}'.format('dog','cat'))
print('Pi {}'.format(3.14159))
```

will return

```
var 1: cat, var 2 dog
Pi 3.14159
```

with general syntax

```
[argument]:[width][.precision]type
```

such that the example

```
print('Pi is {0:8.2f}'.format(3.14159, 2.125))
```

returns

```
Pi is     3.14,
```

in other words, pi to two decimal laces preceded by fives spaces; since, given the format placeholder `{0:8.2f}`: `0` selects the argument relative to its position in the format string, i.e. 3.14159 not 2.125; `8` is the formatted width (where if the width is longer than the number white space is added in front); `2` is the number of decimal places; and `f` is the (float) type. Examples of other common types include `d` (signed integer) and `s` (string) type.

Booleans

Booleans represent binary `True` or `False` statements. They may be returned from the `bool(...)` function or output from Boolean operators (below). For the purpose of control flow (i.e. if) statements (section), the following objects would be considered as False:

- integer or float zero (i.e. `0` or `0.0`)
- `None` statement
- empty lists, dictionaries, tuples, arrays etc. (e.g., `(),[],{}`)

Every other output would be considered `True`.

Dynamic typing

Python variables are not "statically typed". This means you do not need to declare variables before using them, nor declare their type. Every variable in Python is an object, for example, you can declare simple variables within a print statement, and do math on them without first declaring their type, e.g.,

```
my_var=5+2.3
print("the sum of 5 and 2.3 is {}".format(my_var))
```

is the same as

```
print("the sum of 5 and 2.3 is {}".format(5+2.3))
```

1.2.2 Grouping structures

In addition to simple data types, Python provides a range of different structures for storing groups of variables. The key types (ignoring arrays and matrices, for the time being) are lists, tuples and dictionaries. The most important differences to be aware of when reviewing these types of structures is whether they store objects in order, and whether they are mutable.

Mutable and immutable objects

The definition of a mutable object is one that may be changed after creation. All built-in simple Python variable types (int, float, strings, Booleans) are immutable and therefore fixed. This means that, when a different value is assigned to a previously created variable, e.g.,

```
my_var=5
my_var=7
```

the location in memory of these two instances of `my_var` will change, indicating that an entirely new variable has been created. This can be verified by running `id(my_var)` after each line of code.

For group structures, the impact of this property is more noticeable since an attempt to assign a new variable to any location in an immutable group structure, e.g.,

```
my_tuple=(1,2,3)
# attempt to change the first item
my_tuple[0]=4
```

will cause Python to throw an error. The same thing happens if you try to assign a new character to a location in an existing string.

There are, however, many occasions in which changing a data structure can be useful. For example, one can imagine creating a database of patient information where the contact information might change. For these occasions, we have mutable objects: dictionaries and lists.

Lists

A list is an ordered collection of objects. These elements don't have to be of the same type but can be an arbitrary mixture of numbers, strings, or other types of objects.

```
# An empty list
emptylist=[]
#A list of integers
integerlist=[1,2,3,4,5,6]
#A list of strings
stringlist=['string1', 'string2', 'string3']
#A list of mixed data types
mixedlist=[10, "some string", 4.2, 2, 'some other string']
# a 'nested' list (of lists)
```

A list may also contain other lists as sublists, known as nested lists:

```
nestedlist=[['dog','cat','pig'], [1,2,3 ,4], [10, "some string", 4.2, 2,
    'some other string'] ]
```

where there is no requirement for these to contain lists all of the same length. Lists are mutable objects and so may be appended at run time:

```
mixedlist.append('another variable')
```

Or new objects may be inserted into the center of a list, at any time:

```
mixedlist.insert(2,'inserted variable')
```

Tuples

Tuples are immutable lists. They are defined analogously to lists, except that the set of elements is enclosed in parentheses instead of square brackets, and none of the elements of the Tuple may be changed after creation:

```
#empty tuple (parenthesis notation)
mytuple=()
# a mixed tuple
mytuple=(10,"Dog's", 4.2)
```

Use of tuples can be advantageous because they are faster to index than lists. As such, they can be useful in cases where program runtime is important and you know you want to permanently fix the items in that list.

Dictionaries

Dictionaries differ from tuples and lists in that the objects stored have no order. Instead, objects are indexed using keys. Dictionaries are defined using curly bracket notation:

```
#empty dictionary
mydict={}
```

and may be filled one entry at a time:

```
#define one key pair look up at a time
mydict['Course Name']='Machine Learning' #here key is 'Course Name' (in
    square brackets) and object is 'Machine Learning')
mydict['Department']="biomedical engineering"
mydict['Year']=2021
mydict['Number of students']=67
```

or all at once using in-line notation, e.g., `key1:object1,...`:

```
# inline definition
mydict_inline={'Course Name': 'Machine Learning', 'Department': "
    biomedical engineering", 'Year': 2021, 'Number of students': 67}
```

Like lists, dictionaries are mutable, meaning that objects can be changed, for example, if a new student joined after the course started:

```
# incrementing dictionary entry
mydict['Number of students']=68
```

or, new keys may be added at a later time, e.g.,

```
# adding new dictionary entry
mydict['Student Satisfaction Score']=5
```

Keys may be **any immutable type** (this includes tuples):

```
# string as key (most common)
mydict['key']='val1'
#int and float as keys
mydict[5]='val2'
mydict[3.2413]='val3'
#tuple as keys
mydict[(1,2,3)]='val4'
```

However, since dictionaries are unordered, it most often makes sense to use strings. Objects may be **any type**, including lists or other dictionaries,

```
# adding a list as new dictionary entry
mydict['student ids']=['id00001','id00006','id00015']
```

Dictionary elements may be deleted using `del mydict[key]`. Any attempt to index a key that does not exist will raise a `KeyError`.

1.2.3 Operators

So, now that we know what classes of variable we have to play with, what types of operation can we perform on them? In this section, we will look at simple mathematical and Boolean operators.

Math operators

The basic math operators are: addition (+), subtraction (-), multiplication (*) and division (/). The modulus operator (%) returns the integer remainder following division, for example: for a=9 and b=5, a%b=4. Using * twice (**) results in the power operator, e.g., a**b=59049. And the // operator means whole division: a//b=1.

Note that math operators also work on strings, lists, and dictionaries, for example, given two strings: string1='hello' and string2='5', adding (string3=string1+string2) returns 'hello5', multiplying (string4=string1*3) returns 'hellohellohello'. The same operations may be applied to lists as:

```
list1=[1,2,3,4]
list2=[5,6,7,8]
list3=list1+list2
#or
list1+=list2
```

where +=, -=, *= operators are simplifying operations that reduce the amount code needed, for a+=b is equivalent to a=a+b. For mutable objects such as lists, this can be used to append additional items to an existing list. Whereas, for immutable numeric and string variables, the output will be a new variable in memory.

Boolean operators

In contrast to math operators, Boolean operations always return either True or False. They are often used to define if and while control-flow statements (covered in Sect. 1.4). Examples include:

- exactly equals to: ==
- not equal to: !=
- inverse/opposite: not
- object identity: is or is not
- comparisons: greater than >, less than <, greater than or equal to >=, less than or equal to <=
- containment: in or not in

Some examples of the use of Booleans on numeric types include:

```
a=10
print(a==10)
print(a<12)
print(a>20)
```

Using not before a Boolean expression inverts it:

```
a=10
b=12
print(not a==b)
```

To check whether two variables point to the same object, use `is` or `is not`. These differ from `==` and `!=` in that they are checking whether the objects themselves are identical (in memory), as opposed to whether just their *values* are identical. This functionality is best demonstrated using lists:

```
list_a=[1,2,3]
list_b=list_a
```

Here, `list_a` is copied to `list_b`, so they point to the same memory location (and therefore are the same object). If a new `list_c` is subsequently created with the same values as `list_a`, it may be equivalent in value but will not point to the same location in memory:

```
list_c=[1,2,3]
# will return True
print(list_a is list_b)
# will return false
print(list_a is list_c)
```

To check whether an item is in a list, use `in` or `not in`:

```
my_list=[1,2,3,4]
#returns False
print(5 in my_list)
```

Finally, two conditional statements can be considered concurrently with `and`/`or` statements, where, for `and`, both statements must be true for the chained condition to return `True`; whereas, for `or`, only one need be true for the combination to return `True`, e.g.,

```
a=10
b=12
# returns False
print(a == b)
#returns False
print(a< 15 and b < 10)
# returns True
print (a < 15 or b < 10)
```

1.2.4 Exercises

1. Open an IDE and create a) an integer; b) a float with two decimal places; c) a string. Cast the float as an integer and print it out.[8]

[8] The code, exercises and solutions are available from github.com/MachineLearningBiomedicalApplications/notebooks.

2. Use a format string to encapsulate a numeric type within a string.
3. Create a dictionary that translates English to French (or any other language); what other uses for dictionaries can you think of?
   - try indexing dictionary entries with an index; what happens?
   - try accessing different objects from their dictionary keys
   - what happens if you mistype a key or use one that doesn't exist?
4. What is meant by an immutable object? Which Python objects are immutable?
5. Attempt various mathematical operations and print out the answers. Use all the following symbols: `+`, `-`, `*`, `/`, `//`, `%`, `**`. Try also using mathematical operators to combine strings.
6. For variables: `a=5`, `b=5`, evaluate the following with Boolean operations:
   - a is exactly equal to b;
   - twice a is exactly equal to b;
   - a is greater than b;
   - a is b.

1.3. Indexing and slicing

Lists, tuples, and strings are what as known as sequential data types. This means that it is possible to iterate over these objects in order, index individual elements, and slice out variables within a range.

Unlike MATLAB, Python objects are indexed from 0 not 1. Accordingly, the integer corresponding to the second index (third element) of `integerlist` is indexed as `integerlist[2]` and returns the value 3. The principle is exactly the same for strings, for example, the sixth index of `teststr='Hello World'` (`teststr[6]`) returns 'W' since it also counts the space. Indexing may also be done in reverse (counting from the end of the object rather than the beginning), e.g., `integerlist[-1]` would return 6.

```
Index     0 1 2 3 4 5
          ↑ ↑ ↑ ↑ ↑ ↑
integerlist=[1,2,3,4,5,6] #A list of integers
```

It is also possible to slice different ranges, or groups, of elements from lists (strings or tuples) using syntax `my_list[start:stop:step]`, where it is important to note that **slice indexing takes all elements up to, but not including, the last index**. For example, slicing the first five values from `integerlist` can be achieved using syntax `integerlist[:5]`. To return the middle two (of six) elements use: `integerlist[2:4]`. Alternatively, we can use : after the number to slice from the fifth element to the end: `integerlist[4:]`. Similarly to indexing, negative numbers may be used to define the range relative to the end of the array, for example, slicing from the fourth to the penultimate (fifth) as shown here: `integerlist[3:-1]`. Incidentally, there is no fixed requirement for the slice to take every element within a range. Another option is to use the step notation, for example, to select every second item in a range: `integerlist[0:5:2]`.

1.4. Control flow

Like many coding languages, Python offers a range of various types of statements which direct the flow of code, allowing loops, breaks, and conditional statements. In this book we consider `if`, `for`, and `while` statements, but you may also come across `try` statements (which specify exception handlers and/or cleanup code) or `with` statements (which allow execution of initialization and finalization code, prior to running a code block). All control flow statements share a common form. In pseudocode this is:

```
main body of code

control flow (if/for/while/try/with) statement :
    statement
    statement

return to main body of code
```

The most essential features of this structure are:

1. ensure a colon is placed at the end of the conditional statement;
2. follow control flow statements by indented lines.

In Python, the flow of code is almost entirely controlled through code indentation (see Fig. 1.3). These signifies which blocks of code belong to which flow statements. To break out of a loop, therefore, all that is needed is to revert the code back inline with the previous block of code. This is unlike MATLAB which uses `end` statements and C/C++ which contains all control flow within parentheses.

1.4.1 Exercises

1. In your IDE create the list:[9] `vowels=['a', 'b','c','d', 'e']`
   - How would you index the letter ‘d’?;
   - Slice from ‘b’ to ‘d’ inclusive;
   - Append the list with the letter ‘f’.
2. What is the output of the following code?

```
b = "Introduction to Python"
print(b[3:7])
```

[9] The code, exercises and solutions are available from github.com/MachineLearningBiomedicalApplications/notebooks.

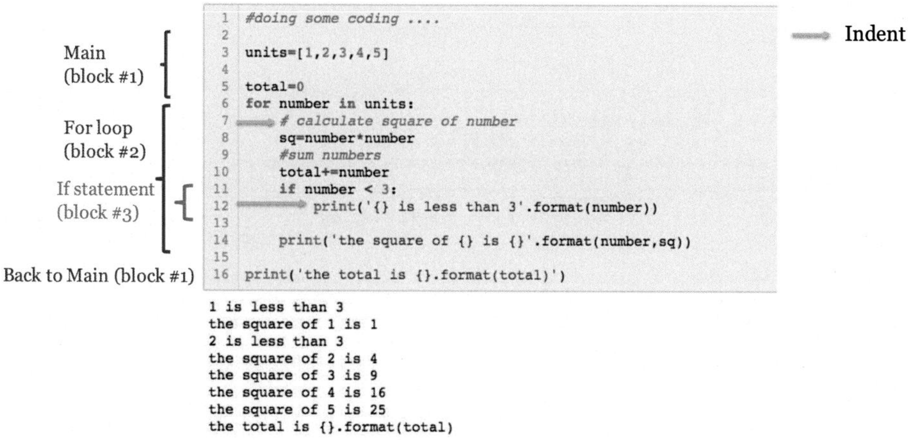

Main (block #1)

For loop (block #2)

If statement (block #3)

Back to Main (block #1)

Indent

```
#doing some coding ....

units=[1,2,3,4,5]

total=0
for number in units:
    # calculate square of number
    sq=number*number
    #sum numbers
    total+=number
    if number < 3:
        print('{} is less than 3'.format(number))

    print('the square of {} is {}'.format(number,sq))

print('the total is {}.format(total)')
```

```
1 is less than 3
the square of 1 is 1
2 is less than 3
the square of 2 is 4
the square of 3 is 9
the square of 4 is 16
the square of 5 is 25
the total is {}.format(total)
```

Figure 1.3 Using indentation to control flow.

3. What is wrong with this code?

```
a = "Introduction to Python"
 a[2]='b'
```

1.4.2 Debugging

Exploring indentation errors provides a useful framework with which to highlight Python exception handling and error messaging since, if the previous code example had contained errors been up, accidentally deleting the indentation in the middle of the loop, the Python interpreter would have thrown an `IndentationError` error (Fig. 1.4) highlighting the offending line, and the location within that line using the ^ symbol. In general, Python error messages should be fairly self-explanatory. However, sometimes you will come up against ones you do not understand. In those circumstances, it is advisable to term to online support forums such as Stack Overflow.[10]

1.5. Conditional (if) statements

Starting with `if`, let's look at the structure of each different type of control flow in turn. In pseudocode, a Python `if` statement takes the following general form:

```
if condition:
    statement
    statement
```

[10] https://stackoverflow.com/.

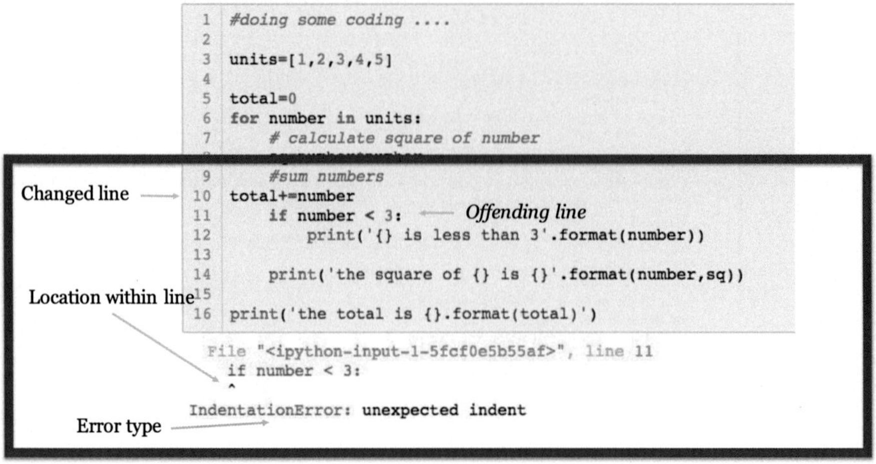

```
#doing some coding ....

units=[1,2,3,4,5]

total=0
for number in units:
    # calculate square of number

    #sum numbers
total+=number
    if number < 3:
        print('{} is less than 3'.format(number))

    print('the square of {} is {}'.format(number,sq))

print('the total is {}.format(total)')
```

```
File "<ipython-input-1-5fcf0e5b55af>", line 11
  if number < 3:
  ^
IndentationError: unexpected indent
```

Figure 1.4 Debugging.

where the conditional statement must evaluate to a Boolean (True/False), but otherwise there are few constraints. Some examples include:

```
BMI=27

if BMI > 25.0:
    print('This person is overweight')
```

or

```
name='John'

if name=='John':
     print("This person's name is John ")
```

All forms of conditional statement (described in Sect. 1.2.3 'Boolean operators') may be used, including the use of `is`. It is also possible to use combinations of conditions, through the use of `and` or `or`:

```
a=10
b=12

if a< 15 and b > 10:
     print('run the following block of code')
```

The `in` operator can also be used to check if a specified object exists within an iterable object container, such as a list:

```
course = "physics"
if course in ["physics", "biology", "chemistry"]:
        print("This course is available")
```

Further, a series of `if` statements can be chained together within `if/else` statements, following the following general structure:

```
BMI=20

if BMI <= 18.5:
     print('This person is underweight')
elif BMI > 18.5 and BMI <=25.0:
     print('This person has normal weight')
elif BMI > 25.0 and BMI <=30.0 :
     print('This person is overweight')
else:
     print('This person is obese')
```

Here, `if` and `else` statements bookmark the beginning and end, and `elif` (else if) conditions are found in the center.

1.6. For statements

For loops iterate over a given sequence, for example, as given by a list:

```
mylist=[10,20,30,40,50]

for item in mylist:
     print(item)
```

For numeric ranges, Python provides function `range(start,end,increment)`:

```
for item in range(0,10,2):
     print(item)
```

where the previous loop would iterate over all values from 0, in steps of 2, up to but not including 10. It is also possible to have multiple `for` loops nested within each other, for example

```
adj = ["red", "big", "fast"]
fruits = ["car", "dog", "bike"]

# for every item in the 'adj' list
for x in adj:
     #loop over the fruits list
```

```
    for y in fruits:
        print(x, y)
```

In some cases you might need both the list item and the index of the loop. In those circumstances it is possible to use enumerate:

```
mylist=['one','two','three','four','five']

for index,item in enumerate(mylist):
    print(index,item)
```

1.6.1 While statements

While loops are similar to if statements in that they evaluate a condition:

```
while condition:
    statement
    statement
```

However, for a while statement, the loop will continue until the condition has been met. In other words, it is important to update the loop variable (or otherwise be sure the condition will be met), else it will carry on indefinitely, e.g.,

```
# we initialize variable count and loop over using a while statement
count = 0
while count < 5:
    print(count)
    #Here count is updated each time
    count += 1
```

1.6.2 Break and continue statements

In some circumstances you may need the option to break out of a loop or skip certain elements of a loop. This can be achieved with: 1) break and 2) continue statements. Here, break will cause a loop to terminate if a certain condition is met:

```
mylist=['Alice', 'Fred', 'Bob', 'John', 'Steve']

for index,item in enumerate(mylist):
    print(item)
    if item=='John':
        break
```

For example, this code would loop through mylist until it reaches the string 'John', where it will stop, break out of the loop and return to the main body of code, whereas, continue will simply skip loop variables that meet certain conditions:

```
for index,item in enumerate(mylist):
    if item=='John':
        continue
```

which would cause the loop to skip over the entry for 'John'.

1.6.3 Looping over dictionaries

So, what do we do when we don't have a sequential data object but instead have a dictionary? Since dictionaries are unordered, it is impossible to iterate through them sequentially by index. Specifically, the following code example would throw an error:

```
mydict={}
mydict['Name']='Dave'
mydict['Age']=23
mydict['job']='Lecturer'
mydict['height']=190
mydict['BMI']=25

for i in range(5):
    print(mydict[i])
```

However, the dictionary class instead provides iterator functions `keys()` and `items()`. For example, the `keys()` iterator supports looping through all dictionary keys, in principle allowing some operation to be performed on each one. In the following code snippet, an `if` condition is simply used to search for a specific key and print:

```
for k in mydict.keys():
    if k=='height':
        print("The person's height is:", mydict[k])
        break
```

Note that it is so common to loop over keys in a dictionary that a shorthand call is also available (that omits explicitly stating the keys method):

```
for k in mydict:
    print(k)
```

Using `items`, it is possible to simultaneously access both key and and value:

```
for k,v in mydict.items():
    print(k,v)
```

1.6.4 List comprehensions

One other example of how we can write in shorthand is list comprehensions. These collapse all the lines of code from a for loop (with just one if statement, and a single output expression) into a single line appended at each end with a square bracket

```
a=[]

for i in range(5):
    if i%2==0:
        a.append('num{}'.format(i))
```

Thus, for the previous list, which prints out numbers in the range 0 to 4 if they are exactly divisible by 2 (and concatenates to the `'num'` string), using a list comprehension, the code may be written in a single line as

```
b=['num{}'.format(i) for i in range(5) if i%2==0]
```

Note that the `if` statement is not a necessary component, so you can have list comprehensions with just `for` loops.

1.6.5 Exercises

1. Write a loop that prints out all numbers in the range 0 to 1000 that are divisible by 3 and 5.
2. Write a function to multiply all numbers in a list.
3. Write a Python function that checks whether a number (e.g., 71) is prime or not.
4. List comprehensions: What will be the output of the following Python code snippet?

```
my_string='123omdkapmfdnfosmxc!!aaaaa'
k = [print(i) for i in my_string if i not in "aeiou"]
```

5. Dictionary iterators: What is the output of the following lines of code?

```
Fr_En = {"parc":"park", "maison":"house"}
En_Fr = {}
En_Fr["park"] = "parc"
En_Fr["house"] = "maison"
En_Fr["park"] = "jardin"

for key in Fr_En.keys():
print(En_Fr[Fr_En[key]])
```

1.7. Functions

Functions allow compact structuring of sections of code that are intended to be used more than once in a program (or indeed multiple programs). A function in Python is defined by a def statement. In pseudocode, the general syntax looks like this:

```
def myfunction(arg1,arg2,arg3):

    body of code to be repeated

    return someval1, someval2
```

which takes input arguments arg1, arg2, and arg3, performs operation(s), and returns outputs variables someval1 and someval2. As with control flow statements, the function definition is *followed by a colon*, and all code within the function is *indented* relative to the def statement. For simple functions the function can returned in one line, e.g.,

```
def sum(x,y):
    return x+y
```

It is also possible to supply optional input arguments with default values, e.g., z in this example:

```
def sum2(x,y,z=0):
    return x+y+z
```

whereby, it is possible to call the function either with, or without, z:

```
a=5; b=10; c=20

sum_of_a_and_b=sum2(a,b)
sum_of_a_b_and_c=sum2(a,b,c)
```

Alternatively, it is possible to specify which exact optional arguments are required through the use of keywords (referencing the specific argument name in the function call):

```
def sum3(x, y, z1=0, z2=0):
    return x - y + z1 - z2

# apply function

a=5; b=10; c=20; d=30

a_minus_b=sum3(12,4)
a_minus_b_minus_d=sum3(42,15,z2=10)
a_minus_b_plusc_minus_d=sum3(42,15,z1=20, z2=10)
```

In all cases the function may take 0 or more input arguments, and may return 0 or more output arguments. For functions where it is not possible to prescribe an exact number of input arguments, arbitrary numbers may be defined using an asterisk:

```
def arbitary_sum(*x):
    mysum=0
    for val in x:
        mysum+=val
    return mysum

mylist=[1,2,3,4,5]

sumlist1=arbitary_sum(*mylist)
# returns same result as
sumlist2=arbitary_sum(1,2,3,4,5)
```

1.7.1 Doc strings

When writing code that includes functions, it is good practice to document the purpose of the function using a 'doc' string after the function definition, indicated by triple quotes.

```
def arbitary_sum(*x):
    ''' This function adds and arbitrary number of input arguments

    input args:
        *x: a list or tuple containing numbers to be summed

    returns:
        mysum: result of adding all input arguments
    '''

    mysum=0
    for val in x:
        mysum+=val
    return mysum
```

1.7.2 Passing by object

In C++ you may have heard the terms 'pass by value' or 'pass by reference' with respect to how arguments are passed to functions. This references how variables are either copied to a new place in memory when they are passed to a function (pass by value) or whether their memory address is passed and shared with the function argument (pass by reference). In the former case, when the argument is changed within the function, the original variable remains unchanged. In the latter case, changing the value of the input argument will also change the value of the original variable.

In Python arguments are strictly 'passed by object', which means that what happens to the variable within a function will depend on whether it is mutable or immutable. For immutable types (ints, floats, tuples, strings) the objects are immutable, hence they cannot be changed at any point whether they are in a function, or in the main body of code. Hence, in effect they will always be passed 'by value'. On the other hand if objects are mutable (lists, dictionaries) then the original values (in the main code body) can and will be changed if the variable is changed in place, for example:

```
def passing_by_object2(names):
    # changed in place using the += operator;
    names += ["Emma", "Maria"]
```

This will also occur if you change (mutate) the objects a container (such as a dictionary/list) points to. Therefore, should you want the original object not to be modified, it is important to assign to a new variable inside the body of the code (even if this has the same name) e.g.,

```
def passing_by_object2(names):
    names = names + ["Emma", "Maria"]
```

By contrast, if this mutating behavior is desired, but perhaps you wish to keep a copy of the original object (during debugging for example), then this can be achieved by making a copy of the original object using the copy module:

```
import copy
mylist_copy=copy.deepcopy(mylist)
```

where modules will be specifically discussed in the next section.

1.7.3 Exercises

1. Write a Python function to multiply all the numbers in a list and return the total.[11]
2. Write a function that takes in a list and returns a new list, generated from the input list by randomly sampling with replacement (hint see `np.choice`
   - allow the user to define the length of the new array;
   - modify the code to generate a set of new lists.

[11] The code, exercises and solutions are available from github.com/MachineLearningBiomedicalApplications/notebooks.

3. What is the output of the following lines of code?

```
def select(aList):
    result = aList[0]
    for i in range(len(aList)):
        if aList[i] < result and aList[i] % 2 != 0:
            result = aList[i]
    return result

myList = [6, -5, 7, 4, -8]

print(select(myList))
```

1.8. Modules, packages, and classes

When working with Python interactively, as we have been doing thus far, all functions that we define are available only within that notebook. This would also be the case if we were to write a simple script within an IDE. Thus, in order to write more complex programs, it is important to be able to write code in carefully organized and structured files that can then be accessed from the main program. To support this, Python has a way to put definitions in a file and use them in a script or in an interactive instance. This type of file is called a module. Groups of related modules can be used to create packages. As Python is open source and utilized by broad communities in research and industry, a wide variety of advanced and well-documented/supported packages for machine learning and statistics exist (discussed in Sect. 1.8.3). There is also scope to create and use your own modules. Let's have a first look at this next.

1.8.1 Python scripts

In Python all code (outside of notebooks) is saved within .py files. These may be used either to encapsulate whole modules and classes, or to store a script, which imports external modules and applies them to some data. Such scripts may either be run interactively (i.e., line by line using the editor window of an IDE) or directly by calling Python from the command line as:

```
python myscript.py
```

1.8.2 Modules

A module is a .py file that contains a collection of functions designed to perform a set of related tasks. For example, we might consider creating a module simplemath.py and filling it with basic math functions:

```
def mysum(x,y):
    return x+y

def mult(x,y):
    return x*y

def divide(x,y):
    return x/y
```

This example is, of course, rather redundant but serves as a simple explanation since we might now imagine calling these functions in a separate Python script:

```
import simplemath as sm # load module

# define variables
x=2; y=5

print('output sum of x and y:', sm.mysum(x,y))
print('output product:', sm.mult(x,y))
print('output quotient:', sm.divide(x,y))
```

Note how the module functions are made available to *any* script by performing an `import`. Here, the name of the module must be kept exactly as it was defined in the .py file the code was stored in. Once imported, functions from the module may then be called simply by prefixing the function name, with the name given to the module when it is imported (here `sm`). It is also possible to just load selective functions from a module using the `from` syntax:

```
from simplemath import divide

print('output sum of x/y:', divide(x,y))
```

Standard modules

Certain modules come packaged with Python as standard.[12] Useful examples include: `copy`, mentioned previously as a means for making copies of variables in memory; `os`, which supports interactions with the operating system (allowing definition of file paths, and changing of the current working directory). Also, `sys`, which allows for the addition or removal of paths from the Python search path; this is therefore useful when you need to add the location of novel user-designed modules:

[12] https://docs.python.org/3/tutorial/stdlib.html.

```
import sys
sys.path.append('/some/path/')
```

Finally, `math` is Python's standard math module, including amongst other functions, operations for rounding up or down:

```
import math
x=2.2 ; y=4

round_up=math.ceil(x)
round_up=math.floor(x)
```

1.8.3 Packages

Python packages are collections of related classes and modules designed to solve some broad category of tasks. A wide variety of externally supported and well-documented packages exist to meet a variety of advanced programming requirements. Examples of some that will be key to this module include:

- NumPy [32][13]—a package for scientific computing with functionality for fast manipulation of arrays, and powerful numerical computing tools [19];
- Matplotlib [20][14]—a plotting label designed to mimic the plotting behavior of MATLAB;
- Scikit Learn[15]—a powerful toolbox with broad implementation of machine learning methodology and intuitive API [6,34];
- Pandas[16]—tool for creating and manipulating complex tabulated data sheets [50];
- Nibabel[17]—a library for reading and writing to medical image-file formats.

We will learn more about these packages in due course, starting with NumPy in the subsequent Sect. 1.9. Note that, where derived code utilizes such packages, it is very important to cite[18] them in the resulting projects and papers.

Installing packages

Assuming you have installed Anaconda, then all the just-listed packages (with the exception of Nibabel) should be already installed. However, for other packages, like Nibabel, there are two ways to install: either through Anaconda:

```
conda install -c conda-forge nibabel
```

[13] http://www.NumPy.org/.
[14] https://matplotlib.org/.
[15] http://scikit-learn.org.
[16] https://pandas.pydata.org.
[17] http://nipy.org/nibabel/.
[18] https://www.scipy.org/citing.html.

or through the python installer package pip:

```
pip install nibabel
```

These commands should be typed into a terminal (or `cmd`) window for your local system. Here, `conda-forge` represents an independent community resource that packages popular Python repositories for installation with Anaconda. Some very popular packages will also be available through the main Anaconda installer through running `conda install <package>`. To update packages, use `pip install <package> --upgrade` or `conda update <package>`.

1.8.4 Classes

Going further, Python is an object-oriented language that allows the structuring of code into classes. This supports a clean and efficient coding style, further improving code readability and reuse. The basic structure of a Python class can be written in pseudocode as

```
class ClassName:
    <statement-1>
    .
    .
    .
    <statement-N>
```

where it is necessary to start classes with an constructor (instantiation function) such as:

```
class MyClass:
    def __init__(self): # constructor
        self.data = []

x=MyClass() # creates new instance of class.
```

The task of constructors is to create an instance of the class and initialize (assign values) to class attributes used elsewhere in the code. In Python the constructor is formed from the `init()` method, and it is always called when an object is created. Beyond the constructor, classes contain attributes and method (function) definitions:

```
class MyClass:

    # creating a class attribute
    my_class_attribute='bananas'
    def __init__(self):
        self.data = []
        #creating an instance attribute
        self.instance_attr = random.randint(1, 100)
```

```
    def f(self): # function -> object method
        return 'hello world'
```

Here, attributes may be defined outside of the constructor (as shown for `my_class_attribute`). This will be the same (`'bananas'`) for every single instance of the class. Alternatively, each instance may have it's own attributes, e.g., `self.instance_attr`, defined inside the constructor or class methods; these describe properties of the object being created, e.g., see the `shape, size, ndim, and dtype attributes` of NumPy matrices in the next section.

Understanding the formatting of Python classes is essential knowledge for development and utilization of advanced Python packages. However, in this book we will stick to relatively simple scripting. We therefore leave investigation of more advanced features to the reader.

1.9. NumPy

NumPy (an acronym for "Numeric Python" or "Numerical Python") is a foundation, open-source library upon which all scientific programming in Python is based. At its core are tools for efficient creation and manipulation of data arrays (including matrices and tensors). Most commonly, NumPy is imported as:

```
import numpy as np
```

using the popular abbreviation `np`.

1.9.1 Arrays

In computational terms an array is a data structure, which is similar to a list, or nested set of list, that collects variables in an ordered way that may be indexed by a tuple. However, in contrast to lists, **all of the values of an array must be of the same type** and (thinking only in 2D for the time being), **each individual row or column must have the same length**.

Creating arrays

Some example methods for array generation are

```
zeros=np.zeros( (3,3) )
ones=np.ones((3,3))
identity = np.eye(3)
empty=np.empty( (3,3) )
```

Here, `zeros` creates an 3×3 array full of zeros (by passing shape as a tuple `(3,3)`); `ones` create an array full of ones; `eye` creates an identity matrix, and `empty` creates an array of fixed shape with uninitialized (very) small nonzero values. Note that, by default, the datatype (dtype) of the created array is float64, but this can be changed during initialization, e.g.,

```
ones=np.ones( (3,3), dtype=np.int16)
```

NumPy arrays may also be initialized from lists:

```
# creating 1-D array
my_array=np.array([1,2,3,4,5,6])
# creating 2-D array
my_matrix=np.array([[1,2,3,4,5,6],[7,8,9,10,11,12]])
```

And, it's also possible to define arrays that evenly sample within a range using `np.arange([start], stop, [step])`, e.g., `np.arange(50,80,5)` samples points in the range `[50-80)`, in steps of 5. This function is commonly used in combination with for loops. Note that, when sampling all integers from zero, only the end point of the range needs be defined, e.g., `np.arange(5)` returns `[0,1,2,3,4]`. When, alternatively, seeking a fixed *number* of values within a range, use `np.linspace(start,end,num)`. Here, `num` determines the number of samples and thus the size of the spacing.

Random number generation

NumPy also has a submodule `np.random`,[19] which creates arrays that follow specific random distributions, including uniformly distributed samples in the range `[0,1)`.

```
rand1=np.random.random((3,3))
```

floats sampled from the standard normal distribution

```
rand2=np.random.randn(3,3)
```

and random integers in some range, e.g., `[5,20)`:

```
rand3=np.random.randint(5,20,(3,3))
```

Note that in each case the returned array has size 3 × 3; however, the functions differ in whether the shape is passed as a tuple or each dimension is passed as a separate argument.

Loading from files

Often, data will come preformated and stored in text files. It is possible to directly load matrices and arrays from text files using the `loadtxt` function:

```
new_mat=np.loadtxt('matrix.txt',delimiter=',')
```

[19] https://numpy.org/doc/1.16/reference/routines.random.html.

Here, the first argument prescribes the path to the file, and the second argument (`delimiter`) defines how values are separated in the file, for example, ',' indicates comma separated values (or csv files) but arrays may equally be stored using white spacing. In the same manner, arrays may be saved as a text file, using `savetxt`, or more efficiently as a `.npy` file using `np.save(filepath, arr)`. NumPy file types may be loaded with `np.load(filepath)`.

1.9.2 Array attributes

Once created, each array object may be described by a range of attributes including `shape` (length of each dimension), `size` (total number of elements), `ndim` (total number of dimensions, `and` `dtype` (the data type of the array); to access these attributes, use the `array.atr` syntax, i.e.:

```
my_array=np.array([[1,2,3],[4,5,6]],dtype=np.int16)
my_array_shape=my_array.shape # returns (2, 3)
my_array_size=my_array.size # returns 6
my_array_size=my_array.dtype # returns dtype('int16')
```

1.9.3 Indexing slicing and iterating

Arrays, like lists, are indexed from 0, or in reverse from the end of the array using negative integers:

```
my_array=np.array([1,2,3,4,5,5,6,7,9,10])

print('the first index of array:',my_array[0])
print('the last index:',my_array[-1])
print('the penultimate index:',my_array[-2])
```

Also, similarly to lists, NumPy arrays may be sliced. However, you must specify a slice for each dimension of the array, i.e.,

```
my_matrix=np.array([[1,2,3,4,5,6],[7,8,9,10,11,12]])

my_slice=my_matrix[1,2:5]
```

returns a 1×3 array, representing the values from the third to fifth columns of the second row. Again, like lists, slicing the range is not inclusive of the last index in the range. Alternatively, to slice a whole row (or column) of the following matrix, use a colon to indicate that values across all columns (or rows) are required, e.g., `my_matrix[0,:]` slices the first row and `my_matrix[:,3]` slices the fourth column. While slicing extracts submatrices in fixed ranges, integer indexing (using lists) allows arbitrary values to be selected from the array, such that `my_matrix[0,[1,3,5]]` returns columns 2, 4, and

6. More examples are given in Fig. 1.5. It is also possible to return all indices from a array, whose values meet certain boolean conditions, e.g.,

```
boolean_cond=(my_matrix>4)
new_matrix=my_matrix2[boolean_cond]
```

This can be useful, for example, when the goal is to mask one array using the values of another (Fig. 1.6).

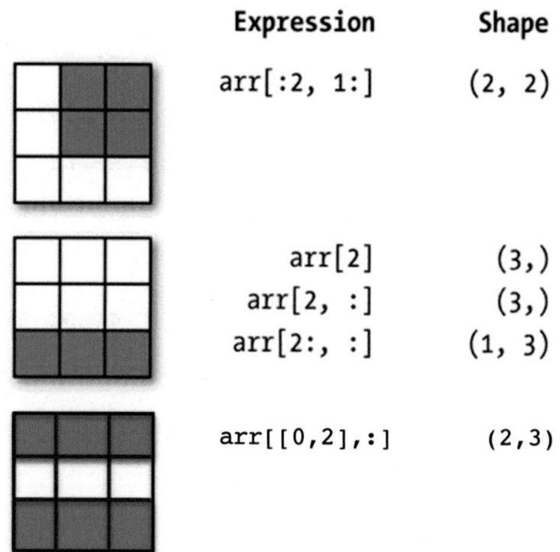

Figure 1.5 Slicing Numpy arrays.

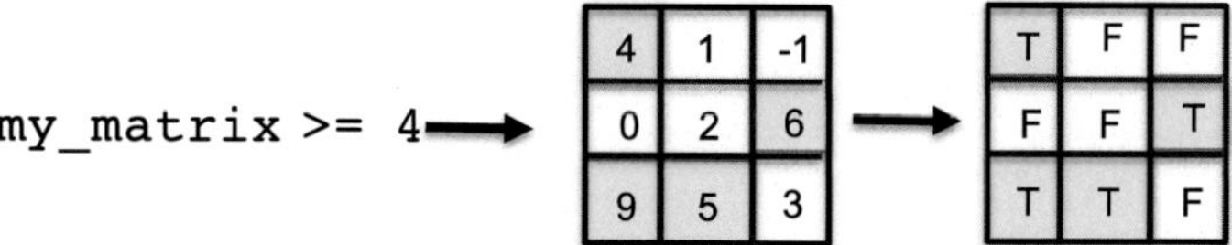

Figure 1.6 Masking arrays.

1.9.4 Reshaping arrays

On regular occasions, throughout this book, it will become necessary to reshape, or flatten an array before operating on it. Using NumPy, array flattening may be achieved using (`ravel` or `flatten`). Here, both functions perform the same general operations. However, whereas `flatten` creates a complete copy of the variable (with new shape) in memory, `ravel` continues to reference the original array. An important difference is that any changes to the flattened array output from a `ravel` operation will change the contents of the original array, whereas this is not the case for `flatten`. Care should

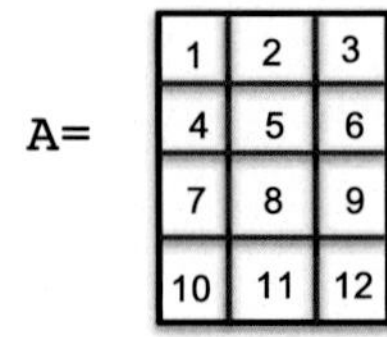


```
print(A.flatten(order="C"))
print(A.flatten(order="F"))
```

```
[ 1  2  3  4  5  6  7  8  9 10 11 12]
[ 1  4  7 10  2  5  8 11  3  6  9 12]
```

Figure 1.7 Array flattening.

therefore be taken to consider which is the desired behavior. However, since `ravel` does not occupy any new memory, it is the faster operation to run.

In both cases the functions offer choices as to how the array is unravelled, through an optional argument "order". Order can have the values "C" (default), "F", and "A" (Fig. 1.7). Here, "C" means to flatten in the same way as would be performed in C/C++, i.e., in row-major ordering such that the row index varies the slowest and the column index the quickest. "F" stands for Fortran column-major ordering and "A" means preserve the C/Fortran style of the original array (where this is saved as an attribute when the array is created).

More general reshaping operations may be implemented using `reshape` and `resize` functions. In this case, `reshape` creates a copy of the array, whereas `resize` modifies the original. It is also possible to concatenate two (or more) arrays together, provided all arrays share (at least one) compatible dimension:

```
np.concatenate((a1, a2, ...), axis=0, ..)
```

Here, `(a1, a2, ...)` are the arrays to concatenate. These must be comparable in shape along the chosen axis.

1.9.5 Broadcasting

Broadcasting is a powerful mechanism within Python that allows combined operations on arrays of (apparently) different sizes, provided the sizes of equivalent dimensions between arrays are either exactly the same or one. What this means is that, if you have two arrays with different numbers of dimensions (e.g., a vector and a matrix), extra dimensions will be added to the smaller array to give it the same dimensionality. Effectively, the smaller array will be copied along the new dimension as many times as is necessary until it has the exact same size as the larger array. Provided all other dimensions agree between the arrays, this will allow them to be operated on together. For example, when summing a (3,4) shaped matrix with a (,4) shaped array (Fig. 1.8), Python will broadcast three copies of the vector in the row dimension until it has shape (3,4). This will allow the two arrays to be summed together.

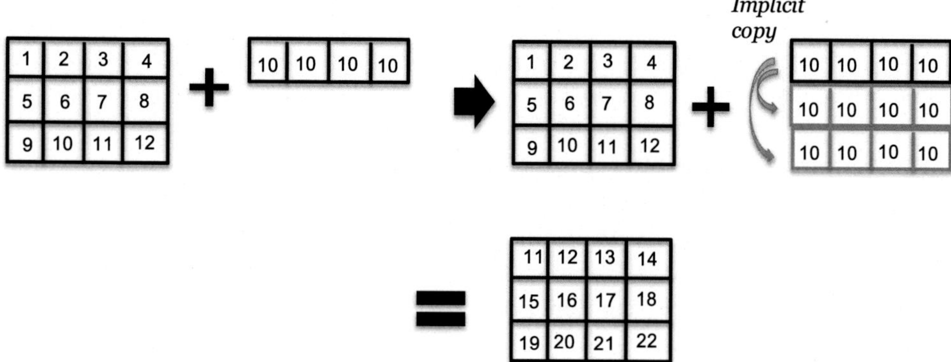

Figure 1.8 Broadcasting.

1.9.6 Exercises

1. Try creating some arrays of your own and checking their attributes e.g.:[20]
   - Create a numpy array from a list with six integer values;
   - Create an 2D array with dimensions 3 × 2 from a nested list;
   - Create a 3 × 4 array full of zeros;
   - Create a random 2 × 4 array of random integers in the range 10 to 20;
   - Create an array that returns every even number from 0 to 20;
   - Print various attributes of these arrays, e.g., shape, size, ndim, dtype.
2. Given the following array

```
X=np.array([[0, 1, 2],[3,4,5],[6,7,8], [9,10,11], [12,13,14],
    [15,16,17],[18,19,20],[21,22,23]])
```

   - Slice the third row, and second and 4th column;
   - Reshape X into a (6,4) matrix;
   - Create a `ones` matrix the same size as X; concatenate with X;
   - Create a new array of size (1,4,1) add it to X using broadcasting;
   - Create an array of size (4,6) and add a row vector to it by broadcasting.
3. Given the following array

```
C = np.array([[16,64],[-25,4]],
          dtype=np.float64)
```

   implement the following matrix operations: `mean`, `std`, `var`, `sum`, `sqrt`, `fabs`, `exp` and `log`.

[20] The code, exercises and solutions are available from github.com/MachineLearningBiomedicalApplications/notebooks.

1.10. A MATLAB to Python cheatsheet

Assuming that many readers may come to this book knowing MATLAB and not Python, we include Table 1.1 which is a cheat sheet summarizing the major similarities and differences. The most important points to recognize are:

- **Python uses indentation** to control flow through the code (thus there are no end statements at the end of if/for/while statements, unlike in MATLAB);
- Python **indexes arrays from 0 not 1.**

Additionally, Python does not require semicolons at the end of each line to prevent the interpreter from printing out the values of each variable. However, their presence will not result in any errors.

1.11. Pandas

Pandas is a Python package for handling tabular data with many similarities to MS Excel. It provides extensive functionality for reading, writing, searching, filtering, and manipulating data from spreadsheets, with interfaces to a range of formats including MS Excel, Comma Separated Value (CSV), and pickle files. Pandas is imported as

```
import pandas as pd
```

In this section we will present a brief introduction to the Pandas package. To learn more, consult one of the online tutorials.[21]

1.11.1 Dataframes

The Pandas module stores the data in a **Dataframe** object. In contrast to Numpy arrays, dataframes can hold data values of different types, such as mixtures of numerical values and text. Additionally, the columns and rows are named, allowing user-friendly access through the name of the feature rather than a numerical index. Examples of the dataframes that store data about 40 university students, including gender, height, and distance to home from the university, are shown in Fig. 1.9.

Creating a dataframe object

Assuming that we have a data matrix, for example, numerical data 'distance' and 'height' stored in numpy array `data`, we can create the dataframe object as

```
df=pd.DataFrame(data,columns=['distance','height'])
```

Note that we named the columns using the attribute `columns` as shown in Fig. 1.9 left. We can also name the rows using the attribute `index`. We can display the dataframe by

[21] https://pandas.pydata.org/pandas-docs/stable/getting_started/tutorials.html.

Table 1.1 MATLAB to Python cheat sheet.

<table>
<tr><th>MATLAB</th><th>Python</th></tr>
<tr><td>% comments are with '%'</td><td># comments are with '#'</td></tr>
<tr><td>% end lines with colon
var_int=5;</td><td># no semi colon
var_int=5</td></tr>
<tr><td>% array creation
C = [1, 2, 3];</td><td># same bar ';'
C = [1, 2, 3]</td></tr>
<tr><td>% indexes from 1
C(1)</td><td># indexes from 0
print(C[0]) # print</td></tr>
<tr><td>% loops
% no need to initialise array
% control flow using end statements
for i=1:10
    A(i) = i;
end</td><td># loops
A=[] # initialize empty array
# control flow using indentation
for i in np.arrange(10):
    A.append(i)</td></tr>
<tr><td>% creating 2D arrays
my_array=[1,2,3 ; 4,5,6]</td><td># creating 2D arrays
my_array=[[1,2,3],[4,5,6]]</td></tr>
<tr><td>% logical or
if a < 15 || b > 10
% logical and
if a < 15 && b > 10</td><td># logical or
if a< 15 or b > 10:
# logical and
if a< 15 and b > 10:</td></tr>
<tr><td>% MATLAB array functionality is
    inbuilt
I = eye(3);</td><td># for Python import NumPy for arrays
import numpy as np
I = np.eye(3)</td></tr>
</table>

df

	gender	height
0	M	183
1	F	163
2	F	152
3	F	157
4	F	157

df2

	distance	height
0	80	183
1	3	163
2	90	152
3	272	157
4	80	157

Figure 1.9 Examples of dataframe objects. Left: the dataframe `df` composed numerical values only. Right: the dataframe `df2` composed of mixture of numerical and text values.

simply typing its name, or, if it has too many rows, we can display only the first five rows by

```
df.head()
```

as shown in Fig. 1.9. The last five rows are displayed by `df.tail()`.

Convert dataframe to numpy array

If the dataframe object contains numerical values, we can convert it to a numpy array using

```
np_array=df.to_numpy()
```

We will of course lose all the names of columns and rows by applying this conversion.

1.11.2 Reading and writing files

Pandas offers interfaces to read and write tabular data with various formats. We can read a CSV file using

```
df=pd.read_csv('distance_height.csv')
```

and the Python specific data format **pickle** can be read by

```
df2=pd.read_pickle('gender_height.pkl')
```

Similarly, we can save dataframe objects to the disk using these formats:

```
df.to_csv('distance_height2.csv')
df2.to_pickle('gender_height2.pkl')
```

1.11.3 Selecting and filtering the data

We can select a column by

```
df['height']
```

and a range of rows (e.g., first five) by

```
df[0:5]
```

In order to select only height for the first five students, we use the function `loc`

```
df.loc[0:4,'height']
```

Alternatively, we can access the elements of the dataframe through their numerical indices using the function `iloc`, for example,

```
df.iloc[0:5,1]
```

will also return height for the first five students. We can also filter the data, for example, if we would like to select only tall students with heights more that 170 cm, we can do that by

```
df[df['height']>170]
```

To select only the distance data for the tall students, we can call

```
df['distance'][df['height']>170]
```

1.11.4 Merging and iterating

We can easily merge the dataframes `df` and `df2` because the rows correspond to the same data samples. We simply copy the column 'distance' from `df` to `df2`:

```
df2['distance']=df['distance']
```

To iterate over the rows of the dataframe, we write a `for` loop in the following way:

```
for index, row in df2.iterrows():
    print(index,row['gender'],row['distance'])
```

In this example, print the index, 'gender' and 'distance' for all rows in the dataframe `df2`.

1.11.5 Exercises

1. Read the file *gender_height.pk1* into a dataframe.[22] Perform the following:
   - Display the first and the last five lines of this dataset;
   - Select the column 'height' and convert it to a numpy array;
   - Create the dataframe object `male_heights` that contains the heights of all the male students;
   - Save the male heights into a CSV file.

[22] Datasets and additional exercises are available from github.com/MachineLearningBiomedicalApplications/notebooks.

2. Read the files *gender_height.pk1* and *'distance_height.csv'* into the dataframes. Perform the following:
   - Merge the files into the same dataframe;
   - Select only the students who live less that 30 miles from the campus;
   - Iterate over the selected students and print out the gender of each.

1.12. Matplotlib

Matplotlib is a plotting library that provides functionality very similar to visulatization in MATLAB. In this section we will briefly introduce line plots, scatter plots, histograms, boxplots, and plotting 2D images. The Matplotlib plotting module `pyplot` is imported as follows:

```
import matplotlib.pyplot as plt
```

1.12.1 Line plots

Line plots are used for plotting of simple functions. We will now describe how to obtain a line plot shown in Fig. 1.10 left.

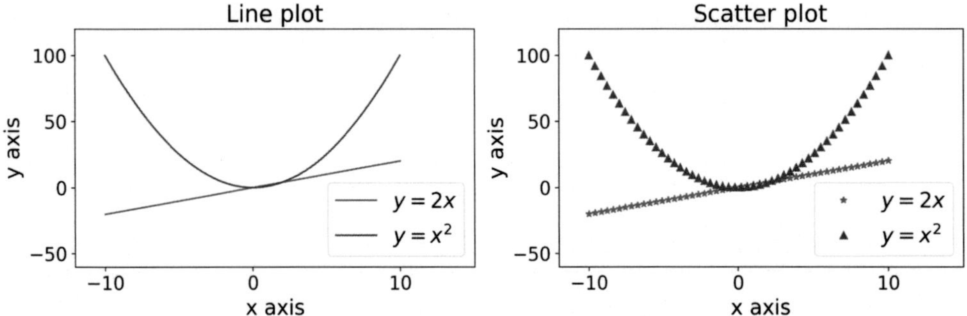

Figure 1.10 Example of a line plot and scatter plot.

Let's start by plotting a the function $y = 2x$. We first need to prepare the data that will be stored in `numpy` arrays. We will create x values as 50 samples of the interval $(-10, 10)$ using `np.linspace` and then calculate the corresponding y values as follows:

```
import numpy as np
x = np.linspace(-10, 10)
y = 2*x
```

We can plot the graph using

```
plt.plot(x,y)
```

It is important to always annotate your plot by adding a title and labeling the axis. Note how we can change the size of the font by setting the parameter `fontsize`:

```
plt.title('Line plot', fontsize = 16)
plt.xlabel('x axis')
plt.ylabel('y axis')
```

To add a second line, for example, $y = x^2$, we simply repeat the same process

```
y2 = x**2
plt.plot(x, y2,'r')
```

Note that this time we have chosen red as the color of the plot by adding the string `'r'` as a third parameter. We also need to annotate the lines that we plotted, and this can be done using the legend:

```
plt.legend(['$y=2x$','$y=x^2$'], loc='lower right')
```

We used symbols `$ $` to create mathematical equations and the parameter `loc` to define the position of the legend in the plot. We can also change the range of values we want to display for each axis:

```
plt.xlim([-12,15])
plt.ylim([-60,120])
```

and choose which values will be displayed on each axis

```
plt.xticks([-10,0,10])
plt.yticks([-50,0,50,100 ])
```

1.12.2 Scatter plots

If we prefer to plot individual data points rather than a joint curve, we can create a **scatter plot** instead. There are two ways to do that. Either we use function `scatter` (note that the color is set by parameter `c`)

```
plt.scatter(x,y)
plt.scatter(x, y2,c='r')
```

or we use the line plot but tell it to use markers rather than a line. These two lines will plot blue stars and red triangles:

```
plt.plot(x,y,'*')
plt.plot(x, y2,'r^')
```

The plot is shown in Fig. 1.10 right.

1.12.3 Subplots

To plot the two plots in one figure next to each other, we use **subplots**. Usually, since the default size of the figure is not suitable for multiple subplots, we therefore resize the figure, before defining the subplots as:

```
# resize figure
plt.figure(figsize=(12,4))
# plot on the left
plt.subplot(121)
plt.plot(x,y)
plt.plot(x, y2,'r')
# plot on the right
plt.subplot(122)
plt.plot(x,y,'*')
plt.plot(x, y2,'r^')
```

Note how we define the subplots using the function `plt.subplot`. We can also use commas, which is useful if we need many plots or use `for` loop to define the subplots:

```
plt.subplot(1,2,1)
```

The first argument sets the number of rows, the second argument the number of columns, and the third argument defines the plot number.

1.12.4 Histograms, barcharts, and boxplots

Matplotlib offers functions for plotting the summary characteristics of the data. Examples of such plots are shown in Fig. 1.11.

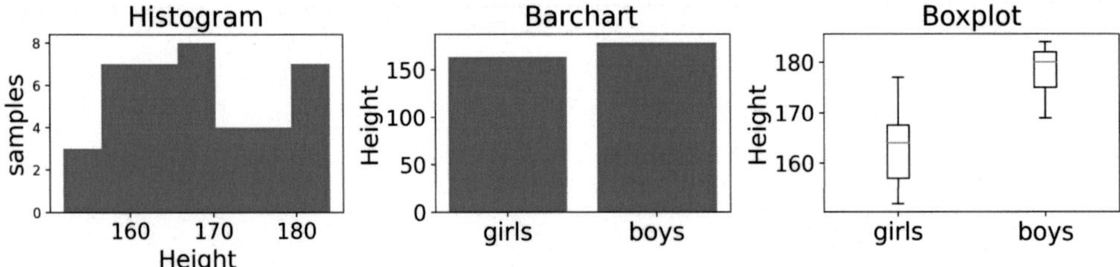

Figure 1.11 Example of the different types of plots available in Matplotlib.

Histogram

The **histogram** of the numerical values, in this case the height of students from Sec. 1.11, can be plotted as

```
import pandas as pd
df=pd.read_pickle('gender_height.pkl')
plt.hist(df['height'], bins=7)
```

In this example we use seven bins to discretize the height values (Fig. 1.11 left).

Barchart

We would also like to plot statistics of the heights of male and female students. First, we will extract the heights for each gender:

```
girls_height = df['height'][df['gender']=='F']
boys_height  = df['height'][df['gender']=='M']
```

Next, we plot the mean height for each gender using a **barchart** (Fig. 1.11 middle):

```
plt.bar([0,1],[girls_height.mean(),boys_height.mean()])
plt.xticks([0,1],['girls','boys'])
```

Note that the function `bar` requires an array of indices, one for each bar, as the first argument, while the second argument represents the heights of the bars. We can name the bars on the x-axis using the function `xticks`.

Boxplot

The Matplotlib function **boxplot** will calculate and display the median, the upper and lower quartiles, and the range of values as shown in Fig. 1.11 right. The input arguments are the arrays of values for each category. We can set the labels for the boxes and y-axis in a similar way as for a barchart:

```
plt.boxplot([girls_height,boys_height])
plt.xticks([1,2],['girls', 'boys'])
plt.ylabel('Height')
```

1.12.5 Images

Two-dimensional images in standard formats can be read from disk using the function `imread` and displayed using `imshow`:

```
image = plt.imread('fetalbrain.png')
plt.imshow(image)
```

In fact, any 2D array can be displayed this way. In this example we create an artificial image and display it, while setting the colormap to grayscale:

```
array = np.zeros([100,100])
array[25:50,25:50]=1
plt.imshow(array,cmap='gray')
```

The results of these commands are shown in Fig. 1.12.

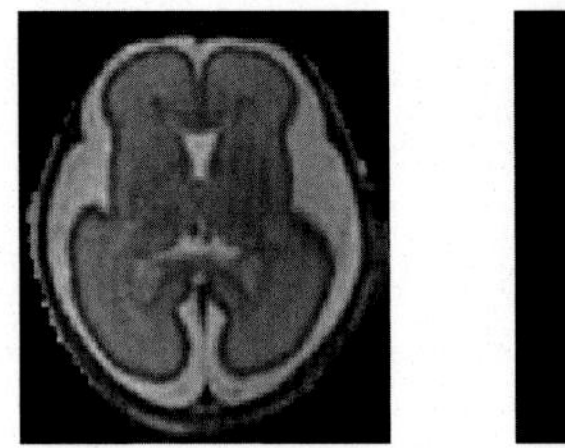 

Figure 1.12 Examples of images displayed in Matplotlib.

1.12.6 Exercises

1. Create the line plot shown in Fig. 1.10 left using the code given in this section. Perform the following tasks:[23]
   - Add a third function $y = \exp(x/2)$ to the plot using a green line. Update the legend;
   - Instead of using a single plot, modify the figure to contain three subplots, with each function in a separate plot;
   - Put the equation for each function in the title of the subplot.
2. Load the student data available in files *gender_height.pk1* and *'distance_height.csv'*, described in Sect. 1.11. Merge the data into a single dataframe. Create the following plots:
   - scatter plot of 'height' and 'distance';
   - histogram of 'distance';
   - barchart of average 'distance' for girls and boys;
   - boxplot of 'distance' for girls and boys;

   Hint: All plots accept dataframes and numpy arrays.
3. Create and display the image shown in Fig. 1.12 right. Change the colormap to 'viridis' and 'jet'.

[23] The code, exercises and solutions are available from github.com/MachineLearningBiomedicalApplications/notebooks.

CHAPTER 2

Machine learning basics

2.1. What is machine learning?

Over the last 50–70 years, computer programs have become more and more important in solving various problems. A traditional way of building a computer program is to write a set of rules and execute them to calculate some outcomes. For example, processes fully determined by laws of physics, such as radioactive decay at a particular time-point, can be predicted according to the simple formula $A = A_0 \exp(-\lambda t)$, where t is time, λ is the decay constant, A_0 is the activity at time $t = 0$, and A the predicted activity at time t. A more sophisticated example is a complex and precise calculation of the path of the Rosetta probe that landed on a comet in 2014 after 10 years of journeying from the Earth.

For many real-life problems though, it is very difficult to write a set of rules because the underlying processes are too complex or not completely understood. Many biomedical applications fall into this category. Let's take the example of brain growth during the last trimester of pregnancy. In a clinical setting we can measure the head circumference as a proxy for the brain size using fetal ultrasound. But how do we know whether the growth is healthy? We need to collect a large number of measurements, also called **samples**, and **learn the pattern** of normal growth from the collected data. For each patient we need to record the gestational age (age from the beginning of the pregnancy) and head circumference, and calculate the growth curve from this dataset. For each new patient, the growth curve determines the normal head circumference depending on the gestational age.

A **machine learning system** is programmed to learn a mathematical **model** from **training data**, and it is therefore **trained** rather than explicitly programmed. In the brain-growth example, the model that needs to be learned is the growth curve, and the training data consists of the gestational age and head circumference for a number of healthy fetuses. The **machine learning task** is to predict the head circumference from the gestational age of a fetus.

In the remainder of this chapter, we will introduce various machine learning tasks, describe them using mathematical notation, and demonstrate how these tasks can be learned using the **scikit-learn library.**

2.1.1 Supervised learning: regression and classification

In **supervised learning** the task is to learn a model from a set of training samples that contain some measured inputs, also called **features**, and expected outputs. If the out-

Machine Learning for Biomedical Applications
https://doi.org/10.1016/B978-0-12-822904-0.00007-8
Copyright © 2024 Elsevier Ltd.
All rights reserved.

puts are **continuous**, they are called **target values,** and a machine learning algorithm that finds a model to predict continuous target values from a set of features is called a **regression**.

Prediction of the brain volume from the gestational age is an example of a regression task. In this case, the feature is the gestational age, and the target value is the brain volume. In a research setting we are able to accurately calculate brain volumes from segmented high-resolution volumetric magnetic resonance images (MRI). Fig. 2.1 shows the prediction of the brain volume from the gestational age in scans of preterm neonates using **linear regression**.

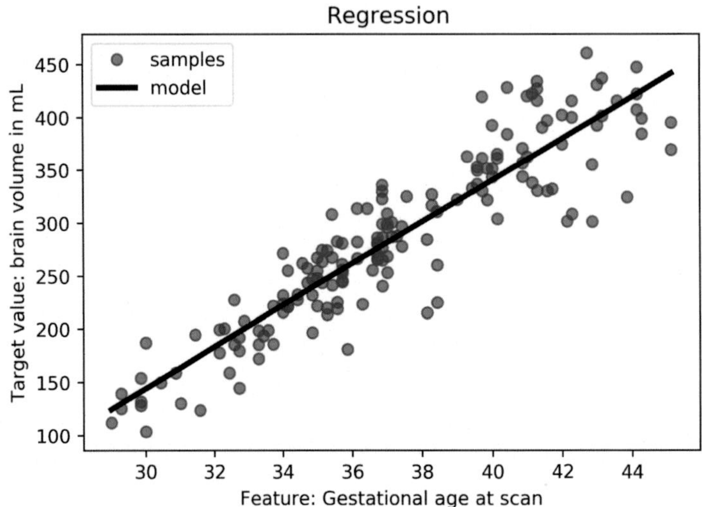

Figure 2.1 Example of a regression problem: prediction of brain volume from gestational age in preterm neonates.

If the expected outputs are **discrete**, they are called **labels,** and the machine learning task is called a **classification**. Diagnosis of heart failure using ultrasound or magnetic resonance imaging is an example of the classification task. Diagnostic measurements include the percentage of blood that the left ventricle can eject at each heartbeat and the global longitudinal strain of the heart between diastole and systole, two features per sample (or a two-dimensional **feature vector**). Our aim is to find a **model** to predict whether the patient is healthy or has heart failure, which we call a **label**. In this case the labels take only two values: label 0 for the healthy patient and label 1 for the patient with heart failure. Our example classification problem is illustrated in Fig. 2.2.

2.1.2 Unsupervised learning: clustering and dimensionality reduction

In **unsupervised** problems the training samples are also characterized by the feature vectors, but outputs are not known, and we look for hidden patterns in the data instead.

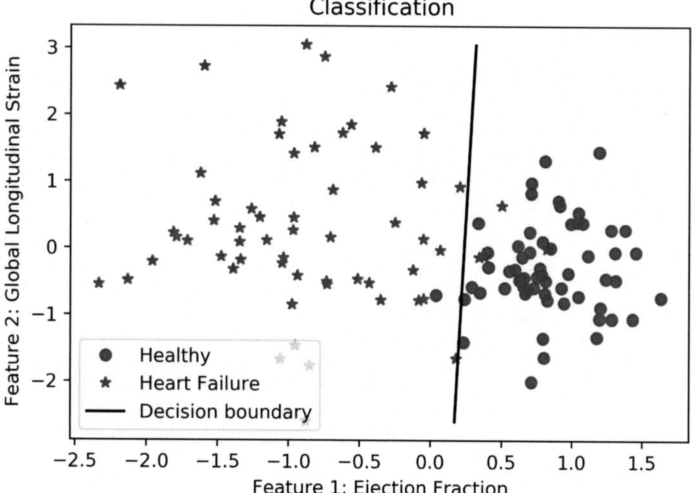

Figure 2.2 An example of a classification problem: diagnosis of heart failure using the ejection fraction and global longitudinal strain, biomarkers calculated from ultrasound or magnetic resonance images.

In **clustering** problems we look for groups of samples with similar feature vectors, and we assign a label to each group, which is called a **cluster**. An example of such a problem is the segmentation of images based on intensity values, such as segmentation of brain tissues on MRI. On a T_1-weighted MRI, the white matter (WM) has the brightest intensity values, grey matter (GM) intensities are medium, and the cerebro-spinal fluid (CSF) is the darkest. On a T_2-weighted MRI, the order of intensities is reversed. Fig. 2.3 shows detection of the clusters of pixels based on feature vectors containing T_1-weighted and T_2-weighted intensity values.

Dimensionality reduction seeks to reduce the number of features in high-dimensional machine learning tasks, while preserving the important characteristics of the data. It can be used for visualization of high-dimensional data or as a preprocessing step for other machine learning tasks. Fig. 2.4 shows the first two principal components of 30 dimensional feature vectors that describe the characteristics of cell nuclei in malignant and benign breast tumors. These characteristics, such as radius, texture, and concavity of the cells, were calculated from digitized images of cells obtained through fine needle aspiration (a type of biopsy).

2.1.3 Mathematical notation

In all machine learning tasks a sample is characterized by a D-dimensional **feature vector**

$$\mathbf{x} = (x_1, ..., x_D)^T.$$

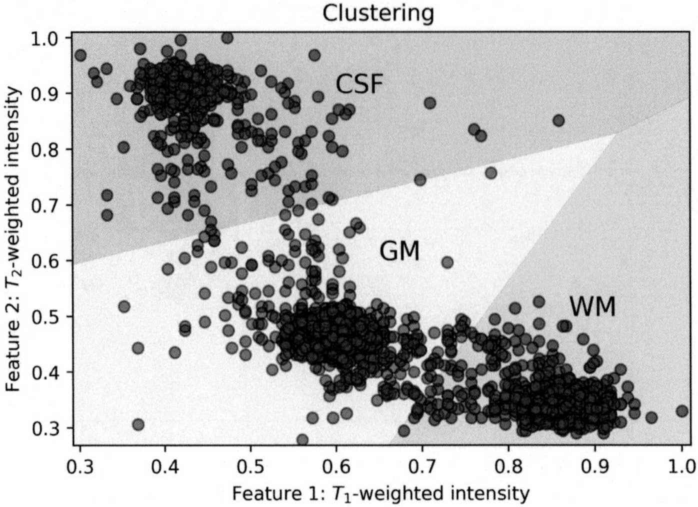

Figure 2.3 An example of a clustering problem: detecting tissue type (WM, GM, CSF) in pixels of brain MRI based on intensity on T_1-weighted and T_2-weighted images.

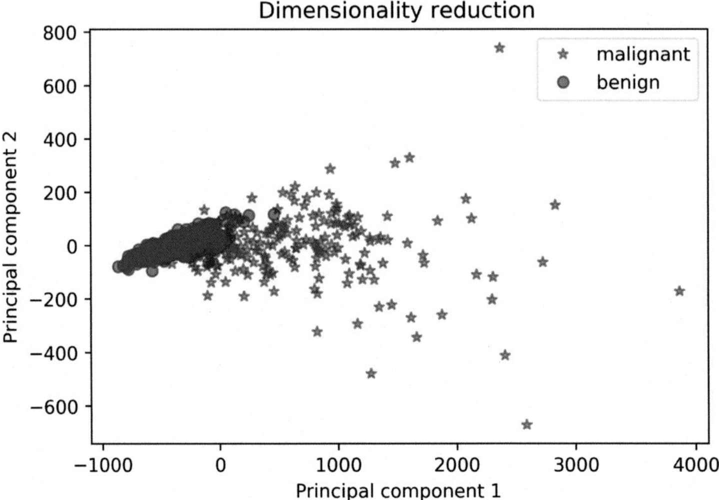

Figure 2.4 An example of a dimensionality reduction: detecting breast cancer from characteristics of cell nuclei obtained through biopsy. Each sample contains 30 different characteristics, which have been reduced to two principal components, enabling visualization of patterns in the data.

We seek to find a mathematical **model** to predict some outputs that can be expressed as a function f

$$\hat{y} = f(\mathbf{x}),$$

where $\hat{y}$ is an output estimated by our model. In the case of regression it is an estimated target value, for classification and clustering it is an estimated label, and for dimensionality reduction it is a transformed feature vector.

Let's assume that we have N training samples with feature vectors $\mathbf{x}_1, ..., \mathbf{x}_N$ defined as follows:

$$\mathbf{x_i} = (x_{i1}, ..., x_{iD})^T.$$

The features of the training samples determine a **feature matrix X** that characterizes the whole training set

$$\mathbf{X} = \begin{pmatrix} \mathbf{x}_1^T \\ \vdots \\ \mathbf{x}_N^T \end{pmatrix} = \begin{pmatrix} x_{11} & \cdots & x_{1D} \\ \vdots & \ddots & \vdots \\ x_{N1} & \cdots & x_{ND} \end{pmatrix}. \tag{2.1}$$

Note that the dimensions of the feature matrix are $N \times D$, with training samples corresponding to the rows of the feature matrix and individual features to the columns of the feature matrix.

In supervised learning we expect an output y_i for each training sample $\mathbf{x_i}$. These outputs determine the **target vector** for regression and the **label vector** for classification as follows:

$$\mathbf{y} = (y_1, ..., y_N)^T. \tag{2.2}$$

To find the mathematical model f, we need to select its mathematical form, which will vary according to the machine learning algorithm. In general, we select our model in advance by choosing a mathematical form of the function f that depends on the feature vector $\mathbf{x}$ and parameter vector θ:

$$\hat{y} = f(\mathbf{x}, \theta). \tag{2.3}$$

For example, the mathematical form of f could be a quadratic function $y = f(x, \theta) = w_0 + w_1 x + w_2 x^2$, and the parameter vector would be composed of its coefficients $\theta = (w_0, w_1, w_2)^T$.

Training the model f can then be mathematically expressed as finding the parameter vector $\hat{\theta}$ that minimizes some **loss function F** for the given training set

$$\hat{\theta} = \arg\min_{\theta} \mathbf{F}(\mathbf{X}, \mathbf{y}, \theta), \tag{2.4}$$

where $\mathbf{y}$ is dropped from the equation for unsupervised tasks. Some of the common loss functions are the sum of squared errors between predicted and expected target values for regression, cross-entropy for predicted and expected labels for classification and within-class variance of the feature vectors for clustering. In our example we could use the sum of squared errors between the given and predicted target values

$$\mathbf{F}(\mathbf{X}, \mathbf{y}, \theta) = \sum_{i=1}^{N} (y_i - w_0 - w_1 x_i - w_2 x_i^2)^2.$$

2.1.4 Summary

In this section we summarize the various machine learning tasks and list machine learning algorithms to learn the tasks covered in this book.
A **machine learning task** is:

Supervised: if we have both the features and the expected outputs for the training samples	**Regression:** if the outputs are continuous **Classification:** if the outputs are discrete
Unsupervised: if we have only features for the training samples	**Clustering:** if the similar features are grouped together to form clusters **Dimensionality reduction:** if the number of features is reduced while preserving important properties of the data.

The **machine learning algorithms** covered in this book:

Regression:	Linear, ridge and lasso regression
	Polynomial regression
	Kernel ridge regression
	Random-forest regression
	(Deep) neural network regression
Classification:	Perceptron
	Logistic regression
	Support-vector classification
	Random-forest classification
	(Deep) neural network classification
Clustering:	K-means
	Gaussian mixture model
	Spectral clustering
Dimensionality reduction:	Principal component analysis
	Independent component analysis
	Laplacian eigenmaps

2.1.5 Exercises

1. Explain how the machine learning approach differs from traditional programming.

2. Explain supervised and unsupervised learning.
3. What is the difference between regression and classification?
4. Explain what is similar and what is different between classification and clustering.
5. What is the purpose of dimensionality reduction?

2.2. Starting with scikit-learn

Scikit-learn is a Python library of machine learning algorithms integrated with Python packages such as Numpy, Matplotlib, and Pandas. It is very intuitive and easy to use. The library can be accessed from Python by importing the module `sklearn`.

In this section we introduce four types of objects available in scikit-learn: **regressor, classifier, clusterer,** and **transformer**, which implement various machine learning algorithms. Scikit-learn offers a user-friendly application interface (API) that requires these objects to implement a set of standard methods to access the machine learning algorithms. Here we list the most important ones:

- `fit` implements fitting the mathematical model f (Eq. 2.3) to the training data composed of feature matrix $\mathbf{X}$ (Eq. 2.1) and, for regressors and classifiers, also an output vector $\mathbf{y}$ (Eq. 2.2);
- `predict` implements prediction of output vector $\hat{\mathbf{y}}$ (Eq. 2.3) for regressors, classifiers, and clusterers;
- `transform` implements feature transformation (Eq. 2.3) for transformers;
- `fit_transform` fits the model and transforms the feature vector for transformers;
- `score` implements an evaluation metric.

In the remainder of this section, we will implement examples of each of the four algorithms. The datasets and the notebook with the code for this section can be downloaded from github.com/MachineLearningBiomedicalApplications/notebooks. They are located in the folder Chapter 2 - Starting with Scikit-learn.

2.2.1 Regression in scikit-learn

We will demonstrate fitting a regression model in scikit-learn using the example of **univariate linear regression** to predict the brain volumes of preterm babies from Sect. 2.1.1. The dataset and the fitted model are presented in Fig. 2.1. This section demonstrates the API of a **regressor** object in `Sklearn`.

Prepare the data

The data is stored in a comma separated values (CSV) file. We will import it using the Pandas package into the dataframe object `df`.

```
import pandas as pd
df = pd.read_csv('neonatal_brain_volumes.csv')
```

By running either `df.head()` or `df.keys()`, we will find that the file contains two columns 'GA' and 'brain volume'. Next, we will convert the dataframe object `df` into a Numpy array `data`.

```
import numpy as np
data = df.to_numpy()
```

We are ready to construct a feature matrix `X` that will hold the gestational age of the baby (GA).

```
X = data[:,0].reshape(-1,1)
```

Note that, by selecting a single column, we obtain a 1-dimensional numpy array; however the `sklearn` functions require a feature matrix formatted as a 2-dimensional array. This conversion is achieved by using the function `reshape(-1,1)`, where `-1` means that the number of rows should stay the same. We now check the dimensions of the feature matrix (note that output is shown by >>>):

```
print('Feature matrix X dimensions: ', X.shape)
print('Number of samples: ', X.shape[0])
print('Number of features: ', X.shape[1])
>>> Feature matrix X dimensions:  (162, 1)
>>> Number of samples:  162
>>> Number of features:  1
```

Finally, we create the target vector `y` containing the brain volumes and print its dimensions. Note that the target vector is a 1-dimensional array.

```
y = data[:,1]
print('Target vector y dimensions: ', y.shape)
>>> Target vector y dimensions:  (162,)
```

Create the model

Next, we choose the linear regression model:

```
from sklearn.linear_model import LinearRegression
model = LinearRegression()
```

Our model will be **univariate** because we have only one feature per sample, though scikit-learn implementation is suitable for any number of features. A univariate linear regression model is given by

$$\hat{y} = w_0 + w_1 x,$$

where x is the feature, $\hat{y}$ is the predicted target value, and $\mathbf{w} = (w_0, w_1)$ is the **parameter vector** we want to find to fit the linear regression model.

Fit the model

In the case of linear regression, the model is fitted by minimizing a sum-of-square-errors loss function

$$F(w_0, w_1) = \sum_{i=1}^{N} (y_i - w_0 - w_1 x_i)^2,$$

where we sum over all training samples. The fitting is performed as follows:

```
model.fit(X,y)
```

We can now check the coefficients of the fitted linear function

```
w0=model.intercept_
w1=model.coef_[0]
```

and find out that the fitted model is

$$\hat{y} = 20x - 445.$$

Note that for the linear regression model the `intercept_` is a scalar, and `coef_` is a 1D array.

Evaluate the model

We can see how well our model fits the data by evaluating a **performance measure**. The `sklearn` offers a function `score` to do that:

```
r2 = model.score(X,y)
```

For regressors, the function `score` returns **R^2 score**

$$R^2 = 1 - \frac{\sum_{i=1}^{N} (y_i - \hat{y}_i)^2}{\sum_{i=1}^{N} (y_i - \bar{y})^2},$$

where $\bar{y}$ denotes the mean of all target values. Note that the numerator is related to the residual variance in the data after the fit, while the denominator is related to the overall variance in the data. R^2 therefore measures the proportion of variance explained by the model. If $R^2 = 1$, then we have a perfect fit. A low R^2 means that the model does not fit the data well. In this example we have calculated the R^2 score for the training dataset, and we therefore obtained a measure of goodness of fit for the model and the training data. We will see later that it is useful to calculate the score for data that was not included in the fitting. Let's find out what is the score for our example:

```
print('R2 score: ', round(r2,2))
>>> R2 score:  0.84
```

We see that 84% of the variance in our data is explained by the linear model that we have fitted.

Predict on new data

We are interested in visualizing the model so we will therefore create a grid that samples the feature space. The following code creates 10 samples that span the values between minimum and maximum of the GA in the training set. Note that we need a 2D array for prediction.

```
x_model_1D = np.linspace(np.min(X),np.max(X),10)
X_model = x_model_1D.reshape(-1,1)
```

Now, we can predict the target values for these new samples:

```
y_model = model.predict(X_model)
```

Plot the result

We will use the `matplotlib.pyplot` to visualize the fitted model:

```
import matplotlib.pyplot as plt
```

First, we plot the training data

```
plt.plot(X,y,'bo')
```

and then the fitted model that we predicted for the samples on a grid spanning the feature space

```
plt.plot(X_model,y_model,'k')
```

The plot is shown in Fig. 2.1 in Sect. 2.1.1.

2.2.2 Classification in scikit-learn

We will now revisit the classification example of detecting heart failure using measures calculated from cardiac MRI or US images from Sect. 2.1.1, and visualized in Fig. 2.2. We will demonstrate how the prediction model can be fitted using the **perceptron** classifier. This section demonstrates the API of a **classifier** object in `sklearn`.

Prepare the data

We will first import the data from a CSV file and check the column names:

```
df = pd.read_csv('heart_failure_data.csv')
df.keys()
>>> Index(['EF', 'GLS', 'HF'], dtype='object')
```

Now, we are ready to create a feature matrix of 2-dimensional feature vectors with EF and GLS measurements. We will also standardize both features to have a zero mean and unit variance across all the training samples. This is implemented in `sklearn` object

StandardScaler. Scaling of the features is important for convergence of the perceptron classifier:

```
from sklearn.preprocessing import StandardScaler
scaler = StandardScaler()
data = df.to_numpy()
X = scaler.fit_transform(data[:,:2])
```

The label vector will be HF which indicates diagnosis of heart failure.

```
y = data[:,2]
```

Create the model

The following code creates the perceptron classifier:

```
from sklearn.linear_model import Perceptron
model = Perceptron()
```

The perceptron model will find the linear decision function, which for our 2-dimensional features $\mathbf{x} = (x_1, x_2)$ takes the following linear form:

$$h(\mathbf{x}) = w_0 + w_1 x_1 + w_2 x_2.$$

The predicted label is decided based on the sign of the decision function

$$\hat{y} = \begin{cases} 1 & \text{if } h(\mathbf{x}) \geq 0 \\ 0 & \text{if } h(\mathbf{x}) < 0. \end{cases}$$

The **decision boundary** is therefore defined by the decision function being zero:

$$w_0 + w_1 x_1 + w_2 x_2 = 0.$$

Fit the model

Just as for linear regression, fitting the perceptron model means finding the weight vector $\mathbf{w} = (w_0, w_1, w_2)$ that best separates the two classes. This is achieved by minimizing the perceptron criterion

$$F(\mathbf{w}) = \sum_{i \in \mathcal{M}} |h(\mathbf{x}_i)|,$$

where $\mathcal{M}$ is the set of all the misclassified samples. Note that for correctly classified samples there is no penalty and for misclassified samples the penalty is equal to the absolute value of the decision function for that sample. The criterion will therefore be zero if all samples are classified correctly, and we will try to minimize misclassifications. The perceptron model is fitted by

```
model.fit(X,y)
```

and the coefficients of the decision function can be accessed as

```
w0=model.intercept_[0]
w1=model.coef_[0][0]
w2=model.coef_[0][1]
```

Note that for the perceptron the `intercept_` is a 1D array and `coef_` is a 2D array. This is to support more than two classes, which requires multiple decision functions. The resulting decision boundary is

$$1 - 4x_1 + 0.15x_2 = 0.$$

Evaluate the model

The classifiers also implement the function `score` to evaluate the performance of the model. The performance measure for classifiers is **accuracy**, a proportion of correctly classified samples. If all samples are correctly classified, the accuracy is 1; if none are correctly classified, the accuracy is 0. We evaluate the performance of our perceptron model as follows:

```
accuracy = model.score(X,y)
print('Accuracy score: ', round(accuracy,2))
>>> Accuracy score:  0.96
```

We can see that 96% of the samples were correctly classified.

Plot the result

We start by plotting the data. We will place the first feature on the x-axis and the second feature on the y-axis, while the two classes are depicted by different markers.

```
plt.plot(X[y==0,0],X[y==0,1],'bo')
plt.plot(X[y==1,0],X[y==1,1],'r*')
```

We evaluate the decision boundary by taking the minimum and maximum of the second feature x_2, applying the equation for the decision boundary to calculate the first feature

$$x_1 = -\frac{w_0 + w_2x_2}{w_i},$$

and plotting the line joining these two points:

```
x2 = np.array([X[:,1].min(), X[:,1].max()])
x1 = -(w0 + w2*x2)/w1
plt.plot(x1, x2, "k-")
```

The plot is presented in Fig. 2.2 in Sect. 2.1.1.

2.2.3 Clustering in scikit-learn

Clustering algorithms are unsupervised and, unlike for classification, the labels are not provided during training. We will demonstrate the API of a **clusterer** object in `sklearn` to perform segmentation of a slice of brain MRI by **k-means** clustering algorithm. We will use the example in Sect. 2.1.2, but with a single image (T1-weighted) for simplicity.

Prepare the data

The slice of T1-weighted MRI that we want to segment is stored in image 'T1.png'. We will load it using `matplotlib.pyplot` function `imread`

```
T1 = plt.imread('T1.png')
```

The object `T1` is a 2D array and is padded with zeroes. We therefore first find all the indices where the image contains non-zero values:

```
ind = T1>0
```

and then vectorize all non-zero values and convert to a 2D-array format needed for `sklearn`:

```
X = T1[ind].reshape(-1,1)
```

Create the model

We choose **k-means** clustering algorithm with three clusters, one for each brain tissue type: WM, GM and CSF.

```
from sklearn.cluster import KMeans
model=KMeans(n_clusters=3)
```

K-means clustering algorithm searches for centers $\mu_1, \ldots, \mu_K$ of the predefined numbers of clusters and assigns each sample to the cluster with the closest center. For 1D features this can be written as

$$\hat{y}_i = \arg\max_k |x_i - \mu_k|. \tag{2.5}$$

Fit the model

K-means clustering finds the cluster centers by minimizing the within-class variance

$$F(\mu_1, \ldots, \mu_k) = \frac{1}{N}\sum_{i=1}^{N}(x_i - \mu_{\hat{y}_i})^2,$$

which is performed using the `fit` function. Clustering is unsupervised and, therefore the feature matrix `X` is the only input argument:

```
model.fit(X)
```

The centers can be accessed as follows:

```
c = model.cluster_centers_
print(c.flatten())
>>> [0.4 0.8 0.6]
```

Predict the labels

The labels are predicted according to Eq. (2.5):

```
y=model.predict(X)
```

Plot the result

To plot the result, we will first create a segmentation image of the correct dimension filled with zeros.

```
segmentation = np.zeros(T1.shape)
```

Next, we will insert the predicted labels at the locations that we remember in logical array `ind`:

```
segmentation[ind] = y+1
```

Note that we need to increase the label number to distinguish the class with label 0 from the background pixels. Finally, we display the segmentation using `matplotlib.pyplot` function `imshow`

```
plt.imshow(segmentation)
```

The original image and the segmentation are shown in Fig. 2.5

2.2.4 Dimensionality reduction in scikit-learn

We will look at **principal component analysis** (PCA) as an example of a dimensionality-reduction method. PCA seeks to find a predefined number of orthogonal directions, along which the data has the greatest variance. It orders these components according to the variance size and creates an orthonormal coordinate system transformation to project the original feature vectors to the reduced dimensional subspace that preserves the most variance in the data. It is therefore considered a feature transformation, and `PCA` is a **transformer** object in `sklearn`.

Let's revisit the example of the breast-cancer dataset to predict whether a tumor is malignant or benign from 30 different properties of cells obtained by a biopsy. This is one of the in-built `sklearn` datasets available in the module `datasets`.

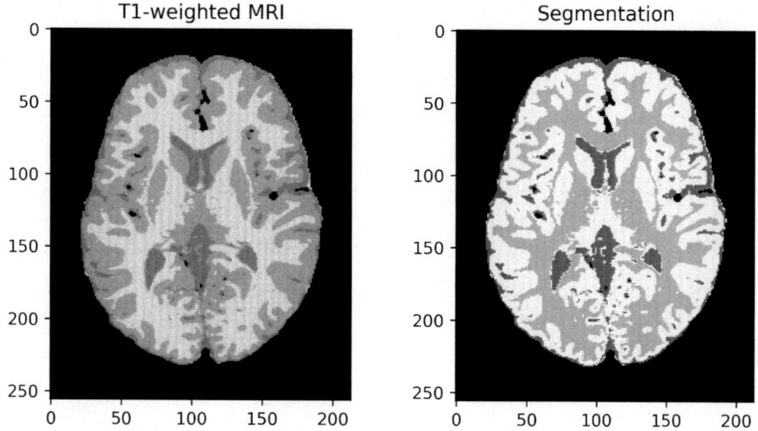

Figure 2.5 Segmentation of T1-weighted brain MRI using k-means clustering.

Prepare the data

The following code loads the breast-cancer dataset and extracts the feature matrix `X` of 30-dimensional feature vectors:

```
from sklearn import datasets
bc = datasets.load_breast_cancer()
X = bc.data

print('We have {} features.'.format(X.shape[1]))
>>> We have 30 features.
```

Create the model

We will now create the model for PCA with two principal components:

```
from sklearn.decomposition import PCA
model = PCA(n_components = 2)
```

Fit the model

After we fit the model to the training data, we are able to access the two principal component vectors as follows:

```
model.fit(X)
pc1 = model.components_[0]
pc2 = model.components_[1]
```

Transform the features

The projection on the first two principal components is performed by

```
y = model.transform(X)
print('We have {} features.'.format(y.shape[1]))
>>> We have 2 features.
```

The breast-cancer data projected on the first two principal components are visualized in Fig. 2.4 in Sect. 2.1.2.

2.2.5 Exercises

1. Predict the GA of a preterm baby from the measurement of the brain volume. Note that the GA and volumes switched the roles: The volume is a feature, and GA is the target value. Write scikit-learn code to create the feature matrix and the target vector, fit the model, calculate the R^2 score, and print out the equation of the fitted model.[1]
2. Find out whether using only the Ejection Fraction (EF) would be sufficient to predict the heart failure (HF). Write scikit-learn code to create the new feature matrix and the target vector, fit the model, calculate the accuracy score, and print the equation of the decision boundary. What is the drop in accuracy compared to using both features (EF and GLS)?
3. Perform k-means clustering to segment the T2-weighted image 'T2.png'. Is the result similar to the T1-weighted MRI?
4. Compare performance of a `Perceptron` classifier to detect breast cancer using the original features and features reduced to two dimensions using PCA.

2.3. Training machine learning models

We have now seen how we can create, fit and evaluate various machine learning models. The question remains, though, which type of model is best suited for a dataset. Let's explore this issue using a simple simulated example of quadratic polynomial regression. Let's assume that the underlying process we want to discover follows a quadratic relationship:

$$y = 2x^2 + 4x + 5.$$

However, in real world the true model is unknown, and we only observe noisy samples generated from this model. We will generate these noisy observations by adding Gaussian noise with standard deviation $\sigma = 3$ to the random samples from this model. The

[1] The skeleton code for the exercises and the datasets can be obtained from github.com/MachineLearningBiomedicalApplications/notebooks.

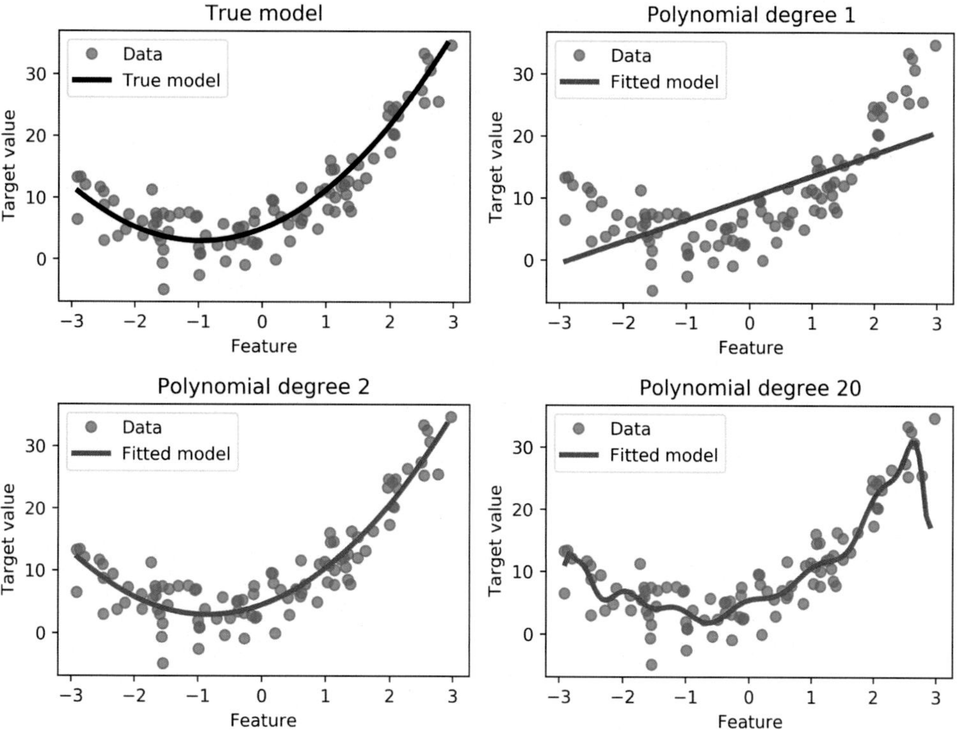

Figure 2.6 Fitting polynomial models of different degrees to the noisy data generated from a quadratic function (top left).

true model and noisy samples are visualized in Fig. 2.6, top left. Our task is to recover the underlying true model from the noisy data. It would be reasonable to choose a family of polynomial functions defined by

$$y = \sum_{j=0}^{M} w_j x^j.$$

We already understand that the coefficient vector $\mathbf{w} = (w_0, ..., w_M)$ can be found by minimizing sum of squared errors to fit the training data (Sect. 2.2.1). But how do we choose the polynomial degree M? The polynomial degree will determine the number of free parameters to fit and therefore the **complexity** of the model. We call such parameters the **hyperparameters** of the model. Different polynomial degrees will result in different models; see examples of $M = 1, 2, 20$ in Fig. 2.6. In the next section we will discuss how to choose the best one.

2.3.1 Underfitting and overfitting

In the case of simple models, such as univariate polynomial regression, we can assess the model visually. We can see in Fig. 2.6 that a polynomial of degree 1 does not capture the quadratic trend in the data and is therefore **underfitting** the data. On the other hand, a polynomial of degree 20 varies too much, seems to fit the noise in the data, and is therefore **overfitting** the data. Finally, the polynomial of degree 2 seems to work very well. This is expected because the underlying true model is quadratic.

2.3.2 Training, validation, and testing

To be able to tune the machine learning models automatically, we need a quantitative measure of how well the model fits. In Sect. 2.2.1 we have seen that R^2 score is a suitable measure for regression models and it measures the proportion of variance in the data explained by the model. If we plot R^2 scores for polynomial fits to the training data (Fig. 2.7), we can see that it increases with the degree of the polynomial. We can clearly identify underfitting for the polynomial fit of degree 1 (linear regression). However, we cannot identify overfitting because increasing the polynomial degree always increases the R^2 score. The solution is to have a separate **validation set** on which we can evaluate the model for each polynomial degree. If we fit the model using the original data (**training set**) but evaluate it using the validation set, the model will overfit to the noise in the training set but not in the validation set. That way we can identify overfitting. In Fig. 2.7 we can see that the R^2 score on the validation set first increases just as on the training set, but soon starts decreasing as the polynomial degree becomes higher. We chose

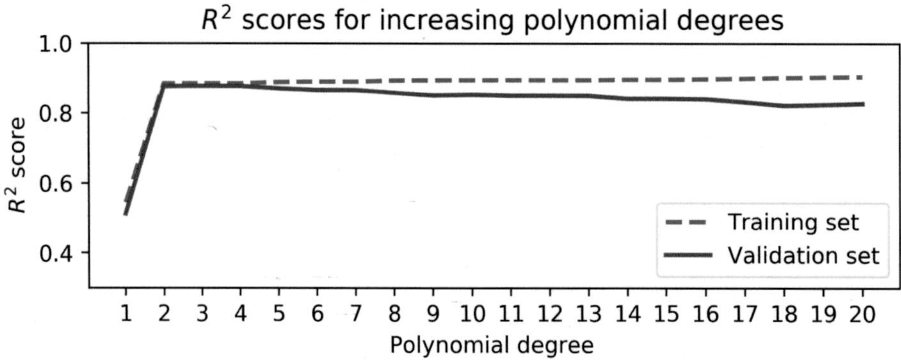

Figure 2.7 Performance of polynomial regression models of various degrees measured by R^2 score on training set and test set.

the hyperparameters (e.g., polynomial degree) by selecting the model that performs best on the validation set. However, there would be still a possibility that the model is overfitted to the validation set as this set was used to choose the hyperparameters and the final performance is overestimated. It is therefore necessary to create a third set, called the **test set**, to evaluate the performance of the model. The purpose of each set is summarized in Table 2.1.

Table 2.1 Types of sets needed for training machine learning algorithms.

training set	fit the model
validation set	find the best hyperparameters
test set	evaluate performance

2.3.3 Cross-validation

In biomedical applications we commonly deal with small datasets available for training. In this scenario, excluding two sets of data is wasteful and undesirable. **Cross-validation** provides a solution to this problem. We first exclude the test set as before, but, instead of excluding the validation set as well, we split the remaining data into k groups (**folds**). We then perform training k times. Each fold becomes a validation set exactly once, while the remaining $k-1$ folds become a training set, to which we fit the model for all different hyperparameter values. We will select the hyperparameters that provide the best performance on the validation set averaged over all k folds. This process is called ***k*-fold cross-validation**.

Once the hyperparameters have been chosen, we will fit the model to all k folds, thus maximising the amount of data available for the training of our final model. The final performance is evaluated on the test set, which is never used during hyperparameter tuning. A schematic diagram of 5-fold cross-validation is presented in Fig. 2.8.

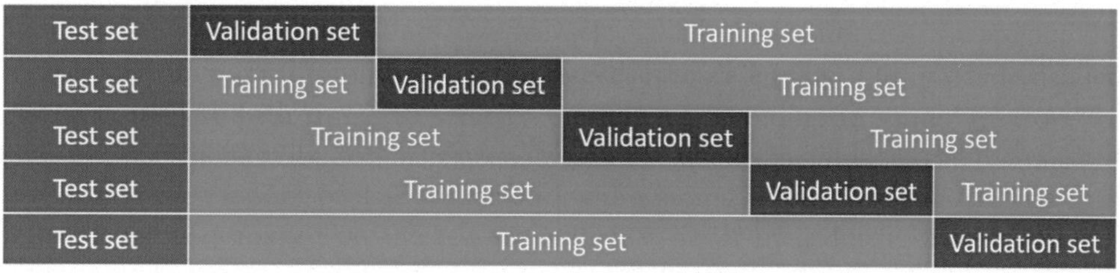

Test set | Validation set | Training set
Test set | Training set | Validation set | Training set
Test set | Training set | Validation set | Training set
Test set | Training set | Validation set | Training set
Test set | Training set | Validation set

Figure 2.8 Schematic diagram of k-fold cross-validation for $k = 5$.

It is very important to ensure that the test set is representative of the whole dataset. One way to deal with this is to **stratify** the test set according to some criterion, for example, that the distribution of target values in the test set is similar to the training set.

2.3.4 Bias and variance

The total error of the fitted model when compared to the true underlying model can be decomposed into three distinct components:

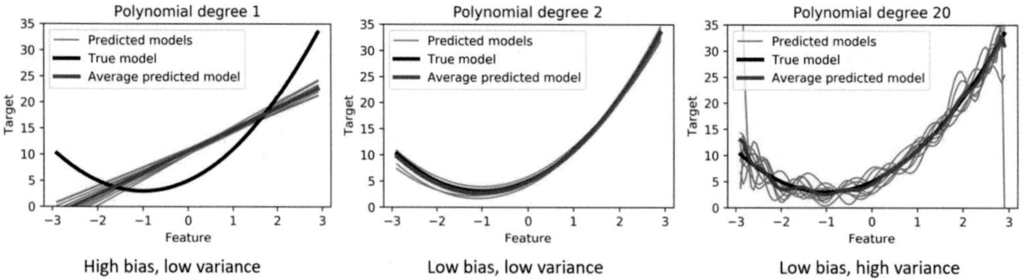

Figure 2.9 Bias and variance of a set of models fitted to a set of random samples.

- **Bias error**: how much, on average, the predicted target values differ from the true model;
- **Variance error**: how much the predicted target values from models trained using different samples vary from each other;
- **Noise**: How much the sample target values differ from the true model.

As the model complexity increases, the bias error will decrease because the model will be flexible enough to capture the true trends in the data. On the other hand, the variance will increase because the increased flexibility of the model also means the potential to overfit to the noise. There is therefore a trade-off between bias and variance, and the optimal model complexity balances both. Noise error is always present in the data and is therefore also called irreducible error.

Let's now demonstrate these concepts using our example. We generate 10 different random datasets from the true model and fit polynomial models of degree M to each of them. The fitted models are depicted in Fig. 2.9 by the green lines. Next, we can calculate the average of the fitted models, depicted by the red line. The true model is depicted by the black line. Bias error is the root-mean-squared error between the average predicted (the red line) and true target (the black line) values, and we see that it decreases with increasing model complexity, in our case the polynomial degree. Variance error, the average squared difference between the individual models (the green lines) and the average model (the red line), increases with the polynomial degree. The optimal model complexity is achieved when the variance is still low, but the bias has already decreased, such as in the case of second-degree polynomial fit.

2.3.5 Training models in scikit-learn

In this section we will show how to train machine learning models in the scikit-learn library on an example of a **univariate polynomial regression**. We will use the simulated dataset described at the beginning of Sect. 2.3 and depicted in Fig. 2.6, top left. We will learn how to:

- Split the data into training set and test set;

- Fit a polynomial model to the training data;
- Tune the hyperparameter polynomial degree using cross-validation;
- Evaluate performance on the test set.

Generate the data

Let's first define our true model $y = 2x^2 + 4x + 5$ as a function:

```
def TrueModel(x):
    return 2*x**2+4*x+5
```

Next, we generate an array of $n = 100$ random features `X` from a uniform distribution with interval $[-3, 3]$. This can be done using `numpy` function `rand`

```
import numpy as np
n=100
X = 6*np.random.rand(n)-3
```

To generate the noisy target values, we first generate the Gaussian noise with $\sigma = 3$ using `numpy` function `randn`

```
noise = 3*np.random.randn(n)
```

The noisy target values `y` will be obtained by calculating the true target values and adding the noise

```
y = TrueModel(X) + noise
```

Finally, the feature matrix `X` is converted to a 2D array

```
X = X.reshape(-1,1)
```

Train test split

Scikit-learn offers a function `train_test_split` to perform the splitting of the dataset. A common pattern is to keep 80% of the data for training and use 20% for testing. This can be set using an option `test_size`. Note that backslash allows splitting a long command over two lines.

```
from sklearn.model_selection import train_test_split
X_train, X_test, y_train, y_test = \
        train_test_split(X,y,test_size = 0.2)
```

If we want to create a representative test set, we can use the `stratify` parameter. In this example we will split the data into seven bins by rounding the feature values, and stratify the test set to have the same proportion of the data from each bin as the training set:

```
bins = np.round(X)
X_train, X_test, y_train, y_test = \
        train_test_split(X,y,test_size = 0.2, \
        stratify = bins)
```

Fitting a polynomial model

Scikit-learn does not directly implement a polynomial regression model. Instead, the polynomial regression is performed in two steps:

1. Polynomial feature transformation—a **transformer** object `PolynomialFeatures` transforms each feature x into a feature vector $(1, x, x^2, ..., x^M)$, where the polynomial degree M is defined by setting the parameter `degree`;
2. Performing multivariate linear regression—a **regressor** object `LinearRegression` fits the model $y = x_0 + x_1 w_1 + ... + x_M w_M$ to the data.

If we combine these two steps, we will have $x_j = x^j$ and therefore create a polynomial model $y = x_0 + w_1 x + ... + w_M x^M$. These two steps are implemented as follows: first we perform the polynomial feature transformation

```
from sklearn.preprocessing import PolynomialFeatures
poly_features = PolynomialFeatures(degree=M)
X_train_poly = poly_features.fit_transform(X_train)
```

and then we create and fit the `LinearRegression`. Note that we do not need intercept in the `LinearRegression` model because we have generated a feature $x^0 = 1$. We will therefore set `fit_intercept=False` when creating the `LinearRegression` object:

```
from sklearn.linear_model import LinearRegression
model = LinearRegression(fit_intercept=False)
model.fit(X_train_poly,y_train)
```

Setting up a model pipeline

It is not always convenient to perform several steps for model training, prediction, and evaluation. In particular, if the model becomes an input to another `sklearn` object, such as hyperparameter search using cross-validation that we will introduce subsequently, the steps need to be unified in a single object. Scikit-learn implements a class `Pipeline` to join multiple **steps** into one model. It implements methods `fit`, `predict`, `score`, and others to offer a unified API with other `sklearn` objects. Next, we join the polynomial feature transformation and multivariate linear regression into a single pipeline:

```
from sklearn.pipeline import Pipeline
pipeline = Pipeline((
("poly_features", PolynomialFeatures(degree=2)),
("lin_reg", LinearRegression(fit_intercept=False)) ))
```

Let's look in detail at the syntax for creating the pipelines. It is in the form `Pipeline(steps)`, where the input argument `steps` is a list of transforms and models to be chained, in the order in which they need to be called. Each step is described by a tuple `(name, model)`, where `name` is a string chosen by the user and `model` is a `sklearn` object. The pipeline can be fitted to the data the same way as other models:

```
pipeline.fit(X_train, y_train)
```

To access the original objects joint in a `Pipeline`, we use attribute `named_steps`. For example, the linear regression object is accessed as:

```
pipeline.named_steps["lin_reg"]
```

and coefficient of the linear regression $w_0, \ldots, w_k$ can be accessed as

```
pipeline.named_steps["lin_reg"].coef_
>>> array([4.98164783, 3.7729512, 1.90766111])
```

We see that we have recovered the model $y = 5 + 3.8x + 1.9x^2$ which is fairly close to our true model.

Cross-validation

If we use a single test set, the performance may vary every time we create a different split. A more robust way is to perform cross-validation, where we split the data into k groups (**folds**). Each fold will be used to measure performance exactly once, while the remaining data are used to fit the model. Average performance over the k folds will be much more robust. If there are no hyperparameters to tune, cross-validation can be used directly to measure the performance of the model. In scikit-learn cross-validation is called using

```
from sklearn.model_selection import cross_val_score
scores = cross_val_score(estimator, X, y, cv=5)
```

where `estimator` is the model we want to fit to the feature matrix `X` and target values/labels `y` (for supervised models only). The optional argument `cv` defines the number of folds. The model returns an array with scores for each fold.

Hyperparameter search using cross-validation

Finally, we will show how we can automatically find the optimal hyperparameters in scikit-learn. One of the most common ways is to train a model for each hyperparameter value and measure its performance using cross-validation. This approach is implemented in `GridSearchCV`. We first need to create a dictionary of the hyperparameter values that we want to try during the search. Because we have a `Pipeline` object, the parameter name is combined of the step name `"poly_features"` and parameter name `"degree"` which are joined by two underscores `__`.

```
parameters = {"poly_features__degree": range(1,20)}
```

Next we create the grid search object

```
from sklearn.model_selection import GridSearchCV
grid_search = GridSearchCV(pipeline, parameters, cv=5)
```

We will now find the optimal polynomial degree automatically, by calling

```
grid_search.fit(X_train, y_train)
```

The best cross-validated score obtained during the grid search can be accessed as

```
grid_search.best_score_
>>> 0.84
```

The model with the best hyperparameters fitted to the training data is

```
best_model = grid_search.best_estimator_
```

and the optimal polynomial degree

```
best_model.named_steps['poly_features'].degree
>>> 2
```

Evaluate performance on the test set

We can evaluate the performance on the test set directly using a trained `GridSearchCV` object by calling its method `score`. It will return the score of the model with the best hyperparameter setting identified during the search and fitted to the whole training set:

```
grid_search.score(X_test,y_test)
>>> 0.91
```

2.3.6 Exercises

1. In Sect. 2.3 you were given code to generate a noisy dataset and fit the second-order polynomial model. Write code to visualize the fitted polynomial curve and the original data. Experiment with the polynomial degree of the fit and observe how the model changes.
2. Perform cross-validation for polynomial fits of different degrees to the simulated dataset and observe how the average R^2 score changes.
3. Load the data `noisy_data.csv` using `pandas`.[2] The file contains two columns:
   - column zero contains features `X`;

[2] The dataset and the skeleton code for this exercise can be obtained from github.com/MachineLearning-BiomedicalApplications/notebooks.

- column one contains target values `y`.

Fit a polynomial model to the data. Perform the following steps:

- Perform stratified train-test split;
- Create a polynomial model using `Pipeline`;
- Use `GridSearchCV` to find the optimal polynomial degree and print out the best cross-validated score;
- Calculate performance on the test set;
- Plot the fitted model;
- Print out the coefficients of the model.

Can you work out what was the underlying polynomial model? *(Hint: the coefficients were whole numbers.)*

CHAPTER 3

Regression

In Chap. 2 we have seen examples of univariate linear regression (Sect. 2.2.1) and univariate polynomial regression (Sect. 2.3). The word **univariate** refers to having only a single feature to predict the target values. In machine learning problems, however, we often wish to combine multiple features to achieve more accurate predictions. Regression that involves multiple features is called **multivariate**.

In this chapter we will demonstrate various multivariate regression models using the example of **predicting the age of preterm babies from volumes of various brain structures** calculated from MRI scans, see Fig. 3.1. The dataset consists of brain structure volumes calculated from 164 MRI scans of preterm babies scanned between 27 and 45 weeks GA gathered by the Developing Human Connectomme Project[1] [13,29]. We will have a detailed look at the algorithms for the segmentation of brain structures in Chap. 6. We will first describe the multivariate linear regression (Sect. 3.1). Next, we will show how we can prevent overfitting using regularization (Sect. 3.2). Finally, we will look at nonlinear multivariate regression (Sect. 3.3).

3.1. Regression basics

In this section we will look at a basic regression technique called multivariate linear regression. First, we describe this regression model in detail (Sect. 3.1.1), then we explain how we train it (Sect. 3.1.2), and finally we investigate its performance in Sect. 3.1.3.

3.1.1 Multivariate linear regression

Multivariate linear regression model is defined as

$$\hat{y} = w_0 + w_1 x_1 + ... + w_D x_D,$$

where $\mathbf{x} = (x_1, ...x_D)^T$ is a feature vector, weight vector $\mathbf{w} = (w_0, w_1, ..., w_D)^T$ forms parameters of the model, and $\hat{y}$ is a predicted target value.

We wish to fit the model (find the weight vector $\mathbf{w}$) to N training samples $\mathbf{x_i} = (x_{i1}, ..., x_{iD})$ with associated target values y_i, where $i = 1, ..., N$. This can be done by minimizing the loss function that measures a **sum of squared errors** between true

[1] www.developingconnectome.org.

Machine Learning for Biomedical Applications
https://doi.org/10.1016/B978-0-12-822904-0.00008-X
Copyright © 2024 Elsevier Ltd.
All rights reserved.

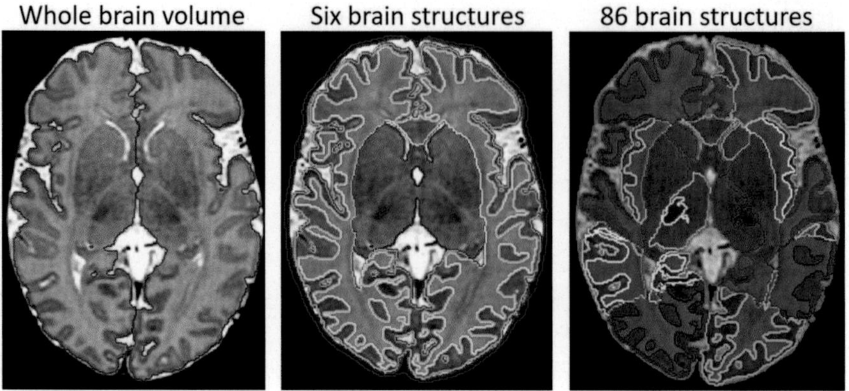

Figure 3.1 Brain volumes for predicting the age of preterm babies from MRI scans. Left: whole brain volume as a single feature; middle: six main structures; right: detailed segmentation resulting in 86 volumes as features.

and predicted target values

$$L(\mathbf{w}) = \frac{1}{2}\sum_{i=1}^{N}(y_i - \hat{y}_i)^2, \tag{3.1}$$

where

$$\hat{y}_i = w_0 + w_1 x_{i1} + \ldots + w_D x_{iD}.$$

In our biomedical example, each sample denoted by index i is a brain MRI scan, and the feature vector $\mathbf{x_i}$ is composed of volumes of brain structures calculated from that scan. Each feature, denoted by index k, represents a volume of a particular brain structure, and the target value y_i is the true GA of the baby at the time of the scan.

Matrix representation

Next, we will construct a feature matrix for regression. Note that we have D features but $D+1$ weights. The weight w_0 is not multiplied by a feature and is often called a **bias** or **intercept**. In order to simplify the equations, we will define a new feature $x_0 = 1$. The model will the simplify to

$$\hat{y} = \sum_{k=0}^{D} w_k x_k.$$

Construction of a feature matrix is described in Sect. 2.1.3. If we add the feature x_0, the feature matrix will become

$$\mathbf{X} = \begin{pmatrix} 1 & x_{11} & \cdots & x_{1D} \\ \vdots & \ddots & \vdots & \\ 1 & x_{N1} & \cdots & x_{ND} \end{pmatrix}. \tag{3.2}$$

Recollect that in Sect. 2.1.3 we defined the target vector as $\mathbf{y} = (y_1, ..., y_N)^T$. We can now also define a **predicted target vector** $\hat{\mathbf{y}} = (\hat{y}_1, ..., \hat{y}_N)^T$ in a matrix form as

$$\hat{\mathbf{y}} = \mathbf{X}\mathbf{w}. \tag{3.3}$$

The sum of squared errors loss (Eq. (3.1)) can be expressed as

$$L(\mathbf{w}) = \frac{1}{2}(\mathbf{y} - \hat{\mathbf{y}})^T(\mathbf{y} - \hat{\mathbf{y}}). \tag{3.4}$$

Substituting $\hat{y}$ according to Eq. (3.3) results in

$$L(\mathbf{w}) = \frac{1}{2}(\mathbf{y} - \mathbf{X}\mathbf{w})^T(\mathbf{y} - \mathbf{X}\mathbf{w}). \tag{3.5}$$

3.1.2 Training linear regression models

Normal equation

The solution $\hat{\mathbf{w}}$ that minimizes the loss given in Eq. (3.5) can be found analytically using

$$\hat{\mathbf{w}} = \left(\mathbf{X}^T\mathbf{X}\right)^{-1}\left(\mathbf{X}^T\mathbf{y}\right) \tag{3.6}$$

and is called the **normal equation**. It can be used on the condition that the $D+1 \times D+1$ square matrix $\mathbf{X}^T\mathbf{X}$ is invertible. We will discuss this condition in more detail in Sect. 3.1.3.

Scikit-learn implements the multivariate linear regression as the object `LinearRegression`, which we have already demonstrated in Sect. 2.2.1 and 2.3.

Gradient descent

If the number of features D is very large, matrix inversion is impractical, and numerical algorithms, such as **gradient descent,** can be employed instead. In this case the solution $\hat{\mathbf{w}}$ can be found iteratively by

$$\hat{\mathbf{w}}^{(n+1)} = \hat{\mathbf{w}}^{(n)} + \eta\mathbf{X}^T\left(\mathbf{y} - \mathbf{X}\hat{\mathbf{w}}^{(n)}\right), \tag{3.7}$$

where n is the iteration number, and η is a learning rate that needs to be set correctly for the algorithm to converge, as demonstrated in Fig. 3.2. The gradient descent (GD) algorithm that uses all the samples at each iteration is called the batch GD. If there is also a very large number of samples N, each GD iteration might be very slow to execute. To

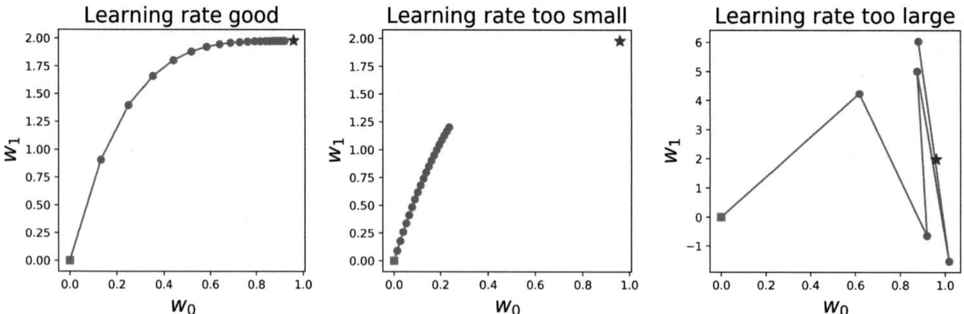

Figure 3.2 Influence of the learning rate η on gradient descent optimization. Red star represents solution $\hat{\mathbf{w}}$ obtained using normal equation; green square is the initial estimate of $\hat{\mathbf{w}}^{(0)}$; and blue circles are estimates $\hat{\mathbf{w}}^{(n)}$ at each iteration n. When learning rate is correctly set, the algorithm converges to the correct solution. If the learning rate is too small, the algorithm will need a very large number of iterations and might stop before reaching the correct solution. If the learning rate is too large, the algorithm will oscillate rather than converge.

solve this problem, we can instead use only one random sample per iteration, and such an algorithm is called the **stochastic GD**. Obviously, this would be very fast, but the solution might become unstable. A good compromise is the **mini-batch GD**, where we use a small subset (a mini-batch) of training samples at each iteration. Comparison of these three types of GD is presented in Fig. 3.3.

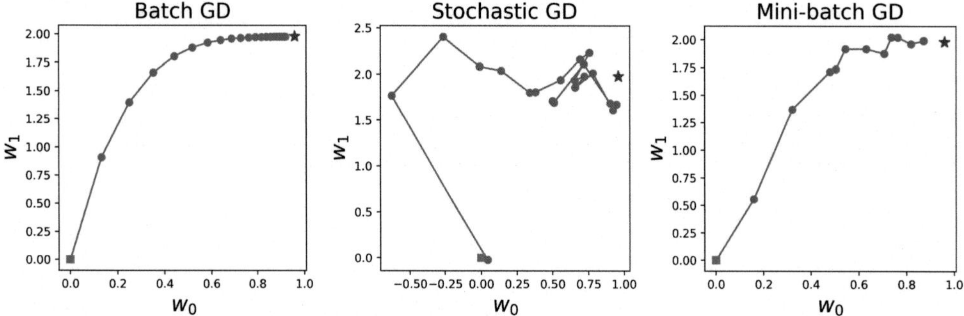

Figure 3.3 Comparison of convergence properties of batch, stochastic, and mini-batch gradient descents.

Scikit-learn implements object `SGDRegressor` to fit the regression models using the stochastic gradient descent. A multivariate linear regression model can be created by

```
from sklearn.linear_model import SGDRegressor
model = SGDRegressor(loss="squared_loss", penalty=None)
```

Derivation of the normal equation

We will now have an in-depth look at the normal equation (Eq. (3.6)). The solution $\hat{\mathbf{w}}$ will be the minimum of the loss function $L(\mathbf{w})$. It is therefore necessary that the first derivative at the minimum is zero:

$$\frac{\partial L(\mathbf{w})}{\partial \mathbf{w}} = 0.$$

To calculate the first derivative of Eq. (3.5), we will first use the product rule and then simplify the expression:

$$\begin{aligned}\frac{\partial L(\mathbf{w})}{\partial \mathbf{w}} &= \frac{\partial \frac{1}{2}(\mathbf{y}-\mathbf{X}\mathbf{w})^T(\mathbf{y}-\mathbf{X}\mathbf{w})}{\partial \mathbf{w}} \\ &= \frac{1}{2}(\mathbf{y}-\mathbf{X}\mathbf{w})^T(-\mathbf{X}) + \frac{1}{2}(-\mathbf{X})^T(\mathbf{y}-\mathbf{X}\mathbf{w}) \\ &= -\mathbf{X}^T(\mathbf{y}-\mathbf{X}\mathbf{w})\end{aligned}$$

We can now set the first derivative to zero and find the expression for $\mathbf{w}$:

$$\begin{aligned}-\mathbf{X}^T(\mathbf{y}-\mathbf{X}\mathbf{w}) &= 0 \\ \mathbf{X}^T\mathbf{X}\mathbf{w} &= \mathbf{X}^T\mathbf{y} \\ \mathbf{w} &= (\mathbf{X}^T\mathbf{X})^{-1}\mathbf{X}^T\mathbf{y}\end{aligned}$$

Implementation of normal equation in NumPy

Let's assume that we have a feature matrix `X` and a target vector `y`. We first need to add the feature $x_0 = 1$ using `np.hstack` to create a new feature matrix `X1` (Eq. (3.2)).

```
x0 = np.ones([X.shape[0],1])
X1 = np.hstack([x0,X])
```

Next we use a series of matrix multiplication using `np.matmul` and matrix inversion `np.linalg.inv` to implement Eq. (3.6)

```
XtX = np.matmul(X1.T,X1)
Xty = np.matmul(X1.T,y)
w = np.matmul(np.linalg.inv(XtX),Xty)
```

We can calculate predicted target values `y_pred` using the estimated weight vector `w` (Eq. (3.3)):

```
y_pred = np.matmul(X1,w)
```

Derivation of gradient descent equation

The update equation for the gradient descent is derived from the first derivative of the loss function as

$$\hat{\mathbf{w}}^{(n+1)} = \hat{\mathbf{w}}^{(n)} - \eta \frac{\partial L(\hat{\mathbf{w}}^{(n)})}{\partial \hat{\mathbf{w}}^{(n)}}. \tag{3.8}$$

We have already derived the first derivative of the sum of squared errors loss $\frac{\partial L(\mathbf{w})}{\partial \mathbf{w}} = -\mathbf{X}^T(\mathbf{y} - \mathbf{X}\mathbf{w})$ which results in Eq. (3.7).

3.1.3 Measuring performance of multivariate regression

The most intuitive measure of performance of the regression model is the **root mean squared error (RMSE)** defined as

$$RMSE = \sqrt{\frac{1}{N}\sum_{i=1}^{N}(y_i - \hat{y}_i)^2}. \tag{3.9}$$

It is closely related to the sum of squared errors loss $L(\mathbf{w})$: $RMSE = \sqrt{\frac{2}{N}L(\mathbf{w})}$. Because it is normalized by the number of samples N and the square root is taken, it offers a meaningful measure of error in units of the target values. For example, when target values represent the GA of a baby in weeks, RMSE is also an average error in weeks. To achieve the best performance of the model, we need to minimize the RMSE and the best possible RMSE is zero. This is in contrast to R^2 score, which measures the proportion of variance in the data explained by the model (see Sect. 2.2.1) that we wish to maximize, and its best possible value is one. In scikit-learn we can calculate the RMSE of a regression model using the function `mean_squared_error`:

```
from sklearn.metrics import mean_squared_error
from sklearn.linear_model import LinearRegression
model = LinearRegression()
model.fit(X_train,y_train)
y_pred_train = model.predict(X_train)
RMSE_train = np.sqrt(mean_squared_error(y_train, y_pred_train))
```

This code calculates how well the model fits the training data, and therefore it measures bias. To identify overfitting, we can use cross-validation, but this time we define a scoring function `scoring=neg_mean_squared_error`:

```
from sklearn.model_selection import cross_val_score
model = LinearRegression()
scores = cross_val_score(model,X_train,y_train,
                scoring='neg_mean_squared_error')
RMSE_CV = np.sqrt(-np.mean(scores))
```

Alternatively, the overfitting can be uncovered by calculating RMSE on the test set that has been excluded from the training:

```
model.fit(X_train,y_train)
y_pred_test = model.predict(X_test)
RMSE_test = np.sqrt(mean_squared_error(y_test, y_pred_test))
```

Intuitively, we could think that larger number of features results in better prediction, but is this really the case? Let's revisit our dataset with volumes of brain structures calculated from 164 MRI scans of preterm babies (Fig. 3.1). The first dataset has a single feature, the second dataset six features, and the third dataset 86 features. Table 3.1 gives `RMSE_train` and `RMSE_CV` (in weeks) for these three datasets.

Table 3.1 Root-mean-squared error obtained by fitting regression model to whole training dataset (`RMSE_train`) and using cross-validation (`RMSE_CV`).

Number of features	1	6	86
`RMSE_train` (weeks)	1.56	1.12	0.68
`RMSE_CV` (weeks)	1.6	1.27	2.08

We can see that RMSE calculated on the training dataset (`RMSE_train`) decreases with more features. However, this is not the case for `RMSE_CV` that has been calculated through cross-validation. The model fitted to six brain volumes has better `RMSE_train` and `RMSE_CV` than model with a single feature, the whole-brain volume. However, the model with 86 features has clearly overfitted to the noise in the data. We can judge this from the small training error (`RMSE_train`) but large cross-validated error (`RMSE_CV`), which shows that the model does not generalize well to unseen data. In fact, the more features we have, the more flexibility the model has because the number of free parameters of the models (weights w_i) grows with the number of features. Multivariate linear regression with a large number of features is therefore prone to overfitting.

How do we decide how many features D are optimal for our model? That depends on the number samples N available for training. The most error-prone part of the normal equation (Eq. (3.6)) is inversion of the matrix $\mathbf{X}^T\mathbf{X}$. The size of this matrix $D+1 \times D+1$ is related to the number of features D. However its rank also depends on the number of samples N and is at most $\min(N, D+1)$ because the size of the matrix $\mathbf{X}$ is $N \times D+1$. Therefore, if we have no more samples than features, $N < D+1$, the matrix $\mathbf{X}^T\mathbf{X}$ is not invertible, and there are many solutions that fit the training data exactly. In that case the scikit-learn object `LinearRegression` will select the solution with the smallest $|\mathbf{w}|$. If the number of samples N is similar to number of features D and $N \geq D+1$, overfitting to noise is very likely. If N is much larger than $D+1$, the model is well conditioned, and the predictions will generalize well.

3.1.4 Exercises

1. The performance of the regression algorithm is measured using RMSE and R^2 score. Describe what these two measures represent.
2. Table 3.2 gives performance measures for three regression models. Decide which of the models has the highest bias, the highest variance, and the best bias-variance trade-off.

Table 3.2 Performance of three different regression models.

	Model 1	Model 2	Model 3
R^2 score training set	0.97	0.85	0.92
R^2 score cross-validation	0.68	0.81	0.89

3. The comma separated values (CSV) file *'GA-brain-volumes-6-features.csv'*[2] contains the GA at scan in the first column and the volumes of six brain structures in the second to seventh column. Perform the following tasks:
   - Load the file using `Pandas` package and extract the feature matrix and target vector. Print out the number of features and samples.
   - Fit the `LinearRegression` model to the data and calculate the RMSE on the whole dataset and using cross-validation, as described in Sect. 3.1.2.
   - Create function `RMSE(model,X,y)` to fit the model to the whole dataset and calculate the RMSE (note that we are not using a test set in this exercise).
   - Create function `RMSE_CV(model,X,y)` to calculate the RMSE using cross-validation.
   - Fit the regression model using stochastic gradient descent implemented in `SGDRegressor` and calculate RMSE and cross-validated RMSE using the functions you created.
4. Implement multivariate linear regression in `NumPy`. Perform the following steps:
   - Split the dataset that you loaded in Exercise 3 into training and test sets, by including the first 120 samples in the training set and the rest in the test set.
   - Implement fitting of the model to the training data in `NumPy` using Eq. (3.6).
   - Predict the target values on the test set according to Eq. (3.3).
   - Calculate the RMSE on the test set.
5. Load the datasets with a single volume and 86 volumes from CSV files *'GA-brain-volumes-1-feature.csv'* and *'GA-brain-volumes-86-features.csv'*. The first column contains GA and the remaining columns contain volumes. Compare the performance of the linear regression with different numbers of features by calculating RMSE on the whole dataset and the cross-validated RMSE (note that we are not

[2] The datasets and the skeleton code for exercises 3–5 are available from github.com/MachineLearning-BiomedicalApplications/notebooks.

using a test set in this exercise). Does combining six volumes as features in a multivariate regression model improve the predictions compared to the single volume? Does using all 86 volumes as features further improve predictions?

3.2. Penalized regression

In the previous section we saw that fitting multivatiate linear regression to datasets with large number of features but limited number of samples can be problematic. However, such datasets are common in biomedical applications. In this section we will describe one of the approaches to tackle this problem called **regularization**. Regularized regression algorithms seek to fit the model to the training data, while also penalizing large weights to prevent overfitting to noise. In this section we will describe two most common penalized regression techniques, **ridge** in Sect. 3.2.1 and **lasso** in Sect. 3.2.2. We will compare them in Sect. 3.2.3.

3.2.1 Ridge regression

Ridge penalty seeks to minimize the weight vector $\mathbf{w}$ by penalizing its squared L_2 norm

$$|\mathbf{w}|_2^2 = \sum_{k=0}^{D} w_k^2.$$

In the context of linear regression, the ridge penalty is added as an extra term to the loss function

$$L(\mathbf{w}) = \frac{1}{2}\sum_{i=1}^{N}\left(y_i - \sum_{k=1}^{D} w_k x_{ik} - w_0\right) + \frac{\lambda}{2}\sum_{k=0}^{D} w_k^2. \tag{3.10}$$

The **hyperparameter** λ defines the weight of the ridge penalty and is usually determined using cross-validation, see Fig. 3.4. In general, if a dataset is prone to overfitting, the ridge linear regression will require higher λ. For datasets with sufficient number of samples, a low λ is required.

To formulate the ridge regression problem in a matrix form, we will expand Eq. (3.5) by the ridge penalty

$$L(\mathbf{w}) = \frac{1}{2}(\mathbf{y} - \mathbf{X}\mathbf{w})^T(\mathbf{y} - \mathbf{X}\mathbf{w}) + \frac{\lambda}{2}\mathbf{w}^T\mathbf{w}. \tag{3.11}$$

The solution that minimizes the loss function $F(\mathbf{w})$ is

$$\hat{\mathbf{w}} = \left(\mathbf{X}^T\mathbf{X} + \lambda\mathbf{I}\right)^{-1}\left(\mathbf{X}^T\mathbf{y}\right), \tag{3.12}$$

where $\mathbf{I}$ is an identity matrix. The gradient descent solution for the ridge regression is

$$\hat{\mathbf{w}}^{(n+1)} = \hat{\mathbf{w}}^{(n)} + \eta\left(\mathbf{X}^T\left(\mathbf{y} - \mathbf{X}\hat{\mathbf{w}}^{(n)}\right) - \lambda\hat{\mathbf{w}}^{(n)}\right). \tag{3.13}$$

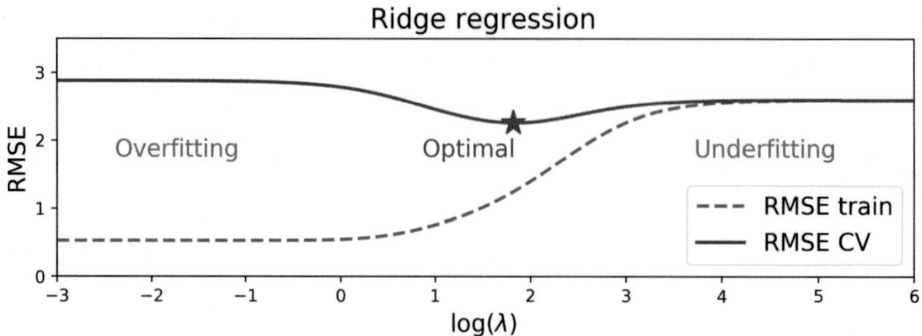

Figure 3.4 Root-mean-squared error of the ridge regression model fitted to a noisy dataset for various values of λ, ranging from 10^{-3} to 10^6. For small values of λ, the model is overfitted, as seen from the high cross-validated RMSE. For large values of λ the model is underfitted, and both training and cross-validated RMSE are high. Optimal λ corresponds to the smallest cross-validated RMSE.

In scikit-learn the ridge regression model can be formulated as follows:

```
from sklearn.linear_model import Ridge
model = Ridge(alpha=1)
```

where `alpha` is the hyperparameter λ. Note that it is important to perform feature scaling using the `StandardScaler` when training the ridge regression model because weights depend on the amplitudes of the features, and different scaling may result in different solutions.

3.2.2 Lasso regression

The lasso penalty minimizes the weight vector **w** by minimizing its L_1 norm

$$|\mathbf{w}|_1 = \sum_{k=0}^{D} |w_k|,$$

where |.| denotes the absolute value. The loss function becomes

$$L(\mathbf{w}) = \frac{1}{2}\sum_{i=1}^{N}\left(y_i - \sum_{k=1}^{D} w_k x_{ik} - w_0\right) + \lambda \sum_{k=0}^{D} |w_k| \tag{3.14}$$

and can be formulated in a matrix form as

$$L(\mathbf{w}) = \frac{1}{2}(\mathbf{y} - \mathbf{Xw})^T(\mathbf{y} - \mathbf{Xw}) + \lambda \mathbf{w}^T \text{sign}(\mathbf{w}), \tag{3.15}$$

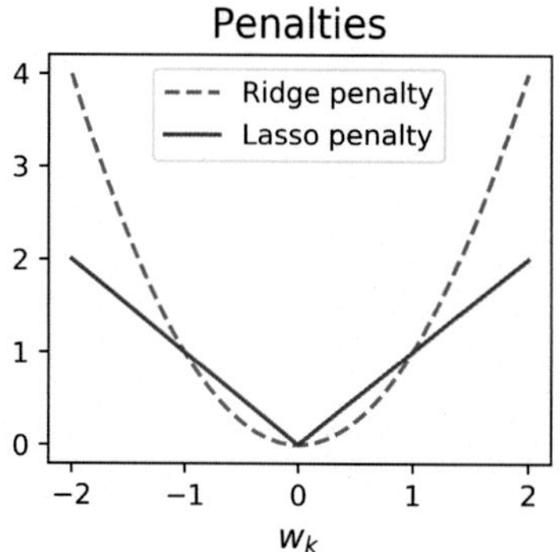

Figure 3.5 Ridge and lasso penalties for a single weight w_k.

where $\text{sign}(\mathbf{w}) = (\text{sign}(w_0), ..., \text{sign}(w_D))^T$ and

$$\text{sign}(w_k) = \begin{cases} 1 & \text{if } w_k > 0 \\ 0 & \text{if } w_k = 0 \\ -1 & \text{if } w_k < 0. \end{cases}$$

The lasso regression does not have an analytical solution and has to be solved using numerical methods. Additionally, the lasso penalty is not differentiable because its derivative is not defined at $w_k = 0$, as can be seen from Fig. 3.5. However, we can still use the gradient descent by calculating a **subgradient**, which is a generalization of the derivative. If we define the first derivative of L_1 norm at $w_k = 0$ to be zero, the subgradient becomes $\text{sign}(\mathbf{w})$, and the gradient descent equation can be written as

$$\hat{\mathbf{w}}^{(n+1)} = \hat{\mathbf{w}}^{(n)} + \eta\big(\mathbf{X}^T\big(\mathbf{y} - \mathbf{X}\hat{\mathbf{w}}^{(n)}\big) - \lambda\text{sign}\big(\mathbf{w}^{(n)}\big)\big). \tag{3.16}$$

In scikit-learn the lasso regression model can be formulated as

```
from sklearn.linear_model import Lasso
model = Lasso(alpha=1)
```

and, as for the ridge model, it is important to scale the features before fitting the lasso model.

3.2.3 Comparison of ridge and lasso penalties

Ridge and lasso penalties both help to decrease the weights, however they have different effect on the resulting solution. In Fig. 3.5 we can observe that for small weights the ridge penalty is weaker than the lasso, and therefore the lasso will more likely push the small weights to zero. On the other hand, the ridge penalty is stronger for larger weights,

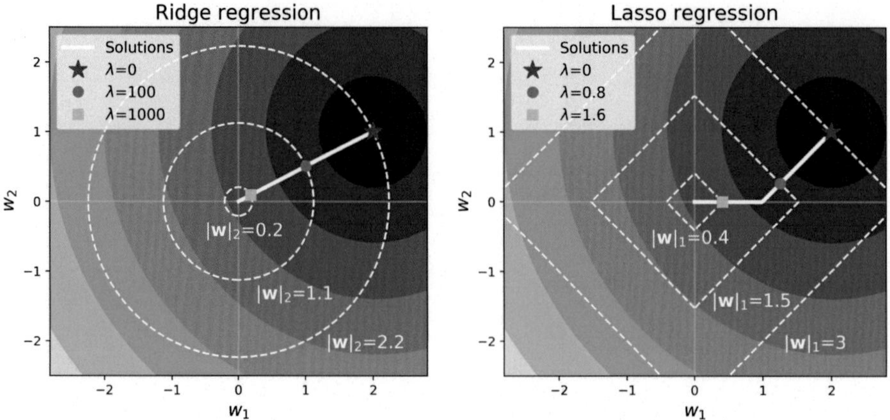

Figure 3.6 Solutions of penalized regression for three different values of λ. The red star represents the nonpenalized solution, and green circle the solution with medium penalty, while large penalty results in a solution close to zero, depicted by a yellow square. For each λ, the solution needs to lie within the circle $|\mathbf{w}|_2 \leq B$ for ridge or the square $|\mathbf{w}|_1 \leq B$ for lasso. The sum of squared error loss is depicted by the background color, with blue representing small values and yellow large values.

and these will decrease faster with ridge than with lasso. Lasso therefore produces more **sparse** weights, by preserving the large weights, while forcing the small weights to zero. On the other hand, the ridge penalty decreases all weights at the same time.

Let's demonstrate this on a simple example where we seek to recover the model $y = 2x_1 + x_2$ from a noisy dataset. The solution to this regression problem is $w_1 = 2$ and $w_2 = 1$, as depicted in Fig. 3.6 by a red star. Because the noise in the dataset is minor, the solution is recovered almost exactly by linear regression with no penalty ($\lambda = 0$). The nonpenalized sum of squared errors loss (Eq. (3.1)) is depicted by the background color and has a minimum (dark blue) around the solution.

The solution for the penalized regression can be also obtained using constrained optimization, where we minimize the sum of squared errors loss (Eq. (3.1)) subject to a constraint $|\mathbf{w}|_2 \leq B$ for ridge and $|\mathbf{w}|_1 \leq B$ for lasso,[3] where for each λ we can find a suitable B. As we increase λ, B decreases, and the solution moves away from the minimum of the sum-of-squared-errors loss towards zero because the size of $\mathbf{w}$ is restricted. In the case of ridge regression, both weights are decreasing proportionally, and the solution follows a straight path to the zero. On the other hand, the lasso penalty decreases the smaller weight w_2 faster, eventually forcing it to zero, while the larger w_1 is still nonzero, thus producing a sparse solution. Due to this property, the lasso penalty is often used for feature selection.

[3] This can be shown using Karush–Kuhn–Tucker conditions.

3.2.4 Training penalized regression models in scikit-learn

In this section we will demonstrate how to tune hyperparameter λ for ridge regression. We first need to define a dictionary of values that we would like to try. We select 100 values for `alpha` on logarithmic scale between 10^{-3} and 10^{3}:

```
params = {"alpha": np.logspace(-3,3,100)}
```

Next we search for optimal `alpha` using `GridSearchCV`, as already shown in Sect. 2.3.5:

```
from sklearn.linear_model import Ridge
from sklearn.model_selection import GridSearchCV

model = Ridge()
gs = GridSearchCV(model, params,
                  scoring='neg_mean_squared_error')
gs.fit(X, y)
```

The optimal parameter can be found as

```
gs.best_estimator_.alpha
>>> 46
```

Because we used `scoring='neg_mean_squared_error'`, cross-validated RMSE can also be extracted directly using

```
np.sqrt(-gs.best_score_)
>>> 1.17
```

The coefficients of the best model can be plotted as

```
plt.plot(gs.best_estimator_.coef_,'*')
```

Optimization of hyperparameter `alpha` for `lasso` is done exactly the same way. Table 3.3 shows that both ridge and lasso penalties reduce overfitting.

Table 3.3 Root-mean-squared error of regression models with ridge, lasso and no penalties calculated on the training set (`RMSE_train`) and using cross-validation (`RMSE_CV`).

Penalty	Ridge	Lasso	None
RMSE_train (weeks)	0.92	1.07	0.68
RMSE_CV (weeks)	1.17	1.27	2.08

Fig. 3.7 shows that ridge and lasso penalties decrease the magnitude of the weights. Lasso forces most weights to zero, resulting in a sparse solution.

Note that in this example we have presented the performance results on a training set only (on the whole set and using cross-validation). Such an approach is suitable for

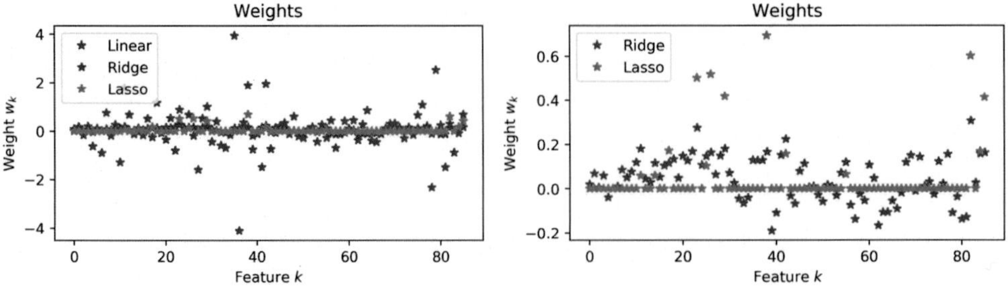

Figure 3.7 Weights $w_0, \ldots, w_D$ of linear regression models with various penalties. Left: ridge and lasso penalties decrease the weights compared to nonpenalized linear regression. Right: lasso penalty, unlike ridge, forces most weights to zero, resulting in a sparse solution.

selecting the best model. The final performance of the model should always be evaluated on a test set that has been excluded from the training as follows:

```
from sklearn.metrics import mean_squared_error
y_pred_test = gs.predict(X_test)
RMSE_test = np.sqrt(mean_squared_error(y_pred_test,y_test))
```

Finally, it is important to note that scikit-learn implementation of ridge and lasso regressions does not penalize the bias term w_0. There is a good reason for it: The bias term is not prone to overfitting, and forcing it to zero decreases the quality of the fit. In other words, very large λ will result in regressor always predicting zero values if all coefficient including bias are penalized. On the other hand, if the bias term is not penalized, large penalty will result in regressor predicting an average of the target values.

3.2.5 Exercises

1. Explain the role of the parameter λ in penalized regression.
2. Explain what is similar and what is different about the ridge and lasso regressions.
3. In Sect. 3.1.2 you were given code to implement the normal equation in Numpy. Amend this code to include the ridge penalty.
4. Fit ridge and lasso regressions to predict GA from 86 structure volumes available in *'GA-brain-volumes-86-features.csv'*.[4] Optimize the hyperparameter λ as described in Sect. 3.2.4. Compare the RMSE of linear regression, ridge and lasso on the whole dataset and using cross-validation. Plot the weights of the three fitted models to see the effect of the penalties.

[4] The dataset and the skeleton code are available from github.com/MachineLearningBiomedicalApplications/notebooks.

3.3. Nonlinear regression

Linear regression models are not always appropriate since there might be nonlinear relationships between features and target values in the data. We have already illustrated this with the example of polynomial regression in Sect. 2.3 and Fig. 2.6. In Fig. 3.8 we plot the true GA of preterm babies against GA predicted from the volumes of six brain structures. Note, that we cannot easily plot the data and the model due to the high dimensionality of the features. In the case of linear ridge regression (Fig. 3.8, left), we can see that for younger babies the model does not fit well, which indicates the nonlinearity of the features.

In the following sections we will describe multivariate nonlinear regression obtained using nonlinear feature transformation (Sect. 3.3.1) and the kernel trick for regression (Sect. 3.3.2).

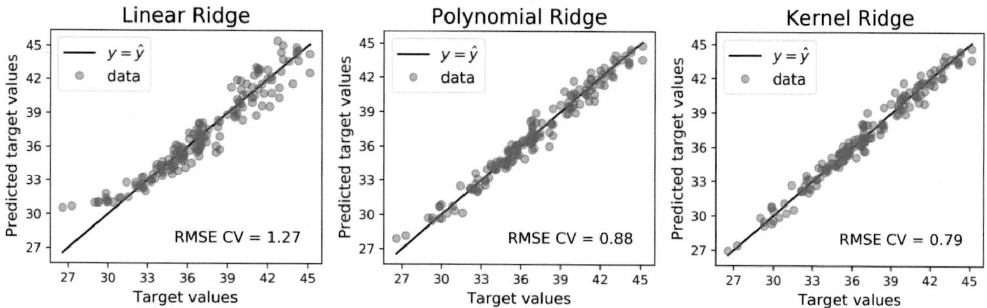

Figure 3.8 Predicted target values plotted against the true target values for prediction of GA from the volumes of six brain structures. Left: linear ridge regression. Middle: polynomial ridge regression. Right: kernel ridge regression with a Gaussian kernel.

3.3.1 Nonlinear feature transformation

In Sect. 2.3 we have seen that univariate polynomial regression can be viewed as a **nonlinear feature transformation** followed by multivariate linear regression. We will now generalize this approach to other nonlinear transformations and multivatiate problems.

Nonlinear feature transformation $\boldsymbol{\phi}$ is a nonlinear function of the original feature vector $\mathbf{x}$. The dimension of the transformed feature vector $\boldsymbol{\phi}(\mathbf{x})$ is often increased compared to $\mathbf{x}$. For example, the univariate polynomial feature transformation of second-degree $\boldsymbol{\phi}(x) = (1, x, x^2)^T$ increases the dimension of the feature vector from one to three. For a two-dimensional feature vector $\mathbf{x} = (x_1, x_2)^T$, the polynomial feature transformation of second degree

$$\boldsymbol{\phi}(x_1, x_2) = \left(1, \sqrt{2}x_1, \sqrt{2}x_2, x_1^2, \sqrt{2}x_1x_2, x_2^2\right)^T$$

increases the dimension to six. Once the features have been transformed, we can apply the univariate linear regression model

$$\hat{y} = \boldsymbol{\phi}(\mathbf{x})^T \mathbf{w}.$$

Due to the increased number of features, we select the loss function with ridge penalty to prevent overfitting, i.e.,

$$L(\mathbf{w}) = \frac{1}{2}\sum_{i=1}^{N}\left(y_i - \boldsymbol{\phi}(\mathbf{x_i})^T \mathbf{w}\right) + \frac{\lambda}{2}\mathbf{w}^\mathbf{T}\mathbf{w}.$$

Similarly we can define matrix representation by constructing the transformed feature matrix

$$\boldsymbol{\Phi} = \begin{pmatrix} \boldsymbol{\phi}(\mathbf{x_1})^T \\ \vdots \\ \boldsymbol{\phi}(\mathbf{x_N})^T \end{pmatrix},$$

and the loss function can be rewritten with the feature matrix as

$$L(\mathbf{w}) = \frac{1}{2}(\mathbf{y} - \boldsymbol{\Phi}\mathbf{w})^T(\mathbf{y} - \boldsymbol{\Phi}\mathbf{w}) + \frac{\lambda}{2}\mathbf{w}^\mathbf{T}\mathbf{w}. \tag{3.17}$$

It became clear that we can work with the transformed feature matrix in exactly the same way as with original feature matrix $\mathbf{X}$, and the solution to Ridge regression is

$$\hat{\mathbf{w}} = \left(\boldsymbol{\Phi}^T\boldsymbol{\Phi} + \lambda\mathbf{I}\right)^{-1}\left(\boldsymbol{\Phi}^T\mathbf{y}\right).$$

In scikit-learn we can fit polynomial Ridge model as follows:

```
from sklearn.preprocessing import PolynomialFeatures
from sklearn.linear_model import Ridge
poly_features=PolynomialFeatures(degree=2)
model = Ridge(alpha = 0.1,fit_intercept=False)
Phi=poly_features.fit_transform(X)
model.fit(Phi,y)
```

The result of the multivariate polynomial fit to the six brain volumes to predict GA is shown in Fig. 3.8, middle. We can see that this model is more accurate for younger babies than the linear model, and the cross-validated RMSE of GAs decreased from 1.27 to 0.88 weeks. The hyperparameters `degree` and `alpha` were tuned using `GridSearchCV`.

3.3.2 Kernel trick

Dual representation

An alternative way to turn a linear model into a nonlinear one is to use the **kernel trick**. First, we will change the parameters of our model $\mathbf{w}$ to a **dual representation** $\mathbf{a}$ defined as

$$\mathbf{w} = \mathbf{\Phi}^T \mathbf{a}. \tag{3.18}$$

Let's now find out what this representation means. First of all, the weight vector $\mathbf{w}$ has dimension D, which is the number of features. The feature matrix $\mathbf{\Phi}$ is $D \times N$, and therefore dimension of the dual representation $\mathbf{a}$ is N, with one parameter a_i **per sample**. Let's now have a look at the new regression model

$$\hat{y} = \boldsymbol{\phi}(\mathbf{x})^T \mathbf{w} = \boldsymbol{\phi}(\mathbf{x})^T \mathbf{\Phi}^T \mathbf{a} = \sum_{i=1}^{N} \boldsymbol{\phi}(\mathbf{x})^T \boldsymbol{\phi}(\mathbf{x_i}) a_i. \tag{3.19}$$

The regression model thus becomes a linear combination of **kernels** κ

$$\kappa(\mathbf{x}, \mathbf{x_i}) = \boldsymbol{\phi}(\mathbf{x})^T \boldsymbol{\phi}(\mathbf{x_i}) \tag{3.20}$$

that define the **similarity** between two feature vectors. In this case we calculate a similarity between a training sample $\mathbf{x_i}$ and a new sample $\mathbf{x}$ for which we would like to evaluate the model. The most common choice for the kernel κ is the **Gaussian kernel**:

$$\kappa(\mathbf{x}, \mathbf{x_i}) = \exp\left(-\frac{|\mathbf{x} - \mathbf{x_i}|_2^2}{2\sigma} \right), \tag{3.21}$$

where $|\mathbf{x} - \mathbf{x_i}|_2 = \sqrt{\sum_{j=1}^{D} (x_j - x_{ij})^2}$ is the Euclidian distance between two feature vectors. The Gaussian kernel is shown in Fig. 3.9. Note that pairs of features with larger distances have smaller similarity κ, while identical feature vectors have the largest similarity.

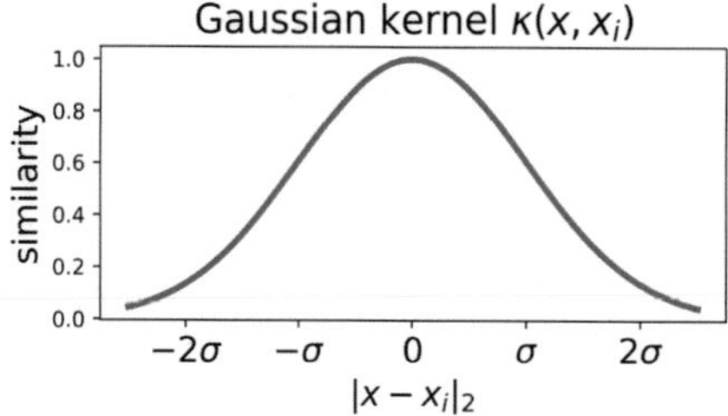

Figure 3.9 Gaussian kernel.

The resulting dual prediction model is a linear combination of kernels placed around the feature vectors

$$\hat{\mathbf{y}} = \sum_{i=1}^{N} a_i \kappa(\mathbf{x}, \mathbf{x_i}). \tag{3.22}$$

An example of the dual prediction model with Gaussian kernel is visualized in Fig. 3.10. We can observe that model becomes smoother as the size of the kernel increases. On the left the kernels are of optimal size, resulting in a smooth and well fitting regression model. In the middle plot, the kernel size is too small and model tends to zero between the samples. In the plot on the right, the kernel is too large and the regression curve underfits the data.

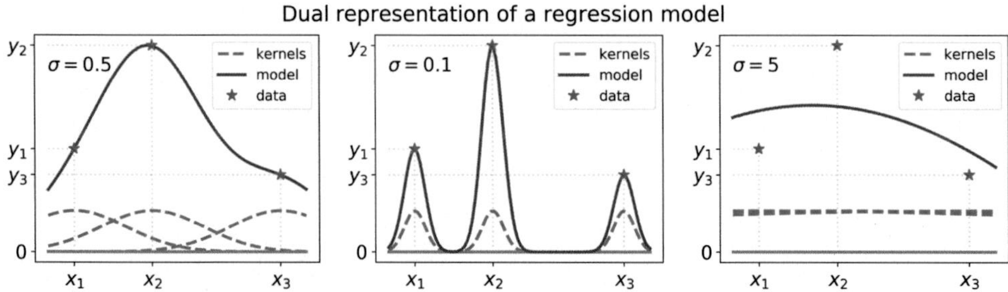

Figure 3.10 Kernel ridge regression with various Gaussian kernel sizes σ. Dashed green lines show kernels $\kappa(\mathbf{x}, \mathbf{x_i})$ centered around each datapoint x_i. Solid red lines indicate the linear combination of the kernels that forms the predicted model (Eq. (3.22)). Hyperparameter λ has been set to 10^{-3}.

Kernel ridge regression

We will demonstrate how we can apply the kernel trick to the regression models using an example of ridge regression. If we introduce the dual representation (Eq. (3.18)) into ridge regression loss (Eq. (3.17)), we obtain

$$L(\mathbf{a}) = \frac{1}{2}(\mathbf{y} - \mathbf{Ka})^T(\mathbf{y} - \mathbf{Ka}) + \frac{\lambda}{2}\mathbf{a}^T\mathbf{Ka}, \tag{3.23}$$

where matrix $\mathbf{K} = \mathbf{\Phi\Phi}^T$ is called the **Gramm matrix**, consisting of elements $\kappa(\mathbf{x_i}, \mathbf{x_j}) = \boldsymbol{\phi}(\mathbf{x_i})^T\boldsymbol{\phi}(\mathbf{x_j})$, the similarities between all pairs of training feature vectors evaluated by the kernel. The solution for dual representation of the kernel ridge regression model is obtained as

$$\hat{\mathbf{a}} = (\mathbf{K} + \lambda\mathbf{I})^{-1}\mathbf{y}. \tag{3.24}$$

Once we have the dual representation $\hat{\mathbf{a}}$, we can make a prediction $\hat{y}$ for a new feature vector $\mathbf{x}$ by first evaluating similarities with all training feature vectors to calculate the vector $\mathbf{k}(\mathbf{x})^T = (\kappa(\mathbf{x}, \mathbf{x_1}), ..., \kappa(\mathbf{x}, \mathbf{x_N}))$ and then applying Eq. (3.19), which can be expressed as

$$\hat{y} = \mathbf{k}(\mathbf{x})^T \hat{\mathbf{a}} = \mathbf{k}(\mathbf{x})^T (\mathbf{K} + \lambda \mathbf{I})^{-1} \mathbf{y}. \tag{3.25}$$

From this result we can see that we do not need to know the original feature transformation $\boldsymbol{\phi}$, and choosing a kernel is sufficient for the kernel ridge regression model.

Kernel ridge regression in scikit-learn

Kernel ridge regression can be fitted in scikit-learn as follows:

```
from sklearn.kernel_ridge import KernelRidge
model = KernelRidge(kernel='rbf',gamma=0.01,
                    alpha=0.0001)
model.fit(X,y)
```

The prediction of GA from six brain structure volumes using `KernelRidge` is shown in Fig. 3.8, right. The hyperparameter `gamma` is equal to $\frac{1}{2\sigma^2}$. The hyperparameters `gamma` and `alpha` were tuned using `GridSearchCV`. The kernel ridge regression model achieved the best cross-validated RMSE of 0.79 weeks and completely removed the bias in predictions for young babies.

Feature transformation or kernel?

One of the advantages of the kernel methods is the intuitive interpretation of the kernel as a similarity between feature vectors. Additionally, it enables the original feature transformations to have very large, possibly infinite, dimension D. This is due to the fact that we invert the matrix $\mathbf{K} + \lambda \mathbf{I}$, which has dimension $N \times N$ related to number of samples. On the other hand, for ridge regression with nonlinear feature transformation, we invert the matrix $\mathbf{\Phi}^T \mathbf{\Phi} + \lambda \mathbf{I}$ with dimension $D \times D$, which is related to the number of features instead. Kernel methods are thus more flexible compared to the parametric models such as polynomials, and are able to model the trends in the data more accurately.

From the point of view of computational efficiency, we should choose between kernel and feature transformation methods depending on whether the bottleneck is a large number of features or a large number of samples. Kernel methods are slow for large datasets, during both fitting and evaluation, because similarity with every single training sample needs to be evaluated when predicting for an unseen sample. On the other hand, if the trend can be captured by a nonlinear model with small number of parameters, such as low-degree polynomial model, both training and evaluation can be very fast.

3.3.3 Exercises

1. The feature transformation to create linear regression is $\boldsymbol{\phi}(x) = (1, x)^T$. Calculate the linear kernel using Eq. (3.20).
2. The feature transformation to create polynomial regression of second degree is $\boldsymbol{\phi}(x) = (1, x, x^2)^T$. Calculate the second-order polynomial kernel using Eq. (3.20).
3. Given three training samples with feature matrix $\mathbf{X} = (-1, 0, 1)$ and target vector $\mathbf{y} = (2, 3, 2)^T$, Gaussian kernel with $\sigma = 1$ and $\lambda = 0$, calculate the dual representation $\mathbf{a}$ (Eq. (3.24)) to fit the kernel ridge regression model. Evaluate the model for the new sample $x = 0.5$ using Eq. (3.25).
4. Fit the polynomial ridge model and kernel ridge regression model with Gaussian kernel in scikit-learn to predict GAs from the volume of the cortex, the first feature given in the file *'GA-brain-volumes-6-features.csv'*.[5] Experiment with parameters `degree`, `gamma`, and `alpha` to observe the effect.
5. Given three training samples with the feature matrix $\mathbf{X} = (-1, 0, 1)^T$ and target vector $\mathbf{y} = (2, 3, 2)^T$, Gaussian kernel with $\sigma = 1$, and $\lambda = 0$, implement the following in `NumPy`:
   - Generate vector $\mathbf{x}$ of 100 samples in the interval $[-1.25, 1.25]$;
   - Calculate and plot the kernels $\kappa(x, x_i)$ (Eq. (3.21)) for these samples;
   - Calculate dual representation $\mathbf{a}$ using Eq. (3.24);
   - Calculate and plot the kernel ridge regression model using Eq. (3.25).
6. Fit the kernel ridge regression model in scikit-learn to predict GAs from six structure volumes available in *'GA-brain-volumes-6-features.csv'*. Optimize the hyperparameters λ and γ using `GridSearchCV`. Compare the cross-validated RMSE for kernel ridge and linear ridge regressions.

[5] The dataset and the skeleton code for exercises 4–6 can be obtained from github.com/MachineLearning-BiomedicalApplications/notebooks.

CHAPTER 4

Classification

In Chap. 2 we introduced linear classification using the perceptron model (Sect. 2.2.2). In this chapter we will describe various linear and non-linear classification methods in detail. In Sect. 4.1 we will cover linear binary and multi-label classifiers, including perceptron and logistic regression. We will also discuss how to correctly evaluate classification models. In Sect. 4.2 we will introduce support vector classifier and apply feature transformation and the kernel trick to turn a linear classifier into nonlinear.

We will demonstrate training classification models using an example of the **prediction of heart failure (HF)** from measurements obtain using cardiac ultrasound, MRI and ECG [36]. We have already introduced this dataset in Sects. 2.1.1 and 2.2.2. The dataset consists of three measurements (features):

- **Ejection fraction (EF)**: the percentage of blood the left ventricle pumps out with each contraction;
- **Global longitudinal strain (GLS):** the percentage of change in length of the heart during the cardiac cycle;
- **QRS interval duration (QRS):** a characteristic of healthy cardiac function obtained from ECG.

These measurements were calculated from examinations of 120 patients with one of the following conditions:

- **Healthy:** No symptoms;
- **Mild Heart Failure:** Symptoms during physical activity;
- **Serious Heart Failure:** Symptoms while resting.

4.1. Classification basics

In this section we will introduce binary and multi-label linear classification techniques. We will look at perceptron and logistic regression models and discuss performance measures for binary and multi-label classifiers.

4.1.1 Binary linear classification

Binary classifiers predict two labels, usually 0 and 1, based on a D-dimensional feature vector $\mathbf{x} = (x_1, ..., x_D)^T$. The prediction is based on a **decision function**, which is the multivariate linear function

$$h(\mathbf{x}) = w_0 + x_1 w_1 + ... + x_D w_D. \tag{4.1}$$

Machine Learning for Biomedical Applications
https://doi.org/10.1016/B978-0-12-822904-0.00009-1
Copyright © 2024 Elsevier Ltd.
All rights reserved.

The **decision boundary** is defined by the decision function being equal to zero $h(\mathbf{x}) = 0$. The binary labels $\hat{y}$ are based on the sign of the decision function: If the value of the decision function is positive or zero, the predicted label is 1. If the value of the decision function is negative, the predicted label is 0.

$$\hat{y} = \begin{cases} 1 & \text{if } h(\mathbf{x}) \geq 0 \\ 0 & \text{if } h(\mathbf{x}) < 0 \end{cases}$$

We have already introduced an example of binary linear classification in Sect. 2.1.1. In this example we predicted whether the patient is healthy or has heart failure (mild or serious) from two features (EF and GLS), see Fig. 2.2. In Fig. 4.1 we visualize the decision function $h(\mathbf{x})$ for this example as a 2D plane embedded in 3D space. The decision boundary $h(\mathbf{x}) = 0$ is a 1D line, defined by the intersection of the decision function with the zero plane. The decision boundary separates the 2D feature space into two regions.

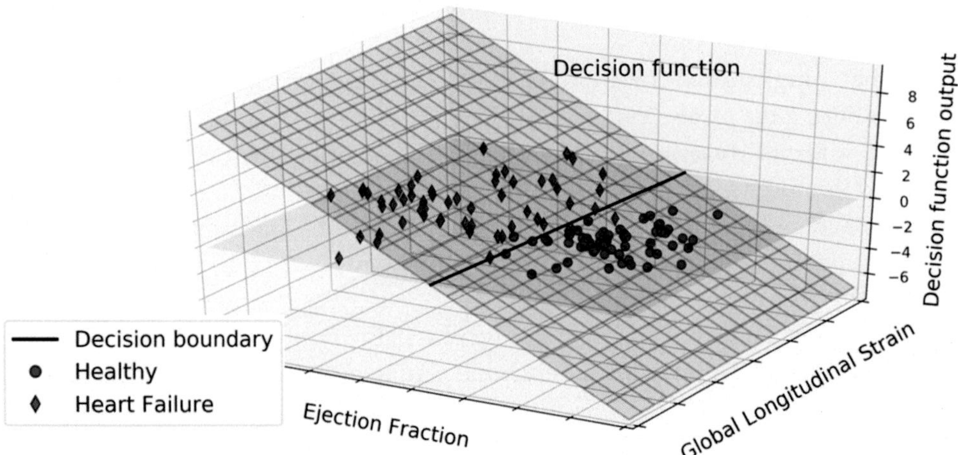

Figure 4.1 Binary classification for 2D feature vectors.

4.1.2 Perceptron

The objective of a binary classification model is to find the decision function (Eq. (4.1)) so that the resulting predicted labels match the training labels as closely as possible. The perceptron model achieves this by penalizing the misclassified labels proportionally to the absolute value of the decision function, called a **perceptron criterion**

$$\hat{\mathbf{w}} = \arg\max_{\mathbf{w}} \sum_{i \in \mathcal{M}} |h(\mathbf{x}_i)|, \tag{4.2}$$

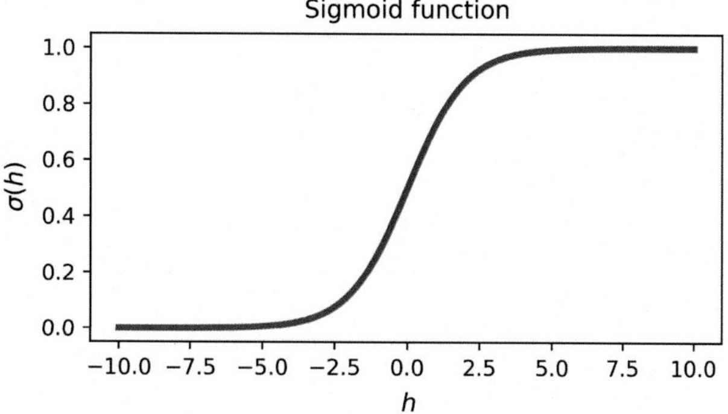

Figure 4.2 Sigmoid function converts output of the decision function h into a probability.

where $\mathcal{M}$ is the set of all misclassified samples. The samples on the wrong side of the decision boundary are penalized proportionally to their distances from the decision boundary. The decision boundary can be found using the **perceptron learning algorithm:**

1. Pick a random training sample $\mathbf{x_i}$;
2. If $y_i = 1$ and $h(\mathbf{x_i}) < 0$, update the parameters of the decision function: $\mathbf{w} = \mathbf{w} + \eta\mathbf{x_i}$;
3. If $y_i = 0$ and $h(\mathbf{x_i}) \geq 0$, update the parameters of the decision function: $\mathbf{w} = \mathbf{w} - \eta\mathbf{x_i}$.

The algorithm iterates between these three steps until convergence. Parameter η is the learning rate, which is usually set to 1. Even though this algorithm works in practice, the convergence is not always guaranteed. This drawback is overcome by the logistic regression model that we will describe next.

4.1.3 Logistic regression

For some samples it might be difficult to decide the correct label because they lie very close to the decision boundary. It is therefore useful to predict not only the label but also the **confidence** in the prediction. Logistic regression converts the output of the decision function h into a probability using a **sigmoid** function σ

$$\sigma(h) = \frac{1}{1 + e^{-h}}.$$

The sigmoid function is depicted in Fig. 4.2. Note that positive values of the decision function result in probabilities between 0.5 and 1, while negative values result in probabilities between 0 and 0.5. If a data point $\mathbf{x}$ lies on the decision boundary $h(\mathbf{x}) = 0$, the resulting probability will be 0.5. The probability that a binary label y is given the feature vector $\mathbf{x}$ can therefore be expressed as a conditional probability and modeled by

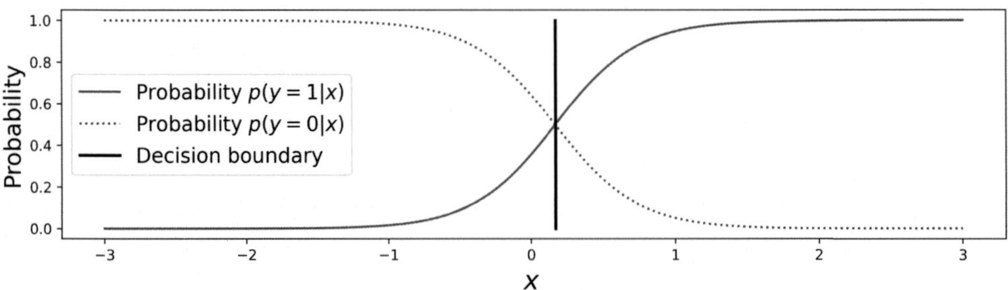

Figure 4.3 Conditional probabilities and the decision boundary for binary classification with 1D feature space.

the sigmoid of the decision function

$$p(y=1|\mathbf{x}) = \sigma\big(h(\mathbf{x})\big)$$
$$p(y=0|\mathbf{x}) = 1 - \sigma\big(h(\mathbf{x})\big).$$

These conditional probabilities are illustrated together with the decision boundary for a 1D feature vector in Fig. 4.3.

Logistic regression finds parameters $\mathbf{w}$ of the decision function by minimising the **cross-entropy** between the training labels y_i and probabilities $p_i = \sigma(h(\mathbf{x}))$ for class 1 to ensure that they are as similar as possible:

$$\hat{\mathbf{w}} = \arg\min_{\mathbf{w}} - \sum_{i=1}^{N} [y_i \ln(p_i) + (1 - y_i) \ln(1 - p_i)]$$

To understand why the cross-entropy loss works, let's consider a single sample with a training label y_i. If $y_i = 1$, the penalty induced by cross-entropy loss for this sample will be $-\ln(p_i)$. This quantity is zero for $p_i = 1$ and tends to infinity as p_i approaches zero. By minimizing this penalty, we will ensure that the predicted probability of label 1 for this sample is high, as prescribed by the training label. On the other hand, if the training label is $y_i = 0$, the penalty $-\ln(1 - p_i)$ will be zero if probability p_i of class 1 is also zero and tends to infinity if it is close to 1.

Cross-entropy is differentiable and can be minimized using numerical methods such as the gradient descent. Unlike for a perceptron, the convergence of the logistic regression model is guaranteed.

In scikit-learn logistic regression is formulated and fitted as follows:

```
from sklearn.linear_model import LogisticRegression
model = LogisticRegression()
model.fit(X_train,y_train)
```

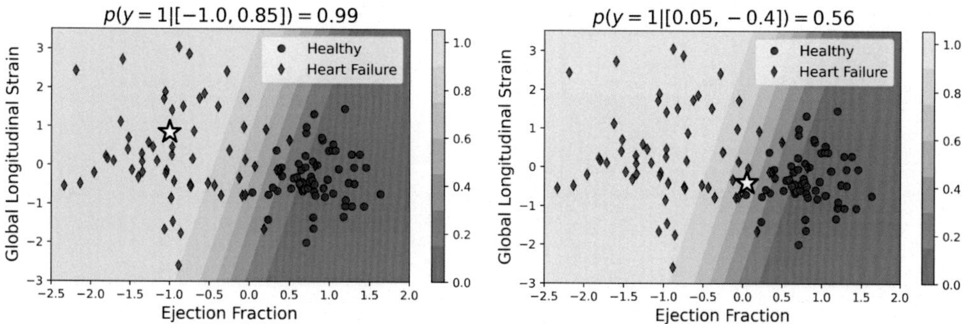

Figure 4.4 Conditional probabilities for heart failure (label 1). Yellow and green colors represent high and low probabilities, respectively. The white star shows a sample with high confidence (left) and low confidence (right).

For the test data, we can obtain probabilistic predictions for all classes

```
p = model.predict_proba(X_test)
```

The predicted probabilities for label zero can be obtained as `p[:,0]` and for label 1 as `p[:,1]`.

In Fig. 4.4 we plotted conditional probabilities for class 1 (heart failure) predicted from two features (EF and GLS). Yellow color represents high probabilities (close to 1) and green color represents low probabilities (close to zero). The two plots show two different samples, plotted by a white star, both with a predicted label 1 (heart failure). However, the confidence in the predicted label is different. The first sample lies in the area of high confidence for heart failure (probability 0.99), while the second one lies close to the decision boundary (probability 0.55). Clearly, we would be more certain that the diagnosis of heart failure for the first case is correct.

4.1.4 Multi-label linear classification

In many applications we wish to assign our samples to more than two classes. For example, we would like to diagnose not only whether a patient has heart failure but also how severe it is. We will therefore have three classes: label 0 for healthy patients, label 1 for cases of mild heart failure, and label 2 for cases of severe heart failure, as described at the beginning of this chapter. We can generalize binary linear classifiers to multi-label classifiers by fitting multiple decision functions. For each class k we have a linear decision function $h_k(\mathbf{x})$ with parameter vector $\mathbf{w_k}$ that separates class k from the rest of the classes.

A multinomial logistic regression model generalizes logistic regression to multiple classes. To predict a label for sample $\mathbf{x}$, we first evaluate the decision functions for

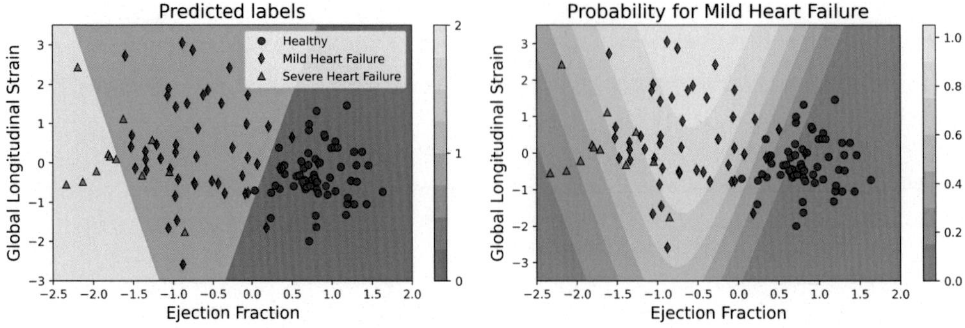

Figure 4.5 Multi-label classification of heart failure. Left: separation of the feature space into three regions: dark green for healthy (label 0), light green for mild heart failure (label 1), and yellow for severe heart failure (label 2). Right: Conditional probabilities for mild heart failure (label 1). Yellow and green colors represent high and low probability, respectively.

each class k (note that we have defined $x_0 = 1$, as in Chap. 3):

$$h_k(\mathbf{x}) = \mathbf{w_k^T x}. \tag{4.3}$$

Outputs of the decision functions are then converted to conditional probabilities $p_k(\mathbf{x}) = p(y = k|\mathbf{x})$ by passing them through the **softmax** function

$$p_k(\mathbf{x}) = \frac{e^{h_k(\mathbf{x})}}{\sum_{j=1}^{K} e^{h_j(\mathbf{x})}}.$$

Finally, we assign the class with highest probability $p_k(\mathbf{x})$ to the sample $\mathbf{x}$:

$$\hat{y} = \arg\max_k p_k(\mathbf{x}).$$

The parameter vectors $\mathbf{w_k}$ for each class-dependent decision function are found by minimizing the **cross-entropy**

$$-\sum_{i=1}^{N}\sum_{k=1}^{K} y_{ik} \ln p_k(\mathbf{x}_i),$$

where y_{ik} is 1 if label $y_i = k$ and zero otherwise.

The classification of patients into healthy or mild or severe heart-failure cases using features EF and GLS is shown in Fig. 4.5. On the left, we can see separation of the feature space into three regions corresponding to the three classes of patients. The plot on the right displays the predicted probability for patients with mild heart failure.

Multinomial logistic regression is implemented in scikit-learn using

```
LogisticRegression(multi_class="multinomial")
```

There is however no need to set the parameter since scikit-learn will automatically detect when we have more than two labels. We will now demonstrate how we fit and plot the logistic regression model to obtain results presented in Fig. 4.5. We can select and fit the model using a standard scikit-learn API

```
model = LogisticRegression()
model.fit(X,y)
```

To plot the classification results, we will predict the labels for the whole 2D feature space. First, we sample the relevant ranges of values for both features

```
import numpy as np
x1 = np.linspace(-2.5, 2, 1000)
x2 = np.linspace(-3, 3.5, 1000)
```

Next, we combine the individual feature vectors into matrices of 2D coordinates, with sizes 1000×1000, suitable for plotting

```
x1, x2 = np.meshgrid(x1, x2.T)
```

However, scikit-learn requires a matrix in shape number of samples $\times$ number of features, which is $1,000,000 \times 2$ in our case. We will achieve this shape by flattening `x1` and `x2` into 1D vectors and concatenating to form a feature matrix

```
Feature_space = np.c_[x1.ravel(), x2.ravel()]
```

Now, we are able to predict the labels for the sampled 2D feature space

```
y_pred = model.predict(Feature_space)
```

Before wc can plot these labels, we need to reshape them back to a 2D grid

```
y_pred = y_pred.reshape(x1.shape)
```

We will plot the result using a `matplotlib` function `contourf` that takes the coordinates and the intensity (color) to be plotted as input arguments

```
import matplotlib.pyplot as plt
plt.contourf(x1, x2, y_pred, cmap = 'summer')
```

The parameter `cmap` determines the colormap for the plot. Finally, we plot the data on and annotate the plot

```
plt.plot(X[y==0,0],X[y==0,1],'bo')
plt.plot(X[y==1,0],X[y==1,1],'rd')
plt.plot(X[y==2,0],X[y==2,1],'g^')
plt.xlabel('Ejection Fraction')
```

```
plt.ylabel('Global Longitudinal Strain')
plt.legend(['Healthy','Mild Heart Failure',
            'Severe Heart Failure'])
plt.title('Predicted labels')
```

To plot the probability for the class 1, we can use the following code:

```
p = model.predict_proba(Feature_space)
p = p[:,1].reshape(x1.shape)
plt.contourf(x1, x2, p, cmap = 'summer')
```

4.1.5 Evaluating performance of classifiers

Accuracy

We have already seen in Sect. 2.2.2 that we can measure the performance of classifiers using the **accuracy** score, which is the proportion of the correctly classified samples. Accuracy works for both binary and multi-label classifiers and is the default classification performance measure in scikit-learn.

We usually measure the accuracy score either on the test set that has been excluded from the training, or using cross-validation on the training set, even though we can also check the accuracy on the whole training set to identify overfitting (see Sect. 2.3). To measure the accuracy using cross-validation, usually done for the purpose of tuning hyperparameters of the model, we can use scikit-learn function `cross_val_score`

```
from sklearn.model_selection import cross_val_score
model = LogisticRegression()
scores = cross_val_score(model, X_train, y_train)
print(round(scores.mean(),2))
>>> 0.89
```

This function will fit a new model for each of the folds (number of folds can be set using parameter `cv`) and output one accuracy score per model. We then print the average score over all folds, which tells us that 89% of samples were correctly classified for the example of the three-class prediction of heart failure (Sect. 4.1.4). To measure accuracy on the test set, we use the default scoring function of the model

```
model.fit(X_train,y_train)
score = model.score(X_test,y_test)
```

Accuracy, however, has some limitations because it depends on the proportion of the data in each class. Let's take an example dataset, with 90% of the samples with label 1 and only 10% with label 0. If classifier assigns 1 to all the samples, it will achieve accuracy 0.9, even though it did not learn how to separate the classes. We call such a dataset **unbalanced**. In cases of unbalanced datasets, good accuracy will depend on proportion of the samples in each class within the dataset.

Sensitivity and specificity

The problem with the accuracy score for unbalanced *binary* dataset can be resolved by calculating the proportion of correctly labeled positive and negative samples, separately. **Sensitivity**, also called **recall**, is the proportion of correctly labeled positive samples (e.g., samples with label 1). In scikit-learn it can be evaluated using the function `recall_score`

```
from sklearn.metrics import recall_score
y_pred_test = model.predict(X_test)
sensitivity = recall_score(y_test,y_pred_test)
```

Specificity, on the other hand, is the proportion of correctly labeled negative samples (e.g., samples with label 0). It is actually identical to the recall score for the negative label. In scikit-learn we can also use `recall_score` to calculate specificity, by setting the positive label to 0

```
specificity = recall_score(y_test,y_pred_test,
                           pos_label=0)
```

Sensitivity and specificity measures can only be applied to binary classifiers. We can generalize sensitivity (recall) to multi-label classification by setting a chosen class as positive and all the other labels as negative. We can calculate the mean recall over all the classes by setting parameter `average='macro'`

```
mean_recall = recall_score(y_test,y_pred_test,
                           average='macro')
```

Similarly, we can also calculate all these measures using cross-validation on the training set by first predicting the labels using `cross_val_predict` and then applying the `recall_score`

```
from sklearn.model_selection import cross_val_predict
y_pred_train = cross_val_predict(model,X_train,
                                 y_train)
sensitivity = recall_score(y_train,y_pred_train)
specificity = recall_score(y_train,y_pred_train,
                           pos_label = 0)
mean_recall = recall_score(y_train,y_pred_train,
                           average='macro')
print('Sensitivity: ', round(sensitivity,2))
print('Specificity: ', round(specificity,2))
print('Mean Recall: ', round(mean_recall,2))
>>> Sensitivity:  0.92
>>> Specificity:  0.98
>>> Mean Recall:  0.95
```

These performance results were calculated for a binary classifier to detect heart failure (Sect. 4.1.3). For multi-label problems, such as three-class heart-failure detection (Sect. 4.1.4), we can efficiently print out recalls for all classes by

```
recalls = recall_score(y_train,y_pred_train,
                       average = None)
print('recalls: ',np.around(recalls,2))
>>> recalls: [0.98 0.88 0.5 ]
```

We can quickly observe that the good accuracy of 89%, which we just calculated, does not reflect relatively poor sensitivity 0.5 for the detection of the severe heart failure, which means that we correctly identify only 50% of the severe cases.

4.1.6 Exercises

1. Explain the role of the sigmoid function in logistic regression.
2. The probabilistic prediction for sample $\mathbf{x}_i$ to belong to class 1 is $p_i = 0.6$. Interpret this result.
3. The training sample $\mathbf{x}_i$ has label $y_i = 0$. Logistic regression predicted p_i close to 1. Approximately evaluate the cross-entropy for this sample and interpret the result.
4. Implement a logistic regression model in scikit-learn to predict heart failure from a single feature, the ejection fraction.[1]
   - Load dataset *heart_failure_data.csv* using Pandas. Select the column `EF` as the feature matrix and the column `HF` as the label vector. Note that the labels are binary. Fit the logistic regression model and plot the data and the decision function. Plot the decision boundary and the conditional probabilities, similarly to Fig. 4.4.
   - A patient with suspicion of heart failure has an MRI scan. The ejection fraction is 40%. Decide whether the patient is likely to experience heart failure and calculate the confidence of this decision.
5. Global longitudinal strain is difficult to estimate correctly due to manual measurements that need to be performed, resulting in poor reproducibility. Researchers believe that GLS could be replaced by duration of the QRS interval extracted from ECG, which is much easier to measure. Load dataset *heart_failure_data.csv* using Pandas. Compare the classifier that predicts heart failure from EF and GLS (Fig. 4.4) with the classifier that predicts HF from EF and QRS. Compare the accuracy, sensitivity, and specificity of the two classifiers.
6. Train a multinomial logistic regression classifier to predict no, moderate, or severe heart failure from EF and GLS (Fig. 4.5). Load dataset *heart_failure_data_complete.csv*

[1] The datasets and the skeleton code for exercises 4–6 can be obtained from github.com/MachineLearningBiomedicalApplications/notebooks.

using Pandas. Calculate the accuracy of this classifier, the recall for each class, and the average recall. Discuss the performance of the classifier.

4.2. Support vector classifier

The Support Vector Classifier (SVC) is a large margin classifier that aims not only to find the decision boundary that correctly splits the samples but also results in the largest separation of the classes. In this section we will introduce the hard-margin and soft-margin support vector classifiers and the kernel trick for nonlinear classification.

4.2.1 Hard-margin support vector classifier

In classification problems where the two classes are linearly separated, there is no unique solution. The hard-margin classifier (Fig. 4.6 left) will choose the decision boundary with the largest distance from the samples of both classes. The decision boundary is determined by **support vectors**, the samples that lie on the margins. In Fig. 4.6 the margins are shown by dashed lines and the support vectors by pink circles.

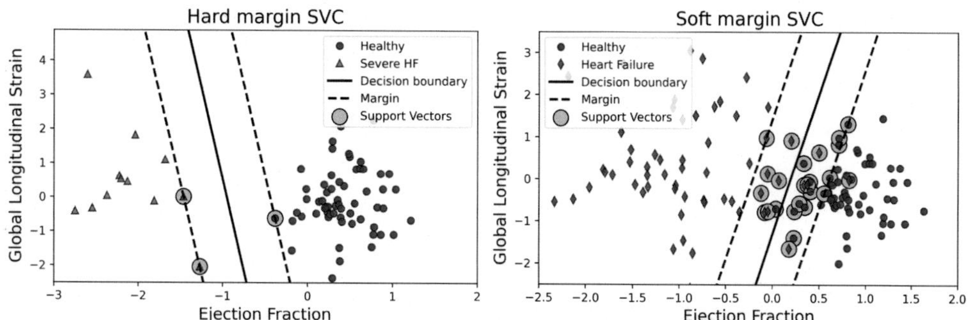

Figure 4.6 Hard-margin and soft-margin support vector classifiers.

The decision function is a multivariate linear function

$$h(\mathbf{x}) = \mathbf{w}^{\mathrm{T}}\mathbf{x} + b.$$

This formulation is equivalent to the formulation in Eq. (4.1), except that the intercept is denoted by b rather than w_0. The decision boundary is determined by

$$h(\mathbf{x}) = 0,$$

while **margins** are defined as

$$h(\mathbf{x}) = \pm 1.$$

We will also rename the negative label from 0 to -1. As before, we predict the label as 1 if the decision function is positive or zero, and -1 if it is negative:

$$\hat{y} = \begin{cases} 1 & \text{if } h(\mathbf{x}) \geq 0 \\ -1 & \text{if } h(\mathbf{x}) < 0. \end{cases} \tag{4.4}$$

The aim of the **hard-margin objective** is to keep the samples on or outside the margins on the correct side of the decision boundary, while keeping the margin as large as possible at the same time. This can be written as

$$\begin{aligned} &\text{minimize} \quad \frac{1}{2}\mathbf{w}^{\mathbf{T}}\mathbf{w} \\ &\text{subject to} \quad y_i h(\mathbf{x}_i) \geq 1 \quad \text{for } i = 1, \ldots, N. \end{aligned}$$

The expression $\mathbf{w}^{\mathbf{T}}\mathbf{w}$ measures the squared magnitude of the slope of the decision function. Smaller slopes mean larger margins. Note the similarity to the ridge penalty. The quantity $y_i h(\mathbf{x}_i)$ is larger than 1 for a positive sample if $h(\mathbf{x}_i) \geq 1$, which ensures that the sample is on or outside the margin and correctly classified. For negative sample we have $h(\mathbf{x}_i) \leq -1$, which again means that it should be on or outside the margin and correctly classified.

The hard-margin objective can be only applied to separable problems and is very sensitive to outliers. Practical implementations therefore use the soft-margin objective that addresses these problems instead.

4.2.2 Soft-margin support vector classifier

We would like to apply the support vector classifier also to nonseparable problems (Fig. 4.6 right) and reduce sensitivity to outliers. We will therefore introduce slack variables ζ_i to allow margin violations. Slack variables ζ_i measure how much sample $\mathbf{x}_i$ violates the margin—see Fig. 4.7. If $\zeta_i = 0$, then the sample is on or outside of the margin, on the correct side of the decision boundary. If $\zeta_i > 0$, then the sample $\mathbf{x}_i$ violates the margin. Note that slack variables are never negative, e.g., $\zeta_i \geq 0$. For the soft-margin SVC the **support vectors** are all the training samples that lie on the margins or violate the margins—see Fig. 4.6 right.

The goal of the **soft-margin objective** is to maximize the margin while minimizing margin violations. The latter is equivalent to minimizing the sum of slack variables $\sum_{i=1}^{N} \zeta_i$, as each slack variable ζ_i is proportional to the distance by which the sample $\mathbf{x}_i$ violates the margin. Similarly to the hard margin objective, maximising the margin is equivalent to minimising the slope of the decision function. Putting this together, soft

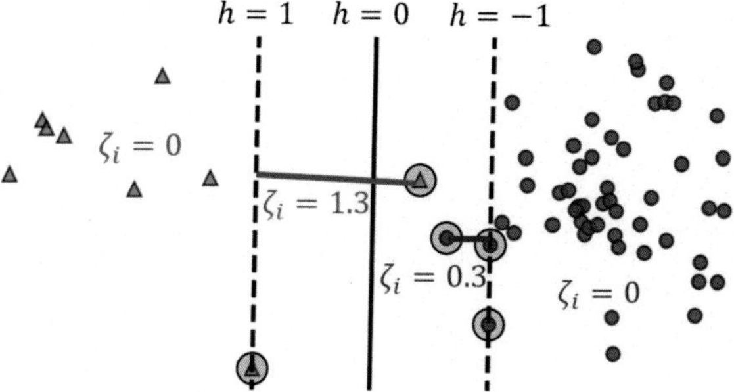

Figure 4.7 Interpretation of slack variables ζ_i.

margin objective can be written as

$$\begin{aligned} &\text{minimize} \quad \frac{1}{2}\mathbf{w}^{\mathbf{T}}\mathbf{w} + C\sum_{i=1}^{N}\zeta_i \\ &\text{subject to} \quad y_i h(\mathbf{x}_i) \geq 1 - \zeta_i, \quad \zeta_i \geq 0 \ \text{ for } i = 1, \ldots, N. \end{aligned}$$

The hyperparameter C represents the trade-off between margin width and margin violations. For large C we will have smaller margins with fewer violations, while for small C we will have larger margins with more violations.

The soft-margin objective has to be minimized numerically, usually using quadratic solvers [7]. Alternatively, we can equivalently express the soft-margin objective as the **hinge loss**

$$\hat{\mathbf{w}} = \arg\min_{\mathbf{w}} C\sum_{i=1}^{N}\max\left(0, 1 - \mathbf{w}^{\mathbf{T}}\mathbf{x} + b\right) + \frac{1}{2}\mathbf{w}^{\mathbf{T}}\mathbf{w},$$

that can be minimized using a gradient descent with subgradients (Sec. 3.1.2).

In scikit-learn the linear support vector classifier model can be formulated as

```
from sklearn.svm import LinearSVC
model = LinearSVC(C=10)
```

Alternatively, it is implemented as a stochastic gradient descent classifier with hinge loss

```
from sklearn.linear_model import SGDClassifier
model = SGDClassifier(loss='hinge', alpha = 0.01)
```

Here, the parameter `alpha` is the hyperparameter for the ridge penalty, and it is equal to $1/C$.

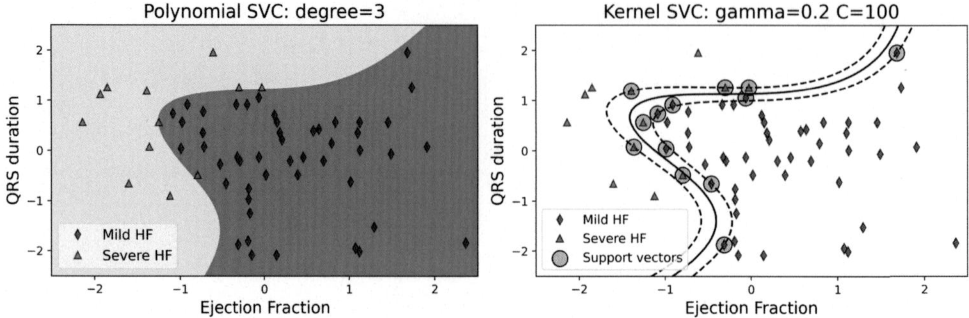

Figure 4.8 Nonlinear support vector classifiers. Left: linear SVC with polynomial feature transformation. Right: kernel SVC with radial basis function (Gaussian) kernel.

4.2.3 Polynomial support vector classifier

Some datasets cannot be well separated using a linear decision boundary. For example, if we wish to distinguish between patients with mild and severe heart failure based on EF and QRS, nonlinear classification will work better, as shown in Fig. 4.8.

Similarly to the regression (Sect. 3.3.1), a linear classifier can be turned into a nonlinear classifier by the application of a nonlinear feature transformation $\boldsymbol{\phi}$. The decision boundary will become

$$h(\mathbf{x}) = \mathbf{w}^{\mathbf{T}}\boldsymbol{\phi}(\mathbf{x}) + b,$$

and hard or soft margin objectives can be applied exactly the same way as before.

In scikit-learn we can implement this as a pipeline of the nonlinear feature transformation, in this case a polynomial of third degree, followed by linear SVC:

```
from sklearn.pipeline import Pipeline
from sklearn.preprocessing import PolynomialFeatures
from sklearn.preprocessing import StandardScaler
from sklearn.svm import LinearSVC
model = Pipeline((
    ("poly_features",PolynomialFeatures(degree=3)),
    ("scaler",StandardScaler()),
    ("svc",LinearSVC())))
```

The fitted polynomial support vector classifier is shown in Fig. 4.8, left.

4.2.4 Kernel support vector classifier

Alternatively we can create a nonlinear support vector classifier by using a **kernel trick**. We have already introduced the kernel trick in the context of ridge regression in Sect. 3.3.2. We will first replace the parameter vector **w** with its dual representation

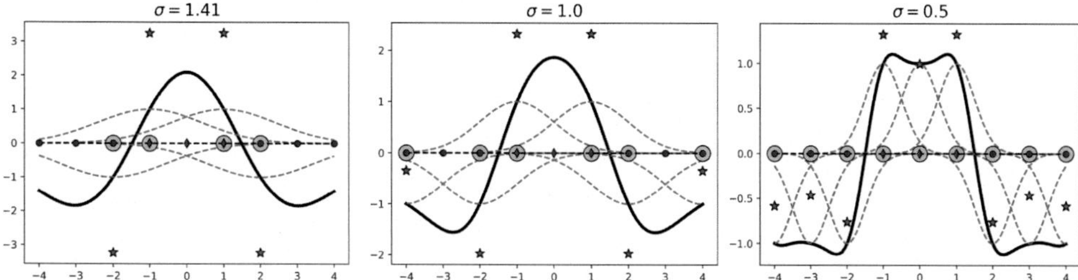

Figure 4.9 Kernel support vector classifier with various Gaussian kernel sizes σ. The positive samples are shown by red diamonds and negative samples by blue circles. Dashed green lines show kernels multiplied by labels $\kappa(\mathbf{x}, \mathbf{x_i})y_i$ centered around support vectors $\mathbf{x_i}$. Green stars show nonzero dual coefficients multiplied by labels $a_i y_i$, $a_i > 0$. Solid black line shows linear combination of the kernels that forms the decision function (Eq. (4.5)).

a, where $a_i \geq 0$:

$$\mathbf{w} = \sum_{i=1}^{N} a_i y_i \boldsymbol{\phi}(\mathbf{x_i}).$$

The decision function then becomes

$$h(\mathbf{x}) = \sum_{i=1}^{N} a_i y_i \kappa(\mathbf{x}, \mathbf{x_i}) + b, \tag{4.5}$$

where $\kappa(\mathbf{x}, \mathbf{x_i}) = \boldsymbol{\phi}^T(\mathbf{x})\boldsymbol{\phi}(\mathbf{x_i})$ is the kernel. The labels are obtained from this formulation the same way as before, by thresholding the decision function (Eq. (4.4)).

Examples of decision functions for Gaussian kernels of various widths and a simple 1D dataset are depicted in Fig. 4.9. The resulting nonlinear decision function $h(\mathbf{x})$ (black line) is a linear combination of the kernels $\kappa(\mathbf{x}, \mathbf{x_i})$ (green dashed lines) placed around the support vectors $\mathbf{x_i}$, $a_i > 0$ (data points in pink circles). Note that we plotted the kernels multiplied by label y_i so they appear positive for class 1 and negative for class -1.

If the dual coefficient a_i is zero, the sample $\mathbf{x}_i$ is outside the margins on the correct side of the boundary and therefore does not influence the decision boundary. If the dual coefficient a_i is positive, then the sample $\mathbf{x}_i$ is either on the margin, within the margin, or on the wrong side of the decision boundary. Then, it is a support vector, and it defines the decision boundary. The nonzero dual coefficients a_i multiplied by the labels y_i are shown with green stars.

We can see how kernels around the positive support vectors drag the decision function above zero, and kernels around negative support vectors drag the decision function below zero. That way, the new samples that are close to the positive samples will be given label 1, and the new samples that are close to mostly negative samples will be given label −1. We can also see that this dataset is not linearly separable, but, using the nonlinear decision function, it can be perfectly separated into two classes. Example of the 2D classification result for kernel SVC is given in Fig. 4.8, right. Here we show the decision boundary (black line), margins (dashed black lines), and support vectors (data points in pink circles) that define the boundary.

The dual hard- and soft-margin objectives can be derived by substituting the dual decision function into the original hard- and soft-margin objectives and in turn be minimized by quadratic programming solvers.

In scikit-learn the kernel support vector classifier is implemented by the class `SVC`:

```
from sklearn.svm import SVC
model = SVC(kernel='rbf', gamma = 0.2, C=1e2)
```

The parameter setting `kernel='rbf'` gives a Gaussian kernel with variance $\sigma^2 = 1/(2\gamma)$, where value γ is set by the parameter `gamma`. Smaller γ will therefore result in a larger kernel and a smoother decision boundary (Fig. 4.9). Hyperparameter `C` regulates the width of the margin by penalizing the margin violations. A smaller `C` will therefore result in a wider margin, more support vectors, and a smoother decision boundary. Multi-label classification is also supported by the object `SVC` and implemented using multiple decision boundaries.

The support vectors of the fitted `SVC` model can be accessed as

```
model.fit(X_train,y_train)
model.support_vectors_
```

and their indices as

```
model.support_
```

The nonzero dual coefficients a_i are accessed as

```
model.dual_coef_
```

and the intercept b as

```
model.intercept_
```

4.2.5 Training a support vector classifier

In this section we will show how to tune and evaluate a kernel support vector classifier in scikit-learn using the example of the prediction of mild or severe heart failure from EF and QRS durations. The dataset and decision boundaries using two different example classifiers are shown in Fig. 4.8.

Before we start tuning our model, we need to exclude the test set so that we are able to measure the performance without any risk of overfitting. We use `train_test_split` to exclude 20% of the data from training and stratify the test set by labels `y` to ensure that there is the same proportion of both classes in the training and test sets:

```
from sklearn.model_selection import train_test_split
X_train, X_test, y_train, y_test = \
train_test_split(X, y, test_size=0.33, stratify=y)
```

Next, we will tune the `SVC` model on the training set using cross-validation. First, we need to define the parameter grid. This time, we aim to tune multiple parameters of SVC at the same time, including the kernel type (linear or Gaussian), the Gaussian kernel size γ, and the regularization parameter C:

```
param = {'C':np.logspace(-3,3,7),
         'gamma':np.logspace(-3,3,7),
         'kernel': ['linear','rbf']}
```

Now, we will search through the grid of models, with different combinations of the parameter settings, to find the one with the highest cross-validated accuracy through `GridSearchCV`, with `SVC` as the model, parameters `param` defined above, and five folds. Note that we did not specify the performance metric, therefore the accuracy, the default metric for classifiers, will be used:

```
from sklearn.model_selection import GridSearchCV
g = GridSearchCV(SVC(),param,cv=5)
g.fit(X_train,y_train)
```

We can access the tuned `SVC` model as `g.best_estimator_`. The cross-validated accuracy and parameters of this model can be viewed as

```
print('Best CV accuracy: ',round(g.best_score_,2))
print('Best C: ',round(g.best_estimator_.C,2))
print('Best gamma: ',round(g.best_estimator_.gamma,2))
print('Best kernel: ',g.best_estimator_.kernel)
>>> Best CV accuracy:  0.95
>>> Best C:  10.0
>>> Best gamma:  1.0
>>> Best kernel:  rbf
```

The final step is to establish the performance of the tuned model on the test set:

```
acc = g.best_estimator_.score(X_test,y_test)
y_test_pred=g.best_estimator_.predict(X_test)
rec = recall_score(y_test,y_test_pred,average=None)
print('Accuracy on test set: ', acc)
print('Recalls: ', rec)
>>> Accuracy on test set:  0.95
>>> Recalls:  [1.   0.75]
```

We can observe that the accuracy on the test set is the same as the cross-validated accuracy on the training set, so the model generalized well on the unseen data. By analysis of the recalls, we can see that the ability of the classifier to identify mild heart failure (label 0) is better than for severe heart failure (label 1). This is not unexpected, as the class 1 is underrepresented, because only 20% patients in this dataset had been diagnosed with severe heart failure.

4.2.6 Exercises

1. What is the role of the support vectors in support vector classification?
2. What is the role of slack variables in soft margin SVC?
3. Provide intuitive interpretation of the mathematical formulation of the decision function through dual representation in kernel SVC. Describe how this decision function is used for label prediction.
4. Train a multi-label kernel support vector classifier to diagnose no, moderate, or severe heart failure from EF and QRS. Load dataset *heart_failure_data_complete.csv* using Pandas.[2] Perform the following steps:
   - Perform a stratified train-test split;
   - Tune parameters of kernel SVC classifier using cross-validation, including kernel type, kernel parameters, and the regularization parameter C.
   - Visualize the classification result and calculate the appropriate performance measures using cross-validation on the training set and on the test set. Analyze the performance of the classifier. How does it perform for different classes?
5. You are given a 1D dataset with the following features and labels:

$$\mathbf{X} = (-4, -3, -2, -1, \ \ 0, \ \ 1, \ \ 2, \ \ 3, \ \ 4)^T$$
$$\mathbf{y} = (-1, -1, -1, \ \ 1, \ \ 1, \ \ 1, -1, -1, -1)^T$$

   - Fit an `SVC` classifier with `gamma=0.1` and `C=1e5`. Plot the data with features on x-axis and labels on y-axis. Plot the decision function and place circles around the support vectors;
   - Plot the Gaussian kernels $\kappa(\mathbf{x}, \mathbf{x_i})$ with variance $\sigma^2 = 1/(2\gamma)$ corresponding to the support vectors, multiplied by their label y_i;
   - Plot the product of dual coefficients and labels $a_i y_i$
   - Calculate and plot the decision function according to Eq. (4.5). Compare it to the decision function returned by the `SVC` model.

   Your final plot should be similar to the ones in Fig. 4.9.

[2] The datasets and the skeleton code for exercises 4 and 5 can be obtained from github.com/MachineLearningBiomedicalApplications/notebooks.

CHAPTER 5

Dimensionality reduction

Modern biomedical data sets are enormous. Consider, for a minute, just one single MRI brain scan, defined on a typical volumetric image grid. This has a resolution of $255 \times 255 \times 180$. If we were to consider each data point as a separate feature, we would have over 11 million features per image. Similarly, genetic samples each record millions of single nucleotide polymorphisms (SNPs) per example, and biometric devices (such as smart watches) record physiological measurements continuously in time. Add to this the fact that biomedical samples are challenging to acquire, and this tends to mean that the numbers of features often vastly outstrip the numbers of examples. This is a problem because, with increasing dimensions, the same amount of data fills the space more and more sparsely, making it easier to fit a separating hyperplane by chance and, in this way, overfit to noise in the training data. In this chapter, we look at techniques for addressing this through linear or nonlinear projection of the data.

5.1. The curse of dimensionality

To better understand the risks associated with having many more features than examples, consider the toy example shown in Fig. 5.1. This simulates the effect of classifying a fixed number of data points as the dimensionality of feature space grows. In this example, we have two classes, shown by red and green markers. Each point is randomly sampled from a normal distribution centered at 0.5, with equal variance for each group. Therefore, the groups should be non-separable. Fig. 5.1, however, shows a case where the classes are separable by chance.

In the top row, we can see that, in one dimension, both groups completely overlap, and classification accuracy is close to random chance (as would be expected). As the feature dimensions grow, the points spread out more, and the classification rates rise. At three dimensions, the classifier reports 75% accuracy. Clearly, the classifier is overfitting to the noise in the data, and this is getting worse as the dimensionality of the feature space increases.

5.2. Low-dimensional embedding: a physical motivation

One way to address the risk of overfitting to noise in high-dimensional data is to reduce the dimensionality of the feature space. In Chapter 8 we will see how this can be addressed by feature selection. Here, however, we focus on dimensionality reduction through linear, or nonlinear, projection. The objective is always to preserve key statistical

https://doi.org/10.1016/B978-0-12-822904-0.00010-8
Copyright © 2024 Elsevier Ltd.
All rights reserved.

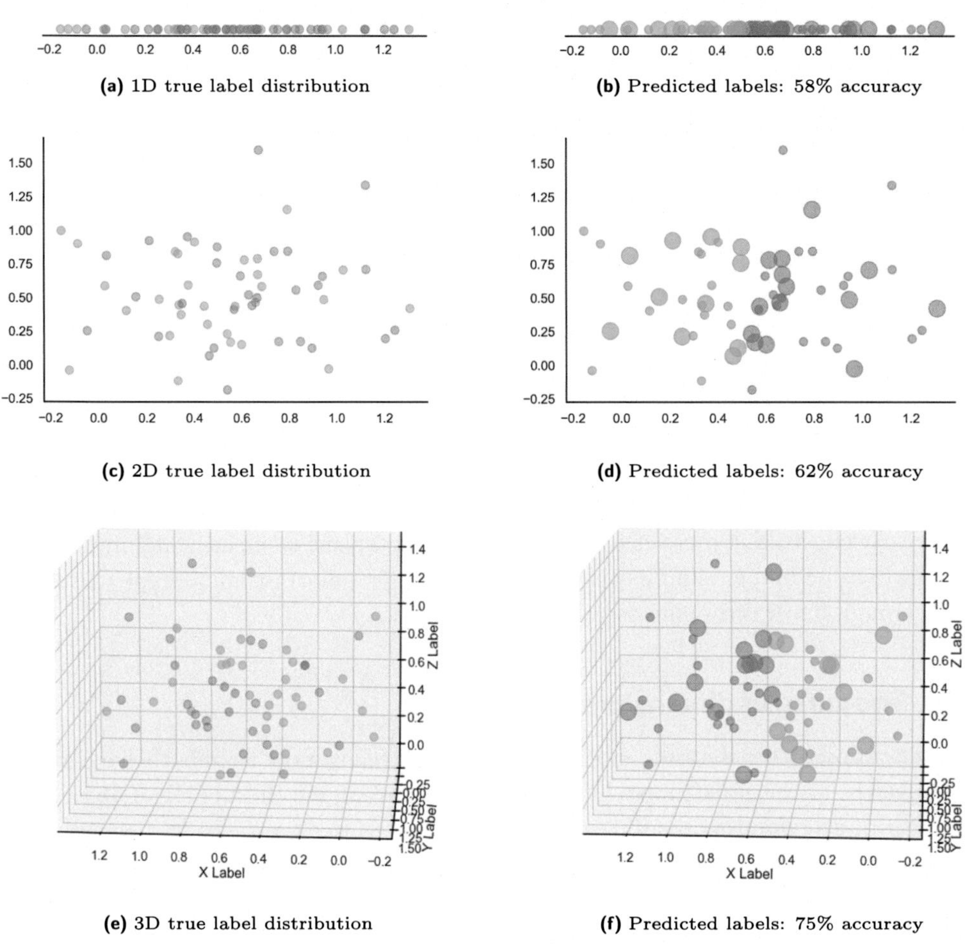

(a) 1D true label distribution

(b) Predicted labels: 58% accuracy

(c) 2D true label distribution

(d) Predicted labels: 62% accuracy

(e) 3D true label distribution

(f) Predicted labels: 75% accuracy

Figure 5.1 Curse of dimensionality toy example: simulating the spreading of randomly generated points as the dimensionality of the space increases. Left column: true labels; right column: predicted labels (larger markers indicate incorrectly classified examples).

or geometric properties of the data. This follows an understanding that real-world data examples are generated by processes constrained by physical laws with few degrees of freedom. For example, think of the series of pictures that goes into building a panoramic photo. You might think that, since each of these photos has 10–20 mega pixel resolution, that it would be a very hard problem for an algorithm to figure out how to map common features between photos to make one seamless final image. In reality, the process of taking these photos is embedded in three dimensions (the pitch, roll and yaw of the camera), and thus the relevant degrees of freedom reflect a much lower-dimensional space (greater than four due to encoding changes in illuminations, etc., but far less than the dimensionality of the images). The same is true for reconstruction of dynamic

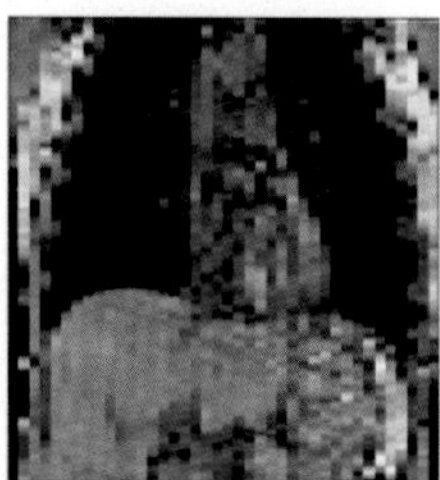
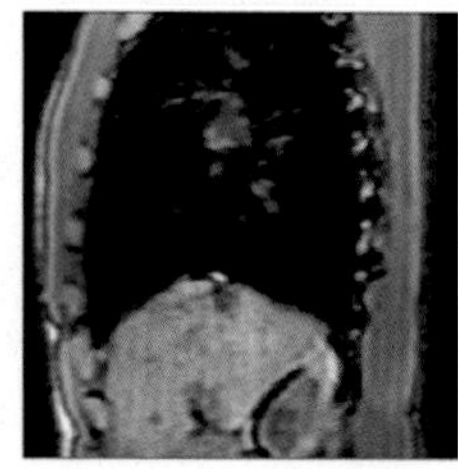
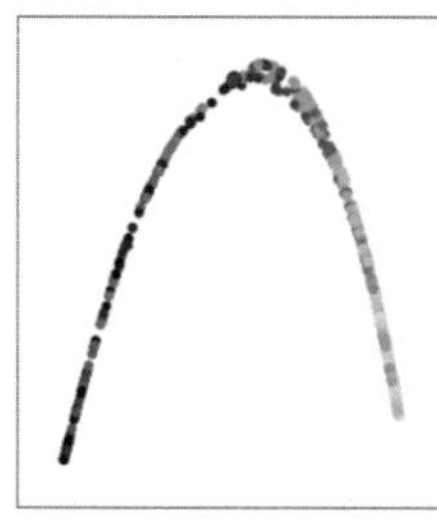

Figure 5.2 Left: a 4D movie of a chest CT is collected as a series of $2D+time$ slices through the volume. The original reconstruction is corrupted by motion. Middle: the image can be sharply reconstructed by identifying which neighboring slices were acquired during the same state of motion. Right: the correct slices can be found through nonlinear (manifold) embedding of the points using manifold learning [8].

scans of the chest (heart and lungs) where manifold learning (described in Sect. 5.6) can similarly be used to reconstruct high-resolution 4D volumes (3 space + 1 time dimension) from dynamically acquired 2D slices (Fig. 5.2).

5.3. Linear transforms

Before we consider nonlinear manifolds, let us start by considering linear embeddings constructed from linear transforms. Mathematically, a linear transform is a function that satisfies the properties of additivity and scalar multiplication, whilst preserving the origin

$$\text{additivity}: \quad T(\mathbf{x_1}+\mathbf{x_2}) = T(\mathbf{x_1}) + T(\mathbf{x_2}) \tag{5.1}$$

$$\text{scalar multiplicity}: \quad T(\alpha\mathbf{x}) = \alpha T(\mathbf{x}). \tag{5.2}$$

In simple terms, this means that linear transforms preserve the linear properties of the vector space. In other words, they map data points from one Euclidean domain to Euclidean subspace. Practically, the action of any matrix on a vector is a linear transform. For example, the action of $\mathbf{A} = \left(\begin{smallmatrix} 3 & 0 \\ 0 & 1 \end{smallmatrix}\right)$ represents a scale along the x-axis by a factor of 3 (see Fig. 5.3), as follows:

$$\begin{pmatrix} x' \\ y' \end{pmatrix} = \begin{pmatrix} 3 & 0 \\ 0 & 1 \end{pmatrix} \begin{pmatrix} x \\ y \end{pmatrix} \tag{5.3}$$

$$= \begin{pmatrix} 3x + 0y \\ 0x + 1y \end{pmatrix} \tag{5.4}$$

$$= \begin{pmatrix} 3x \\ 1y. \end{pmatrix} \tag{5.5}$$

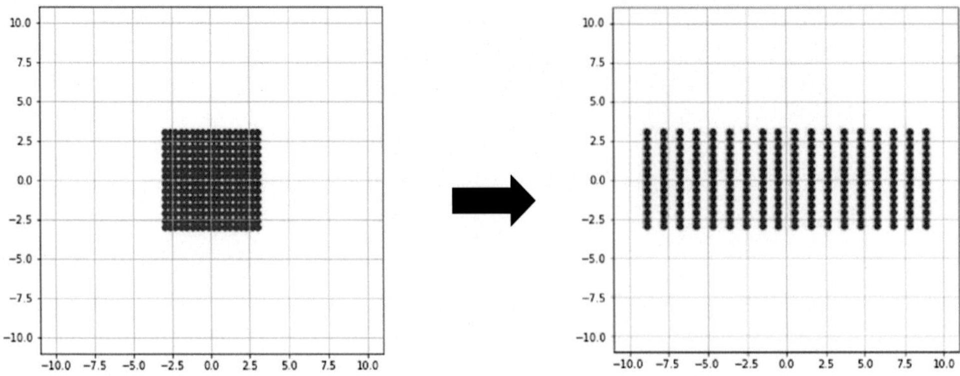

Figure 5.3 The action of $\mathbf{A} = \begin{pmatrix} 3 & 0 \\ 0 & 1 \end{pmatrix}$ is a scale along the axis of magnitude 3.

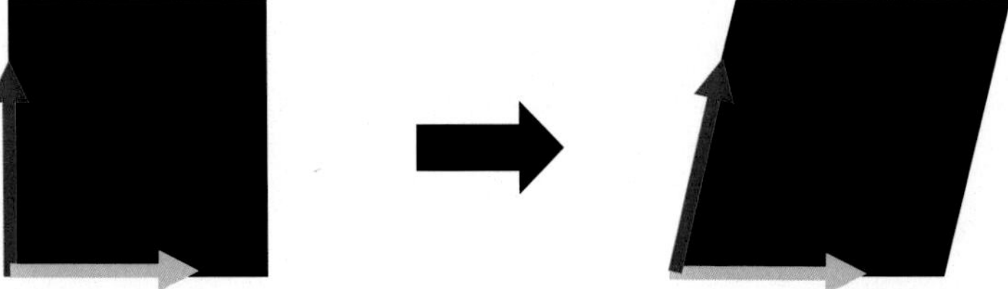

Figure 5.4 Eigenvectors are vectors whose directions do not change under a linear transform. In this example of a horizontal shear transform, the yellow vector is an eigenvector and the red vector is not.

5.3.1 Eigenvalues and eigenvectors

An eigenvector of a given linear transform is defined as a direction that remain unchanged (with the exception of a scale factor) following application of a linear transform. For example, observe the shearing operation shown in Fig. 5.4, the red vector (initially in the y direction) changes direction under the operation of the transform, whereas the yellow arrow (in the direction of the x axis) does not. In this case, the yellow vector is an *eigenvector,* and the degree to which an eigenvector ($\mathbf{v}$) is scaled by a transform is represented by its *eigenvalue* (λ). We can represent this relationship in matrix form as

$$\mathbf{Av} = \lambda \mathbf{v}, \tag{5.6}$$

which presents a way to estimate the eigenvectors and values of $\mathbf{A}$ by rearranging the equation, bringing everything to one side and extracting the common factor of $\mathbf{v}$[1]

$$\mathbf{Av} - \lambda \mathbf{v} = 0 \tag{5.7}$$

[1] $\mathbf{I}$ represents the identity matrix.

$$(\mathbf{A} - \lambda\mathbf{I})\mathbf{v} = 0. \tag{5.8}$$

We enforce that $\mathbf{v}$ must be nonzero. This means that $(\mathbf{A} - \lambda\mathbf{I})$ must be singular, with the determinant equal to zero

$$|\mathbf{A} - \lambda\mathbf{I}| = 0. \tag{5.9}$$

This expression is known as the *characteristic equation*.

Matrix determinant

A determinant is a scalar value, derived as a function of a matrix, that is nonzero only if the matrix is invertible and represents an isomorphic transformation (one-to-one) such that all points in the original domain are mapped to exactly one location in the second domain. For a 2×2 matrix $\mathbf{B} = \left(\begin{smallmatrix} a & b \\ c & d \end{smallmatrix}\right)$, the matrix determinant may be estimated as:

$$det\mathbf{B} = |\mathbf{B}| = ad - bc. \tag{5.10}$$

Example: eigenvector calculation

To estimate the eigenvectors and eigenvalues of the horizontal scaling operation $\mathbf{A} = \left(\begin{smallmatrix} 3 & 0 \\ 0 & 1 \end{smallmatrix}\right)$, first substitute for $\mathbf{A}$ in the characteristic equation and calculate the determinant

$$|\mathbf{A} - \lambda\mathbf{I}| = \begin{pmatrix} 3 & 0 \\ 0 & 1 \end{pmatrix} - \lambda \begin{pmatrix} 1 & 0 \\ 0 & 1 \end{pmatrix} \tag{5.11}$$

$$= \begin{vmatrix} 3-\lambda & 0 \\ 0 & 1-\lambda \end{vmatrix} = 0 \tag{5.12}$$

$$= (3-\lambda)(1-\lambda) = 0. \tag{5.13}$$

This tells us that the solutions (roots) are $(3-\lambda) = 0$ and $(1-\lambda) = 0$; thus, the eigenvalues of $\mathbf{A}$ are $\lambda_1 = 3$ and $\lambda_2 = 1$. Now, estimate the eigenvectors by substituting into Eq. (5.8) for λ, starting with $\lambda = 3$

$$\begin{pmatrix} 3-3 & 0 \\ 0 & 1-3 \end{pmatrix} \begin{pmatrix} v_1 \\ v_2 \end{pmatrix} = 0. \tag{5.14}$$

Multiplied out this gives

$$\rightarrow 0v_1 + 0v_2 = 0 \tag{5.15}$$

$$\rightarrow 0v_1 - 2v_2 = 0, \tag{5.16}$$

which implies v_2 must be zero (since $2 \times v_2$ cannot equal 0, unless $v_2 = 0$). Thus, the eigenvector corresponding to $\lambda_1 = 3$ (defined up to an arbitrary scale factor k) is

$$\mathbf{v} = \begin{pmatrix} k \\ 0 \end{pmatrix} \tag{5.17}$$

This represents a scale along the x-axis. Similarly, the eigenvector corresponding to eigenvalue $\lambda_1 = 1$ is estimated from

$$\begin{pmatrix} 3-1 & 0 \\ 0 & 1-1 \end{pmatrix} \begin{pmatrix} v_1 \\ v_2 \end{pmatrix} = 0 \tag{5.18}$$

$$\rightarrow 2v_1 + 0v_2 = 0 \tag{5.19}$$

$$\rightarrow 0v_1 - 0v_2 = 0, \tag{5.20}$$

where Eq. (5.20) implies v_1 must be zero (from $2v_1 = 0$). Thus, the eigenvector corresponding to $\lambda_2 = 1$ represents a scale along y

$$\mathbf{v} = \begin{pmatrix} 0 \\ k \end{pmatrix} \tag{5.21}$$

Since the eigenvalue = 1, this equates to a unit scale, resulting in the overall effect of a stretch along x.

Eigenvectors of symmetric matrices

If instead we have a matrix with an off-diagonal term, such as $\mathbf{A_2} = \left(\begin{smallmatrix} 2 & 1 \\ 1 & 2 \end{smallmatrix}\right)$, the characteristic equation is expanded as:

$$\begin{vmatrix} 2-\lambda & 1 \\ 1 & 2-\lambda \end{vmatrix} = (2-\lambda)(2-\lambda) - 1 = 0 \tag{5.22}$$

$$\lambda^2 - 4\lambda + 4 - 1 = 0 \tag{5.23}$$

$$\lambda^2 - 4\lambda + 3 = 0 \tag{5.24}$$

$$(3-\lambda)(1-\lambda) = 0. \tag{5.25}$$

Thus, once more, the eigenvalues are $\lambda_1 = 3$ and $\lambda_2 = 1$. For $\lambda_1 = 3$ the corresponding eigenvector can be calculated from

$$\begin{pmatrix} 2-3 & 1 \\ 1 & 2-3 \end{pmatrix} \begin{pmatrix} v_1 \\ v_2 \end{pmatrix} = 0 \tag{5.26}$$

$$\rightarrow -v_1 + v_2 = 0 \rightarrow v_1 = v_2 \tag{5.27}$$

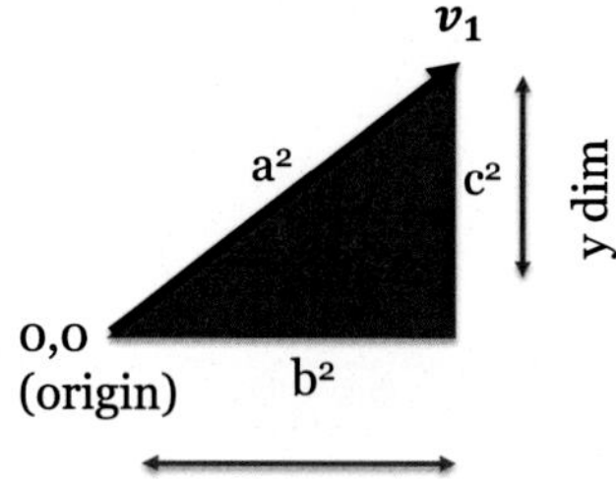

Figure 5.5 Pythagoras' theorem: $a^2 = b^2 + c^2$.

$$\rightarrow 0v_1 - 2v_2 = 0 \rightarrow v_1 = v_2, \tag{5.28}$$

which suggests that v_1 is any constant multiple of

$$\mathbf{v_1} = \begin{pmatrix} 1 \\ 1 \end{pmatrix}. \tag{5.29}$$

Following the same procedure[2] for eigenvalue $\lambda_2 = 1$ returns

$$\mathbf{v_2} = \begin{pmatrix} 1 \\ -1 \end{pmatrix}. \tag{5.30}$$

Unit eigenvectors

Going forward, we will see that, for PCA we always want *unit* eigenvectors. To normalize we first need to use the Pythagorean theorem for the magnitude of a vector. Specifically, the magnitude of $\mathbf{v_1}$ as shown in Fig. 5.5 is determined from $a = \sqrt{b^2 + c^2}$. For the previous example, where $v_1 = \binom{1}{1}$ and $v_2 = \binom{1}{-1}$, the magnitude in both cases is $\sqrt{2}$.[3] Thus, the normalized eigenvector is

$$\mathbf{v_1} = \frac{1}{\sqrt{2}} \begin{pmatrix} 1 \\ 1 \end{pmatrix}. \tag{5.31}$$

Following the same procedure[4] for eigenvalue $\lambda_2 = 1$ returns

$$\mathbf{v_2} = \frac{1}{\sqrt{2}} \begin{pmatrix} 1 \\ -1 \end{pmatrix}. \tag{5.32}$$

[2] **Exercise:** try this for yourself.
[3] Since $\sqrt{1^2 + 1^2} = \sqrt{1^2 + (-1)^2} = \sqrt{2}$.
[4] **Exercise**: try this for yourself.

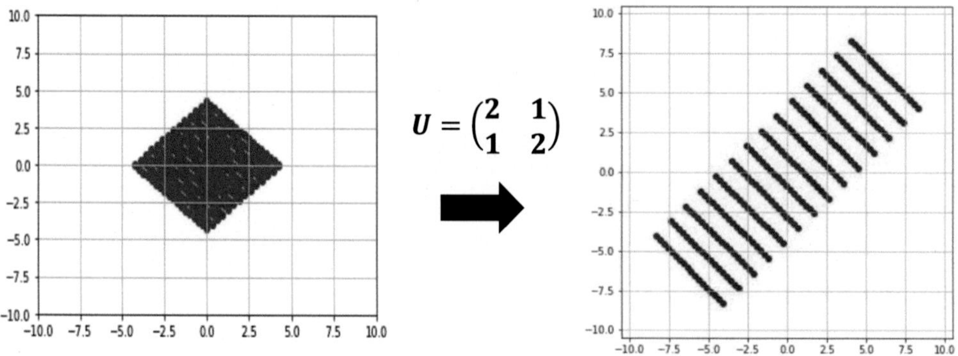

Figure 5.6 A scale along the $\mathbf{v} = \begin{pmatrix} 1 \\ 1 \end{pmatrix}$ axis of magnitude 3.

Matrix diagonalization

We can see from Fig. 5.6 that this represents the same transformation as before (a stretch of 3 along one axis and 1 along the other) but this time along the $\mathbf{v_1} = \begin{pmatrix} 1 \\ 1 \end{pmatrix}$ and $\mathbf{v_2} = \begin{pmatrix} 1 \\ -1 \end{pmatrix}$ axes. Thus, eigenvectors $\mathbf{v_1}$, $\mathbf{v_2}$ represent the same transform in a rotated coordinate basis. More specifically, it can be shown that the eigenvectors of any real symmetric matrix $\mathbf{A_2}$ form an orthogonal basis from which the matrix may be diagonalized

$$\mathbf{A_2 V} = \mathbf{\Lambda V} \tag{5.33}$$

$$\rightarrow \mathbf{V}^{-1}\mathbf{A_2 V} = \mathbf{V}^{-1}\mathbf{V \Lambda} \tag{5.34}$$

$$= \mathbf{\Lambda} \tag{5.35}$$

$$= \mathbf{A} \tag{5.36}$$

Here, Eq. (5.33) is a matrix equivalent of Eq. (5.6), the columns of $\mathbf{V}$ represent all eigenvectors of $\mathbf{A_2}$, and $\mathbf{\Lambda}$ is a diagonal matrix of all eigenvalues. For the example of this case, $\mathbf{A_2} = \begin{pmatrix} 2 & 1 \\ 1 & 2 \end{pmatrix}$; $\mathbf{A} = \mathbf{\Lambda} = \begin{pmatrix} 3 & 0 \\ 0 & 1 \end{pmatrix}$.

5.4. Principal component analysis

Using this principle, PCA works by estimating the eigenvectors of the (symmetric) data covariance matrix to return a reduced orthogonal eigenbasis that represents the directions of maximal variance in the data. As a demonstration of how this works, consider once again our neonatal brain-volume data set, which pairs brain volumes of babies with their gestational age at the time of the scan. We see from Fig. 5.7a that the growth patterns of various regions are highly correlated. This means that knowledge of one strongly informs prediction of the other, meaning that consideration of both features is redundant. In PCA the objective is therefore to search for the vector $\mathbf{v_1}$ which, once

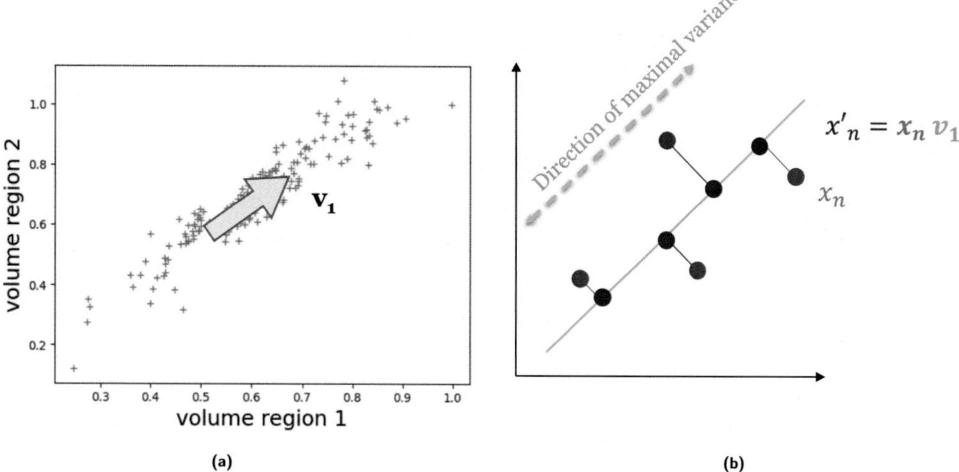

Figure 5.7 a) Growths of various brain regions are highly correlated; the goal of PCA is to project all data onto one direction u_1 (yellow arrow); b) the optimal direction (green line) is the one for which variance will be maximized, once (blue) data points are projected onto it.

data is projected onto it (Fig. 5.7b), returns the largest estimate of variance of any direction through the feature space. We can do this by considering the eigenvectors of the data covariance matrix.

5.4.1 Estimation of the data covariance matrix

The covariance matrix is a symmetric matrix whose entries represent the variance between all elements of a data set, whereby elements we may interchangeably refer to the features of the data set or the examples, themselves. For example, if we assume that our data set $\mathbf{X} \in \mathbb{R}^{100\times 4}$ has 100 examples each with 4 features, we can either estimate the covariance between examples as

$$\mathbf{C} = \frac{1}{N-1}\mathbf{X}_C\mathbf{X}_C^T, \tag{5.37}$$

where in this case $\mathbf{C}$ will have shape 100×100, or we estimate the covariance between features as

$$\mathbf{C} = \frac{1}{N-1}\mathbf{X}_C^T\mathbf{X}_C, \tag{5.38}$$

with shape 4×4. Importantly, in each instance we assume the data has first been mean centered: $\mathbf{X}_C = \mathbf{X} - \bar{\mathbf{X}}$, by subtracting either the mean per example (for Eq. (5.37)) or the mean per feature (for Eq. (5.38)). For dimensionality reduction, we are always interested in the latter, i.e., covariance between features. In this case, our covariance matrix looks like

$$C = \begin{pmatrix} \mathrm{cov}_{11} & \mathrm{cov}_{12} & \mathrm{cov}_{13} & \mathrm{cov}_{14} \\ \mathrm{cov}_{21} & \mathrm{cov}_{22} & \mathrm{cov}_{23} & \mathrm{cov}_{24} \\ \mathrm{cov}_{31} & \mathrm{cov}_{32} & \mathrm{cov}_{33} & \mathrm{cov}_{34} \\ \mathrm{cov}_{41} & \mathrm{cov}_{42} & \mathrm{cov}_{43} & \mathrm{cov}_{44} \end{pmatrix}, \tag{5.39}$$

with variance of each individual feature (cov_{11}, cov_{22}, cov_{33}, cov_{44}, cov_{55}) on the diagonal and covariances between different features ($\mathrm{cov}_{12}, \mathrm{cov}_{13}, \mathrm{cov}_{14}, \mathrm{cov}_{21}, ...$) stored on the off diagonal. In this representation, the variance estimates the spread of values along a single feature dimension, whereas covariance is a measure of shared information between features. The covariance matrix is symmetric, which means its eigenvectors form a novel orthogonal basis set that better represents the variance between features.

5.4.2 Deriving PCA

We know from trigonometry that the projection of data point $\mathbf{x}_n$ onto $\mathbf{v_1}$ may be estimated as $|\mathbf{x_n}|\cos\theta$ and that the scalar (dot) product of these two vectors is

$$\mathbf{x_n v_1} = |\mathbf{x_n}||\mathbf{v_1}|\cos\theta. \tag{5.40}$$

Thus, by rearranging Eq. (5.40), we see that the dot product is equivalent to the scalar projection, provided that $|\mathbf{v_1}| = 1$,

$$|\mathbf{x_n}|\cos\theta = \frac{\mathbf{x_n v_1}}{|\mathbf{v_1}|}. \tag{5.41}$$

Putting this altogether, for PCA we are seeking the direction $\mathbf{v_1}$ for which the variance across all projected data points is maximized. Thus, assuming that we first normalize our eigenvectors ($\mathbf{v_1} = \mathbf{v_1}/|\mathbf{v_1}|$), we can represent the variance of points projected on $\mathbf{v_1}$ as

$$\frac{1}{N-1}(\mathbf{X}_C\mathbf{v_1})^T(\mathbf{X}_C\mathbf{v_1}) = \mathbf{v_1}^T\mathbf{C}\mathbf{v_1}. \tag{5.42}$$

To find the direction that maximizes the projected variance, we must take the derivative of the variance w.r.t. $\mathbf{v_1}$. At the same time, we enforce a plausible solution by constraining the estimated eigenvectors to have unit magnitude. This constraint is implemented through the method of Lagrange multipliers:

$$\mathcal{L}(\mathbf{v_1}, \lambda_1) = \mathbf{v_1}^T\mathbf{C}\mathbf{v_1} + \lambda_1(1 - \mathbf{v_1}^T\mathbf{v_1}). \tag{5.43}$$

Optimizing for $\nabla_{\mathbf{v_1}}\mathcal{L}(\mathbf{v_1}, \lambda_1) = 0$, this then reduces to

$$\mathbf{C}\mathbf{v_1} = \lambda_1\mathbf{v_1}, \tag{5.44}$$

meaning that $\mathbf{v_1}$ must be an eigenvector of $\mathbf{C}$, where eigenvalue $\lambda_1 = \mathbf{v_1}^T\mathbf{C}\mathbf{v_1}$ equates to the magnitude of the variance along that direction.

Extending to higher dimensions

We can extend this process to higher dimensions by constraining the next choice of eigenvector to be orthogonal to $\mathbf{v}_1$.[5] This time, therefore, we need two Lagrange multipliers, λ_2 and ϕ, where λ_2 constrains the magnitude of the second eigenvector to 1 and ϕ ensures that $\mathbf{v}_2$ is orthogonal to $\mathbf{v}_1$ ($\mathbf{v}_2{}^T\mathbf{v}_1 = 0$),

$$\mathcal{L}(\mathbf{v}_2, \lambda_2, \phi) = \mathbf{v}_2{}^T\mathbf{C}\mathbf{v}_2 + \lambda_2(1 - \mathbf{v}_2{}^T\mathbf{v}_2) - \phi\mathbf{v}_2{}^T\mathbf{v}_1. \tag{5.45}$$

Now, when taking the derivative with respect to $\mathbf{v}_2$, and left multiplying through by $\mathbf{v}_1$:

$$\mathbf{C}\mathbf{v}_2 \quad -\lambda_2\mathbf{v}_2 \quad -\phi\mathbf{v}_1 \quad = 0 \tag{5.46}$$

$$\mathbf{v}_1\mathbf{C}\mathbf{v}_2 \quad -\lambda_2\mathbf{v}_1{}^T\mathbf{v}_2 \quad -\phi\mathbf{v}_1{}^T\mathbf{v}_1 \quad = 0 \tag{5.47}$$

$$0 \quad -0 \quad -\phi\mathbf{v}_1{}^T\mathbf{v}_1 \quad = 0. \tag{5.48}$$

The first two terms must be zero since, by the orthogonality constraint, $\mathbf{v}_2\mathbf{v}_1 = 0$, and, since $\mathbf{v}_1{}^T\mathbf{v}_1 = 1$, Eq. (5.48) tells us that ϕ must also be 0. This means that all terms in ϕ must disappear, leaving us again with an eigenvector equation, this time for $\mathbf{v}_2$:

$$\mathbf{C}\mathbf{v}_2 = \lambda_2\mathbf{v}_2 \tag{5.49}$$

5.4.3 Estimating PCA from the eigenvectors of the data covariance matrix

Extrapolating across all dimensions, the matrix equation for eigendecomposition of $\mathbf{C}$ can be written as[6]

$$\mathbf{C}\mathbf{V} = \mathbf{V}\mathbf{\Lambda}. \tag{5.50}$$

Here, $\mathbf{\Lambda}$ is a diagonal matrix of eigenvalues

$$\Lambda = \begin{pmatrix} \lambda_1 & 0 & \dots & 0 \\ 0 & \lambda_1 & \dots & 0 \\ \vdots & \vdots & \ddots & \vdots \\ 0 & 0 & \dots & \lambda_m \end{pmatrix} \tag{5.51}$$

where eigenvalues represent the proportion of data variance described by each corresponding eigenvector (or *principal component*). It is common practice to organize principal components in descending order of magnitude, such that λ_1 corresponds to the largest eigenvalue, λ_2 the second largest eigenvalue, all the way down to λ_m (the smallest eigenvalue). When sorting eigenvalues, it is also important to permute the columns of $\mathbf{V}$ to preserve the correct relationship between eigenvalues and eigenvectors.

[5] Since covariance matrix is symmetric and thus eigenbasis is orthogonal.

[6] Where the specific order of matrix multiplication here is important.

5.4.4 Estimating PCA using singular value decomposition

Often the covariance matrix will not be of full rank (several eigenvalues will be zero). This is particularly likely to be the case when the matrix is estimated from nonsquare data matrices with high numbers of features. In these cases, computation becomes unstable, and it is better practice to instead implement PCA using singular value decomposition (SVD). SVD generalizes eigendecomposition to matrices of any shape. For example, for $\mathbf{X} \in \mathbb{R}^{n \times m}$,

$$\mathbf{X} = \mathbf{U}\mathbf{\Sigma}\mathbf{V}^T \tag{5.52}$$

SVD factorizes $\mathbf{X}$ into $\mathbf{U} \in \mathbb{R}^{n \times n}$, $\mathbf{V} \in \mathbb{R}^{m \times m}$ and $\mathbf{\Sigma} \in \mathbb{R}^{n \times m}$. Here, $\mathbf{U}$ and $\mathbf{V}$ are the left and right singular vector matrices, with each component vector having unit magnitude, and being orthogonal to one another[7]; $\mathbf{\Sigma}$ represents a rectangular diagonal matrix of singular values (σ_i). The maximum number of nonzero singular values is determined by the matrix rank $r \leq \min(m, n)$.

The relationship between PCA and SVD can be seen if we substitute Eq. (5.52) into our expression for the eigenvectors and values of our covariance matrices[8]

$$\begin{aligned}
\mathbf{X}_C\mathbf{X}_C^T\mathbf{U} &= \mathbf{U}\mathbf{\Sigma}V^T(\mathbf{U}\mathbf{\Sigma}\mathbf{V}^T)^T\mathbf{U} \\
&= \mathbf{U}\mathbf{\Sigma}\mathbf{V}^T\mathbf{V}\mathbf{\Sigma}\mathbf{U}^T\mathbf{U} \\
&= \mathbf{U}\mathbf{\Sigma}^2\mathbf{U}^T\mathbf{U} \\
&= \mathbf{U}\mathbf{\Sigma}^2.
\end{aligned} \tag{5.53}$$

Thus, $\mathbf{U}$ reflect the eigenvectors of data covariance matrix $\mathbf{X}_C\mathbf{X}_C^T$. Likewise, $\mathbf{V}$ represents the eigenvectors of $\mathbf{X}_C^T\mathbf{X}_C$

$$\begin{aligned}
\mathbf{X}_C^T\mathbf{X}_C\mathbf{V} &= (\mathbf{U}\mathbf{\Sigma}\mathbf{V}^T)^T\mathbf{U}\mathbf{\Sigma}\mathbf{V}^T\mathbf{V} \\
&= \mathbf{V}\mathbf{\Sigma}^2\mathbf{V}^T\mathbf{V} \\
&= \mathbf{V}\mathbf{\Sigma}^2.
\end{aligned} \tag{5.54}$$

In both cases, covariance matrices share r nonzero eigenvalues ($\mathbf{\Sigma} \in r \times r$), and these are related to the SVD singular values as[9]

$$\lambda_i = \frac{\sigma_i^2}{n-1}. \tag{5.55}$$

[7] Such that $\mathbf{U}^T\mathbf{U} = \mathbf{I}$ and $\mathbf{V}^T\mathbf{V} = \mathbb{I}$.

[8] Temporarily dropping the $\frac{1}{n-1}$ normalization term for visualization purposes.

[9] Here, we put the normalization term back in.

5.4.5 Implementing PCA in Python

Whether you implement PCA using the covariance method or from SVD, implementation always starts in the same way: You must *demean the data matrix*. Following this, eigenvectors and eigenvalues are estimated using either SVD or the covariance method. Assuming the data matrix $\mathbf{X}$ has shape $(n_{examples}, m_{features})$ and we are interested in the covariance between features not examples, then PCA may be run from the following steps:

1. Mean center the data matrix $\mathbf{X}_C = \mathbf{X} - \bar{\mathbf{X}}$ using `numpy.mean`. Make sure to specify which axis you want to average over (in this case you are looking for a mean value for each feature).
2. Estimate the principal components either through:
   a. The covariance method:
      - Estimate the data covariance matrix using Eq. (5.38), implemented using `numpy.matmul(..)`.
      - Estimate the eigenvector and eigenvalues of the data covariance matrix using `Lambda,U=numpy.linalg.eig(...)`.
      - This will return *unsorted* eigenvalues (`Lambda`) and eigenvectors (`U`).
      - Sort eigenvalues and eigenvectors into descending order using `numpy.argsort`.[10]

   b. The SVD method:
      - Estimate the singular vectors and values using `U,Lambda,VH=numpy.linalg.svd(...)`.
      - This will return *sorted* left singular vectors (`U`), right singular vectors (`VH`[11]) and singular values (`Lambda`)
      - calculate eigenvalues from singular values by implementing Eq. (5.55).
3. Project the data matrix onto the new basis: $\mathbf{Y} = \mathbf{X}_C \mathbf{V}$

5.4.6 PCA for dimensionality reduction

For datasets that have more features than examples, the action of projecting all points onto their PCA components ($\mathbf{Y} = \mathbf{X}_C \mathbf{U}$) reduces feature dimensionality automatically since the total number of nonzero components is *at most* equal to the size of the smallest dimension of the data matrix (matrix rank $r \leq \min(m, n)$). Often, the rank of the data covariance matrix will be even less as a result of correlation between features. For example, when predicting neonatal brain age from the volume of various regions, we see strong correlation in their trends of growth (Figs. 5.7a and 5.8a). A cumulative distribution of the values of PCA eigenvalues derived from the full data set (Fig. 5.8b) shows

[10] `numpy.argsort` will return the indices that sort an array in *ascending* order. This can be inverted and used to permute the eigenvalue and eigenvector matrices.

[11] Here, `VH` corresponds to $\mathbf{V}^T$; thus, columns of `U` and rows of `VH` are the singular vectors.

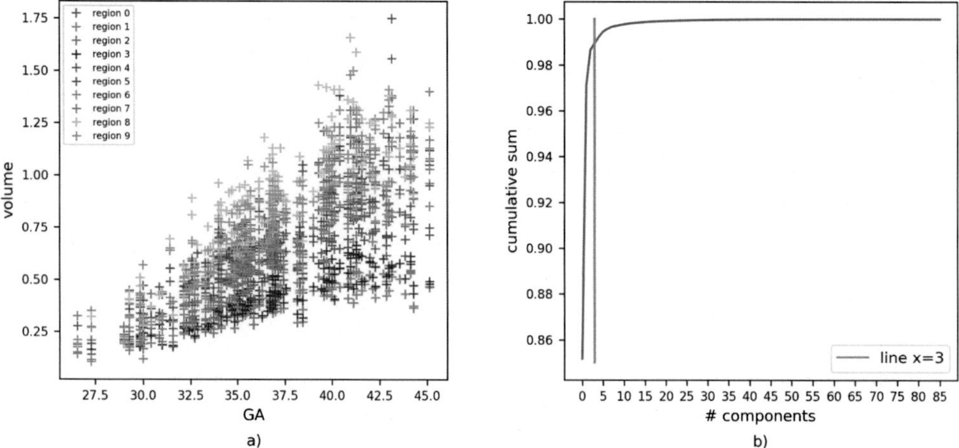

Figure 5.8 a) Volumes of ten neonatal brain regions plotted against GA. b) Cumulative distribution of the PCA eigenvalues.

that almost all of the data variance can be described by just three eigenvalues. Thus, we could project $\mathbf{X}_C$ onto just three eigenvectors and still capture the most meaningful variation in the data. Although there is no strict guide, a good rule of thumb is to choose the set of PCA eigenvectors that represent some significant proportion (e.g., 90%) of the total data variance.

5.4.7 Implementing PCA in scikit-learn

As with all models, PCA is straightforwardly implemented using a few calls to scikit-learn. The PCA object is derived from `class sklearn.decomposition` and takes an optional argument `n_components`, which determines the number of components that are returned from the model. For example, fitting PCA to a randomly generated matrix of shape `(10,2)`

```
from sklearn.decomposition import PCA
import numpy as np

# creating a random matrix of shape (10,2)
random_data=np.random.uniform(0,10,(10,2))

#instantiate model
model=PCA(n_components=2)
# fit the model
# note PCA is unsupervised (only Features for fitting!)
model.fit(random_data)
```

```
# or simultaneously fit the model
# and use it to transform the data
projected_data=model.fit_transform(random_data)
```

Key attributes that can be returned from the PCA model include: `model.explained_variance_ratio_`, which returns explained variance (lambdas) as a proportion of total variance; `model.singular_values_`, which returns the singular values and `model.components_`, which returns the PCA components.

5.4.8 PCA exercises

1. Estimate on paper the eigenvalues and *unit* eigenvectors of the matrices
   a. $\mathbf{A} = \begin{pmatrix} 0 & 1 \\ -2 & -3 \end{pmatrix}$
   b. $\mathbf{A} = \begin{pmatrix} 2 & 2 \\ 5 & -1 \end{pmatrix}$.
2. Using data from "GA-structure-volumes-preterm.csv",[12] implement from scratch the covariance and SVD methods for PCA decomposition (see 5.4.5):
   a. First load the data; we suggest slicing just the first ten features initially to make it easier to debug

   ```
   import pandas as pd

   #  first load data
   df = pd.read_csv(
   "GA-structure-volumes-preterm.csv",header=None)
   structure_volumes = df.values
   #  Load first 10 features
   Features = structure_volumes[:,1:11]
   # load labels
   Labels = structure_volumes[:,0]
   ```

   b. Mean center the data.
   c. Implement the covariance method:
      (i) estimate the data covariance matrix.
      (ii) evaluate the eigenvectors and values of the covariance matrix.
      (iii) sort eigenvalues and eigenvectors in descending order.
      (iv) project all data onto the PCA eigenspace.
   d. Implement the SVD method:
      (i) return the singular vectors and values of the *mean centered* data matrix.
      (ii) project all data onto the correct singular vectors.

[12] This dataset, skeleton code and solutions for exercises 2–4 are available from github.com/MachineLearningBiomedicalApplications/notebooks.

(iii) calculate the magnitude of the explained variance from the singular values using Eq. (5.55).
(iv) compare singular vectors and explained variance with the results from the covariance method; they should be the same.

e. implement PCA using scikit-learn and verify you get the same results.

3. Now, using all the features from "GA-structure-volumes-preterm.csv", train a simple `LinearRegression()` model to predict the target variable (GA).

a. evaluate performance using `sklearn.model_selection.cross_val_score`

4. Perform PCA-based dimensionality reduction to improve performance by

a. using scikit-learn to fit a PCA model of the data

b. using PCA attribute `explained_variance_ratio_` to return the ordered and normalized eigenvalues.

c. plot the cumulative distribution using `np.cumsum` to return the cumulative sum of eigenvalues. Identify the optimal number of eigenvalues (see Fig. 5.8b for the solution).

d. fit a new PCA model, setting `n_components` to the values chosen in using the plot to identify the optimal number of eigenvalues chosen in part c.. Project the original data matrix onto these components using scikit-learn's `fit_transform` function

e. Evaluate regression model on this reduced data set; cross-validated performance should improve.

5.5. Independent component analysis

In contrast to PCA which searches for a coordinate basis that aligns with the main sources of variance in the data, Independent Component Analysis (ICA) instead searches for a basis whose eigenvectors are maximally independent. A famous use of ICA is in the 'cocktail party problem', where the objective is to unmix sound recordings from a mixture of various sources (e.g., microphone recordings at various locations in a crowded room of people speaking). In medical applications, ICA is commonly applied to electrophysiological or functional brain recordings.

5.5.1 Statistical independence

To fully understand what it means to extract 'independent' signals, we must first revise probability theory. Consider the table shown in Fig. 5.9. This simulates the outcome of a survey of 100 people. Here, participants were asked whether they were suffering from any of the following illnesses: Cancer (C), Heart disease (H), Diabetes (D), Mental health illness (M), or none of the above (N). The responses were grouped by age bracket (< 20 years, 20–40 years, 40–60 years, 60–80 years, > 80 years). The sum of all values in the table adds up to 100.

Let's say that we are interested in the *marginal* probability of selecting a participant at random from a specific age bracket. This can be written in general terms as $P(age_i) = \frac{r_i}{N}$, i.e. the marginal probability of any age in the table is the row total (r_i) as a fraction of all participants. For the probability of selecting a participant aged under 20, we therefore get $P(<20) = \frac{r_1}{N} = \frac{2+1+3+5+14}{100} = \frac{25}{100}$ (Fig. 5.9b (orange row)). If we are interested in the marginal probability that an individual suffers from heart disease, we instead need the column total (Fig. 5.9c): $P(H) = \frac{c_2}{N} = \frac{1+6+0+6+3}{100} = \frac{16}{100}$.

Joint probabilities summarize the chances of two of more events co-occurring. For example, if we want the joint probability that we sample an individual aged 60–80 with mental health illness, we need the total from the cell at the intersection of these two options: c_{ij} (shown in pink in Fig. 5.9d). The joint probability is then the cell value divided by the total number of samples: $P(60-80, M) = \frac{c_{44}}{N} = \frac{4}{100}$.

Finally, *conditional probability* measures the probability of one event occurring given that another event has already occurred. For example, to calculate the probability of an individual suffering from mental illness given that you already know they are aged 20–40, it is first necessary to take the subset of examples corresponding to participants of age 20–40 (Fig. 5.9e (row highlighted in orange)) and then estimate the proportion of examples that have mental health illness *relative to the row total*: r_i. Hence, $P(M|20-40) = \frac{c_{24}}{r_2} = 6/30 = 1/5$. If our interest was instead in the conditional probability of age given disease status, then we would express the conditional probability as the cell total relative to the column total, e.g., $P(20-40|m) = \frac{c_{24}}{c_4} = 6/20$

Independent variables are variables for which *knowledge of one gives us no information of the value of the other.* In the case of mental health and age groups, we can see that the marginal probabilities of selecting an individual with mental health illness from any age group are always $P(M| < 20) = P(M|20-40) = P(M|40-60) = P(M|60-80) = P(M| > 80) = 1/5$. Further, the marginal probability of selecting an individual with mental health illness irrespective of age (Fig. 5.9f (blue column)) is also $P(M) = \frac{20}{100} = \frac{1}{5}$. So, $P(M|20-40) = P(M)$—the addition of age doesn't impact our certainty at all. Another feature of independent events is that their joint probability is equal to the product of the marginals. This is derived from the product rule: $P(A, B) = P(A|B)P(B)$, where, if independent $P(A|B) = P(A)$, then $P(A, B) = P(A)P(B)$.

5.5.2 Independence and correlation

Perhaps a more intuitive way of understanding independent events is that they are uncorrelated. Fig. 5.10 simulates the correlation–independence relationship for various functions. In Fig. 5.10a, two completely out-of-phase sinusoids are completely nonoverlapping, and so their correlation is close to 0. In this case they are also independent. By contrast, two completely overlapping signals, such as those shown in Fig. 5.10b, are completely correlated, and therefore not independent. Take caution, however, as uncorrelated events are not necessarily independent. Correlation is a summary of linear

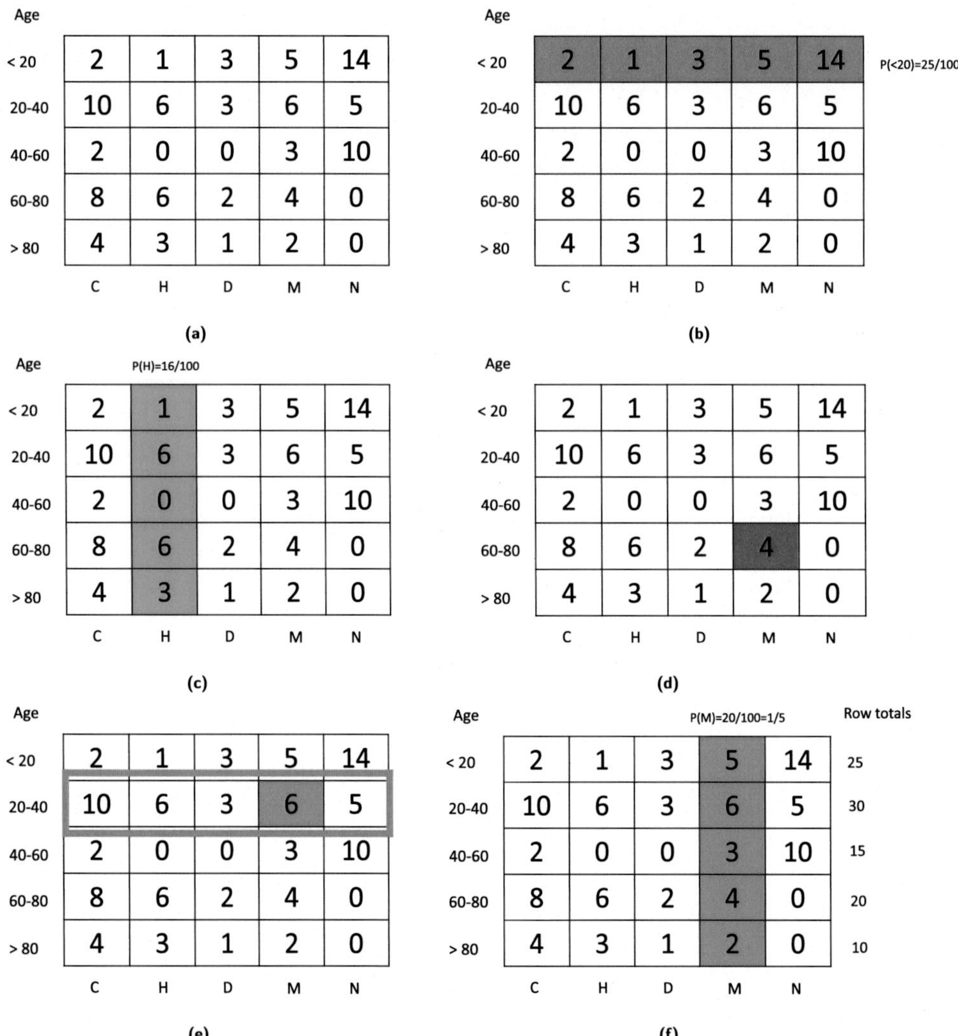

Age	C	H	D	M	N
< 20	2	1	3	5	14
20-40	10	6	3	6	5
40-60	2	0	0	3	10
60-80	8	6	2	4	0
> 80	4	3	1	2	0

Figure 5.9 a) A toy example simulating 100 individuals with self-reported illnesses; b) marginal probability of selecting participant under 20; c) marginal probability of selecting participant with heart disease; d) joint probability of selecting an individual that has cancer and is age 60–80 years; e) conditional probability of selecting an individual reporting mental health illness if they are known to be 20–40 years of age; f) independence can be shown then conditional probabilities are equal to the marginals; here, the marginal probability of sampling an individual with mental illness from any group is 1/5 and $P(M) = 1/5$.

dependencies

$$\rho_{x,y} = \frac{(X - \mu_X)(y - \mu_Y)}{\sigma_X \sigma_Y} = \frac{E(X, Y) - E(X)E(Y)}{\sigma_X \sigma_Y} \tag{5.56}$$

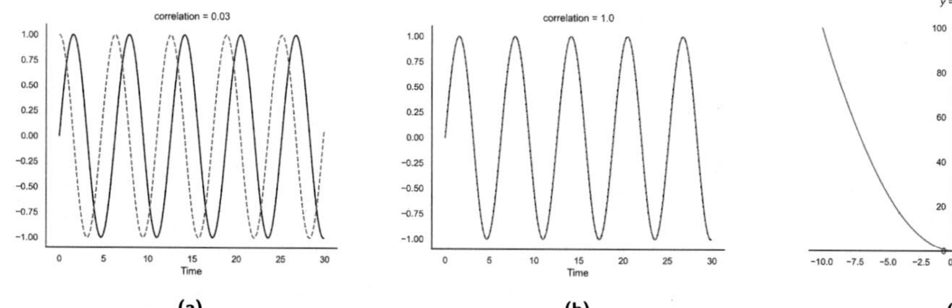

Figure 5.10 a) Two sinusoids completely out of phase have zero correlation and are independent; b) signals that are completely in phase have perfect correlation and thereby dependence; c) the equation $y = x^2$ has zero correlation but *is not independent*.

As such Fig. 5.10c highlights a case where the nonlinear function $y = x^2$ is completely uncorrelated;[13] however, y is completely determined by x so they are not independent.

5.5.3 A mathematical definition

The assumption of ICA is that the available data ($\mathbf{X}_M$) represents a mixture of source signals ($\mathbf{S}$), with mixing coefficients $\mathbf{M}$

$$\mathbf{X}_M = \mathbf{M}\mathbf{S}. \tag{5.57}$$

Thus, each sample from $\mathbf{X}_M$ is a linear combination of the n original source signals

$$X_M(t) = \sum_{i}^{n} M\, S_i(t). \tag{5.58}$$

The objective through ICA optimization is therefore to learn the unmixing matrix $\mathbf{W}$ whose coefficients unmix the data $\mathbf{X}$ and recover the sources $\mathbf{S}$

$$\mathbf{S} = \mathbf{M}^{-1}\mathbf{X} = \mathbf{W}\mathbf{X}. \tag{5.59}$$

This is achieved by assuming the source signals are *independent* and *non-Gaussian*.

Why must signals be non-Gaussian?

Let's say that our sources come from two mean-centered Gaussian signals with unit variance: $\mathbf{S} \sim \mathcal{N}(0, 1)$, i.e., $\mathbf{S}$ will have a circular distribution centered on the origin[14]

[13] Since $E(X, Y) = E(X) = 0$.
[14] And $\mathbf{S}\mathbf{S}^T = \mathbb{I}$, since $\mathcal{N}(0, 1)$ is equivalent to the identity matrix.

(see Fig. 5.11). In this case $\mathbf{X} = \mathbf{MS}$ is also Gaussian with zero mean and covariance:

$$\mathbf{XX}^T = (\mathbf{MS})(\mathbf{MS})^T = \mathbf{MSS}^T\mathbf{M}^T = \mathbf{MM}^T. \tag{5.60}$$

Our goal with ICA is to be able to predict unique sources. However, if the original source signals are Gaussian, we can imagine a situation where we propose a new coefficients matrix $\mathbf{M}'$ through a rotation $\mathbf{R}$ such that $\mathbf{M}' = \mathbf{MR}$. In this case we would observe the effect of a new mixture $\mathbf{X}' = \mathbf{M}'\mathbf{S}$, which, if we are to distinguish the effect of $\mathbf{M}'$ from $\mathbf{M}$, would require that the distribution we observe with $\mathbf{X}'$ differs from that of $\mathbf{X}$. Unfortunately, in the case of Gaussian variables, this becomes impossible because the covariance of $\mathbf{X}'$ is indistinguishable from that of $\mathbf{X}$[15]

$$\mathbf{X}'\mathbf{X}'^T = \mathbf{M}'\mathbf{SS}^T\mathbf{M}'^T = \mathbf{MRSS}^T\mathbf{R}^T\mathbf{M}^T = \mathbf{MRR}^T\mathbf{M}^T = \mathbf{MM}^T. \tag{5.61}$$

If we cannot find a unique $\mathbf{M}$ then we cannot find a unique $\mathbf{W}$ and we cannot recover the original sources. Thus, the signals must be non-Gaussian.

Another explanation may be achieved through the central limit theorem, which states

"The distribution of a sum of independent random variables tends toward a Gaussian distribution"

In other words, a mixed signal will be more Gaussian than that of either of its component signals. We can use this to form the basis of an algorithm to separate the components. What we are looking for is that each source be represented as a linear sum of the mixed signals $\mathbf{S} = \mathbf{A}^{-1}\mathbf{X} = \mathbf{WX}$, with coefficients given by the inverse of our mixing matrix. We can therefore try different linear combinations of mixtures, until we find the most non-Gaussian combination. While there are many ways to encourage non-Gaussianity, one of the most stable (used by the popular FastICA algorithm [21]) is to optimize for the negative entropy of the distribution, since

"a Gaussian variable has the largest entropy among all random variables of equal variance [9]".

Estimates of negative entropy are less sensitive to outliers than standard measures of non-Gaussianity such as Kurtosis and provide a measure which is zero for a Gaussian variable and always nonnegative.

5.5.4 Preprocessing for ICA

Regardless of which optimization method is used, a key preprocessing step is the whitening of the mean-centered data-covariance matrix. Whitening is related to PCA and works by transforming the original input data $\mathbf{X}_C$ into form $\mathbf{Y}$, where $Cov(\mathbf{Y}) = \mathbf{I}$. This is achieved through SVD of the original covariance matrix $Cov(\mathbf{X}_C) = \mathbf{C}_X =$

[15] Using the fact that for orthogonal matrices $\mathbf{R}^T = \mathbf{R}^{-1}$, such that $\mathbf{RR}^T = \mathbb{I}$.

$\mathbf{E\Sigma E}^{-1}$. Specifically, rewriting

$$\mathbf{C}_X = \mathbf{E\Sigma E}^{-1} \rightarrow \mathbf{\Sigma} = \mathbf{E}^{-1}\mathbf{C}_X\mathbf{E} \tag{5.62}$$

We want to learn the prewhitening matrix $\mathbf{P}$ that transforms $\mathbf{X}_C$ (as $\mathbf{Y} = \mathbf{PX}$) into a distribution where the data covariance matrix is diagonal and all eigenvalues are 1 ($Cov(\mathbf{Y}) = \mathbf{I}$).

Prior to whitening, we do know that $\mathbf{\Sigma}$ multiplied by its inverse is the identity ($\mathbf{\Sigma\Sigma}^{-1} = \mathbb{I}$); thus, we can define:

$$\mathbf{\Sigma}^{-1}\mathbf{\Sigma} = \mathbf{\Sigma}^{-1}\mathbf{E}^{-1}\mathbf{C}_X\mathbf{E} \rightarrow \mathbf{I} = \mathbf{\Sigma}^{-1}\mathbf{E}^{-1}\mathbf{C}_X\mathbf{E}. \tag{5.63}$$

Rewriting $\mathbf{\Sigma}^{-1}$ as $\mathbf{\Sigma}^{-1/2}\mathbf{\Sigma}^{-1/2}$ and reordering[16]:

$$\mathbf{I} = \mathbf{\Sigma}^{-1/2}\mathbf{E}^{-1}\mathbf{C}_X\mathbf{E\Sigma}^{-1/2}. \tag{5.64}$$

We need the covariance (rewritten in terms of $\mathbf{P}$ and $\mathbf{X}$) to be the identity:

$$Cov(\mathbf{Y}) = \frac{1}{(n+1)}\mathbf{PXX}^T\mathbf{P}^T = \mathbb{I}, \tag{5.65}$$

and, since both Eqs. (5.64) and (5.65) are equal to the identity, we can equate them:

$$\frac{1}{(n+1)}\mathbf{PXX}^T\mathbf{P}^T = \mathbf{\Sigma}^{-1/2}\mathbf{E}^{-1}\mathbf{C}_X\mathbf{E\Sigma}^{-1/2}. \tag{5.66}$$

Replacing $\frac{1}{(n+1)}\mathbf{XX^T}$ with $\mathbf{C}_X$,

$$\mathbf{PCP}^T = \mathbf{\Sigma}^{-1/2}\mathbf{E}^{-1}\mathbf{C}_X\mathbf{E\Sigma}^{-1/2} \tag{5.67}$$

We can see from the symmetry on the left and right sides[17] that this means that $\mathbf{P} = \mathbf{\Sigma}^{-1/2}\mathbf{E}^T$. Typically $\mathbf{P}$ is also premultiplied by $\mathbf{E}$ in order to rotate data back to its original orientation. Thus, we define:

$$\mathbf{P} = \mathbf{E\Sigma}^{-1/2}\mathbf{E}^T. \tag{5.68}$$

Thus, essentially whitening performs the transformations summarized in Fig. 5.11. First multiplication by $\mathbf{E}$ rotates the data distribution into alignment with principal axes (decorrelating interactions between features (see Fig. 5.11b). Then, the variance is squeezed along the dimensions where it is larger than one, and stretched along dimensions where it is less than one (see Fig. 5.11c). Then, data is rotated back to its original orientation.

[16] This is possible since $\mathbf{\Sigma}$ is a diagonal matrix of singular values; thus, both matrices are diagonal and commute.

[17] $\mathbf{E}$ is orthonormal ($\mathbf{E}^T = \mathbf{E}^{-1}$) since it is an eigenvector of a real, symmetric matrix.

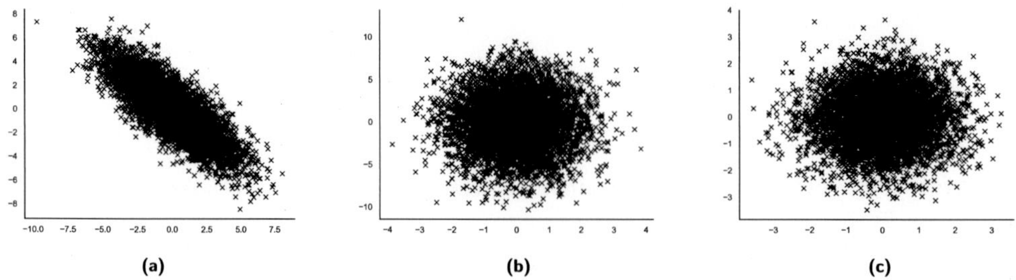

Figure 5.11 Whitening works to transform data into a distribution with diagonalized, and variance-normalized covariance a) original data; b) data is first rotated into alignment with the principal axes; b) variance in each axis is then normalized to one.

This transform can be used to generate a new *orthogonal* mixing matrix $\tilde{\mathbf{A}}$ (from Eq. (5.57), by swapping $\mathbf{X}$ for $\mathbf{Y}$):

$$\mathbf{Y} = \mathbf{E}\boldsymbol{\Sigma}^{-1/2}\mathbf{E}^T\mathbf{X} \tag{5.69}$$

$$= \mathbf{E}\boldsymbol{\Sigma}^{-1/2}\mathbf{E}^T\mathbf{A}\mathbf{S} \qquad = \tilde{\mathbf{A}}\mathbf{S}, \tag{5.70}$$

where, orthogonality may be seen through the fact that $\tilde{\mathbf{A}}$ is the whitened form of $\mathbf{A}$. Whitening therefore reduces the number of parameters that are needed to be estimated during ICA optimization, since all orthogonal matrices are symmetric, it is sufficient to estimate only the values of the upper or lower diagonal triangle of the matrix. In some cases, it can also be useful to implement PCA based dimensionality reduction—throwing away all eigenvectors of $\mathbf{C}_X$ with small eigenvalues—to reduce the impact of noise [21].

5.5.5 Implementing ICA in scikit-learn

Scikit-learn implements the FastICA [21], in a very similar way to PCA (Sec. 5.4.7), namely,

```
from sklearn.decomposition import FastICA

#instantiate model
model=FastICA(n_components=2, whiten='unit-variance')
# fit the model to data X and transform data
model.fit_transform(X)
```

Here, `n_components` and `whiten` are tunable input parameters. The model is set to whiten by default. The class has attributes including `model.components_`, which returns the original source signals, and `model.whitening_`, which returns the whitening transform.[18]

[18] Unless `whiten=False`.

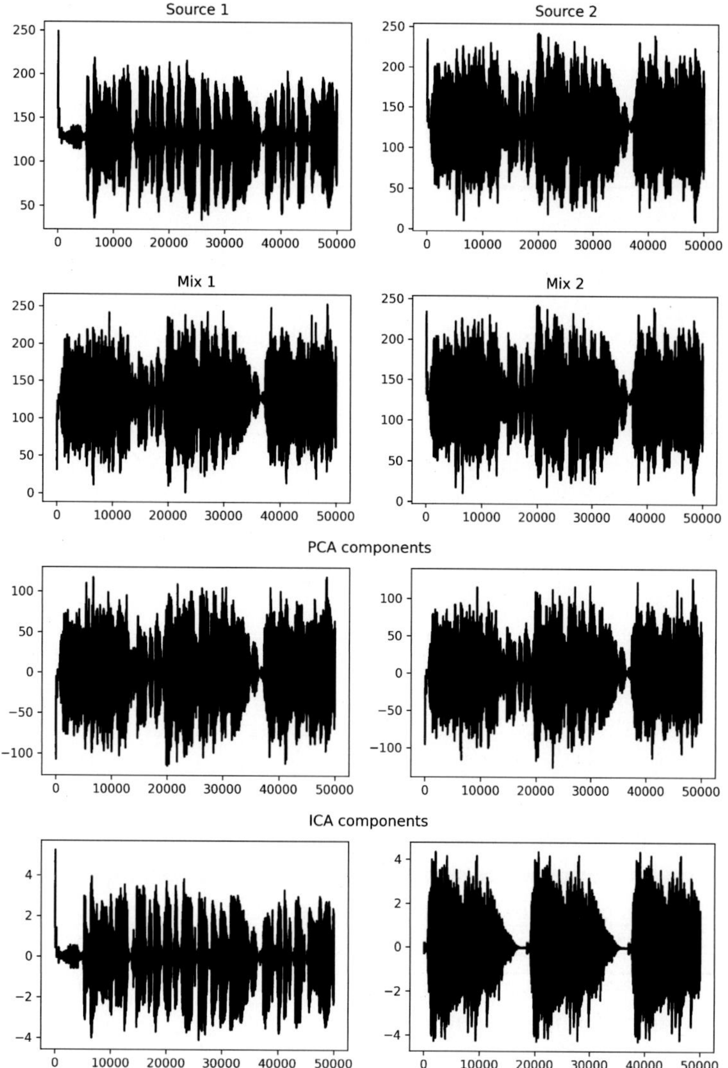

Figure 5.12 Comparing ICA and PCA for unmixing audio signals. From top to bottom: source signals, mixed signals (linear combination of sources), results of PCA decomposition, results of ICA decomposition.

5.5.6 Comparing PCA and ICA

The different objectives of PCA and ICA are summarized very clearly in Fig. 5.12 (implemented as Exercise 5.5.8). Here, two source audio signals are linearly combined into a mixed signal. We see that, while ICA is able to recover the original signals, PCA cannot. This is because PCA assumes the components are Gaussian distributed, whereas

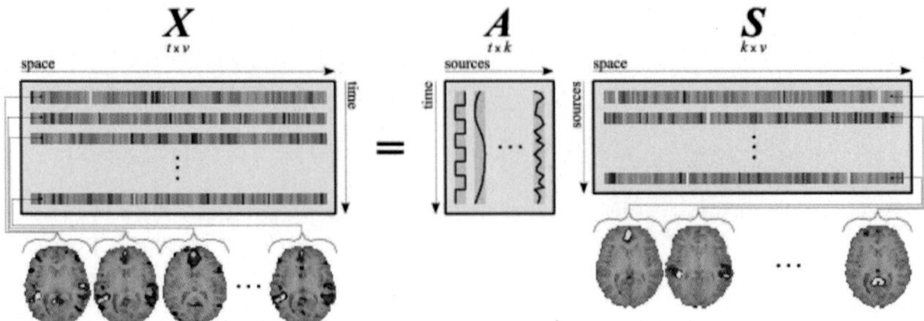

Figure 5.13 ICA decomposition expressed in terms of fMRI signal components.

ICA makes the exact opposite assumption. Thus, PCA is suitable for dimensionality-reduction tasks where the assumptions are that the directions of maximal variance are interpretable and of key importance. On the other hand, ICA is most often used for problems where it can be assumed that the recorded data represent a mixture of source signals.

5.5.7 Biomedical applications of ICA

A very common use of ICA is to isolate source signals from electrophysiological or functional recordings of the brain. Here, $\mathbf{X}_M$ might represent neuronal recordings measured from electroencephalogram (EEG) electrodes, or indirect measures of brain activity recorded from various locations in the brain, as done in functional MRI (fMRI). In the case of fMRI, most often spatial ICA is implemented, which means that the underlying assumption is that the source signals represent nonoverlapping regions of the brain that share a common pattern of brain activity (Fig. 5.13). Then, the loading coefficients $\mathbf{A}$ may be interpreted as the time series of those patterns of activity. In this way, ICA can also be used to remove nuisance signals, e.g., generated through physiological processes (breathing, cardiac pulsation) or motion [41].

5.5.8 ICA exercises

1. Given the table in Fig. 5.9, calculate:
   a. the conditional probability that an individual aged 60–80 has had heart disease;
   b. the joint probability of sampling someone who is under 20 and suffers from diabetes;
   c. the marginal probability of having had cancer.
2. Given the two mixed audio files "mix1.wav" and "mix2.wav":[19]

[19] Datasets and solution is available from github.com/MachineLearningBiomedicalApplications/notebooks.

a. Create a data matrix $\mathbf{X}_M \in \mathbb{R}^{m \times t}$ where m is the number of samples (2) and t is the length of the timeseries

```
from scipy.io import wavfile

# Load first signal
samplingRate, signal1 = wavfile.read('Data/mix1.wav')

# Load second signal
samplingRate, signal2 = wavfile.read('Data/mix2.wav')

# stack both signals into the matrix X
X = np.stack((signal1,signal2),axis=0)
```

b. Estimate the whitening transform of $\mathbf{X}$.[20]

c. Using scikit-learn, decompose $\mathbf{X}$ using PCA and ICA. Which one recovers the original signals and why?

5.6. Manifold learning

In some circumstances, linear embedddings are insufficient to model the underlying distribution of the data. Take the toy example of Fig. 5.14. Here, a uniform distribution of points, generated originally in 2D (Fig. 5.14a), is subsequently rolled up into a 3D structure (Fig. 5.14b). We can see from the black dashed arrow (Fig. 5.14b) that Euclidean distances create shortcuts between points that were originally distant on the plane. For this reason, PCA and ICA embeddings will always fail to recover the data structure of nonlinearly distributed points: A 2D PCA embedding of the swiss roll dataset will specifically collapse all points onto a plane that projects through the main directions of variance through the data (Fig. 5.14c). What we instead need is to recover the *geodesic* distances (Fig. 5.14b (red dashed arrow)) that follow the curve of the *manifold*. Scikit-learn offers several approaches for doing this [2,3,11,39,46,47,51], each with slightly different techniques for approximating the underlying geodesic distances.[21] In this chapter, we will focus on Laplacian eigenmaps [2], also known as spectral embedding, which is one of the most intuitive to understand.

[20] Useful numpy functions for this include: `np.linalg.inv` (to estimate matrix inverses); `scipy.linalg.fractional_matrix_power` (to estimate $\mathbf{D}^{-1/2}$); and `np.linalg.multi_dot` to multiply three matrices together.

[21] https://scikit-learn.org/stable/modules/manifold.html.

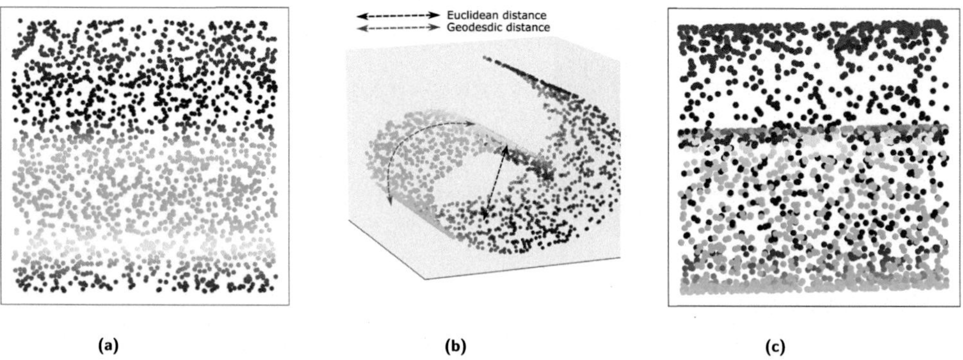

Figure 5.14 Motivating manifold learning with the swiss roll mode: a)A distribution of points on a 2D plane; b) the effect of wrapping the plane up into a 'swiss roll' in three dimensions; c) the results of projecting all points onto the first PCA component.

5.7. Laplacian eigenmaps

In essence, a manifold is a topological space for which Euclidean distances are only meaningful locally. Thus, one way to approximate geodesic distances, along a manifold, is to first construct a *k-Nearest Neighbor* (kNN) graph, which connects each point with its *k* closest points by Euclidean distance. In this way, geodesics along the manifold may be approximated by stepping from neighbour to neighbour, and summing the Euclidean distances between each. Fig. 5.15 shows a toy example for a simple oscillating 1D function.

Thus, Laplacian eigenmaps work by constructing and binarizing a k-NN graph, otherwise known as the adjacency matrix: **A**. This is then used calculate the graph Laplacian: $\mathbf{L} = \mathbf{D} - \mathbf{A}$, where **D** is the *degree* matrix calculated by summing the total number of neighbors of each node ($D_i = \sum_j Aij$). This represents a discrete approximation of the Laplace operator, whose eigenvectors reflect the *spectra* (or harmonics) of the graph. One way to intuitively understand the links between the eigenvectors of the graph Laplacian and the geodesics across the surface of a manifold is to understand that the roots of the Laplacian represent equilibrium solutions for diffusion of some quantity across the graph. As such, the eigenvectors corresponding to the smallest nonzero eigenvalues reflect a random walk across the manifold, such that points having similar values in the eigenvector space must also be close together on the manifold. In this way, it is possible to use the eigenvectors of the graph Laplacian to 'unwrap' the manifold into a lower-dimensional Euclidean space.

5.7.1 Calculation of the graph Laplacian

Estimation of the graph Laplacian may be broken down into the following steps:

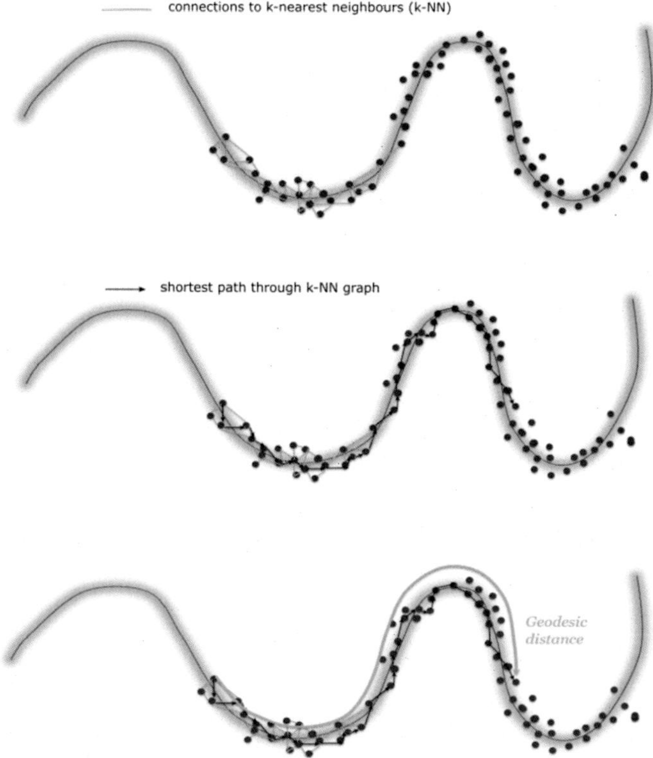

Figure 5.15 Geodesic distances through k-NN graph. Top: green edges connect the 3 nearest neighbors of every point from the distribution; Middle: black arrows indicate the shortest path through the graph; Bottom: for correct choice of k this will approximate a geodesic along the manifold.

1. Construction of the *adjacency* matrix through calculation of squared Euclidean distances between all data points: $SSD_i = \sum_j (\mathbf{x}_i - \mathbf{x}_j)^2$;
2. Set all but the k smallest distances in each row to zero; then set all remaining values to 1;
3. Calculate the *degree* matrix by summing the total number of neighbors of each node: $\mathbf{D} = \sum_j \mathbf{A}$; then
4. Subtract the adjacency matrix from the degree matrix to return the graph Laplacian: $\mathbf{L} = \mathbf{D} - \mathbf{A}$

For a data set of N examples, $\mathbf{A}$ should be a $N \times N$ shaped matrix, where each row represents each node and the entry each column indicates which examples are neighbors of that node. The first step in calculation is therefore to estimate the squared distances between all points (since we are interested only in the magnitude of the separation and not the direction). $\mathbf{A}$ is initialized with all zeros; then, each row is populated with 1 s in the columns that represent the closest neighbors of that node.[22] Finally, we need **A** to be symmetric, or otherwise the derivation of the Laplacian will not hold. Thus, the matrix **A** is symmetrized as $A_{ij} = A_{ji}$.

Let's step through the following simple example for the data matrix **X** with 6 examples, each with 2 features:

$$\mathbf{X} = \begin{pmatrix} 4 & 3 \\ 1 & 3 \\ 4 & 4 \\ 2 & 2 \\ 3 & 0 \\ 2 & 0 \end{pmatrix}. \tag{5.71}$$

To calculate the adjacency matrix **A**, we must first estimate the sum of square distances (SSD) between all points. Let us do this for just the first data point. We write the calculation in the style of Python broadcasting as:

$$\mathbf{x}_0 - \mathbf{X} = \begin{pmatrix} 4 & 3 \\ 4 & 3 \\ 4 & 3 \\ 4 & 3 \\ 4 & 3 \\ 4 & 3 \end{pmatrix} - \begin{pmatrix} 4 & 3 \\ 1 & 3 \\ 4 & 4 \\ 2 & 2 \\ 3 & 0 \\ 2 & 0 \end{pmatrix} = \begin{pmatrix} 0 & 0 \\ 3 & 0 \\ 0 & -1 \\ 2 & 1 \\ 1 & 3 \\ 2 & 3 \end{pmatrix}. \tag{5.72}$$

To calculate the SSD for this point, we need to square[23] and sum the distances:

$$\sum_j (\mathbf{x}_0 - \mathbf{X})^2 = \sum_j \left(\begin{pmatrix} 0 & 0 \\ 3 & 0 \\ 0 & -1 \\ 2 & 1 \\ 1 & 3 \\ 2 & 3 \end{pmatrix} * \begin{pmatrix} 0 & 0 \\ 3 & 0 \\ 0 & -1 \\ 2 & 1 \\ 1 & 3 \\ 2 & 3 \end{pmatrix} \right) = \sum_j \begin{pmatrix} 0 & 0 \\ 9 & 0 \\ 0 & 1 \\ 4 & 1 \\ 1 & 9 \\ 4 & 9 \end{pmatrix} = \begin{pmatrix} 0 \\ 9 \\ 1 \\ 5 \\ 10 \\ 13 \end{pmatrix}. \tag{5.73}$$

[22] Note that it is common practice to binarize **A**; however, weighted adjacency matrices can also be used.
[23] $*$ Represents element-wise multiplication.

Expanding this to all rows, we obtain a symmetric matrix of distances between all pairs of points:

$$\sum_j (\mathbf{X}_i - \mathbf{X})^2 = \begin{pmatrix} 0 & 9 & 1 & 5 & 10 & 13 \\ 9 & 0 & 10 & 2 & 13 & 10 \\ 1 & 10 & 0 & 8 & 17 & 20 \\ 5 & 2 & 8 & 0 & 5 & 4 \\ 10 & 13 & 17 & 5 & 0 & 1 \\ 13 & 10 & 20 & 4 & 1 & 0 \end{pmatrix}. \tag{5.74}$$

However, once we set the k-nearest neighbors of each node to zero, this will lose symmetry. For example, setting $k = 2$, we first highlight the two smallest distances for each row in red:

$$\sum_j (\mathbf{X}_i - \mathbf{X})^2 = \begin{pmatrix} 0 & 9 & 1 & 5 & 10 & 13 \\ 9 & 0 & 10 & 2 & 13 & 10 \\ 1 & 10 & 0 & 8 & 17 & 20 \\ 5 & 2 & 8 & 0 & 5 & 4 \\ 10 & 13 & 17 & 5 & 0 & 1 \\ 13 & 10 & 20 & 4 & 1 & 0 \end{pmatrix}. \tag{5.75}$$

Importantly, we ignore the distance between each point and itself and notice that the closest neighbors of the first row (with distances of 1 and 5) are not necessarily the distances highlighted in the first column. To create the adjacency matrix, we must first set the highlighted distances to 1 and all remaining distances to 0:

$$\mathbf{A} = \begin{pmatrix} 0 & 0 & 1 & 1 & 0 & 0 \\ 1 & 0 & 0 & 1 & 0 & 0 \\ 1 & 0 & 0 & 1 & 0 & 0 \\ 0 & 1 & 0 & 0 & 0 & 1 \\ 0 & 0 & 0 & 1 & 0 & 1 \\ 0 & 0 & 0 & 1 & 1 & 0 \end{pmatrix}. \tag{5.76}$$

Since this is no longer symmetric, it is necessary to fix $A_{ij} = A_{ji}$ for all columns and rows (where, this time, edits are highlighted in red):

$$\mathbf{A}_{sym} = \begin{pmatrix} 0 & 1 & 1 & 1 & 0 & 0 \\ 1 & 0 & 0 & 1 & 0 & 0 \\ 1 & 0 & 0 & 1 & 0 & 0 \\ 1 & 1 & 1 & 0 & 1 & 1 \\ 0 & 0 & 0 & 1 & 0 & 1 \\ 0 & 0 & 0 & 1 & 1 & 0 \end{pmatrix}. \tag{5.77}$$

As a result, some nodes now have more than two neighbors. The degree matrix calculates the total number of neighbors for each node (by summing each row *or* each column):

$$\mathbf{D} = diag(\sum_j \mathbf{A}_{sym}) = \begin{pmatrix} 3 & 0 & 0 & 0 & 0 & 0 \\ 0 & 2 & 0 & 0 & 0 & 0 \\ 0 & 0 & 2 & 0 & 0 & 0 \\ 0 & 0 & 0 & 5 & 0 & 0 \\ 0 & 0 & 0 & 0 & 2 & 0 \\ 0 & 0 & 0 & 0 & 0 & 2 \end{pmatrix}. \tag{5.78}$$

Finally, the Laplacian matrix is calculated as:

$$\mathbf{L} = \mathbf{D} - \mathbf{A}_{sym} = \begin{pmatrix} 3 & -1 & -1 & -1 & 0 & 0 \\ -1 & 2 & 0 & -1 & 0 & 0 \\ -1 & 0 & 2 & -1 & 0 & 0 \\ -1 & -1 & -1 & 5 & -1 & -1 \\ 0 & 0 & 0 & -1 & 2 & -1 \\ 0 & 0 & 0 & -1 & -1 & 0 \end{pmatrix}. \tag{5.79}$$

5.7.2 Deriving the embedding solution

From the graph Laplacian, we need to calculate the coordinates of a new space in which Euclidean distances approximate geodesics along the manifold. This objective can be summarized by the following cost function:

$$C = \sum_{i,j} (y_i - y_j)^2 \mathbf{A}_{ij}, \tag{5.80}$$

where $\mathbf{A}_{ij}$ indexes the symmetric adjacency matrix (dropping the '*sym*' notation for clarity) and y_i and y_j represent the coordinates of the lower-dimensional Euclidean space that we're trying to find. It is hoped that you can see that this cost function is minimized if we place points that are close together in the original data close together in the new low-dimensional space because $\mathbf{A}_{ij}$ is nonzero only when $(x_i - x_j)^2$ is low. At the same time, we must avoid the trivial solution where all points get mapped onto a single location (i.e., either $y_i = 0$ or $y_i = y_j$). We can find a solution by multiplying out our cost function and substituting for $\mathbf{D}_{ii} = \sum_j \mathbf{A}_{ij}$[24] as follows:

$$C = \sum_{i,j} (y_i - y_j)^2 \mathbf{A}_{ij} \tag{5.81}$$

$$C = \sum_{i,j} (y_i^2 + y_j^2 - 2y_i y_j) \mathbf{A}_{ij} \tag{5.82}$$

[24] And through using the symmetry $\mathbf{D}_{jj} = \sum_i \mathbf{A}_{ij}$.

$$C = \sum_i y_i^2 \mathbf{D_{ii}} + \sum_j y_j^2 \mathbf{D_{jj}} - 2\sum_{i,j} y_i y_j \mathbf{A}_{ij} \tag{5.83}$$

$$C = \mathbf{y}^{\mathbf{T}}\mathbf{D}\mathbf{y} - \mathbf{y}^{\mathbf{T}}\mathbf{A}\mathbf{y} \tag{5.84}$$

$$C = \mathbf{y}^{\mathbf{T}}\mathbf{L}\mathbf{y} \tag{5.85}$$

Thus, we need the $\mathbf{y}$ that minimizes $\mathbf{y}^{\mathbf{T}}\mathbf{L}\mathbf{y}$ subject to the constraint that $y_i \neq 0$. We have seen this before for PCA in Eq. (5.43), with the exception that in this case we are looking to *minimize* and not maximize the objective function. From this we know that the solution to this optimization problem is the Laplacian eigenvector corresponding to the smallest eigenvalue. However, this is zero and corresponds to the constant eigenvector $\mathbb{1}$, making it also undesirable because it corresponds to the solution $y_i = y_j$. Solutions are therefore given by the eigenvectors corresponding to the N smallest nonzero eigenvalues. More specifically, for a 2D embedding, you need the two smallest nonzero eigenvalues. Unlike PCA, there is no need to project data onto the eigenvectors—*the Laplacian eigenvectors are the embedding.*

5.7.3 The normalized graph Laplacian

Strictly speaking, most implementations of Laplacian eigenmaps do not use $\mathbf{L} = \mathbf{D} - \mathbf{A}$, but instead seek solutions to the generalized eigenvector problem $\mathbf{Ly} = \lambda\mathbf{Dy}$. This corresponds to estimating eigenvectors of the normalized graph Laplacian $\mathbf{L} = \mathbf{D}^{-1/2}\mathbf{D} - \mathbf{A}\mathbf{D}^{-1/2}$. If the graph is very regular and most vertices have approximately the same degree, then the normalized Laplacian and unnormalized Laplacian will generate very similar results. However, if the degrees in the graph are very broadly distributed, it is more stable to use a normalized Laplacian. By default, this is the approach taken by scikit-learn.

5.7.4 Implementing Laplacian eigenmaps in scikit-learn

Laplacian eigenmaps may be implemented in scikit-learn using the `SpectralEmbedding` function from the `manifold` class. As for PCA and ICA, it is possible to tune the dimensionality of the embedding using the `n_components` argument. Another key hyperparameter for tuning is k, i.e., the number of neighbors retained in the adjacency matrix $\mathbf{A}$. This is defined through the `n_neighbors` argument.

```
from sklearn.manifold import SpectralEmbedding

# set embedding dimensionality=2 and k-NN to 10
model=SpectralEmbedding(n_components=2,n_neighbors=10)
# fit and transform the data
Z = model.fit_transform(X)
# Z is an N x 2 dimensional embedding of X
```

In scikit-learn you have the choice of implementing a binary or weighted adjacency matrix, set by the `affinity` argument. By default, the method is set to `affinity='nearest_neighbors'`, the binary implementation; however, `affinity='rbf'` will populate **A** with values calculated from a Gaussian radial basis function (RBF) of the form: $e^{\gamma||x_i - x_j||^2}$ (where the scaling parameter: $\gamma = \frac{1}{2\sigma^2}$ may be set with argument: `gamma`).

5.7.5 Manifold learning exercises

Working with the Swiss roll data set,

```
import matplotlib.pyplot as plt
from mpl_toolkits.mplot3d import Axes3D # for 3D plotting
import numpy as np

def create_spiral(M, num_rotations):
    """ Take 2D manifold M and output 3D spiral
    made from curling up M in 3D space """
    N = M.shape[0]
    r = np.exp(M[:,1] * num_rotations) * 0.5
    theta = M[:,1] * (2 * np.pi) * num_rotations
    X = np.zeros((N, 3))
    X[:,0] = M[:,0] * 6
    X[:,1] = r * np.cos(theta)
    X[:,2] = r * np.sin(theta)
    return X

# 2000 random points scattered in [0,1]^2
N=2000
X_m = np.random.random((N, 2))

# create 'swiss roll' dataset
X = create_spiral(X_m, 1.2)

# some helpful plotting functions
fig = plt.figure(figsize=(16,8))
ax = fig.add_subplot(121, projection='3d')
# plot data rolled in 3D
_ = ax.scatter(X[:,0], X[:,1], X[:,2], c=X_m[:,1], marker='o')

ax = fig.add_subplot(122)
```

```
#plot original 2D data
_ = ax.scatter(X_m[:,0], X_m[:,1], c=X_m[:,1], marker='o')
```

Consider 2D `X_m` as the 'underlying degrees of freedom'. Think of the 3D `X` as the high-dimensional data we have measured.[25]

1. First, implement PCA to embed `X` in 2D. Plot the transformed data. Check if your result replicates the result shown in Fig. 5.14c (allowing for differences in the random distribution of the data).

2. Now, implement Laplacian eigenmaps from scratch with the steps

- **i** Initialize **A** using `np.zeros(N,N)`;
- **ii** Calculate the sum of square distances between all points—insert `1` at the locations of the closest points for each row of **A**;
- **iii** Symmetrize **A** (hint: use `np.maximum(..)`);
- **iv** Calculate **D** as $\mathbf{D} = \sum_j \mathbf{A}$ (hint: This will output a vector and use `np.diag(..)` to turn this into a matrix);
- **v** Estimate **L**;
- **vi** Use `np.eigh(L, eigvals=(1,2))` to return the eigenvectors corresponding to the two smallest nonzero eigenvalues.[26]
- **vii** plot the Laplacian embedding.[27]

3. Compare your implementation with the result obtained using scikit-learn. Remember that scikit-learn will not return the same result as for the 'from-scratch' implementation due to the use of the normalized graph Laplacian.

4. (optionally) Try editing your scikit-learn implementation to make use of `affinity='rbf'`.

5. (optionally) Try some of the alternative manifold learning methods offered by scikit-learn, such as t-distributed stochastic neighbor embedding (t-sne) [47] or Isomap [46].

[25] Skeleton code and solution is available from github.com/MachineLearningBiomedicalApplications/notebooks.

[26] Where here we assume that you have only 1 nonzero eigenvector; in fact, this will depend on the connectivity of your adjacency matrix, which in turn depends on the tuning of k—we suggest using a relatively high number, e.g., $k = 20$.

[27] Reminder: This is given by the eigenvectors of the Laplacian.

CHAPTER 6

Clustering

In Chap. 2 we have shown that the dataset can be clustered into groups of similar samples (Sect. 2.2.3). We have seen in Sects. 2.1.2 and 2.2.3 that unsupervised image segmentation is one of the important applications of clustering algorithms. In particular, we have seen how k-means clustering can be used to segment brain MRI into white matter (WM), grey matter (GM), and cerebrospinal fluid, either using a single feature (T1-weighted pixel or voxel intensity in Fig. 2.5) or a pair of features (T1- and T2-weighted intensities in Fig. 2.3). More advanced segmentation algorithms that often contain a clustering algorithm within their pipeline can delineate multiple structures or objects in the image, as we have seen in the example of 86 brain structures in Chap. 3 and Fig. 3.1.

In this chapter we will revisit k-means clustering algorithm in Sect. 6.1 and introduce the Gaussian mixture model in Sect. 6.2. In Sect. 6.3 we will describe spectral clustering, which is particularly suitable for high-dimensional nonlinear feature spaces.

6.1. K-means clustering

Clustering is an unsupervised machine-learning task, where training labels are not given. We therefore need to split the samples into groups according to some predefined criterion. One of the simplest ideas is to minimize variances within the clusters as much as possible. Formally, **within-cluster variance** σ_W^2 can be expressed as a sum of cluster variances σ_k^2 weighted by the size $\frac{n_k}{N}$ of the cluster k

$$\sigma_W^2 = \sum_{k=1}^{K} \frac{n_k}{N} \sigma_k^2, \tag{6.1}$$

where n_k is the number of samples in the cluster k, K is the number of clusters and N is the number of all samples.

6.1.1 K-means algorithm

So, how can we minimize the within-cluster variance σ_W^2? First, let's write down the expression for variance of the cluster k:

$$\sigma_k^2 = \frac{1}{n_k} \sum_{i \in S_k} |\mathbf{x}_i - \boldsymbol{\mu}_k|^2$$

Machine Learning for Biomedical Applications
https://doi.org/10.1016/B978-0-12-822904-0.00011-X

Copyright © 2024 Elsevier Ltd.
All rights reserved.

Note that $\mathbf{x}_i$ is a multidimensional feature vector for sample i, $\boldsymbol{\mu}_k$ is the multidimensional mean for the cluster k, and $|.|$ denotes the Euclidean distance. If we expand the expression for σ_W^2 (Eq. (6.1)) by expressing directly the variance of each cluster, we will see that within-cluster variance is actually an average squared distance of each sample to its cluster center:

$$\sigma_W^2 = \frac{1}{N}\sum_{i=1}^{N} |\mathbf{x}_i - \boldsymbol{\mu}_{y_i}|^2,$$

where y_i is the label assigned to the sample i. This intuitively gives an iterative algorithm to minimize the within-cluster variance. We will iterate between assigning the cluster with the closest feature mean to each sample

$$y_i = \arg\min_k |\mathbf{x}_i - \boldsymbol{\mu}_k| \tag{6.2}$$

and recalculating the means of the clusters

$$\boldsymbol{\mu}_k = \frac{1}{n_k}\sum_{i \in S_k} \mathbf{x}_i. \tag{6.3}$$

We start the process with random initialization of the cluster means $\boldsymbol{\mu}_k$. Fig. 6.1 shows how this procedure finds the clusters of voxels belonging to WM, GM, and CSF in T1- and T2-weighted MRI.

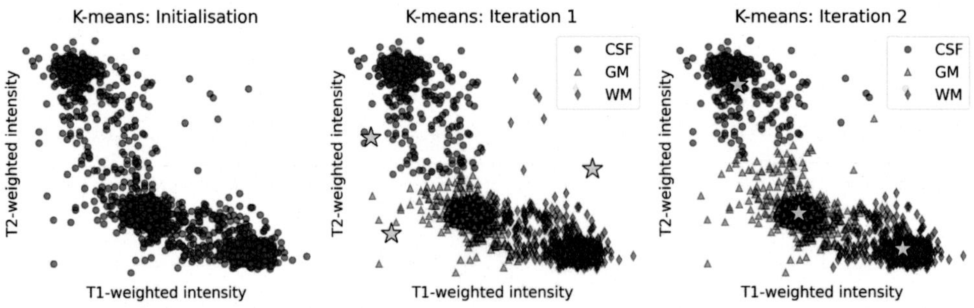

Figure 6.1 K-means clustering. Left: The data, T1- and T2-weighted intensities of a brain MRI image, are shown by blue circles. Middle: the initial random cluster means and resulting cluster memberships (Eq. (6.2)). Right: updated cluster means (Eq. (6.3)) and resulting cluster memberships (Eq. (6.2)). The cluster means are indicated by yellow stars.

6.1.2 K-means in sklearn

We have already shown in Sect. 2.2.3 how to fit the scikit-learn `kmeans` model to a one-dimensional segmentation problem. Here, we will expand it to 2D feature space. First, we will load the T1- and T2-wighted MRI slices

```
import matplotlib.pyplot as plt
T1 = plt.imread('T1.png')
T2 = plt.imread('T2.png')
```

Assuming that the brain tissues have been extracted and the nonbrain tissues padded by zeros, we identify all nonzero values

```
ind = T1>0
```

Next, we select only nonzero values and stack them into a $N \times 2$ feature matrix

```
import numpy as np
X = np.stack((T1[ind],T2[ind])).T
print(X.shape)
>>> (3180, 2)
```

The dataset can now be plotted as in Fig. 6.1. left:

```
plt.plot(X[:,0],X[:,1],'bo')
```

We then fit the three-cluster `kmeans` model to the feature matrix `X` and predict the labels `y`

```
from sklearn.cluster import KMeans
model=KMeans(n_clusters=3)
model.fit(X)
y = model.predict(X)
```

The clustering result, similar to the one shown in Fig. 6.1, right, can be plotted as

```
plt.plot(X[y==0,0],X[y==0,1],'bo')
plt.plot(X[y==1,0],X[y==1,1],'g^')
plt.plot(X[y==2,0],X[y==2,1],'rd')
```

If we wish to display the segmented brain image instead, we can use the code identical to the 1D case described in Sect. 2.2.3.

6.1.3 K-means in NumPy

To further understand K-means algorithm, we will now show how to implement it in `NumPy`. First, we define the distance function that calculates distances of the samples from the cluster centers:

```
def dist(k):
    return np.sum((X-mu[k])**2,axis=1)
```

Next, we randomly initialize the cluster means and iterate between calculating the labels `y` (Eq. (6.2)) and the cluster means `mu` (Eq. (6.3)):

```
mu = np.random.rand(3,2)
for i in range(10):
    y=np.argmin([dist(0),dist(1),dist(2)],axis=0)
    mu[0]=np.mean(X[y==0,:],axis=0)
    mu[1]=np.mean(X[y==1,:],axis=0)
    mu[2]=np.mean(X[y==2,:],axis=0)
```

Here, we used 10 iterations for simplicity, but we can instead stop the algorithm when the cluster means do not change any more. We can then plot the means of the three clusters as follows:

```
plt.plot(mu[:,0],mu[:,1],'y*')
```

6.1.4 Exercises

1. Describe the concept of a clustering algorithm and illustrate it with an example of the k-means.
2. Load the Wisconsin Breast Cancer dataset described in Sect. 2.1.2 using `sklearn.datasets.load_breast_cancer()`. The dataset contains 30 features. Perform k-means clustering to 2 clusters in the full 30-dimensional space. To display your result, reduce the dataset to 2 dimensions using PCA. Create a figure with two 2D plots, the first one displaying results of clustering and the second the original ground truth labels that you obtained from the dataset.
3. Implement 2-cluster K-means algorithm in `NumPy`. Segment image *cells.tiff* into 2 clusters. Explore how the initialization of the means affects the result.[1]

6.2. Gaussian mixture model

We will now introduce another clustering approach using the Gaussian Mixture Model (GMM). It models clusters as Gaussian distributions, and it is therefore suitable for elongated clusters and has potentially nonlinear cluster boundaries. Fig. 6.2, left, is an intensity histogram of a T1-weighted MRI image. The peaks correspond to the mean intensities of WM, GM, and CSF. Note that nonbrain tissues have been removed and padded with zeros.

The key assumption of the Gaussian mixture model is that the feature values for each cluster are drawn from a Gaussian distribution. This is shown in Fig. 6.2, middle. T1-weighted MRI intensities x for brain-tissue class k follow the Gaussian distribution

$$p(x|y=k) = G(x, \mu_k, \sigma_k^2) = \frac{1}{\sqrt{2\pi}\sigma} e^{\frac{(x-\mu_k)}{2\sigma_k^2}}, \tag{6.4}$$

[1] The skeleton code for exercises 2 and 3, as well as the image *cells.tiff* is available from github.com/MachineLearningBiomedicalApplications/notebooks.

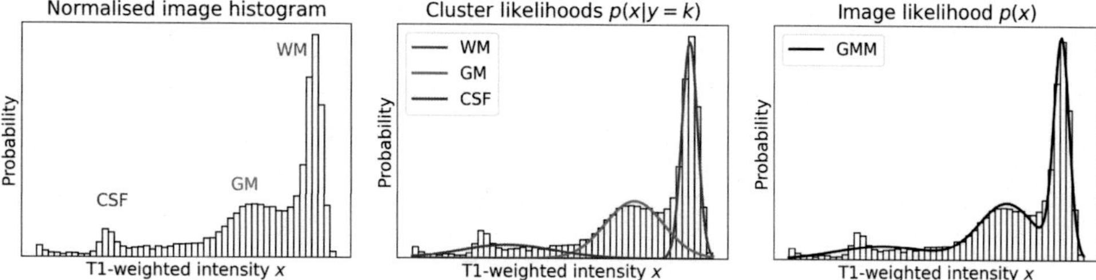

Figure 6.2 GMM clustering. Left: Normalized histogram of T1-weighted intensities of a brain MRI image. The peaks correspond to the three tissues. Middle: likelihood functions for each of the three clusters (red, green and blue lines) fitted to the image histogram. Right: overall likelihood for image intensities (black line), modeled as GMM, fitted to the image histogram.

with mean μ_k and variance σ_k^2. The intensity values of the whole MRI image are therefore drawn from a mixture of Gaussian distributions (the **Gaussian Mixture Model**, GMM)

$$p(x) = \sum_{k=1}^{K} c_k G(x, \mu_k, \sigma_k^2) \tag{6.5}$$

as visualized in Fig. 6.2, right. The mixing coefficients c_k represent the proportion of samples assigned to class k, and they sum to one $\sum_{k=1}^{K} c_k = 1$. The cluster dependent conditional probability $p(x|y=k)$ and the overall image probability $p(x)$ of observing an intensity value x are referred to as **likelihoods**.

6.2.1 GMM algorithm

The purpose of the GMM clustering algorithm is to fit the Gaussian Mixture Model (Eq. (6.5)) to the histogram of observed image intensities (Fig. 6.2, right). In other words, we want to maximize the likelihood $p(X|\phi)$ of observing a particular set of image intensities $X = \{x_1, ..., x_N\}$, given the parameters of GMM $\phi = \{\mu_k, \sigma_k, c_k\}_{k=1}^{K}$. Therefore, to fit a GMM to the image intensity distribution, we need to find the GMM parameters $\hat{\phi}$ that maximize the likelihood of observing intensities X

$$\hat{\phi} = \arg\max_{\phi} p(X|\phi).$$

If we assume that the voxel intensities x_i are independent of each other, we can multiply the individual likelihoods $p(X|\phi) = \Pi_{i=1}^{N} p(x_i|\phi)$, which will change to the sum if we take a logarithm of this expression. By using Eq. (6.5), we get a sum of log-likelihoods of the individual voxel intensities:

$$\hat{\phi} = \arg\max_{\phi} \sum_{i=1}^{N} \log p(x_i|\phi) = \arg\max_{\phi} \sum_{i=1}^{N} \log \sum_{k=1}^{K} c_k G(x, \mu_k, \sigma_k^2). \tag{6.6}$$

We can minimize the log-likelihood by setting the derivatives with respect to the Gaussian mixture parameters to zero, and this way we will arrive at a two-step iterative algorithm. In the first step we calculate the **posterior probabilities** $p_{ik} = p(y_i = k|x_i, \phi)$, which are in fact probabilistic segmentations for individual tissues (Fig. 6.3):

$$p_{ik} = \frac{c_k G(x, \mu_k, \sigma_k^2)}{\sum_{k=1}^{K} c_k G(x, \mu_k, \sigma_k^2)}.$$

In the second step we update GMM parameters ϕ

$$\mu_k = \frac{\sum_{i=1}^{N} p_{ik} x_i}{\sum_{i=1}^{N} p_{ik}}, \qquad \sigma_k^2 = \frac{\sum_{i=1}^{N} p_{ik}(x_i - \mu_k)^2}{\sum_{i=1}^{N} p_{ik}}, \qquad c_k = \frac{\sum_{i=1}^{N} p_{ik}}{N}.$$

The algorithm iterates between these two steps until the change in the log-likelihood (En. (6.6)) is below a specified threshold.

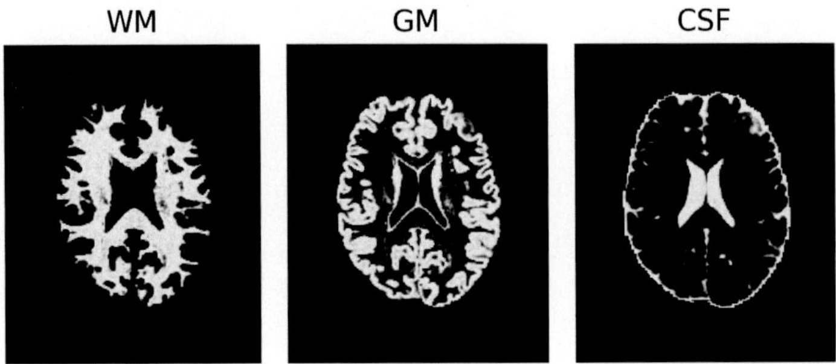

Figure 6.3 Probabilistic segmentation $p_{ik} = p(y_i = k|x_i, \phi)$ in GMM clustering of the three brain tissues k.

6.2.2 GMM in sklearn

Gaussian mixture model is implemented in scikit-learn using the object `GaussianMixture`. We will now explore this model for a MRI segmentation example of the three brain tissues. The 1D feature matrix `X` will therefore be

```
ind = T1>0
X=T1[ind].reshape(-1,1)
```

and we can display the image histogram (Fig. 6.2, left) as

```
plt.hist(X,bins=50,density=True,color='w',ec='k')
```

Note that we have 50 bins, and the histogram is normalized to have area of 1 by setting `density=True`. Next we fit the GMM with three clusters. The code also shows how to access the means μ_k, variances σ_k and mixing proportions c_k:

```
from sklearn.mixture import GaussianMixture

model=GaussianMixture(n_components=3)
model.fit(X)
m = model.means_
s = model.covariances_
w = model.weights_
```

We can then plot the weighted cluster likelihoods $c_k p(y = k|x)$, depicted in Fig, 6.2, middle, as follows:

```
from scipy.stats import norm
x = np.linspace(X.min(), X.max(),100)
for i in range(3):
    l = w[i]*norm.pdf(x, m[i], np.sqrt(s[i]))
    plt.plot(x,l.flatten())
```

The overall image likelihood $p(X|\phi)$, displayed in Fig. 6.2 right, is our fitted Gausian mixture model (Eq. (6.5)), and it can be evaluated using function `score_samples`

```
l = np.exp(model.score_samples(x.reshape(-1,1)))
plt.plot(x,l)
```

Finally, we will show how to plot the probabilistic segmentations p_{ik}, shown in Fig. 6.3, returned by the model using the function `predict_proba`:

```
p = model.predict_proba(X)
for k in range(3):
    pk = p[:,k]
    post2D = np.zeros_like(T1)
    post2D[ind]=pk
    plt.subplot(1,3,k+1)
    plt.imshow(post2D)
```

6.2.3 Exercises

1. What is a Gaussian Mixture Model? How can it be used to perform clustering?
2. For a training data point x_i, the likelihood that this point was generated from a mixture of Gaussian distributions with parameters $\phi = (\mu_k, \sigma_k, c_k)_{k=1,\dots,K}$ can be expressed as

$$p(x_i|\phi) = \sum_{k=1}^{K} c_k G(x_i, \mu_k, \sigma_k),$$

where $G(x, \mu, \sigma^2) = \frac{1}{\sqrt{2\pi}\sigma} e^{\frac{(x-\mu)^2}{2\sigma^2}}$. Explain the meaning of

a. $p(x_i|\phi)$;
b. $\phi = (\mu_k, \sigma_k, c_k)_{k=1,\dots,K}$;
c. $G(x_i, \mu_k, \sigma_k)$.

3. Load the Wisconsin Breast Cancer dataset described in Sect. 2.1.2 using `sklearn.datasets.load_breast_cancer()`. Perform GMM clustering to 2 clusters in the full 30-dimensional space. Reduce the dataset into 2 dimensions using PCA, and plot the clustering result in 2D.[2]
4. Load a 2D brain MRI image saved in a pickle format as *slice.p* and display the image. Perform GMM clustering of this dataset, and display the segmentation result. Use code from Sect. 6.2.2.
5. Explore the GMM model that you fitted to the 2D brain MRI image in the previous exercise. Use code from Sect. 6.2.2.
   a. Predict the posterior probabilities for each class and display, similarly to Fig. 6.3;
   b. Plot posterior probabilities as the function of image intensities;
   c. Plot likelihoods for each cluster as the function of image intensities, similarly to Fig. 6.2, middle:
   d. Plot likelihoods for whole image the function of image intensities, similarly to Fig. 6.2 right.

6.3. Spectral clustering

Spectral clustering [49] allows us to correctly separate highly nonlinear clusters, such as the moon dataset from scikit-learn library. In Fig. 6.4, left, we can see that the GMM fails to separate the moons. To solve this problem, we can perform nonlinear manifold embedding and perform clustering in the embedded space.

6.3.1 Spectral clustering algorithm

The spectral clustering algorithm consists of two steps:
1. Perform nonlinear manifold embedding using a Laplacian eigenmap (Sect. 5.7)
2. Perform K-means clustering in the embedded space

In Sect. 5.7 we have already described how we perform manifold embedding using a Laplacian eigenmap. We first create a symmetric k-nearest neighbor (kNN) graph, shown for the moon example in Fig. 6.4, middle. In this case we used $k = 5$ nearest neighbors, resulting in two disconnected graphs, which correctly define the two moon-shaped clusters. The edges in the graph correspond to values 1 in the affinity matrix $\mathbf{A}$, which means that the two samples are close to each other. A zero in the affinity matrix mean no edge, so the corresponding pair of samples are not the nearest neighbors. Next,

[2] The skeleton code for exercises 3–5, as well as the image *slice.p* is available from github.com/Machine-LearningBiomedicalApplications/notebooks.

we calculate the manifold embedding using eigen-decomposition of the graph Laplacian $\mathbf{L} = \mathbf{D} - \mathbf{A}$, where $\mathbf{D}$ is the diagonal *degree* matrix with number of nearest neighbours (or edges) for each node on diagonal, and zeros elsewhere. The new embedded space is defined by the eigenvectors corresponding to the predefined number of the smallest eigenvalues, except for the first one which is always zero.

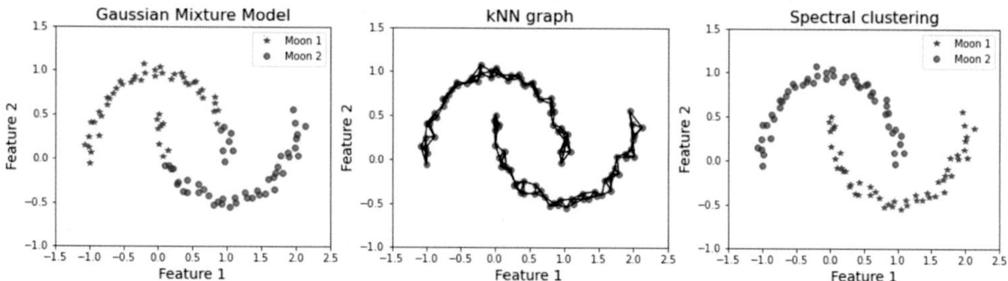

Figure 6.4 Clustering of the moons dataset. Left: GMM fails to correctly separate the moons. Middle: k-nearest neighbor graph used to build the nonlinear manifold embedding using a Laplacian eigenmap. Right: Spectral clustering correctly separates the moons.

The graph Laplacian has one zero eigenvalue for each connected component of the graph. For this reason the smallest eigenvalue is always zero because there is at least one connected component and the first eigenvector is therefore excluded from the embedding. In our moons example, we have two connected components in the graph. The graph Laplacian therefore has two zero eigenvalues, but one of them is excluded. The first embedded dimension therefore has a zero eigenvalue and contains two discrete values only that identify the two moon-shaped clusters—see Fig. 6.4, right.

In Sect. 5.7 we have used the unnormalized graph Laplacian $\mathbf{L} = \mathbf{D} - \mathbf{A}$. This is suitable when degrees of the nodes of the graph (e.g., the number of edges in each node in unweighted graphs) are similar between the nodes. This is obviously the case for kNN graph because each node has a degree of approximately k. When degrees of the nodes vary, it is better to normalize the graph Laplacian, for example, by multiplying it by the inverse of the matrix $\mathbf{D}$

$$\mathbf{L} = \mathbf{D}^{-1}(\mathbf{D} - \mathbf{A}).$$

6.3.2 Spectral clustering in scikit-learn

In scikit-learn the spectral clustering algorithm is implemented in the object `SpectralClustering`. This object implements manifold embedding using a Laplacian eigenmap with normalized Laplacian, followed by k-means clustering.

We will now demonstrate how we obtain the clustering result presented in Fig. 6.4, right. First, we generate the moon dataset

```
from sklearn.datasets import make_moons
X, l = make_moons(n_samples=100, noise=0.05)
```

Next, we create the spectral clustering object. We set the number of dimensions of the nonlinear embedding using parameter `n_components` and the number of clusters (one for each moon), using parameter `n_clusters`. To create the affinity matrix using kNN graph, we set the parameter `affinity` to `'nearest_neighbors'`, and choose the number of nearest neighbors using `n_neighbors`:

```
from sklearn.cluster import SpectralClustering
model=SpectralClustering(n_components=3, n_clusters=2,
                         affinity='nearest_neighbors',
                         n_neighbors=5)
```

Finally, we fit the model, predict the labels, and plot the clustered data:

```
y = model.fit_predict(X)
plt.plot(X[:,0][y==0], X[:,1][y==0], "r*")
plt.plot(X[:,0][y==1], X[:,1][y==1], "bo")
```

In scikit-learn we are also able to choose other types of affinity matrices to construct a Laplacian eigenmap. Symmetric k-NN graph is only one way to construct spectral embedding. The affinity matrix can be constructed from any measure of similarity between the pairs of samples. For example, Euclidean distances d between pairs of samples can be converted to similarities a using a Gaussian kernel

$$a = e^{\gamma d^2}.$$

This is implemented in scikit-learn by

```
model=SpectralClustering(affinity='rbf', gamma=0.0001)
```

Finally, it is also possible to precompute the affinity matrix `A` and input it during fitting instead of the feature matrix `X`:

```
model=SpectralClustering(affinity='precomputed')
y = model.fit_predict(A)
```

6.3.3 Clustering MRI images of term and preterm babies

One of the advantages of spectral clustering algorithm is that we do not need to have Euclidian distances between the samples to perform clustering. In this example we will show how we can cluster T2-weighted brain MRI images of babies. One example of such image is shown in Fig. 6.5, right.

While we cannot measure distance between two brain MRI images, we can calculate the similarity (or affinity) between them in the following way: First, we will align them

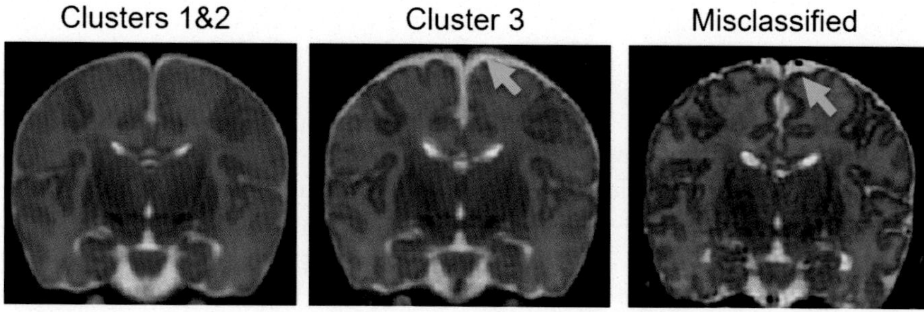

Figure 6.5 Brain MRI of term and preterm babies. Left: average MRI image for babies from cluster 1 and 2. Middle: average MRI image for babies from cluster 3. Right: MRI image of a term baby in cluster 3, which contains mostly preterm babies. Yellow arrows point to enlarged volumes of CSF, which is typical in preterm babies.

to a neonatal brain atlas (which may look similar to Fig. 6.5, left), so that all images are in the same orientation, and also of approximately similar global shape. Because MRI signals are not quantitative, we cannot calculate the Euclidian distance, but we can instead calculate normalized cross-correlation (NCC) to measure the similarity between two images. In this example the NCC will always be positive, with a maximum value 1, because the images are aligned and all have similar T2-weighted contrast. We can therefore input NCC between each pair of images directly to the affinity matrix **A**. This means that we will have a fully connected weighted graph with a single connected component.

We will now apply clustering to brain MRI images of 68 term and preterm neonates. Since the affinity matrix **A** has been precomputed and saved to a file, we can therefore load it using `pandas` package as shown here:

```
import pandas as pd
df = pd.read_csv('babies.csv', header=None)
A = df.to_numpy()
print(A.shape)
>>> (68, 68)
```

Note that the affinity matrix is of size $n \times n$, where n is the number of samples. Each element of the matrix gives NCC between a pair of brain MRI images.

We will perform spectral clustering using a 3D Laplacian eigenmap embedding and k-means clustering with three clusters. It is often not obvious how the parameters of spectral clusterning should be chosen, we therefore selected this setting because it provided stable results with different randomly assigned initial cluster centers in a k-means algorithm (Sect. 6.1). We implement the clustering in scikit-learn using object `SpectralClustering` with `'precomputed'` affinity matrix `A`:

```
from sklearn.cluster import SpectralClustering
```

```
model=SpectralClustering(n_components=3,n_clusters=3,
                        affinity='precomputed')
y = model.fit_predict(A)
```

Now, we would like to visualize our clustering result. However, we do not have a low-dimensional space that we could plot. We will therefore use object `SpectralEmbedding` that will return the coordinates of 3D manifold into which we embedded our brain MRI images using a Laplacian eigenmap. Then, we are able to plot our clusters in the first two dimensions shown in Fig. 6.6, left:

```
from sklearn.manifold import SpectralEmbedding
embedding=SpectralEmbedding(n_components=3,
                           affinity='precomputed')
X = embedding.fit_transform(A)
plt.plot(X[:, 0][y==0], X[:, 1][y==0], "r*")
plt.plot(X[:, 0][y==1], X[:, 1][y==1], "bo")
plt.plot(X[:, 0][y==2], X[:, 1][y==2], "g^")
```

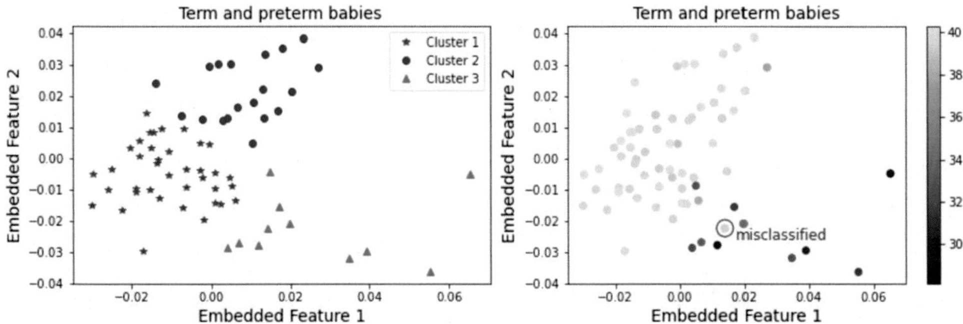

Figure 6.6 Brain MRI of babies in embedded space obtained using the Laplacian eigenmap, first two dimensions. Left: Three clusters obtained by spectral clustering. Right: Age at birth for each baby is color-coded from blue (preterm) to yellow (term). Note that clusters 1 and 2 correspond to term babies and cluster 3 to preterm babies. Red circle highlights a term baby misclassified in cluster 3.

Finally, we will investigate whether the clusters of images we found have some meaningful interpretation. In Fig. 6.6, right, we color-coded the spectral embedding by gestational age at birth (GAB). We can see that cluster 3 corresponds to preterm babies (GAB$<$37), while clusters 1 and 2 correspond to term babies (GAB$\geq$37).

To visualize what kind of features the spectral clustering discovered, we can create an average of all images in different clusters. In Fig. 6.5 we see that images in clusters 1 and 2 (Fig. 6.5, left) have less CSF than images in cluster 3 (Fig. 6.5, middle). This is a common feature resulting from preterm birth. On closer inspection we can see that there is a term baby sample in cluster 3, highlighted by the red circle in Fig. 6.6, right.

Even though this baby was not born preterm, the corresponding image (Fig. 6.5, right) shows that this baby has more CSF, similar to preterm babies, which may be the reason why it was assigned to the preterm cluster.

6.3.4 Exercises

1. The file *structures_first_second_scan.csv* contains volumes of 86 brain structures calculated from 36 MRI scans of preterm babies. Some of these scans were acquired shortly after birth in the preterm period (GA<37) and others at term equivalent age (GA≥37). Perform spectral clustering of the volumes into two clusters to identify which scans were acquired at preterm period and which at term-equivalent age. Display the clustering result.[3]
2. The file *babies.csv* contains the affinity matrix of pairwise similarities calculated using NCC, as described in Sect. 6.3.3. Perform 3D spectral clustering of the babies into three clusters and display it similarly to Fig. 6.6, left. Use code from Sect. 6.3.3. Display the first two coordinates of the embedded space color coded by gestational age at birth (GAB), similarly to Fig. 6.6, right. You can find the GAB in the file *ages.csv*.

[3] The skeleton code and datasets for exercises 1 and 2 are available from github.com/MachineLearning-BiomedicalApplications/notebooks.

CHAPTER 7

Decision trees and ensemble learning

Ensemble learning is a branch of machine learning that seeks to improve model accuracy and/or generalization by combining predictions from several learners. The idea is to train multiple complementary models, each returning slightly different solutions, with the view that over enough trials the consensus solution will improve the prediction of edge cases. Over the course of the chapter, a variety of different approaches to ensemble learning will be studied, including *homogeneous ensembles*: bagging, random forests and boosting, which merge predictions from models trained with the same class of method; and stacked generalization (or *heterogeneous ensembles*) which merge predictions estimated by a range of methods. Before doing so, we must learn about the most popular class of base models used by homogeneous ensembles: the *decision tree*. These are simple and intuitive machine learning models, capable of adapting to a range of regression or classification problems.

7.1. Decision trees

The basic idea behind decision trees is to stack a series of *weak* learning models one on top of another with the goal of learning a single strong generalizable, model (Fig. 7.1). Specifically, each node in the tree asks a simple question of the data. If the response for a given example is true, its passes down one branch of the tree (e.g., the right side

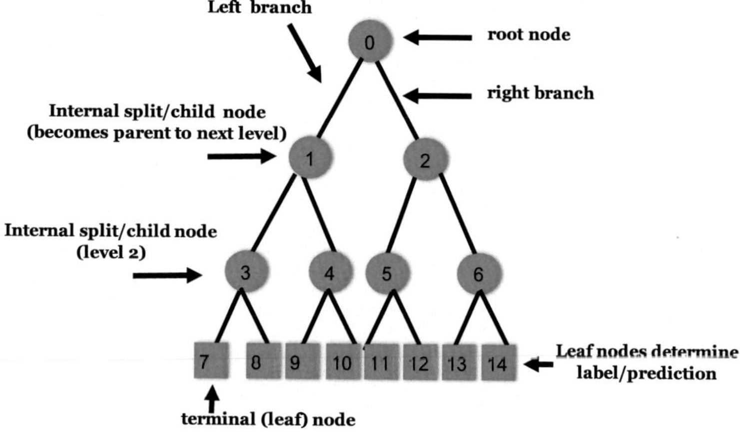

Figure 7.1 Decision tree.

Machine Learning for Biomedical Applications
https://doi.org/10.1016/B978-0-12-822904-0.00012-1

Copyright © 2024 Elsevier Ltd.
All rights reserved.

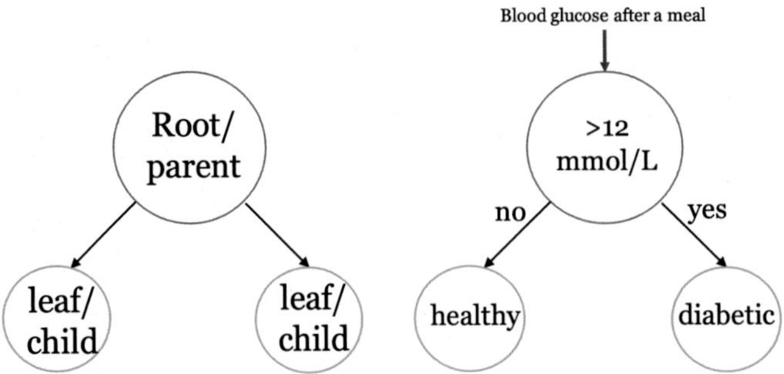

Figure 7.2 Example decision stump.

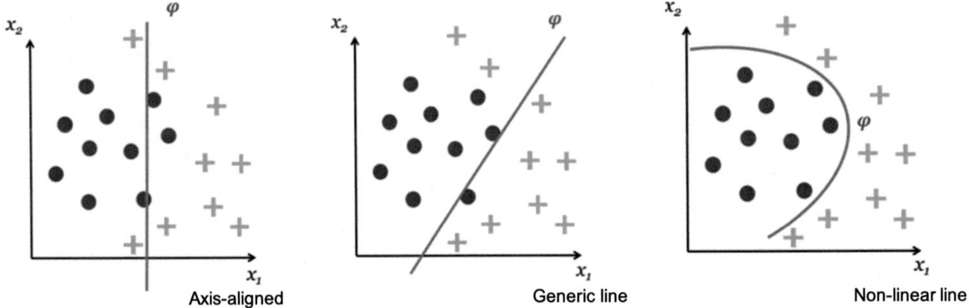

Figure 7.3 Examples of simple weak learning rules for classification.

of Fig. 7.2); if it is false, it passes down the other. Each weak learner in a tree is known as *a decision stump.*

7.1.1 Decision stumps

Learning rules for trees may take many forms including linear (Fig. 7.3 center) and non-linear fits (Fig. 7.3 right) [10]; however, most often, classification trees nodes implement axis-aligned learning rules, which make predictions by thresholding on a single feature (Fig. 7.3 left). This is the approach taken in scikit-learn.

A biomedical example of such a decision stump is shown for classification for diabetes in Fig. 7.2. Here, a decision is made by optimizing a threshold on blood glucose levels. All examples with blood glucose less than 12 mmol/L are considered healthy and pass down the left branch. All remaining examples are labeled as diabetic and pass down the right. It is expected that, for most problems, such a simple learning rule will result in many misclassified examples. Therefore, the role of subsequent decision stumps in the tree is to further refine the prediction.

7.1.2 Stacking stumps into trees

Fig. 7.4 presents a simple cartoon of a nonlinearly separable multiclass classification problem. Here, we have five classes: pink asterisks, yellow question marks, red plus signs, blue crosses and dark green open circles. The objective is to separate these based on two features: x_1 and x_2. A decision tree may achieve this by stacking axis-aligned decision stumps one after another. In this example, the root node splits first on x_1 (orange dotted line). This broadly separates the blue crosses and dark green open circles, from red plus signs, pink asterisks and yellow question marks. In the second level (green dotted line), the second stump thresholds on x_2, splitting pink asterisks from yellow crosses. In the final level (black dotted line), a second threshold on x_1 splits the red plus signs from these partitions. At this stage, each leaf in the tree is assigned a label, based on the majority class of all training examples that reach that leaf. In this way, leaf nodes may determine the prediction for each new example that reach that leaf at test time.

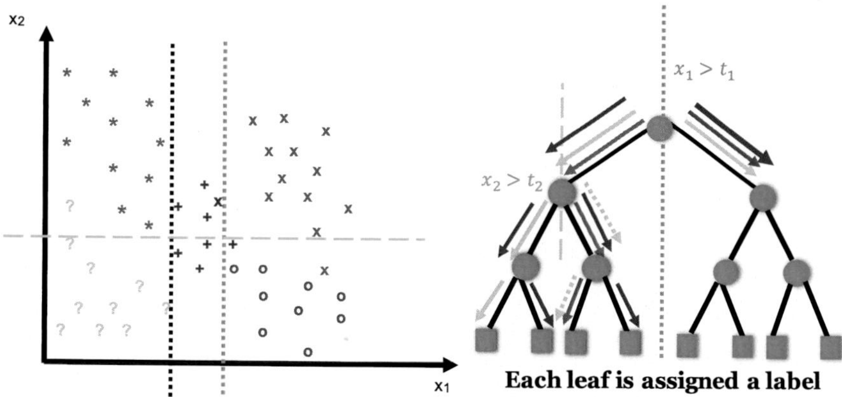

Figure 7.4 Decision tree classifier. Here, each subsequent decision stump seeks to further separate the examples into separate classes.

Regression trees are implemented very similarly (Fig. 7.5[1]). However, rather than partitioning examples into classes, each stump assigns a constant-valued prediction of the dependent variable (y-axis) to some range of values of the independent variable (x-axis). For example, given the oscillating function in Fig. 7.5, the first node in the decision tree would partition the graph at $X = 1.24$ (blue line) since it is clear that the mean value of the dependent variable is higher for the first part of the range ($y = 1.4$) than the second half ($y = -0.4$ (gold lines)). Looking at the right branch, the next node then splits at ($x = 4.03$ (teal line)), where the first part of the range is lower with a mean ($y = -0.95$) and the second part is higher with ($y = 0.27$). For the third split (on the left branch), the stump thresholds at $X = 3.36$ (red line) with $y = 0.57$ for the left leaf

[1] Adapted from https://scikit-learn.org/stable/auto_examples/ensemble/plot_adaboost_regression.html.

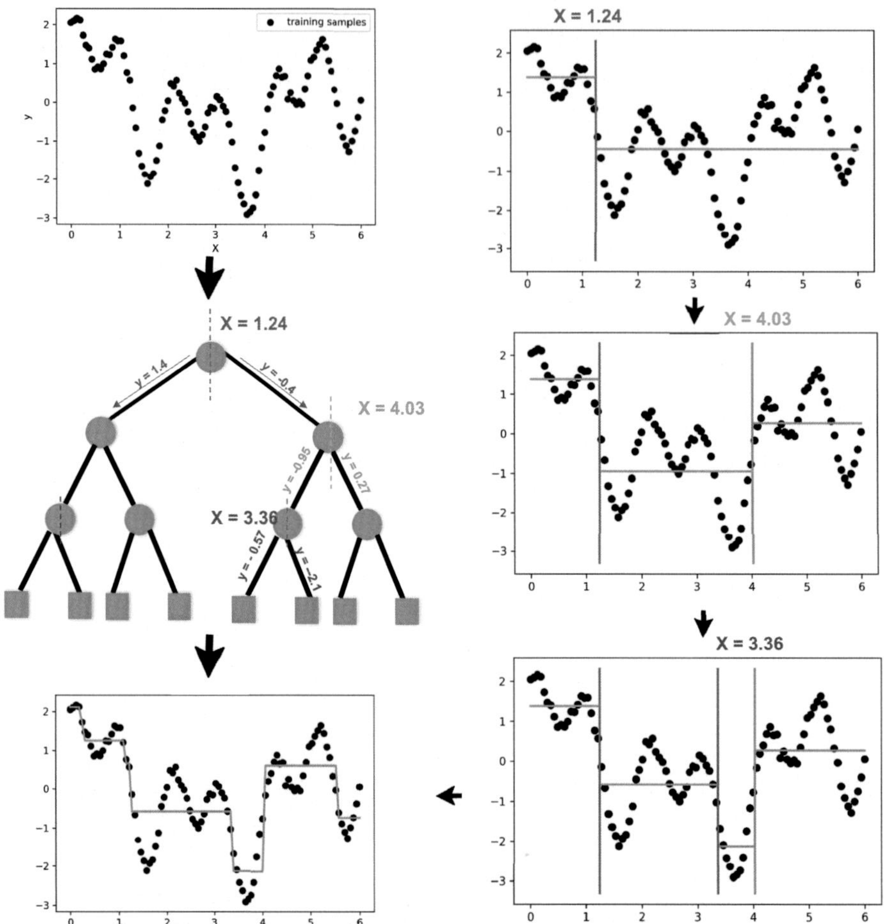

Figure 7.5 Decision tree regression. Left) decision trees fit piecewise constant approximations to nonlinear functions; Right) shows how the fit evolves over three levels of the decision tree (shown on the left); here, the first split is at $X = 1.24$ (fitting $y = 1.4$ to the left branch and $y = 0.4$ to the right branch); the second split is at $X = 4.03$ and the third at $X = 3.36$. The plot on the bottom left shows the data points in black and the final decision tree fit in gold.

and $y = 2.1$ for the right leaf. By continuing in this way, increasing tree depth would allow for better and better fits to the curve for finer and finer ranges of x. Therefore, it's important to be careful since, the deeper the tree, the more likely it is to fit to spurious noise in the data. This is true of both regression and classification models.

7.1.3 Decision tree learning rules

So, decision trees partition up the feature space into distinct sections and assign each section a different prediction. But, how does the model decide which feature, and

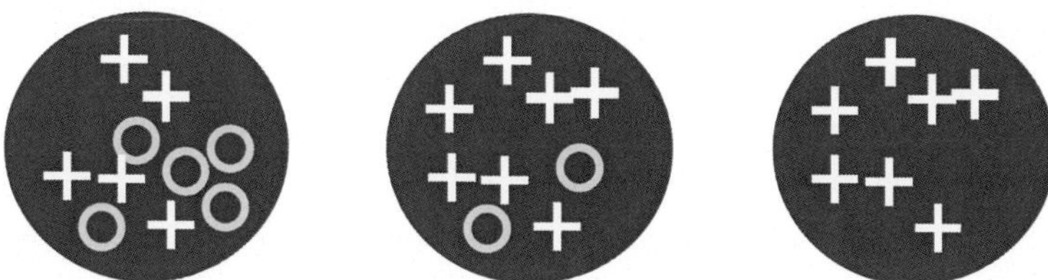

Figure 7.6 Entropy for a two-class problem. From left to right: maximum entropy, intermediate entropy and minimum entropy.

which threshold, to make at each stage?

Like all machine learning models, decision tree splits are parameterized via optimizing a cost function, where the appropriate choice of cost varies for classification and regression. Typical regression losses include costs that we have seen before, specifically mean square error (MSE) and mean absolute error (MAE), where, since trees fit a constant y for each branch, this equates to the value that is, on average, closest to the ground-truth values of the data points within that range.

Decision tree classifiers focus more on measures of node purity than on accuracy scores or counts of false positives/negatives. Specific examples include: *information gain*, which represents the decrease in entropy obtained after a dataset is split on an attribute; and 2) *gini impurity*, which reflects how mixed the classes are following the split. Let's look at these in more detail, starting with a definition of entropy.

Entropy: is an estimate of the amount of disorder in a system. It is calculated for decision tree classifiers, by considering the distribution of labels over all classes, at each node j, as

$$H(S_j) = -\sum_{y_k \in Y} p(y_k) \log_2 p(y_k). \tag{7.1}$$

Here, Y are the class labels (e.g., $\{0, 1\}$ for a binary problem), and $p(y_k)$ is the proportion of examples that have class k, for the node under consideration (j).

Calculating entropy for decision tree nodes acts as a proxy for how cleanly separated data examples are for that split. For example, Fig. 7.6 demonstrates three class label partitions, for a two-class classification problem. In the left case, the group contains 5 examples of each class, with equal proportions $p(y_1) = p(y_2) = 5/10 = 0.5$; this returns maximum entropy $H = -(0.5 \log_2 0.5 + 0.5 \log_2 0.5) = 1$. The second group contains 2 circles and 7 plus signs, with proportions $p(y_1) = 2/9$ and $p(y_2) = 7/9$, with entropy $H = -(2/9 \log_2 2/9 + 7/9 \log_2 7/9) = 0.7642$. The third group *only* has plus signs making its entropy equal to zero ($H = -(1 \log_2 1 + 0) = 0$); this is the minimal possible entropy, meaning that the proposed split is pure. The objective of decision tree classifiers, therefore, is to return leaf nodes with zero entropy.

Information gain for a classification tree node is a measure of the change in entropy of the system when data is split from the parent node into the two child nodes. It is estimated as the relative difference between the entropy of the parent $H(S_j)$ and a weighted sum of the entropies of the children $(H(S_j^i))$:

$$I(S_j) = H(S_j) - \sum_{i \in L,R} \frac{|S_j^i|}{|S_j|} H(S_j^i). \tag{7.2}$$

Here, $|S_j|$ represents the number of samples reaching the parent node, and $|S_j^i|$ represents the number of samples in each child node. As the objective is to reduce entropy for each subsequent level of the tree, *information gain must be maximized.*

Gini impurity, on the other hand, takes a simpler approach, estimating instead the probability of misclassifying an example, based solely on the class probabilities $p(y_k)$. More specifically, it is computed by multiplying the probability of labeling class $p(y_k)$, with the probability $\sum_{k \neq i} p(y_i) = 1 - p(y_k)$ of labeling a different class, summed over all classes. This can be reduced to

$$\begin{aligned} Gini_i &= \sum_k^K p(y_k)(1 - p(y_k)) \\ &= \sum_k^K (p(y_k) - p(y_k)^2) \\ &= \sum_k^K p(y_k) - \sum_k^K p(y_k)^2 \\ &= 1 - \sum_{y_k \in Y} p(y_k)^2. \end{aligned} \tag{7.3}$$

As this represents the impurity of a single node, the full cost of any proposed split must be estimated by combining estimates of impurity, for the left and right splits, as the weighted sum

$$I(S_j, \theta_j) = \sum_{i \in L,R} \frac{|S_j^i|}{|S_j|} Gini_i. \tag{7.4}$$

For Gini, a perfect separation results in a score of 0, whereas the worst case split (that results in 50/50 classes in each group) results in a score of 0.5 (for a 2-class problem). Therefore, in contrast to information gain, *Gini impurity must be minimized.* Note that, for data sets containing many categorical variables, information gain is biased in favor of attributes with more categories; thus, the Gini index is the criterion favored by scikit-learn.

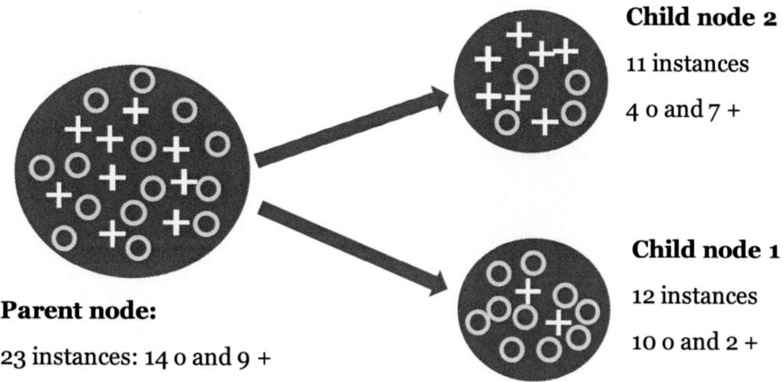

Figure 7.7 Decision stump classifier toy example.

Example

Let's work through the simple example shown in Fig. 7.7. Here, a parent node with 14 circles and 9 plus signs (23 instances in total) is split into two child nodes, with the first containing 10 circles and 2 plus signs, and the second containing 4 circles and 7 plus signs.

Before calculating information gain, we need to calculate the entropy of the parent and children using Eq. (7.1). This returns the entropy for the parent as

$$H(S_j) = -\left(\frac{14}{23}\log_2\frac{14}{23} + \frac{9}{23}\log_2\frac{9}{23}\right) = 0.966, \tag{7.5}$$

for child 1 as

$$H(S_j^1) = -\left(\frac{10}{12}\log_2\frac{10}{12} + \frac{2}{12}\log_2\frac{2}{12}\right) = 0.650, \tag{7.6}$$

and for child 2 as

$$H(S_j^2) = -\left(\frac{4}{11}\log_2\frac{4}{11} + \frac{7}{11}\log_2\frac{7}{11}\right) = 0.946. \tag{7.7}$$

Applying Eq. (7.2), and inserting these values, returns an information gain of

$$I_{IG}(S_j) = 0.966 - \left(\frac{12}{23}\times 0.650 + \frac{11}{23}\times 0.946\right) = 0.174. \tag{7.8}$$

Here, $|S_j| = 23$, $|S_j^1| = 12$ and $|S_j^2| = 11$. Doing the same for Gini impurity instead implements

$$I_{gini}(S_j) = \frac{12}{23}\times Gini_1 + \frac{11}{23}\times Gini_2, \tag{7.9}$$

where

$$Gini_1 = 1 - (10/12 \times 10/12 + 2/12 \times 2/12) = 0.278 \tag{7.10}$$

$$Gini_2 = 1 - (4/11 \times 4/11 + 7/11 \times 7/11) = 0.463. \tag{7.11}$$

Therefore

$$I_{gini}(S_j) = \frac{12}{23} \times 0.278 + \frac{11}{23} \times 0.463 = 0.366. \tag{7.12}$$

7.1.4 Training and testing decision trees

So, the example functions provide a means to assess what split results in the optimal cost for a given feature; but, how do we decide which feature to choose at each node in a tree?

The basic idea behind decision tree optimization (see Algorithm 7.1) is, at each tree node, to search through all features and all possible thresholds on features (τ) to find the best possible cost, where the range of thresholds would be defined simply by all unique values of the data for that feature: $\{x_1, x_2, ...x_k\}$. These thresholds, features and splits are stored, and, then, this procedure is repeated for each subsequent node/stump until either the maximum tree depth (D_{max}) is reached or a threshold on the minimum number of examples per leaf (N_{min}) is exceeded.

Algorithm 7.1 Fitting a classification decision tree using the Gini index.

```
for j in J do                                              ▷ for each node i in the tree
    I_opt = 1
    for k in K do                                          ▷ iterate over all features
        for τ in x_k do                                    ▷ and all possible thresholds
            I(S_j, k) = Σ_{i∈L,R} (|S_j^i| / |S_j|) Gini_i
            if I(S_j, k) < I_opt then
                I_opt ← I(S_j, k)                          ▷ store the best loss
                k^j_opt ← k
                τ^j_opt ← τ
                S^j_opt ← S_j          ▷ and feature, threshold and split with best loss
            end if
        end for
    end for
    if |S_j^i| < N_min ∨ d < D_max then break              ▷ termination criterion
    end if
end for
```

Once the tree is trained, a label is assigned to each leaf node, based on the labels of the training examples that reach that leaf. For classification, this equates to the class of the most common training label within that leaf; for regression, the leaf values is derived from some function of the data (such as the mean). Testing is then performed by passing unseen examples through the tree, using the stored thresholds and features at each node to decide which branches the test examples pass down. The final prediction, for each test example, is then obtained by assigning the values stored at each leaf.

7.1.5 Decision trees with scikit-learn

To implement decision trees in scikit-learn, you may implement either a `DecisionTreeClassifier` or `DecisionTreeRegressor`. As with all scikit-learn supervised learning models, these take a data matrix `X`, of shape N (examples) $\times$ M (features), and a label matrix `y`, of length N:

```
from sklearn.tree import DecisionTreeClassifier
classifier = DecisionTreeClassifier()
classifier.fit(X,y) # here y stores classes

from sklearn.tree import DecisionTreeRegressor
regressor = DecisionTreeClassifier()
regressor.fit(X,y) # here y stores continuous variables
```

In addition to the default constructors (as just shown), scikit-learn offers a range of tunable parameters including: the `criterion` argument, which tunes the choice of learning rule; and a selection of parameters designed to control for overfitting including: `max_depth`, which limits total tree depth; `min_samples_split` and `min_samples_leaf`, which control for the minimum number of training examples allowed for internal nodes and leaf nodes, respectively; `max_features`, which limits the choice of features available to each decision stump to a subset of the total (where this is important for training decision forests, Sect. 7.2.5). Finally, `ccp_alpha` supports pruning away of terminal nodes that do more to fit to noise than improve the quality of the prediction.

7.2. Ensemble learning

Decision trees make for highly intuitive learning models; however, they are prone to overfitting since, the deeper the tree, the more nonlinear the model and the greater chance of fitting to noise. While this may partly be addressed through judicious choice of hyperparameters, further gains may be achieved by ensembling (combining) predictions across a large number of trees. As we will see in this section, ensembles can improve the generalization of predictions by averaging away isolated errors.

7.2.1 Motivation

Take this toy example, where we have a test set for which the ground truth is class "1" for all ten examples:

$$y = \{1, 1, 1, 1, 1, 1, 1, 1, 1, 1\} \tag{7.13}$$

Let's assume that we train three classifiers A, B and C, and these return different predictions, each with 30% error

$$\hat{y}_A = \{1, 1, 0, 1, 1, 1, 1, 1, 0, 0\} \tag{7.14}$$
$$\hat{y}_B = \{0, 1, 1, 1, 1, 0, 1, 1, 0, 1\} \tag{7.15}$$
$$\hat{y}_C = \{1, 1, 1, 0, 0, 1, 1, 0, 1, 1\}. \tag{7.16}$$

Each model makes mistakes on different examples. This means that, if we fuse the predictions across all three models through majority voting (assigning each example the label predicted most commonly across all constituent models), then the resulting prediction is 90% accurate

$$\hat{y}_{ensemble} = \{1, 1, 1, 1, 1, 1, 1, 1, 0, 1\}. \tag{7.17}$$

By contrast, if we instead had the following three highly correlated prediction models:

$$\hat{y}_D = \{1, 1, 0, 1, 1, 1, 1, 1, 0, 0\} \tag{7.18}$$
$$\hat{y}_E = \{1, 1, 1, 1, 1, 1, 1, 1, 0, 0\} \tag{7.19}$$
$$\hat{y}_F = \{1, 1, 0, 1, 0, 1, 1, 0, 0, 0\}, \tag{7.20}$$

then the potential gains through ensembling will be much less (or zero), i.e.,

$$\hat{y}_{corr_ensemble} = \{1, 1, 0, 1, 1, 1, 1, 1, 0, 0\}. \tag{7.21}$$

The logic behind ensembles is therefore that, when decisions of *uncorrelated* prediction models are fused, the resulting prediction will have higher accuracy than any individual model.

7.2.2 Classes of ensemble learning

Ensemble methods come in several forms that can be broadly classed as *homogeneous* or *heterogeneous*, with the subtypes *parallel* and *sequential* models.

Homogeneous models combine predictions from models trained on the same class of a machine learning method. For scikit-learn, the default base learning model is the decision tree, however, in principle, any classifier or regression model may be used. By contrast, heterogeneous models combine predictions trained from a variety of machine learning models. Colloquially, these methods are more often known as stacking models.

Parallel and sequential models reference the way in which the component models are trained and combined. *Parallel learners*, like the majority voting example already described, train large numbers of base learners independently and then combine them to smooth away the impact of isolated errors. The objective is to learn models that are as uncorrelated as possible. Averaging uncorrelated errors away (as seen for the majority voting example above) reduces model variance, improving accuracy and generalization. However, it's important to be conscious of the fact that, if predictions are stable, then parallel ensembling may even lead to a degradation of the result. In addition to voting, parallel methods include *bagging* and *random forests*.

Sequential models, on the other hand, train weak learners one after another, up-weighting the importance of wrongly predicted examples in each subsequent round. Combining in this way enables methods to optimize the complementarity of base learners, to collectively reduce the bias of the model and to improve the performance on edge cases. The family of methods known as *boosting* are examples of sequential learners.

7.2.3 Bagging

Bagging (short for **b**ootstrap **agg**regat**ing** [4]) is an example of a parallel homogeneous ensemble that seeks to reduce model variance by training a large number of decision trees, on other samples than those in the original data set. It seeks to leverage the statistical property that, for independent random variables, the sampling distribution of the mean is $\frac{1}{T}$ times the variance, where T is the number of trained models, i.e.,

$$var(\bar{Y}) = \frac{var(Y)}{T}. \tag{7.22}$$

In other words, the act of averaging will naturally reduce the variance of the model. However, if we have only one training data set, where do all these independent samples come from?

It turns out that we can generate any number of new datasets through a process known as *bootstrapping*. Here, the idea is that, given some data set $\mathbf{X}$ with N examples, we can create T new data sets ($\mathbf{X_b}^i$, $i = \{0, 1, 2...T\}$) by sampling with replacement. In this way, each example from $\mathbf{X}$ might be sampled, once, several times or not at all, with the result that, even though the total number of examples within each bootstrapped sample remains N, the composition of each $\mathbf{X_b}^i$ will be different (see the example in Sect. 7.2.4). Importantly, it can be shown that, for large-enough sample sizes, bootstrap sampling will closely approximate any sampling distribution estimated from the full population [26].

Accordingly, the idea of bagging is to take repeated bootstrapped samples from the training data and use each these to train a different predictive model (typically, a decision tree). Once trained, predictions for each test example are returned from all models in the ensemble and aggregated using either majority voting (for classification) or averaging (for regression).

7.2.4 Exercise: bootstrap sampling

To visualize what a boostrapped data set looks like, open your IDE, `import numpy as np`, and copy and paste the following function:

```
def bootstrap_sample(dataset):
    ''' Sample from the dataset with
    replacement:
        input:
            dataset: shape (N,M)
        output:
            samples: shape (N,M)
    '''
    n_sample = dataset.shape[0]
    indices=np.random.choice(n_sample, n_sample,
                                replace=True)

    return dataset[indices]
```

Then, create a random data set with 10 rows (examples) and 3 features (columns). Pass the data set through the pasted function a few times and observe how the output changes. You will see that the output is fixed to the same shape as the input, which is the default setup for bagging and forests.[2]

7.2.5 Random forests

While bagging seeks to optimize uncorrelated models solely by training on different bootstrapped samples from the data, random forests [5] further increase randomization by presenting each node of the tree with a random subset of the total available features. In this way, each decision stump is trained—maybe without seeing the optimal feature for that level—forcing each tree to find several different solutions to each classification problem, increasing randomization, adding redundancy and further reducing correlations in the predictions across all trees. The overall effect is to further reduce model variance and the chance of overfitting. Unlike bagging, and boosting (see Sect. 7.2.8), random forests always build ensembles of trees.

[2] Skeleton code and the solution is available from github.com/MachineLearningBiomedicalApplications/notebooks.

7.2.6 Training bagging and forests with scikit-learn

To implement bagging and forests with scikit-learn, import the models from the `ensemble` base class, e.g., for classification,

```
from sklearn.ensemble import BaggingClassifier
from sklearn.ensemble import RandomForestClassifier

n_trees=50

# create a bagged ensemble of 50 decision trees
clf=BaggingClassifier(DecisionTreeClassifier(),
                      n_estimators=n_trees)

# create a random forest of 50 trees
# with 30% of the total number of features
clf=RandomForestClassifier(n_estimators=n_trees,
            max_features=0.3)
```

You should see that the first argument of the bagging classifier is the choice of base model, whereas, for forests there is no choice. In both cases, we can control the size of the ensemble using `n_estimators`.

The arguments of the random forests class parallel those of the decision tree class, with `max_features` specifically determines the degree of undersampling of the features at each node. In this example, the use of a float (`0.3`) sets the number of randomly selected features to 30% of the total available. For full options, on all arguments, see the scikit-learn documentation.

7.2.7 Out-of-bag error

One advantage of training bagged ensembles is that it is possible to return an estimate of the likely generalization by testing each tree on the examples that were left out during bootstrap sampling. These are known as *out-of-bag (oob)* samples. For large enough data sets, this can be shown to be approximately 37%.

Once all models are trained, out-of-bag predictions for each training example may be combined, using averaging or majority voting; then, a final score may be calculated from the accuracy (classification) or error (regression) across all examples. To track oob error using scikit-learn, set `oob_score=True`, when instantiating your model, e.g.,

```
# track oob error during training
clf=BaggingClassifier(DecisionTreeClassifier(),
    n_estimators=n_trees, oob_score=True)
```

The oob performance can then be returned after training using the `oob_score_` attribute:

```
# train model
clf.fit(X,y)
# report oob score
print("the oob score is {}".format(clf.oob_score_))
```

7.2.8 Boosting

Boosting contrasts with bagging and forests in that it trains weak learners serially, one after another. After each model is fit, misclassified examples are identified and given higher importance for subsequent rounds.

To see how this works, see the toy example in Fig. 7.8. In this case, the various classes of example are indicated by pluses or minuses. As we can see from Fig. 7.8a, perfect separation would require a nonlinear decision boundary.

Figs. 7.8b–f simulate the process of boosting. In Fig. 7.8b an initial axis-aligned decision stump is fit shown by the red box. This correctly classifies two red crosses and all of the minus class. However, three red crosses are misclassified as belonging to the blue class. Fig. 7.8c shows how boosting upgrades the misclassified examples in the second round, ensuring that these are correctly classified by the second classifier (shown in Fig. 7.8d); however, now three blue cross are misclassified and so boosted for the third round. The third and final classifier in the ensemble is shown in Fig. 7.8e. This trains an axis-aligned classifier on the vertical axis, correctly classifying the upweighted cross and minus class. We can see that, when all three classifiers in the ensemble are combined (with weightings as in Fig. 7.8f) the final result achieves correct classification for all examples.

In this way boosting can learn precise, nonlinear prediction models that significantly improve the accuracy of the ensemble relative to individual base learners. Boosting can be shown to improve model bias *and* variance. The reason for this is that it can be shown that, even when training performance has saturated, boosting continues to refine predictions at the margins by further and further optimizing the losses of each base learner [42]. In other words, it seeks to make the margins between classes bigger and bigger, similarly to the behavior of support vector machines.

7.2.9 Adaboost

There are many variants of boosting that differ primarily in the way they combine and weight the components during training. Here, we will focus on one of the earliest and best known, Adaboost [15], where we will assume each weak learner is an axis-aligned decision stump, similar to that shown in Fig. 7.8.

The Adaboost classifier (Algorithm 7.2) starts by giving all examples in the training set equal weights ($w_i^t = \frac{1}{l}n$). Then, for each tree or stump, the algorithm first estimates $\mathbf{p}^t$ (which represents normalized weights, or probabilities, for each example). These

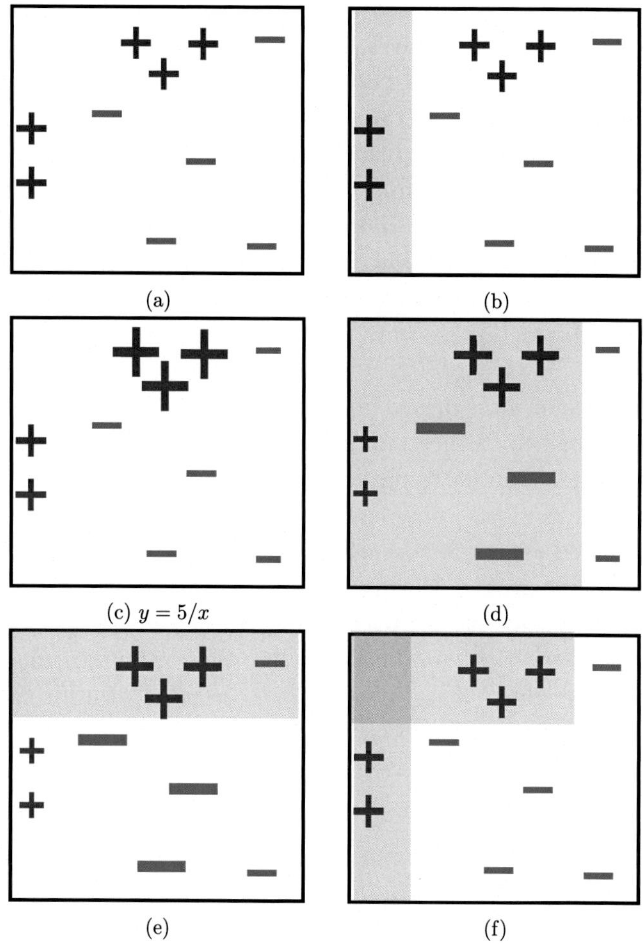

Figure 7.8 Boosting toy example.

Algorithm 7.2 Adaboost classifier.

Given $\mathbf{x}_i \in \mathbf{X}$ and $y_i \in \{0, 1\}$

Assign all n examples equal weight $w_i^t = 1/n$

for t in E **do** ▷ for each tree t in the ensemble

  $\mathbf{p}^t = \mathbf{w}^{\mathbf{t}} / \sum_i^n w_i^t$ ▷ convert weights into probabilities

  $f_t(\mathbf{X}, \theta) =$ `train_stump`$(\mathbf{p}, \mathbf{X}, \mathbf{y})$ ▷ train decision stump

  $\epsilon \leftarrow \sum_i^n p_i^t |f_t(\mathbf{x}_i, \theta) - y_i|$ ▷ calculate the error

  $\beta_t \leftarrow \frac{\epsilon}{1-\epsilon}$

  $w_i^{t+1} \leftarrow w_i^t \beta_t^{1-|f_t(\mathbf{x}_i, \theta) - y_i|}$ ▷ update weights

end for

---

weights are then passed to the weak learner for that iteration, directing it to minimize the cost relative to that probability distribution—in other words, it will learn a weighted cost that will pay more attention to correctly classifying higher weighted examples. After that, an error (ϵ) is calculated over all the examples as a weighted sum, where $|f_t(\mathbf{x}_i, \theta) - y_i|$ will be 0, if the predicted label ($f_t(\mathbf{x}_i, \theta)$) has the same class as the true label (y_i), and will be 1 otherwise. Therefore, there is zero contribution to the error from correctly classified examples, and the contribution from incorrectly classified examples is larger for examples that have been upweighted in previous rounds. Note that the error is never allowed to dip below 0.5 or 50% accuracy because this would mean it performs worse than random chance. If this occurs, the tree or stump is reset and a different weak learner is fit.

In the next step, that error is turned into a β_t value, bounded between 0 and 1, with smaller β_t corresponding to smaller error. This is used to re-weight examples for the next round of boosting. Counter to the toy example in Fig. 7.8, the actual effect is to downweight correctly classified examples (since $|f_t(\mathbf{x}_i, \theta) - y_i|$ is 1 for incorrect predictions, which makes the exponent zero and reduces the β_t term to 1). This indirectly upweights misclassified examples, during probability estimation in the next round because probability is estimated by normalizing over the sum of weights. The lower the overall error, the smaller the β_t and hence the more correctly classified examples for that round are downweighted. Finally, at the end, the prediction for each example, is aggregated from the predictions across all base learners as a weighted majority vote.

Regression (Algorithm 7.3) [12] starts similarly but diverges at the point where the error is calculated. Typically a range of choices are offered for estimation of the loss including absolute error, mean squared error or exponential. An average loss is then estimated across training samples, and used to estimate the β_t parameter. Similarly to classification, the smaller the loss, the more the weight is reduced for the correctly predicted examples. The final prediction is calculated as a weighted median across all models in the ensemble.

7.2.10 Boosting with scikit-learn

Scikit-learn implements Adaboost [15] and gradient boosting [16]. For example, to create a classifier instance of Adaboost implement:

```
from sklearn.ensemble import AdaBoostClassifier

n_trees=50

# create a boosted ensemble of 50 trees
clf=AdaBoostClassifier(DecisionTreeClassifier(),
n_estimators=n_trees)
```

Algorithm 7.3 Adaboost regression.

Given $\mathbf{x}_i \in \mathbf{X}$ and $y_i \in \{0, 1\}$
Assign all n examples equal weight $w_i^t = 1/n$
for t in E **do** ▷ for each tree t in the ensemble
 $\mathbf{p} \leftarrow \mathbf{w}^t / \sum_i^n w_i^t$ ▷ convert weights into probabilities
 $f_t(\mathbf{X}, \theta) =$ `train_stump`$(\mathbf{p}, \mathbf{X}, \mathbf{y})$ ▷ train decision stump
 $D \leftarrow sup|f_t(\mathbf{x}_i, \theta) - y_i|$
 $L \leftarrow \frac{|f_t(\mathbf{x}_i, \theta) - y_i|}{D}$ ▷ calculate loss with D as normalizing factor
 $\bar{L} = \sum_i^n L_i p_i$ ▷ average loss
 $\beta_t \leftarrow \frac{\bar{L}}{1-\bar{L}}$
 $w_i^{t+1} \leftarrow w_i^t \beta_t^{1-L_i}$ ▷ update weights
end for

Similarly to bagging, it is possible to pass any choice of base estimator, where the default is a decision tree with `max_depth=1`—in other words, an axis-aligned decision stump. As before, the size of the ensemble is controlled with `n_estimators`.

7.2.11 `GridSearchCV` for ensembles

One important point to be aware of, when optimizing ensemble methods in scikit-learn, is the various ways in which parameters of their base models are passed to `GridSearchCV`. Normally, the grid search function accepts parameter ranges in the form of a dictionary, where the argument to be optimized is supplied as a dictionary key (i.e., see for the `n_estimators` parameter next). For base learners you additionally need to specify these arguments pre-fixed with the `base_estimator__` keyword; this is shown subsequently for the `min_samples_leaf` parameter of a `DecisionTreeClassifier`, optimized as part of the bagging ensemble

```
from sklearn.tree import DecisionTreeClassifier
from sklearn.ensemble import BaggingClassifier
from sklearn.model_selection import GridSearchCV


#form parameter dictionary
param_dist = {"base_estimator__min_samples_leaf":
                [1, 5, 10], #parameter of base model
              "n_estimators":
              [ 50,100,250,500] # parameter of ensemble model
              }


# instantiate model
model=BaggingClassifier(DecisionTreeClassifier())
```

```
#create an instance of GridSearchCV
grid = GridSearchCV(estimator=model, param_grid=param_dist)
# run grid search on the training data
grid.fit(X, y)

# create model using optimized parameters
model=BaggingClassifier(base_estimator=
    DecisionTreeClassifier(min_samples_leaf=
    grid.best_estimator_.base_estimator_.min_samples_leaf),
    n_estimators=grid.best_estimator_.n_estimators)
```

7.2.12 Feature importance

Another powerful aspect of tree-based ensembles is that they balance performance with interpretability very well. Since decision stumps make predictions by thresholding individual features, it becomes very easy to trace which features are most discriminative for a prediction simply by assessing how useful each was when training decision stumps in the ensemble. Such importance rankings are especially meaningful for biomedical problems, where it is vital that automated decisions are supported by clinically interpretable justifications. Knowledge of the most discriminative features for a problem can generate potential biomarkers of disease progression, or support the construction of mechanistic models of biological processes or the progression of disease. Importance rankings can also be used for feature selection prior to use in other models (see Chap. 8 for more details).

Scikit-learn calculates the importance of decision trees by calculating the degree to which each feature decreases the node impurity that is accumulated throughout the entire tree. Importance for ensembles of trees therefore reflects the mean importance across all trees and can be retrieved from each model using the `feature_importances_` attribute of random-forest and boosting methods.

A visual example of how feature importances can aid interpretation and translation of machine learning findings is shown in Fig. 7.9. This shows importance values returned from a random forest trained to predict gestational age from neonatal brain MRI features (volumes of 86 regions). The plot in Fig. 7.9a shows the mean and standard deviations of importance for the top 20 regions,[3] where statistics were calculated from the distribution of feature importances across all trees in the ensemble.[4] Fig. 7.9b shows

[3] See https://github.com/MIRTK/DrawEM/blob/master/label_names/ALBERT/all_labels_LUT_ITKSNAP.txt for the mapping between regional keys and anatomical structures.

[4] See https://scikit-learn.org/stable/auto_examples/ensemble/plot_forest_importances.html for more details.

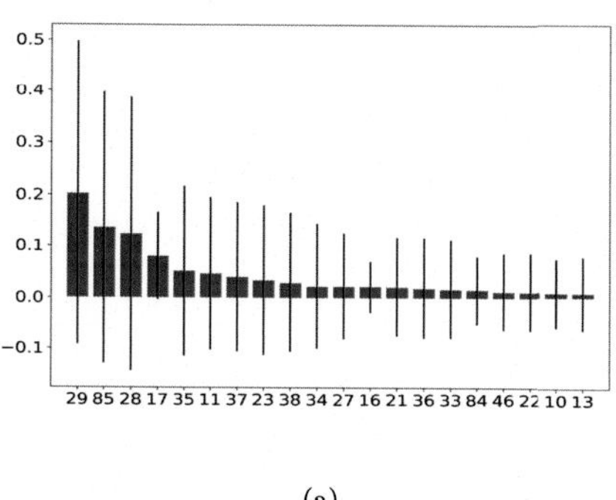

(a)

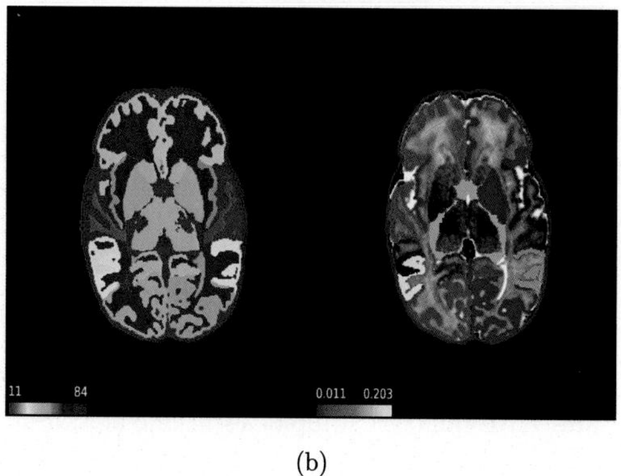

(b)

Figure 7.9 Importances for the GA prediction task: a) distribution of importance scores for the top 20 regions (ordered from biggest to smallest); b) importance values projected back onto an exemplar brain image: left-hand image with all 86 regions (color reflecting the key of the region); right-hand image encodes importances of the top 20 regions.

these importances projected back onto an exemplar brain image, where the left-hand image shows an image of all 86 regions and the right shows the importance of the top 20 regions. As one can see, the grey-matter regions (particularly, the temporal and frontal areas) are most important for this task. This reflects the literature because we know that these regions expand rapidly during late gestation [17].

7.2.13 Heterogeneous ensembles

In contrast to homogeneous ensembles, heterogeneous ensembles stack predictions made from various classes of machine learning model. In principle, this allows for the leveraging of complementary advantages across various types of solutions, for example, combining linear and nonlinear models.

The basic framework of a stacking algorithm is shown in Fig. 7.10. Here, training data $\mathbf{X}$ and labels $\mathbf{y}$ are passed to 3 different models—these could be anything, e.g., a random forest, support vector machine or a logistic regression. Each model outputs a prediction: $\hat{\mathbf{y}}^1$, $\hat{\mathbf{y}}^2$, $\hat{\mathbf{y}}^3$; these predictions form the data that is input to the second level (meta) learning model, which combines them to output a single final prediction $\hat{\mathbf{y}}$. The meta model might be something as simple as majority voting but could equally likely be any other learning model (e.g., a second forest, SVM or logistic regression).

7.2.14 Stacked generalization in biomedical imaging

Stacking has seen broad application within the biomedical literature. Some examples include FIX (FMRIB's ICA X-Noisifier) [41], from the Oxford Centre for Functional MRI of the Brain (FMRIB), which classifies ICA components (derived from fMRI) into either signal or noise, using an ensemble of SVMs, K-NN classifiers and decision

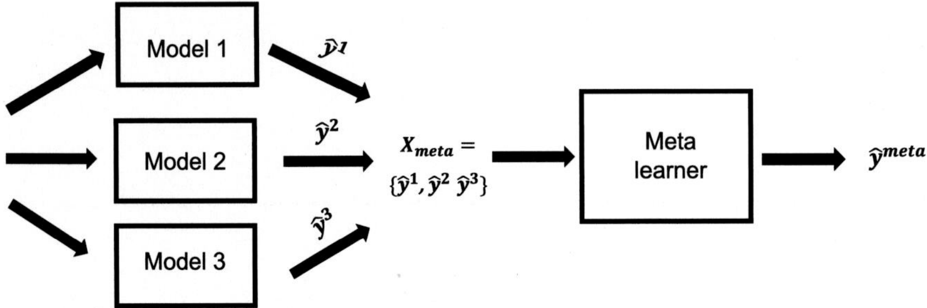

Figure 7.10 The basic setup of a stacking algorithm.

trees, stacked with a random forest. Another example is EMMA [24], which stacks an ensemble of separately trained deep learning-segmentation models through a simple majority vote. Here a range of very different architectures are trained and combined to improve the performance of brain-tumor segmentation. Finally, Rasero et al. [37] seek to condense and combine a vast amount of features from multimodal MRI to build a sensitive prediction of fluid intelligence and other metrics of cognition.

7.2.15 Exercises

Complete the following exercises to test your understanding of how to implement decision trees and ensembles using scikit-learn.

1. Calculate the information gain and Gini index for the split in Fig. 7.11.
2. Using the neonatal brain dataset *'GA-brain-volumes-86-features.csv'* with 86 regional brain volumes:[5] fit a scikit-learn decision tree regression model to predict the target variable (gestational age (GA) in the first column),
   - Split the data set into training and test sets, by including the first 120 samples in the training set and the rest in the test set.
   - Try fitting a tree with the default parameters and reporting the goodness of fit using `score`.
   - Use scikit-learn's `GridSearchCV` to optimize the parameters for: `criterion`, `max_depth`, and `min_samples_leaf`.
3. Fit a `BaggingRegressor`, `RandomForestRegressor` and `AdaboostRegressor` using decision trees as the base model:
   - Set parameters to the optimal values found for Exer. 2;

[5] The datasets, skeleton code and solution is available at github.com/MachineLearningBiomedicalApplications/notebooks.

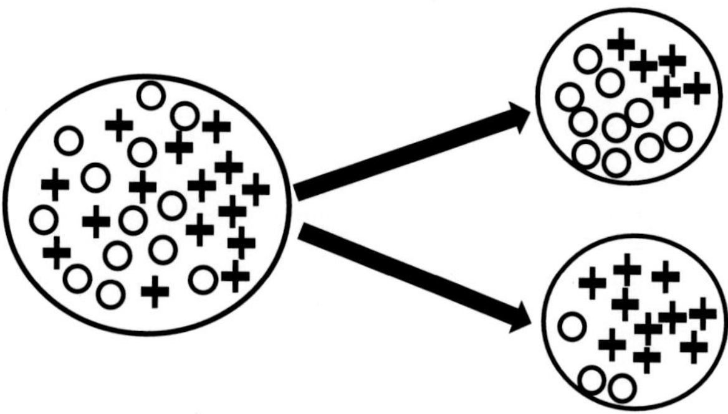

Figure 7.11 Example for Exercise 1.

- Use `GridSearchCV` to optimize the parameters for each model. Keep `criterion` fixed, but optimize `max_depth`, `min_samples_leaf` and `n_estimators`.[6] Which method performs best?
- Return the most important features from each model and plot as shown in Fig. 7.9a (this will require importances to be sorted in decreasing magnitude).

[6] Hint: `max_depth` is likely to be less than 10, and `n_estimators` for bagging and forests will likely be much higher than for boosting, in fact, hundreds for parallel ensembles and units or tens for boosting.

CHAPTER 8

Feature extraction and selection

In the previous chapters we have shown how to train machine learning models using features that have been extracted from biomedical datasets. In many cases we extracted features using dedicated application specific techniques. For example, in Chap. 3 the brain MRI of newborn babies was segmented into 86 structures (Fig. 3.1) and the volumes of these structures were used as features for the machine learning algorithms. We have reduced the number of features from 86 to only 6 to prevent overfitting using the domain knowledge—we simply added volumes of structures depending on the brain tissue type (WM, GM, CSF, ...). Other examples of features extracted using dedicated techniques based on the clinical knowledge include ejection fraction and global longitudinal strain calculated from cardiac MRI or ultrasound, or QRS duration calculated from ECG, which we used in Chap. 4.

In this chapter we describe some more generally applicable techniques for extracting (Sect. 8.1) and selecting (Sect. 8.2) features from medical images and signals. This is often called feature engineering. In the following chapters we will see that modern state-of-the-art machine learning based on deep neural networks helps us to bypass this step by directly learning features from the data. Nevertheless, feature extraction and selection still plays an important role in many applications, in particular, if we have small datasets or if we want to control and interpret the types of features that drive the machine learning models.

8.1. Feature extraction

A **feature** is a measurable property of an observed phenomenon that should ideally be informative, discriminative, and independent. Some features can be observed directly, for example, a patient's age, blood pressure, or history of diseases. Other features can be directly measured from the data, such as the head circumference of a fetus on an ultrasound image, cardiac ejection fraction, or tumor diameter on an MRI image. These features are often measured manually in clinical practice.

Feature extraction is a type of dimensionality reduction where a large number of values in signals or images are reduced to a more manageable number of features that still accurately capture the original data. In other words, we aim to extract new salient features from high-dimensional data and remove redundant information. This way we can reduce overfitting and improve accuracy and computational efficiency of the machine learning models.

Machine Learning for Biomedical Applications
https://doi.org/10.1016/B978-0-12-822904-0.00013-3
Copyright © 2024 Elsevier Ltd.
All rights reserved.

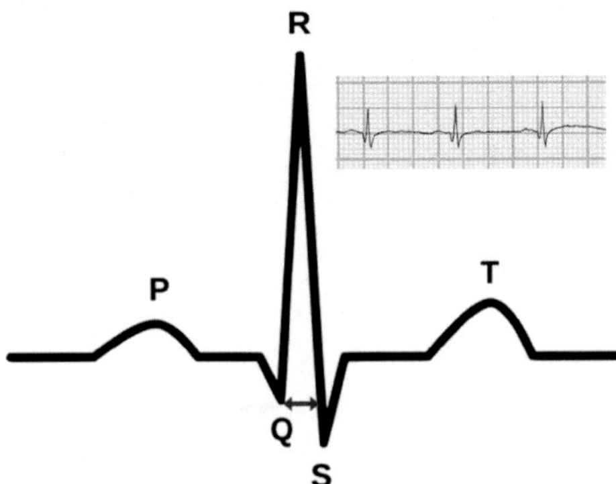

Figure 8.1 Schematic ECG waveform. Red arrows show the QRS interval duration. The real ECG signal is shown on the pink background.

In this section we will give a brief overview of several types of features that can be extracted from the biomedical signals and images. **Morphological features** describe geometric aspects of the objects, such as length, area, or volume. **Texture descriptors** look at statistical properties of the signal or image values. **Transform-based features** provide features in other domains, such as frequency domain.

8.1.1 Morphological features

We have already seen several types of morphological features, for example, the volumes of brain structures (Fig. 3.1) or QRS interval duration in an ECG wave (Fig. 8.1). Morphological features can contain some basic measurements, such as **length, peak height, area, maximum diameter, surface area** A, or **volume** V. **Compactness** C measures how spherical the volume is:

$$C = 36\pi \frac{V^2}{A^3}.$$

An equivalent measurement in 2D would contain the ratio of the area and circumference. Another group of measurements can be extracted using PCA (Sect. 5.4). The eigenvalues correspond to the **length** L **of the major** and **minor axis** in 2D, and an additional **least axis** in 3D, e.g.,

$$L_{\text{major}} = 4\sqrt{\lambda_{\text{major}}}.$$

The ratio of minor and major axes lengths measures **elongation,** and the ratio of least and major axis length measures **flatness.**[1] We have seen various 2D morphological

[1] For a detailed description of morphological imaging features, see Image biomarker standardization initiative reference manual at https://arxiv.org/abs/1612.07003.

features in the Breast Cancer Wisconsin dataset (Sect. 2.1.2). Note that extraction of morphological features usually requires segmentation of the object to create the region of interest. We have already explored clustering for segmentation in Chap. 6.

8.1.2 Texture descriptors

Texture descriptors are summary statistics of signal values or image intensities. They can be calculated from the whole dataset, signal segments or image patches, or segmented regions of interest. These descriptors include simple statistical measures, such as **mean, median, variance, interquartile range, minimum, maximum, coefficient of variation, kurtosis,** and **entropy**.

For 2D and 3D images one of the powerful techniques to characterize texture is through the **Grey Level Co-occurrence Matrix (GLCM)**. GLCM expresses how combinations of discretized intensities (grey levels) of neighboring pixels or voxels are distributed along one of the image directions. Fig. 8.2 shows an example GLCM calculated in x and y directions. For each pair of pixels with intensities (i,j), we add 1 to the position (i,j) in the GLCM matrix.

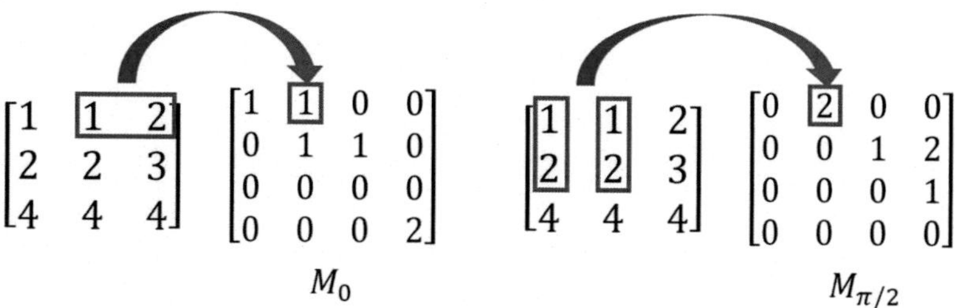

Figure 8.2 Grey level co-occurrence matrix. Each element of M_ϕ contains the count of neighboring intensity pairs (i,j) in direction ϕ. Left: GLCM in x-direction ($\phi = 0$ rad). Right: GLCM in y-direction ($\phi = \pi/2$ rad).

If we normalize the GLCM matrix by the overall number of intensity pairs, it can be interpreted as 2D probability distribution $p(i,j)$. Then we can calculate several summary statistical measures that characterize the texture of the image:

- **contrast:** $\sum_{i,j=0}^{l-1}(i-j)^2 p(i,j)$
- **dissimilarity:** $\sum_{i,j=0}^{l-1}|i-j|p(i,j)$
- **homogeneity:** $\sum_{i,j=0}^{l-1}\frac{1}{1+(i-j)^2}p(i,j)$
- **energy:** $\sqrt{\sum_{i,j=0}^{l-1}p(i,j)^2}$
- **correlation:** $\sum_{i,j=0}^{l-1}\frac{(i-\mu_i)(j-\mu_j)}{\sigma_i\sigma_j}p(i,j)$,

where i and j are discretized intensity levels, l is the number of levels, $\mu_i = \sum_{i,j=0}^{l-1} ip(i,j)$, $\mu_j = \sum_{i,j=0}^{l-1} jp(i,j)$, $\sigma_i^2 = \sum_{i,j=0}^{l-1}(i-\mu_i)^2 p(i,j)$ and $\sigma_j^2 = \sum_{i,j=0}^{l-1}(j-\mu_j)^2 p(i,j)$.

GLCM matrix can be calculated using the `skimage` function `greycomatrix` as follows:

```
from skimage.feature import graycomatrix
glcm = graycomatrix(image, [3], [0], 64)
```

Note that the variable `image` should be of type `'uint8'` or `'int8'` so that it contains a small number of discretized levels. The second input argument is the distance between neighboring pixels, in this case 3, and the third argument is the direction, in this case x-direction (0 rad). This command will therefore produce a matrix similar to Fig. 8.2, left. Final argument is the number of discretised intensity levels, in this case 64, which means levels 0, .., 63.

The statistical measures of GLCM can be calculated using command

```
from skimage.feature import graycoprops
c = graycoprops(glcm, 'contrast')
```

In this case we calculated the contrast measure, but all the other measures listed can be obtained in a similar way. Fig. 8.3 shows an example of GLCM matrices for histological images from PatchCamelyon dataset.[2] We can see how different textures in the images with healthy and cancerous tissue result in different GLCM distributions.

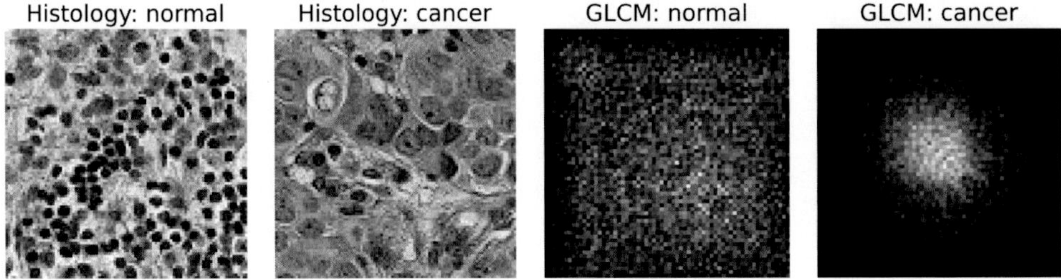

Figure 8.3 Symmetric grey level co-occurrence matrix calculated from histological images in the x-direction.

8.1.3 Transform based features

A classical transformation for extraction of features from signals is the **Discrete Fourier Transform (DFT)**. The signal $s(t)$, which is normally defined as a function of time t, is transformed into $f(u)$ in a **frequency domain**

$$f(u) = \sum_{t=0}^{N-1} s(t)e^{-2\pi iut/N}, \quad u = 1, ..., N-1,$$

where $f(u)$ are the complex transformed coefficients of the signal s that tell us how much of each frequency u is present in the signal s, N is the number of samples, and

[2] https://github.com/basveeling/pcam.

$e^{-2\pi iut/N} = \cos(-2\pi ut/N) + i\sin(-2\pi ut/N)$ are periodic basis functions corresponding to various frequencies. By frequency of a periodic function, we mean the number of times it repeats per unit of time. In Fig. 8.4, left, we show a segment of 1000 samples of an ECG signal from the PhysioNet MIT-BIH Arrhythmia Database.[3] We can see that the signal is approximately periodic and in this time segment we observe ten ECG waves. Fig. 8.4, right, shows the magnitude of the first few complex Fourier coefficients. We can observe a peak at frequency 10 (shown in red) that corresponds to the 10 waves in the ECG segment. We can also infer that each wave consists of $1000/10 = 100$ samples on average.

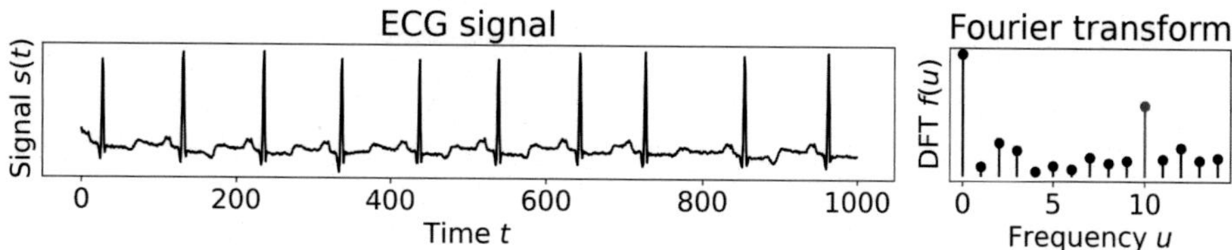

Figure 8.4 Fourier transform of ECG signal. Left: ECG segment with 1000 samples. Right: Magnitude of the DFT coefficients of this segment. Peak coefficient of frequency 10, corresponding to 10 ECG waves in the image, is highlighted in red.

Fourier transform can be calculated using `scipy` object `fft`

```
from scipy.fft import fft
f=fft(signal)
```

The magnitude of the coefficients displayed in Fig. 8.4, right, can be obtained by:

```
import numpy as np
magnitude = np.abs(f)
```

The Discrete Wavelet Transform (DWT) is another popular transform applied to extract features from signals and images. DWT decomposes the signal into **approximation coefficients** that represent a low-resolution version of the data and **detail coefficients** that contain the residual information—see Fig. 8.5.

The DWT of a 1D signal can be calculated using the PyWavelets package `pywt`:

```
import pywt
(ca, cd) = pywt.dwt(signal,'db1')
```

where `ca` are approximation coefficients and `cd` are detail coefficients, shown for the ECG signal in Fig. 8.5, left. We also need to set the type of wavelet we want to use, in this case Daubechies 1 `'db1'`. For 2D images we can use command `dwt2`:

[3] www.physionet.org/physiobank/database/mitdb.

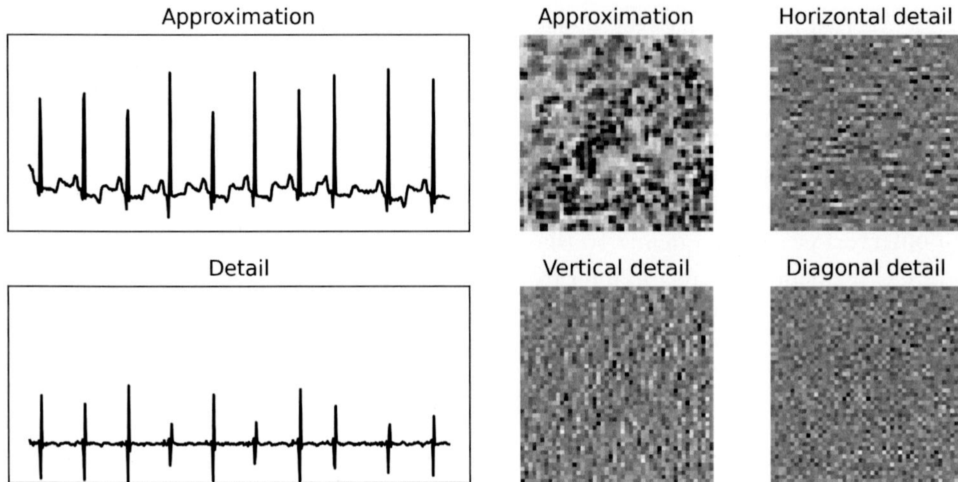

Figure 8.5 Single level DFT. Left: Transformed ECG signal (Fig. 8.4, left). Right: Transformed histological image of normal tissue (Fig. 8.3, left).

```
ca, (cdh, cdv, cdd) - pywt.dwt2(image, 'db1')
```

where `cdh`, `cdv`, and `cdd` are horizontal, vertical, and diagonal detail coefficients, shown for the histological image in Fig. 8.5, right.

So far, we have described single-level DWT. It is however common to perform DWT at multiple resolution levels. Multi-level DWT will further decompose approximation coefficients for the current level to the approximation and detail coefficient of the next lower resolution level. We can perform such decomposition either a predefined number of times, or until the we have a single approximation coefficient. Multi-level DWT can be implemented using command `wavedec`:

```
from pywt import wavedec
ca3, cd3, cd2, cd1 = wavedec(signal, 'db1', level=3)
```

shown here for 1D signal and 3 levels.

Note that the DFT and DWT do not offer dimensionality reduction. In fact, the dimensionality of the data is preserved after transformation, and the inverse DFT and DWT can be used to reconstruct the original data without any loss. We might therefore need to reduce the dimensionality of the transformed data before training machine learning models. One way to do that is to calculate summary statistics, similarly to texture descriptors in Sect. 8.1.2. An alternative is to use one of the feature selection algorithms which will be covered in Sect. 8.2.

8.1.4 Classification of histological images

We will now demonstrate how we can classify histological images based on texture. We will use PatchCamelon dataset, which contains healthy and cancerous breast tissue histological samples (Fig. 8.3).

Training data

We select 1,500 images to train a classifier, and another 150 for testing. These data are available in the file *histological_data.npz*.[4] We can load this data as follows:

```
import numpy as np
data = np.load('histological_data.npz')
```

The training images are of size 96 × 96 pixels and are stored in a 3D array `X_train`:

```
X_train.shape
>>> (1500, 96, 96)
```

The images contain intensity values between 0 and 1:

```
print(X_train.min(),X_train.max())
>>> 0 1
```

The binary training labels `y_train` indicate whether the sample is cancerous (label 1) or not (label 0).

Feature extraction

We will now create a function `getGLCMfeatures` to extract two texture descriptors, contrast and dissimilarity, from gray level co-occurrence matrix. First, we need to convert the image into type `'uint8'` with a small number of gray levels, which we choose to be 64. Then, we calculate GLCM matrix `glcm` in the x-direction and choose the distance between pairs of values to be three pixels. Finally, we calculate contrast `c` and dissimilarity `d`:

```
from skimage.feature import graycomatrix, graycoprops
def getGLCMfeatures(im):
    im = np.round(im*63).astype('uint8')
    glcm = graycomatrix(im, [3], [0])
    c = graycoprops(glcm, 'contrast')[0, 0]
    d = graycoprops(glcm, 'dissimilarity')[0, 0]
    return c, d
```

We will now extract these two texture descriptors from all training images and input them into the feature vector `features_train`:

[4] Available from gin.g-node.org/MachineLearningBiomedApplications/data.

```
features_train = []
for im in X_train:
    features_train.append(getGLCMfeatures(im))
features_train = np.asarray(features_train)
```

Training classifier

Next, we will create and train a `LogisticRegression` classifier to predict whether an image contains cancerous tissue or not:

```
from sklearn.preprocessing import StandardScaler
from sklearn.linear_model import LogisticRegression
scaler= StandardScaler()
features_train=scaler.fit_transform(features_train)
model = LogisticRegression()
model.fit(features_train,y_train)
```

Evaluate performance

Finally, we evaluate the performance of the classifier on the test data `X_test, y_test`. First, we need to extract the texture descriptors from the test images:

```
features_test  = []
for im in X_test:
    features_test.append(getGLCMfeatures(im))
    features  = np.asarray(features_test)
features_test=scaler.fit_transform(features_test)
```

and then we can calculate the performance measures on the test set:

```
from sklearn.metrics import recall_score
def PerformanceMeasures(model,X,y):
    accuracy = model.score(X,y)
    y_pred = model.predict(X)
    sensitivity = recall_score(y,y_pred)
    specificity = recall_score(y,y_pred,pos_label=0)
    print('Accuracy:    ', round(accuracy,2))
    print('Sensitivity: ', round(sensitivity,2))
    print('Specificity: ', round(specificity,2))

PerformanceMeasures(model,features_test,y_test)
>>> Accuracy:     0.79
>>> Sensitivity:  0.8
>>> Specificity:  0.78
```

We have obtained a good classifier that generalized on the test set with approximately 80% accuracy. Sensitivity and specificity are very similar to accuracy, indicating that we have a well-trained classifier.

8.1.5 Exercises

1. What is feature extraction?
2. What are morphological features? Define compactness, elongation, and flatness.
3. Calculate gray level co-occurrence matrix in the x-direction from the following image:

$$\begin{bmatrix} 1 & 1 & 5 & 6 & 8 \\ 2 & 3 & 5 & 7 & 1 \\ 4 & 5 & 7 & 1 & 2 \\ 8 & 5 & 1 & 2 & 5 \end{bmatrix}$$

4. What are the DFT coefficients?
5. Describe coefficients obtained using
   - single-level 2D Discrete Wavelet Transform;
   - multi-resolution 1D Discrete Wavelet Transform.
6. Load histological data described in Sect. 8.1.4 from the file *histological_data.npz*.[5] The data contains the training and testing histological images and labels. Extract gray level co-occurrence matrix based statistical measures (Sect. 8.1.2) from the images. Train a classifier to predict cancer from these images. Which combination of GLCM measures performs the best?

8.2. Feature selection

In Sect. 8.1 we described techniques for extracting features from biomedical signals and images. It is however not always obvious which of the extracted features are the most predictive and therefore most suitable to train our machine learning models. In this section we will describe the **feature selection** techniques that will help us to select the most predictive features, while removing redundant and noisy features. Feature selection is in fact another dimensionality reduction technique that improves performance and reduces the complexity of the machine learning models, leading to more generalizable, easier to train models that are less prone to overfitting.

To illustrate these concepts, let's revisit the example of predicting the age of a baby from MRI brain scans, presented in Chap. 3 (Fig. 3.1). Each 3D MRI contains around one million voxels, and intensities of these voxels could be considered as features. However, to predict age directly from these features using classical machine learning

[5] Available from gin.g-node.org/MachineLearningBiomedApplications/data.

techniques is a nearly impossible task: Not only is the dimensionality of the problem huge, but these raw features are not necessarily meaningful because the brains vary in position and shape and MRI intensities are not quantitative. We have therefore extracted a much smaller number of meaningful morphological features, 86 volumes of brain structures. We have seen in Chap. 3 that this number of features, though greatly reduced, could still lead to overfitting. We have already shown how to prevent overfitting using regularization (Sect. 3.2, ridge or lasso), dimensionality reduction techniques (Sect. 5.4, PCA) and ensemble learning (Chap. 7).

In this section we will cover several feature-selection techniques, including univariate feature selection, model-based feature selection, and recursive feature elimination. We will show that feature selection not only prevents overfitting, but also offers ways to calculate the importance of features and interpret the trained machine learning models.

8.2.1 Feature importances

To be able to select the best features, we need a way to calculate the **importance** of each feature for the prediction task. We will consider two types of methods:

- **Univariate feature importances** measure how well each individual feature predicts the target value;
- **Model-based feature importances** are extracted from fitted machine learning models.

Examples of univariate feature importances are Pearson's correlation coefficient and mutual information between the feature x_k and the target value y. To select features using **linear regressors or classifiers**, we fit a multivariate linear model as a prediction or decision function:

$$y = w_0 + w_1 x_1 + \ldots + w_D x_D.$$

If the features are normalized, for example, using a standard scaler, the absolute values of the coefficients w_k can be considered as feature importances because they measure how much each feature x_k contributes to the prediction model. In scikit-learn we can access coefficients through

```
model.coef_
```

In **tree-based methods** we measure how much each feature decreases the impurity in a tree. For an ensemble of trees, such as random forest, we average these decreases in impurities over all trees to obtain feature importances. In scikit-learn the tree-based methods return the feature importances through

```
model.feature_importances_
```

While, in the univariate approach, each feature is considered separately, the model-based approaches also consider relationships between features and are therefore better able to discover complex predictive combinations of features and remove redundant features.

8.2.2 Univariate feature selection

Pearson's correlation coefficient

Pearson's correlation coefficient measures the strength of the linear relationship between two variables. If there is a strong linear relationship, the correlation coefficient is close to 1 or -1, and 0 means no linear relationship. In the case of univariate feature selection, these variables are the feature x_k and the target value y.

In Fig. 8.6 we generated five features with different levels of noise and non-linearity. The first two features are linear, but the feature 0 has significantly more noise than the feature 1, and consequently lower correlation coefficient C. The feature 2 has the same amount of noise as the feature 1 but is slightly nonlinear. In this case the correlation coefficient is still high, though lower than for the feature 1. The feature 3 is highly nonlinear and not unique (e.g., there can be multiple correct target values for a single feature), and in this case the correlation coefficient is close to zero. Finally, the feature 4 is only noise, resulting in $C = 0$.

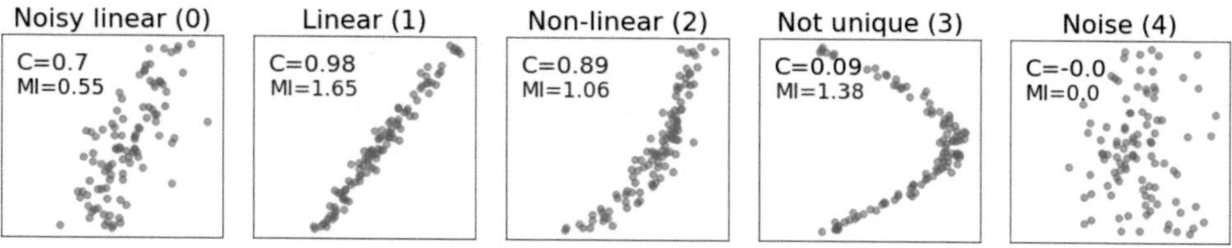

Figure 8.6 Simulated features with various levels of nonlinearity and noise. The correlation (C) and mutual information (MI) between each feature and the target value is given. High values are highlighted in red.

Scikit-learn implements feature selection using the F-value, which is closely related to Pearson's correlation coefficient. The F-value is a statistic that measures whether the slope of the univariate linear regression is different from zero. It is positive for both positive and negative linear relationships. The F-value can be calculated in scikit-learn using the function `f_regression`. The features with the highest F-values can be selected using a selector object `SelectKBest`:

```
from sklearn.feature_selection import SelectKBest, \
                                      f_regression
selector = SelectKBest(f_regression, k=3)
```

The `selector` object that we created selects three features that are most highly correlated with the target values. It is a transformer object, and we can therefore fit it and transform the feature matrix using function `fit_transform`:

```
X_selected = selector.fit_transform(X, y)
```

We can access the indices of the selected features using

```
ind = selector.get_support(indices=True)
print('Selected features: ',ind)
>>> Selected features:  [0 1 2]
```

The selected three best features 0, 1 and 2 (highlighted in red in Fig. 8.6) are linearly related to the target values. Feature selection for classification can be implemented in a similar manner, except that the F-value is calculated using object `f_classif`.

Mutual information

Mutual information (MI) measures how much information two variables have in common. Mutual information importance is decreased primarily by noise, but not by nonlinearity or nonuniqueness, as we can see in Fig. 8.6. Actually, the highly nonlinear, nonunique feature 3 has a higher MI with target values than the close-to-linear feature 2.

Scikit-learn implements scoring function `mutual_info_regression` to calculate the MI of each feature x_k with the target value y. If we use `SelectKBest` to select top three features, the linear and nonlinear features 1, 2, and 3 with the least amount of noise will be selected:

```
from sklearn.feature_selection import \
                              mutual_info_regression
selector = SelectKBest(mutual_info_regression, k=3)
X_selected = selector.fit_transform(X, y)
ind = selector.get_support(indices=True)
print('Selected features: ',ind)
>>> Selected features:  [1 2 3]
```

Mutual information-based feature selection for classification can be implemented in a similar manner, using a scoring function `mutual_info_classif`.

8.2.3 Model-based feature selection

In model-based feature selection, we fit a machine learning model to our data and then use feature importances from the model to select features. We will cover two models—lasso regression and random forest.

Lasso

We have already shown in Sect. 3.2.2 that applying the L1 norm during training introduces sparsity to the model and therefore directly provides feature selection. We will now demonstrate how features can be selected using the lasso regression. Note that the L1 penalty can be added to the classification models too.

We use the scikit-learn object `LassoCV` because it automatically tunes hyperparameter `alpha` using cross-validation. The selector object `SelectFromModel` selects all the features for which the absolute values of coefficients `model.coef_` are larger than the predefined threshold. Note that the features need to be normalized, for example, by the standard scaler, for this method to work well:

```
from sklearn.linear_model import LassoCV
from sklearn.feature_selection import SelectFromModel
selector = SelectFromModel(LassoCV(), threshold=0.01)
X_selected = selector.fit_transform(X, y)
ind = selector.get_support(indices=True)
print('Selected features: ',ind)
>>> Selected features:  [1 2]
```

The model selected the features 1 and 2, which are both linear or close-to-linear and with low noise—see Fig. 8.6.

Random forest

If we use the random forest model as an input of `SelectFromModel` object, it will select features with importances `model.feature_importances_` larger than a predefined threshold:

```
from sklearn.ensemble import RandomForestRegressor
from sklearn.feature_selection import SelectFromModel
selector = SelectFromModel(RandomForestRegressor(),
                           threshold=0.01)
X_selected = selector.fit_transform(X, y)
ind = selector.get_support(indices=True)
print('Selected features: ',ind)
>>> Selected features:  [1 2 3]
```

Note that this model selected the highly nonlinear feature 3, even though it does not have a unique relationship to the target values. This relationship can be resolved in combination with unique relationships provided by the features 1 and 2. We can see that the random forest regressor can successfully use highly nonlinear features.

8.2.4 Recursive feature elimination

The recursive feature elimination algorithm iteratively eliminates the least important features, based on the feature importances calculated by a fitted machine learning model. It iterates between these two steps:

- Fit the model to the current set of features;
- Eliminate the least important feature.

The algorithm ranks all the features from the most important (the ones that were removed last) to the least important (the ones that were removed at the very beginning).

We choose the number of features we want to select, or instead keep removing features while the cross-validated performance of the model keeps improving.

In the following example code, we use ridge regression as a ranking model together with scikit-learn object `RFECV`, which automatically determines the number of selected features that produce the best cross-validated performance of the model:

```
from sklearn.linear_model import Ridge
from sklearn.feature_selection import RFECV
selector = RFECV(Ridge())
X_selected = selector.fit_transform(X, y)
ind = selector.get_support(indices=True)
print('Selected features: ',ind)
>>> Selected features:  [1 2]
```

The model selected the low noise close-to-linear features 1 and 2, which is to be expected since ridge is a linear regression model.

8.2.5 Selecting brain structure volumes to predict age from scans

We will now revisit the example of predicting the age of the baby from the volumes of 86 brain structures segmented from an MRI image (Fig. 3.1). We have seen in Chap. 3 (Table 3.3) that linear regression overfitted this dataset and that this could be rectified by introducing the ridge or lasso penalty. Here, we will show that feature selection is an alternative technique that allows us to fit a linear regression model that will generalize well on unseen data.

Table 8.1 shows the performance of linear regression models with features selected from 86 volumes of brain structures using various feature-selection methods. Because we are comparing models, we show the root-mean-squared error (RMSE) calculated on the training set and using cross-validation. We can see how selection of a small number of features prevents overfitting while optimizing the performance of the model.

Table 8.1 Root-mean-squared error calculated on the training set (RMSE) and using cross-validation (RMSE_CV) for linear regression models with various feature-selection techniques: univariate with Pearson's correlation coefficient; model-based with lasso scoring model; recursive feature elimination with linear regression scoring model; no selection.

Feature-selection method	Univariate correlation	Model Lasso	RFE Lin Reg	None
Selected features	2	6	4	86
RMSE (weeks)	1.25	1.07	1.12	0.68
RMSE_CV (weeks)	1.33	**1.18**	1.21	2.08

We will now demonstrate how we can tune a feature selection model in scikit-learn. We will show an example of model-based feature selection using lasso to optimize a simple linear regression model. First, we load our data[6]:

```
df = pd.read_csv("GA-structure-volumes-preterm.csv",header=None)
data = df.to_numpy()
X = data[:,1:]
X = StandardScaler().fit_transform(X)
y = data[:,0]
```

Next, we split our data into training and test sets, while stratifying by the age at scan `y` rounded to the closest week:

```
from sklearn.model_selection import train_test_split
bins = np.round(y)
X_train, X_test, y_train, y_test = \
train_test_split(X,y,test_size=0.2, stratify=bins)
```

Next, we define our model, which will consist of a selector `SelectFromModel` with the lasso scoring model and the linear regression. We will join this two objects into one model using the `Pipeline`:

```
from sklearn.linear_model import LinearRegression
from sklearn.linear_model import Lasso
from sklearn.pipeline import Pipeline

model = Pipeline((
("selector", SelectFromModel(Lasso())),
("lin_reg", LinearRegression()) ))
```

There are two parameters of our model that we need to tune: the regularization parameter `alpha` for the scoring model `Lasso` accessed through attribute `estimator` of the selector `SelectFromModel`; and the `threshold` on the coefficients of the linear model that will be used to select the features. We will create the parameter grid `par` to test various values of these parameters, and fit `GridSearchCV` object to find ones that results in the best cross-validated score:

```
par={"selector__estimator__alpha": np.logspace(-2,3,5),
     "selector__threshold": np.linspace(0,0.5,6)}
grid = GridSearchCV(model, par)
grid.fit(X_train,y_train)
```

[6] The data can be obtained from github.com/MachineLearningBiomedicalApplications/notebooks.

The tuned model is stored in `grid.best_estimator_`. We will now evaluate performance of this model on the test set:

```
y_pred_test = grid.best_estimator_.predict(X_test)
RMSE = np.sqrt(mean_squared_error(y_pred_test,y_test))
```

The indices of the selected features can be accessed as

```
selector = grid.best_estimator_.named_steps['selector']
selector.get_support(indices=True)
```

8.2.6 Interpretation of machine learning models

An added benefit of feature selection is that we learn which features are informative for our prediction task. In our simulated example (Fig. 8.6), the highly predictive low-noise features 1 and 2 were selected by all the methods. In addition, the nonlinear feature 3 was selected by techniques that can deal with nonlinearity (mutual information, random forest). The feature 4 that contained only noise was never selected.

However, we need to be careful in cases when we have highly correlated features in our dataset. In this case the feature-selection methods might select one representative feature and discard the other correlated features even if they are highly predictive, in particular, if we use lasso or recursive feature elimination. Let's now compare top-ranking features selected from 86 brain structure volumes using different selection techniques. To do that, we will first load the names of the labels for the 86 brain structures and write a function that will list the selected structures:

```
names = pd.read_csv('labels', header=None, sep='\t')


def PrintFeatureNames(labels):
    for i in range(labels.size):
        print(names.loc[labels[i],1])
```

Now, we will check the top four features that have highest correlation with age at scan `y`:

```
selector = SelectKBest(f_regression, k=4)
X_selected = selector.fit_transform(X, y)
ind = selector.get_support(indices=True)
PrintFeatureNames(ind)
>>> Frontal lobe right GM
>>> Frontal lobe left GM
>>> Parietal lobe right GM
>>> Parietal lobe left GM
```

Next let's apply model based selection using Lasso:

```
selector = SelectFromModel(LassoCV(), threshold=0.5)
X_selected = selector.fit_transform(X, y)
ind = selector.get_support(indices=True)
PrintFeatureNames(ind)
>>> Gyri parahippocampalis posterior right GM
>>> Lateral occipitotemporal gyrus posterior left GM
>>> Parietal lobe left GM
>>> CSF
```

And finally let's have a look at recursive feature elimination with linear regression as a scoring model:

```
selector = RFECV(LinearRegression())
X_selected = selector.fit_transform(X, y)
ind = selector.get_support(indices=True)
PrintFeatureNames(ind)
>>> Superior temporal gyrus middle right GM
>>> Brainstem
>>> Frontal lobe right GM
>>> Caudate nucleus right
```

We can see that features selected by different models are very different from each other. The features most correlated with age at scan are frontal and parietal GM on both sides of the brain, but only one of these features has been selected by the other two models, perhaps because it made the other three highly correlated features redundant. Generally, we see that GM volumes are most predictive of age at scan, though the model based selector has also chosen CSF and RFE selector have chosen deep brain structures brainstem and caudate. Choosing complementary features turns out to be a good strategy: while selection of 4 features most correlated with age at scan resulted in linear regression with CV RMSE 1.39 weeks, model based selection and RFE achieved better CV RMSE of 1.19 and 1.21 weeks respectively (see Table 8.1). The feature importances from these three models are displayed in Fig. 8.7.

8.2.7 Exercises

1. What is the purpose of feature selection in machine learning?
2. List different types of feature importances and describe how they are calculated.
3. Explain recursive feature elimination.
4. Load the dataset of 86 brain structure volumes of 164 preterm babies stored in the file *GA-structure-volumes-preterm.csv* and another file *labels* that contains the names of 86 brain structures.[7]

[7] The data can be obtained from github.com/MachineLearningBiomedicalApplications/notebooks.

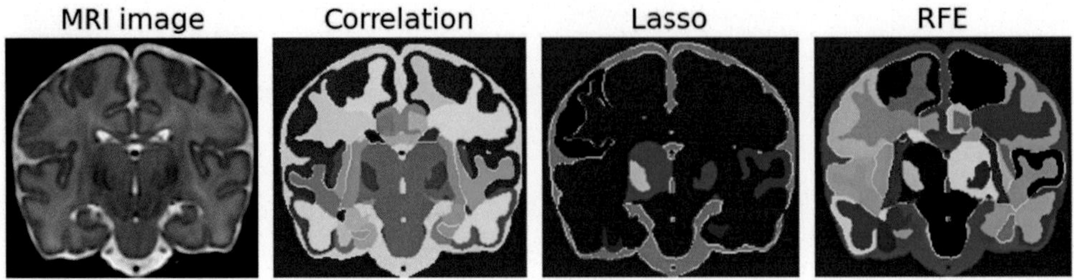

Figure 8.7 Feature importances for volumes of brain structures to predict age at scan. High importances shown in red, low importances in blue. Left: the original MRI image. Correlation: Pearson correlation coefficient between structure volumes and age at scan. Gray matter regions are the most highly correlated with age. Lasso: Absolute values of lasso regression weights. RFE: Ranking of the features by recursive feature-elimination algorithm.

a. Select four features most predictive of age at scan using the F-value and mutual information and print out their names. Do you obtain the same or different features? Can you explain why?

b. Perform model-based feature selection using the lasso model and fit linear regression to the selected features. Calculate performance of your model. Experiment with different thresholds for lasso coefficients to see which one results in the best performance. Print out the names of the selected features.

c. Fit recursive feature elimination with cross-validation (`RFECV`) and ridge ranking model with `alpha=45` to select features. Fit the ridge model with `alpha=45` to the selected features, calculate performance, and print the number and names of the selected features.

CHAPTER 9

Deep learning basics

Modern deep learning is based on **neural networks**, which are one of the most versatile family of machine learning models. They can perform linear and nonlinear classification, regression, or dimensionality reduction, and are indeed the basis of the incredible success of modern deep learning.

In this chapter we will introduce the basic building blocks necessary for understanding and implementing deep neural networks. Section 9.1 will introduce the concept of an **artificial neuron**, which is the smallest unit from which the neural networks are built. In Sect. 9.2 we will introduce **Pytorch**, the most modern library for implementation and training of the neural networks. We will conclude the chapter with the concept of **single-layer perceptron** in Sect. 9.3. Throughout the chapter we will demonstrate that linear classifiers and regressors are in fact examples of single-layer neural networks. Using these simple examples, we will show how we can create regression, binary, and multi-label classification using neural networks.

9.1. An artificial neuron

Neural networks were inspired by how brains work. They are composed of artificial neurons that interact with each other. Fig. 9.1 shows a diagram of an artificial neuron. Inputs x_j represent sensory information or the activity of other neurons that are connected with this artificial neuron through synapses w_j. The weights w_j multiply the inputs x_j, and therefore represent the strength of the synaptic connections. The incoming signals are then collected in the body of the neuron, and their sum z is passed through an activation function $f(z)$ resulting in the activity (or firing) of the neuron.

The simplest neural network is composed of a single artificial neuron (Fig. 9.1). In this case, the inputs x_j are simply the input features, and the output $\hat{y}$ is the predicted target value or label.

The artificial neuron can be written mathematically as

$$z = \sum_{j=0}^{D} w_j x_j \tag{9.1}$$

$$\hat{y} = f(z), \tag{9.2}$$

where $\mathbf{w} = (w_0, ..., w_D)^T$ are the parameters of the model and index j represents the individual input features. We fit this model by finding the optimal weight vector $\hat{\mathbf{w}}$ that

Machine Learning for Biomedical Applications
https://doi.org/10.1016/B978-0-12-822904-0.00014-5
Copyright © 2024 Elsevier Ltd.
All rights reserved.

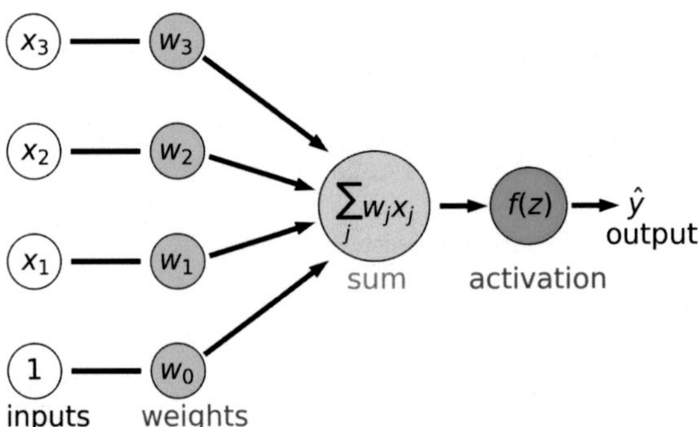

Figure 9.1 An artificial neuron. Inputs x_j are multiplied by learnable weights w_j (synaptic connections). Their sum $z = \sum_j x_j w_j$ is then passed through the activation function $f(z)$ to determine the neuron output $\hat{y}$.

minimizes some suitable loss $L(\mathbf{w})$. We have already seen several examples of artificial neuron models, as we show in the next section.

9.1.1 Artificial neuron examples

Perceptron

The perceptron model that we described in Sect. 4.1.2 is an example of a single artificial neuron binary classifier. For the perceptron model the sum z (Eq. (9.1)) is in fact the decision function $h(\mathbf{x})$ (Eq. 4.1), the activation function $f(z)$ is the *heaviside* function (Fig. 9.2, middle) and the loss function is the perceptron criterion (Eq. (4.1)). The perceptron model is however not commonly used in deep learning because of difficulties with training due to its nondifferentiable activation function.

Linear regression

Linear regression (Sect. 3.1) is an example of a single artificial neuron regressor, where we choose the identity $f(z) = z$ as an activation function (see Fig. 9.2, left) and therefore the sum z is identical to the output $\hat{y}$. The loss function L is the *sum-of-squared-error loss*

$$L(\hat{\mathbf{y}}) = \frac{1}{2} \sum_{i=1}^{N} (y_i - \hat{y}_i)^2, \tag{9.3}$$

where index i represents the individual training samples and $\hat{\mathbf{y}} = (\hat{y}_1, ..., \hat{y}_N)^T$ represents the predicted target values.

Logistic regression

Logistic regression (Sect. 4.1.3) is another example of a single artificial neuron binary classifier. The sum z is the decision function h, and the activation $f(z)$ is the sigmoid function σ, shown in Fig. 9.2, right. The output of the logistic regression single-layer perceptron is not directly the label $\hat{y}_i$, but the probability $\hat{p}_i = f(z_i)$ for class 1, as we explained in Sect. 4.1.3. We use the *cross-entropy loss*

$$L(\hat{\mathbf{p}}) = -\sum_{i=1}^{N}\left[y_i \log(\hat{p}_i) + (1 - y_i)\log(1 - \hat{p}_i)\right] \tag{9.4}$$

to train the logistic regression model. This loss is a function of the predicted probability vector $\hat{\mathbf{p}} = (\hat{p}_1, ..., \hat{p}_N)^T$. It is convex and differentiable and therefore commonly used for deep learning classification. The predicted labels can be obtained by thresholding the probabilities $\hat{p}_i$ at 0.5.

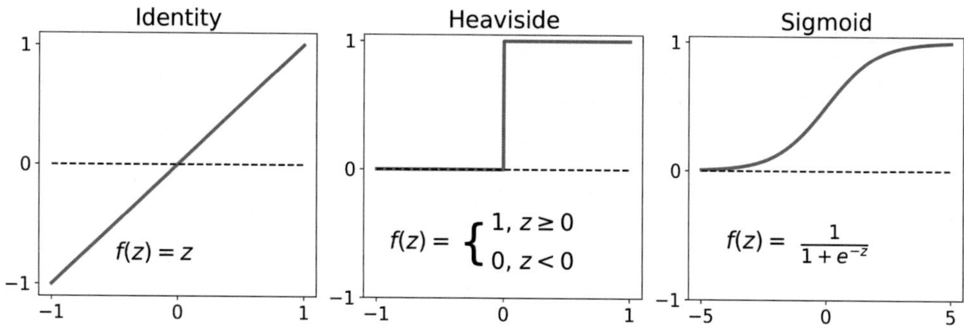

Figure 9.2 Activation functions $f(z)$. Left: identity used in linear regression. Middle: Heaviside used in perceptron. Right: sigmoid used in logistic regression.

9.1.2 Training an artificial neuron

The artificial neuron can be trained using the gradient descent (Eq. 3.8), as explained in Sect. 3.1.2. The gradient descent iteratively updates the weights $\mathbf{w}$ for a number of **epochs**. Each epoch n is split into two steps:

1. **Forward pass: Predict outputs.** Using currently estimated weights $\mathbf{w}^{(n)}$, predict the target values $\hat{y}_i^{(n)}$ (or probabilities $\hat{p}_i^{(n)}$) using Eqs. (9.1) and (9.2):

$$\hat{y}_i^{(n)} = f\left(\sum_{j=0}^{D} w_j^{(n)} x_{ij}\right), \tag{9.5}$$

where x_{ij} is the jth feature of the sample i.

2. **Backward pass: Update model parameters.** Calculate the partial derivatives $\frac{\partial L(\mathbf{w})}{\partial w_j}$ of the loss L with respect to the individual weights w_j with the current estimate of the predictions $\hat{y}_i^{(n)}$ or $\hat{p}_i^{(n)}$, and update the weights using the gradient descent

equation (Eq. (3.8)):

$$w_j^{(n+1)} = w_j^{(n)} - \eta \frac{\partial L(\mathbf{w}^{(n)})}{\partial w_j^{(n)}}. \tag{9.6}$$

To perform the backward pass (Eq. (9.6)), we need to calculate the partial derivatives of the loss with respect to the weights. However, the mean-squared-error loss L for regression (Eq. (9.3)) is a function of predicted target values $\hat{y}_i$ and the cross-entropy loss L for binary classification (Eq. (9.4)) is a function of predicted probabilities $\hat{p}_i$, which we evaluated in the forward pass (Eq. (9.5)). We therefore need to use the sum and chain rules to calculate these derivatives.

The loss $L(\mathbf{w})$ can be written as a sum of losses for the individual samples:

$$L(\mathbf{w}) = \sum_{i=0}^{N} L_i(\mathbf{w}).$$

We can therefore calculate the partial derivatives by first using the sum rule

$$\frac{\partial L(\mathbf{w})}{\partial w_j} = \sum_{i=0}^{N} \frac{\partial L_i(\mathbf{w})}{\partial w_j},$$

followed by the chain rule

$$\frac{\partial L_i(\mathbf{w})}{\partial w_j} = \frac{\partial L_i}{\partial \hat{y}_i} \cdot \frac{\partial \hat{y}_i}{\partial z_i} \cdot \frac{\partial z_i}{\partial w_j} = \frac{\partial L_i}{\partial \hat{y}_i} \cdot \frac{\partial f}{\partial z_i} \cdot x_{ij},$$

where $z_i = \sum_{j=0}^{D} w_j x_{ij}$ (Eq. (9.1)).

Training linear regression

For the linear regression, we have the sum-of-squared-errors loss with

$$L_i = \frac{1}{2}(y_i - \hat{y}_i)^2,$$

and the derivative is

$$\frac{\partial L_i}{\partial \hat{y}_i} = -(y_i - \hat{y}_i),$$

which represents the error in the predicted target value. The activation function f is identity (Fig. 9.2, left), therefore,

$$\frac{\partial f}{\partial z_i} = 1.$$

The partial derivative of the sum-of-squared-error loss with respect to the weights, therefore is

$$\frac{\partial L(\mathbf{w})}{\partial w_j} = -\sum_{i=0}^{N}(y_i - \hat{y}_i)x_{ij}. \tag{9.7}$$

We have already derived a similar equation in a matrix form in Sect. 3.2.4.

Training logistic regression

Logistic regression is trained by minimizing the cross entropy loss with

$$L_i = -y_i \log(\hat{p}_i) - (1 - y_i)\log(1 - \hat{p}_i),$$

and the partial derivative

$$\frac{\partial L_i}{\partial \hat{p}_i} = -\frac{y_i}{\hat{p}_i} + \frac{1 - y_i}{1 - \hat{p}_i} = \frac{-(y_i - \hat{p}_i)}{\hat{p}_i(1 - \hat{p}_i)}.$$

The activation function is sigmoid $f(z) = \sigma(z)$ (Fig. 9.2 right), with the derivative

$$\frac{\partial \sigma}{\partial z_i} = \sigma(z_i)\big(1 - \sigma(z_i)\big) = \hat{p}_i(1 - \hat{p}_i).$$

The partial derivative of the cross entropy loss with respect to the weights, therefore, is

$$\frac{\partial L(\mathbf{w})}{\partial w_j} = -\sum_{i=0}^{N}(y_i - \hat{p}_i)x_{ij}. \tag{9.8}$$

Note the similarity to Eq. (9.7).

From Eqs. (9.7) and (9.8), it becomes obvious why we need the forward pass (Eq. (9.5)) to train the artificial neuron: We need the latest predicted outputs to be able to calculate the derivatives of the loss and update the weights during the backward pass (Eq. (9.6)).

9.1.3 Exercises

1. Describe the following components of the artificial neuron:
   a. Inputs;
   b. Weights;
   c. Activation function;
   d. Output.
2. Which losses and activation functions can you use to create a single artificial neuron classifier and regressor?
3. Describe the main steps for training the artificial neuron.

4. Given an artificial neuron with the sum-of-squared-error loss and sigmoid activation function, calculate the following:
   a. Given the feature vector $\mathbf{x_i} = (x_{i1}, ..., x_{iD})$, give the prediction $\hat{p}_i$.
   b. Given the true label y_i, give the expression for the loss L_i for this sample.
   c. Calculate the derivative of the loss L_i with respect to the weight w_j. Note that derivative of the sigmoid function is $\frac{\partial \sigma(z)}{\partial z} = \sigma(z)(1 - \sigma(z))$.
   d. Give the update equation for the weight w_j of the artificial neuron model.

9.2. Starting with Pytorch

In this section we will introduce the Pytorch environment [33] and implement our first neural network, consisting of a single artificial neuron.

9.2.1 Install Pytorch

Installing Pytorch is very simple. Assuming that you have already installed your Python and Anaconda environments as recommended in Chap. 1, you now need to go to the Pytorch website

pytorch.org/get-started/locally/

The website will automatically detect your system and provide the command for installation that you need to copy to your command line window, which can be accessed for example through the application called Anaconda Prompt. Once you installed Pytorch, you can import it in your Jupyter notebook, or another preferred Python environment using command

```
import torch
```

By default Pytorch will run on the CPU, and this will be sufficient for the example code in this chapter. For more computational intensive deep learning problems, we usually need access to a GPU to speed up computations. To do that, we need to explicitly send our data and models to the available CUDA device. You can check whether you have CUDA available on your computer by calling

```
print('Cuda available:', torch.cuda.is_available())
>>> Cuda available: True
```

9.2.2 PyTorch tensors

PyTorch tensors are multidimensional arrays that are used to store the data and the parameters (weights) of the deep learning models. They are very similar to `NumPy` arrays, but have some additional features, including the ability to run on a GPU, and features to enable automatic differentiation. We can create a random tensor of a particular shape by calling

```
import torch
tensor = torch.rand(2, 2, 2)
print(tensor)
>>> tensor([[[0.9697, 0.8595],
             [0.3722, 0.4119]],
            [[0.1956, 0.0055],
             [0.0683, 0.2933]]])
```

In comparison, the `NumPy` array can be created in very similar way

```
import numpy as np
np_array = np.random.rand(2, 2, 2)
print(np_array)
>>> [[[0.57826831 0.2639664 ]
      [0.95591113 0.67079702]]
     [[0.24742113 0.62599913]
      [0.46188619 0.43755346]]]
```

We can access the elements of tensors through indexing just like the `NumPy` arrays:

```
tensor[0,0,0]
>>> tensor(0.9697),
```

print out the shape:

```
tensor.shape
>>> torch.Size([2, 2, 2]),
```

and easily convert `NumPy` arrays to tensors and the other way:

```
tensor2 = torch.from_numpy(np_array)
np_array2 = tensor.numpy()
```

A useful function to change the shape of the tensor, while not copying the data, is `view`:

```
tensor.view(2,4)
>>> tensor([[0.1443, 0.7539, 0.1976, 0.9701],
            [0.5931, 0.3545, 0.8707, 0.5207]])
```

By default the tensors are stored on CPU:

```
tensor.device
>>> device(type='cpu')
```

but unlike `NumPy` arrays the PyTorch tensors can be sent to the GPU device:

```
if torch.cuda.is_available():
    tensor = tensor.to('cuda')
tensor.device
>>> device(type='cuda', index=0)
```

9.2.3 Autograd

An important feature of PyTorch is that it offers automatic differentiation to enable training of neural networks. If a tensor stores parameters that we want to learn, we can set the `tensor` attribute `requires_grad` to `True`:

```
a = torch.tensor([1.0,2.0], requires_grad=True)
```

Let's say that we want to minimize the sum of squares of the tensor `a`, mathematically written as

$$L(a_1, a_2) = a_1^2 + a_2^2.$$

This can be implemented as

```
b=a**2
loss=b.sum()
```

If we now call the function `loss.backward()`, PyTorch will calculate the gradients

$$\left[\frac{\partial L}{\partial a_1}, \frac{\partial L}{\partial a_2}\right] = \left[\frac{\partial(a_1^2 + a_2^2)}{\partial a_1}, \frac{\partial(a_1^2 + a_2^2)}{\partial a_2}\right] = [2a_1, 2a_2].$$

Because we have set $[a_1, a_2] = [1, 2]$ the gradients will be $[2, 4]$. Let's test it in PyTorch:

```
loss.backward()
print(a.grad)
>>> tensor([2., 4.])
```

PyTorch does automatic differentiation by creating a computational graph, shown for our example in Fig. 9.3, top. When tensors `b` and `loss` are created, PyTorch automatically creates functions `grad_fn` that calculate the gradients during the backward pass:

```
print('b: ', b)
print('loss: ', loss)
>>> b:  tensor([1., 4.], grad_fn=<PowBackward0>)
>>> loss:  tensor(5., grad_fn=<SumBackward0>)
```

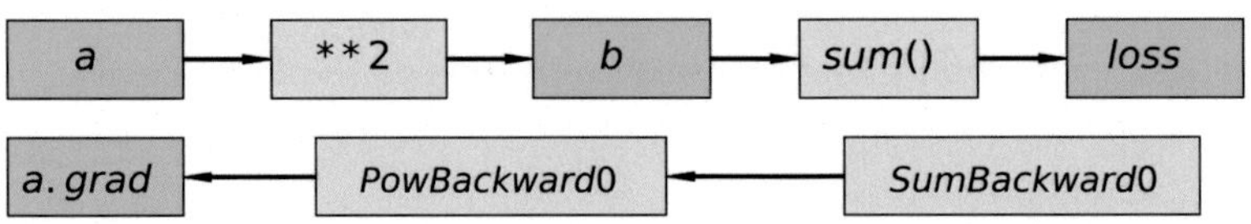

Figure 9.3 Automatic differentionation in PyTorch (Autograd). Top: computational graph. Bottom: computation of the gradients during the backward pass.

When the function `loss.backward()` is called, the functions stored in `grad_fn` will calculate the gradients by moving backward through the computational graph, as shown in Fig. 9.3, bottom.

Note that gradients `grad` are only evaluated for the leaf nodes of the computational graph, and these leaf nodes do not have the gradient function `grad_fn` because there are no gradients to propagate further. We run the function `backward()` on the root of the computational graph (in our case `loss`), which must be a scalar. Additionally, all tensors must be of type `float`.

9.2.4 Creating models in PyTorch

Regression in PyTorch

Now we are ready to create our first neural network model. PyTorch offers the module `torch.nn` with functionality to create neural network models with various architectures. Our first model will be a single-neuron linear regressor with only one linear layer, which implements Eq. (9.1):

```
torch.nn.Linear(D, 1)
```

Note that this layer has D inputs and one output. We will now revisit the univariate regression example of predicting the brain volume of the newborn baby depending on their gestational age, introduced in Sect. 2.1.1. For this reason our model will have only one input feature $D = 1$.

Our neural network, a single artificial neuron regressor, which we will be named `ANRegressor`, will be derived from the base class `torch.nn.Module` as follows

```
import torch.nn as nn
class ANRegressor(nn.Module):
    def __init__(self):
        super(ANRegressor, self).__init__()
        self.layer = nn.Linear(1, 1)
    def forward(self, x):
        x = self.layer(x)
        return x
```

This model implements two functions:

- `__init__` to construct the model, which calls the base class constructor using the function `super` and defines the neural network architecture;
- `forward` to perform the forward pass, which calculates the output of the network.

The backward pass does not need to be implemented because it is performed automatically by Autograd. We can create our neural network model by calling the constructor and storing it in a variable `net`

```
net = ANRegressor()
print(net)
>>> ANRegressor(
    (layer): Linear(in_features=1, out_features=1,
                    bias=True)
    )
```

We can print the learnable parameters of the network:

```
    for parameter in net.parameters():
        print(parameter)
    >>> Parameter containing:
        tensor([[-0.3753]], requires_grad=True)
    >>> Parameter containing:
        tensor([0.1840], requires_grad=True)
```

These parameters correspond to weight w_0 and w_1 of the univariate linear regression model $\hat{y} = w_0 + w_1 x$.

Finally, we need to define the **loss function** which will be minimized to fit the model. The most common loss for regression models is the mean-squared-error loss (Eq. (9.3))—and this loss function is available in `torch.nn` module as:

```
loss_function = torch.nn.MSELoss()
```

Binary classification in PyTorch

Similarly, we can also create an artificial neuron classifier that implements logistic regression. For this we will also need one linear layer, just like for the linear regression, but in addition to that we need a sigmoid activation function, which is available at `torch.nn` module as

```
    torch.nn.Sigmoid()
```

The activation function is added to the `__init__` and `forward` functions:

```
        class ANClassifier(nn.Module):
        def __init__(self):
                super(ANClassifier, self).__init__()
                self.layer = nn.Linear(2, 1)
                self.sigmoid = nn.Sigmoid()


        def forward(self, x):
                x = self.layer(x)
                x = self.sigmoid(x)
                return x
```

We can create an instance of a binary classifier `net2` as

```
net2 = ANClassifier()
print(net2)
>>> ANClassifier(
    (layer): Linear(in_features=2, out_features=1,
                    bias=True)
    (Sigmoid): Sigmoid()
    )
```

Note that in this case we assume two input features and one output feature for the linear layer, so this network is suitable for the binary classification example from Sect. 2.1.1 to predict heart failure from the ejection fraction and global longitudinal strain. The classifier is trained by minimizing a binary cross-entropy loss (Eq. (9.4)), which can be defined in PyTorch as follows:

```
loss_function2 = torch.nn.BCELoss()
```

9.2.5 Training models in PyTorch

Once we have created our neural network model, we need to fit it to our data. We will demonstrate the training using linear regression to predict brain volume from the gestational age of a baby, introduced in Sect. 2.1.1. Training binary classification model requires the same steps as regression.

Prepare training data

First, we will load the data into `NumPy` arrays and standardize the features using `StandardScaler` as usual. Note that both the feature matrix `X` and the target vector `y` are reshaped into 2D arrays.

```
import pandas as pd
from sklearn.preprocessing import StandardScaler
data = pd.read_csv('neonatal_brain_volumes.csv').to_numpy()
X = StandardScaler().fit_transform(data[:,0].reshape(-1,1))
y = data[:,1].reshape(-1,1)
```

We need to convert the feature matrix `X` and target vector `y` to PyTorch tensors and make sure that they are of type `float`.

```
X = torch.from_numpy(X).float()
y = torch.from_numpy(y).float()
```

Define the optimizer

Next, we define the optimizer as a stochastic gradient descent with learning rate $\eta = 0.2$ (see Sect. 3.1.2). The optimizers are available in the module `torch.optim`:

```
optimizer = torch.optim.SGD(net.parameters(), lr=0.2)
```

Training

The training of the network is performed through a predefined number of iterations called **epochs**. During each epoch, we update the network using gradient descent. The following code shows how the training is implemented. For our simple case of linear regression, we perform the training in a `for` loop with 10 epochs:

```
epochs = 10
for n in range(epochs):
    # 1. Clear gradients
    optimizer.zero_grad()
    # 2. Forward pass: predict outputs
    prediction = net(X)
    # 3. Compute loss
    loss = loss_function(prediction, y)
    # 4. Backward pass: calculate gradients
    loss.backward()
    # 5. Update network parameters
    optimizer.step()
```

In step 1, the gradients are set to zero. In step 2, the forward pass predicts the outputs $\hat{y}_i^{(n)}$ (Eq. (9.5)). In step 3, the MSE loss between the true and predicted targets is calculated using Eq. (9.3). In step 4, the backward pass calculates the gradients of the MSE loss (Eq. (9.7)). Finally, in step 5, the network parameters w_j are updated using Eq. (9.6).

Plot the results

Fig. 9.4 illustrates how the network fitted the model to the data to predict brain volume from the normalized age of a baby. We can plot the fitted regression model as follows:

```
import matplotlib.pyplot as plt
# plot data
plt.scatter(X, y)
# predict outputs
prediction=net(X)
# plot model
plt.plot(X, prediction.data,'r')
```

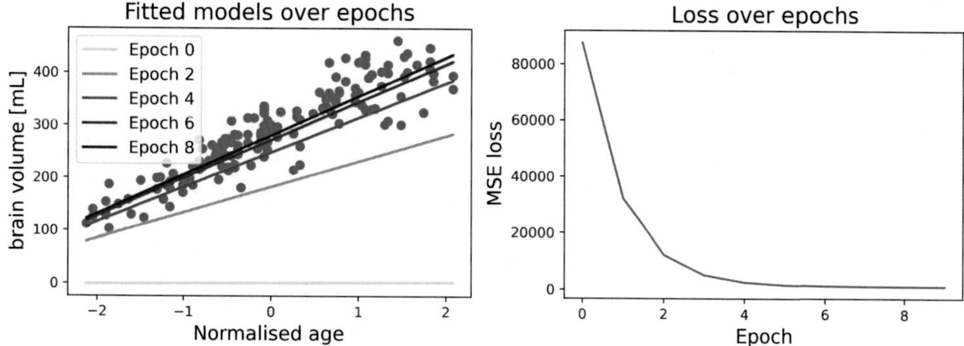

Figure 9.4 Linear regression in PyTorch. Left: Fitted linear model calculated in different epochs. The model fits the data better as the number of epochs increases. Right: MSE loss is descreasing with increasing epochs.

Note that we can plot the PyTorch tensors that do not require gradients directly, but the predicted target values had to be accessed through `prediction.data` because the tensor `prediction` requires gradients.

Evaluation

The performance of the model needs to be evaluated on the test set that has been excluded from the training. Let's assume that that our test set consists of feature matrix `X_test` and target vector `y_test`, which are both PyTorch tensors. We can then predict outputs on the test set as

```
prediction_test = net(X_test)
```

and calculate the loss on the test set as

```
mse = loss_function(prediction_test, y_test).data
```

If we wish to evaluate the root-mean-square error (for regression models only), we can simply take the square root of the mean squared error loss

```
rmse = torch.sqrt(mse)
```

9.2.6 Summary: creating and training neural networks

Here, we recap the steps we need to train a neural network in PyTorch:

1. Convert the training data to Pytorch tensors of type `float`.
2. Define the model architecture derived from `nn.Module`:
   a. In function `__init__` define the layers and parameters.
   b. In function `forward` define the operations of the forward pass.
3. Create an instance of the network, loss function, and optimizer.

4. Create the training loop over the epochs. Inside the loop:
   a. Clear gradients: `optimizer.zero_grad();`
   b. Forward pass: predict the output of the network, `prediction=net(inputs);`
   c. Calculate the loss `loss=loss_func(prediction, outputs);`
   d. Backward pass: calculate the gradients `loss.backward();`
   e. Update the weights using the optimiser `optimizer.step()`.

9.2.7 Exercises

1. Practice working with PyTorch tensors.[1] First, create and display a PyTorch tensor:
   - Create a NumPy array with values `[1,...,12]`. *Hint:* You can use `np.linspace`;
   - Convert it to a PyTorch tensor;
   - Print out the tensor as a matrix of size 3×4.

   Next, learn how to concatenate two Pytorch tensors:
   - Create two random Pytorch tensors with sizes $1 \times 2 \times 4 \times 4$ and $1 \times 5 \times 4 \times 4$;
   - Concatenate them on the second axis using `torch.cat` (*Hint:* axis are numbered from 0);
   - Print the dimensions of the concatenated tensor.
2. Practice using the Autograd feature of PyTorch:
   - Create a Pytorch tensor `y` with values `[0,1]`;
   - Create another Pytorch tensor `p` with values `[0.5,0.5]`. Set `requires_grad` to `True`;
   - Implement cross-entropy loss $L = -y_0 \log(p_0) - y_1 \log(p_1)$;
   - Print out the loss value;
   - Calculate the gradients of the loss with respect to `p` and print them out;
   - Verify that they are correct.
3. Load the file *neonatal_brain_volumes.csv*. The file contains the age of the baby in the first column and the brain volume in the second column. Follow the PyTorch code in this section to fit a linear regression model to predict brain volume from the age. Plot the training data and the fitted model.
4. Load the file *heart_failure_data.csv*. The file contains the cardiac indices EF and GLS in the first two columns. The third column contains a binary label indicating the diagnosis of heart failure (label 1). Implement a binary linear classifier in PyTorch to predict heart failure from EF and GLS, using the code given in this section. Plot the classification result.

[1] The skeleton code, solutions and data for excercises 1-4 are available from github.com/MachineLearningBiomedicalApplications/notebooks.

9.3. Single-layer perceptron

A single-layer perceptron consists of multiple neurons organized in one layer. These neurons share the same input features, but each of them produces a different output, as illustrated in Fig. 9.5.

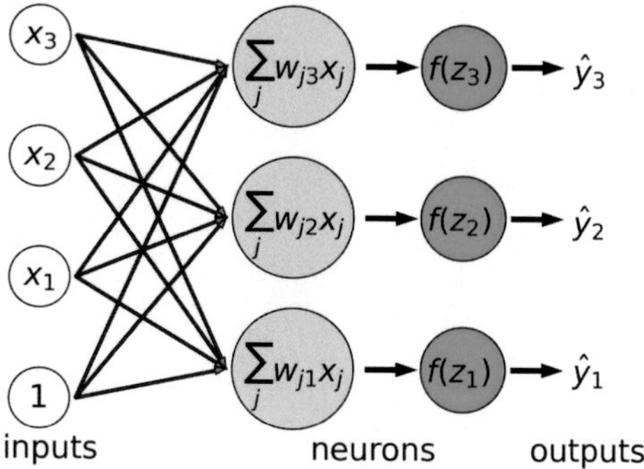

Figure 9.5 A single-layer perceptron consisting of three artificial neurons. The model has three inputs and three outputs. Each neuron k is mathematically defined as $\hat{y}_k = f(z_k)$, $z_k = \sum_j w_{jk}x_j$. For simplicity, the individual weights have been dropped from the diagram as compared to the diagram of the artificial neuron in Fig. 9.1.

The multi-output single-layer perceptron model can be mathematically written as

$$z_k = \sum_{j=0}^{D} w_{jk}x_j \tag{9.9}$$

$$\hat{y}_k = f(z_k), \quad k = 1, ..., K, \tag{9.10}$$

where the neuron k has the weight vector $(w_{0k}, ..., w_{Dk})^T$ and the output $\hat{y}_k$. Eq. (9.9) can be conveniently rewritten in a matrix formulation as

$$\mathbf{z} = \mathbf{W}\mathbf{x}, \tag{9.11}$$

where the matrix $\mathbf{W}$ with shape $K \times (D+1)$ represents the weights of the neurons, K is the number of outputs in the output vector $\hat{\mathbf{y}} = (\hat{y}_1, ..., \hat{y}_K)^T$, and D is the number of input features arranged in the feature vector $\mathbf{x} = (1, x_1, ..., x_D)$. Eq. (9.11) represents one **linear layer**, also called a **fully connected layer**, because all inputs contribute to all outputs. The linear layer with D inputs and K outputs (Eq. (9.11)) is implemented in PyTorch as

```
torch.nn.Linear(D, K)
```

Each output of the linear layer z_k is passed through the same activation function f (Eq. (9.10)) to obtain $\hat{y}_k$.

9.3.1 Training the single-layer perceptron

The training is performed using the forward and backward pass, similarly to the artificial neuron explained in Sect. 9.1.2. In the forward pass we evaluate the predicted output vector $\hat{\mathbf{y}}$ using

$$\hat{y}_{ik}^{(n)} = f\left(\sum_{j=0}^{D} w_{jk}^{(n)} x_{ij}\right), \tag{9.12}$$

and in the backward pass we update the weights according to

$$w_{jk}^{(n+1)} = w_{jk}^{(n)} - \eta \frac{\partial L(\mathbf{W}^{(n)})}{\partial w_{jk}^{(n)}}. \tag{9.13}$$

These equations are direct extensions of Eqs. (9.5) and (9.6).

9.3.2 Multi-label classification

An important application of the single-layer perceptron is multi-label linear classification, such as *multinomial logistic regression* (Sect. 4.1.4). By fitting a single decision function h to the training data, we can only perform binary classification. We need multiple decision functions h_k (Eq. 4.3) to perform multi-label classification. Each of these decision functions corresponds to one artificial neuron, with $z_k = h_k$.

The activation function for multinomial logistic regression is **softmax** defined as

$$\hat{p}_k = \frac{e^{z_k}}{\sum_{j=1}^{K} e^{z_j}}$$

Note that softmax is different from the other activation functions because it uses all the linear-layer outputs z_j, $j = 1, ..., K$ to calculate the output class probabilites $\hat{p}_k$. This is visualized in Fig. 9.6, left.

We have discussed in Sect. 4.1.4 that multinomial logistic regression is optimized using the **cross-entropy loss**

$$-\sum_{i=1}^{N}\sum_{k=1}^{K} y_{ik} \ln p_k(\mathbf{x}_i),$$

where the labels y_i have to be converted to **one-hot vectors** $(y_{i1}, ..., y_{iK})^T$ where y_{ik} is 1 if label $y_i = k$ and zero otherwise. This way they can be related to predicted probability vectors $(p_1(\mathbf{x}_i), ..., p_K(\mathbf{x}_i))^T$ where $\mathbf{x}_i = (x_{i1}, ..., x_{iD})^T$ is the feature vector of a training

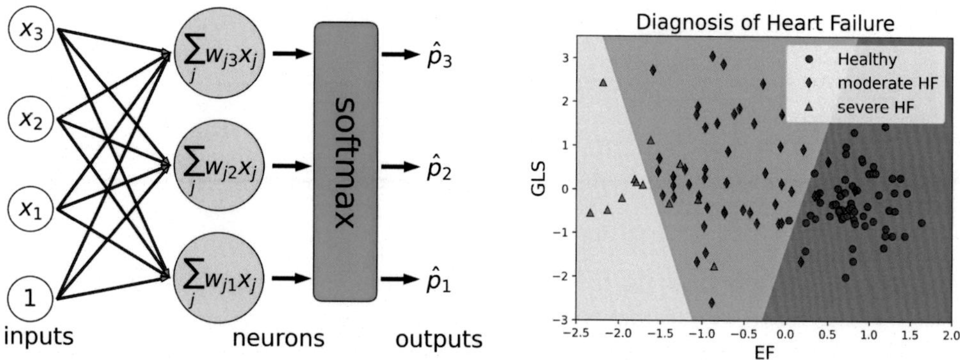

Figure 9.6 Multinomial logistic regression as a single-layer perceptron. Left: the network diagram. The input features x_j are passed through a linear layer composed of three neurons, one for each class label. The outputs of the linear layer z_k are passed through the softmax to convert them to the output class probabilities $\hat{p_k}$. Right: the result of a multi-label classification that predicts a 3-class heart failure diagnosis (healthy, moderate, and severe) from two cardiac imaging indices (EF and GLS), implemented in PyTorch as a network with a single linear layer, softmax, and the cross-entropy loss.

sample i. An example of one-hot encoding is shown here:

$$\begin{pmatrix} 0 \\ 1 \\ 2 \\ 1 \end{pmatrix} \rightarrow \begin{pmatrix} 1 & 0 & 0 \\ 0 & 1 & 0 \\ 0 & 0 & 1 \\ 0 & 1 & 0 \end{pmatrix}$$

9.3.3 Linear multi-label classification in PyTorch

Network architecture

To implement a linear multi-label classifier in PyTorch, we need to create a class with one linear layer, with the number of output features equal to the number of labels. For example, to predict 3-class diagnosis of heart failure (healthy, mild, or severe) from two cardiac indices (EF and GLS), visualized in Fig. 9.6, right, we need a network composed of one linear layer with two input and three output features, which we can implement as follows:

```
class MultiLabelClassifier(nn.Module):
    def __init__(self):
        super(MultiLabelClassifier, self).__init__()
        self.layer = nn.Linear(2, 3)
    def forward(self, x):
        x = self.layer(x)
        return x
```

```
net = MultiLabelClassifier()
```

Cross-entropy loss

The loss will be set to cross-entropy using the in-built function

```
loss_function = torch.nn.CrossEntropyLoss()
```

Note that we did not include the softmax activation in our network. This is because `CrossEntropyLoss` includes the softmax. For numerical reasons, it actually implements log-softmax `torch.nn.LogSoftmax` followed by negative log-likelihood loss `torch.nn.NLLLoss`.

Training

The classification network is trained using the same code as shown in Sect. 9.2.5 for regression:

```
optimizer = torch.optim.SGD(net.parameters(), lr=0.2)
epochs = 500
for i in range(epochs):
    optimizer.zero_grad()
    prediction = net(X)
    loss = loss_function(prediction, y)
    loss.backward()
    optimizer.step()
```

The forward pass through the network `net(X)` returns the outputs of the linear layer $\mathbf{z}$ (Eq. (9.11)), which are often called **logits**. We can convert logits `prediction` to labels $\hat{\mathbf{y}}$ directly by taking the maximum

```
    y_pred = torch.argmax(prediction, dim=1)
```

If we wish to predict the probabilities $\hat{\mathbf{p}}$, we can convert the logits as follows:

The `loss_function` is an instance of the `CrossEntropyLoss`, which requires logits as the first argument and class labels numbered from 0 to $K-1$ (not one-hot) as the second argument. Note that logits `prediction` have to be of type `float`, while the labels `y` must be `long`. The result of the training for our example of prediction of 3-class heart failure is shown in Fig. 9.6, right.

Predicting on new data

We will now show how we can use the network to predict the label on a new datapoint. In the following example code, we have created a new tensor `x` of the correct shape and type so that we can apply the forward pass that predicts the logits z. Note that logits can take both positive and negative values. After we pass them through softmax, we obtain class probabilities p, which are between 0 and 1 and add up to 1. The predicted label y corresponds to the class with the highest probability:

```
# create input feature vector
x = torch.tensor((0,0)).reshape(1,2).float()
print('Input x: ',x)
# predict logits
z = net(x)
print('Logits z: ', z.data)
# probabilities
p=torch.nn.functional.softmax(z,dim=1)
print('Probabilities p: ', p.data)
# labels
y = torch.argmax(z, dim=1)
print('Label y: ', y)
>>> Input x:  tensor([[0., 0.]])
>>> Logits z:  tensor([[ 0.18,  1.30, -2.30]])
>>> Probabilities p:  tensor([[0.24, 0.74, 0.02]])
>>> Label y:  tensor([1])
```

Evaluating performance

PyTorch does not provide functionality for evaluating the performance of the models. We therefore have to implement it ourselves or use another package, such as scikit-learn. Here we show how to implement calculation of accuracy. First we perform forward pass to obtain predicted logits and calculate the predicted labels y_pred. The accuracy can be easily evaluated by comparing predicted and true labels, converting the logical values to float and calculating the mean value:

```
pred=net(X)
y_pred = torch.argmax(pred, dim=1)
accuracy = (y_pred==y).float().mean()
print(accuracy)
>>> tensor(0.91)
```

Of course, we need to evaluate the accuracy on training and validation sets to monitor training, and, after the model is trained, we calculate the final performance on the test set that was completely excluded from the training. We will provide full details through a real-world example in Sect. 10.3.

9.3.4 Limitations of the single-layer perceptron

The key limitation of the models presented in this chapter is that they consist of a single linear layer. This means, that these models are inherently linear and therefore might not adapt well to complex real-world problems. In Chap. 10 we will show how this limitation can be overcome by building networks of neurons organized in multiple layers, which are interleaved with nonlinear activation functions. Such deep nonlinear models are extremely flexible and can adapt to any real-world situation. This flexibility is one of the key factors in the success of the modern deep learning.

9.3.5 Exercises

1. What is the main difference between a single neuron and a single-layer perceptron?
2. Describe the activation function and the loss that we use to create multi-label classification.
3. Load dataset *heart_failure_data_complete.csv*.[2] Create and train a multi-label single-layer perceptron classifier in PyTorch, to diagnose no, moderate, or severe heart failure from EF and QRS. Calculate the accuracy and plot the classification result on the training set. Follow the code from Sect. 9.3.3.

[2] The data, skeleton code and solution are available from github.com/MachineLearningBiomedicalApplications/notebooks.

CHAPTER 10

Fully connected neural networks

The flexibility of the neural networks comes from combining many artificial neurons into a single machine-learning model organized in multiple layers. In fact, neural networks are universal approximators, and can learn a good approximation of a function of any complexity, given a sufficient number of learnable parameters.

In this chapter we will show how we can build flexible **fully connected neural networks**. We will introduce the architecture of fully connected neural networks in Sect. 10.1. In Sect. 10.2 we will describe how neural networks are trained using **backpropagation** [40]. In the final section 10.3 we will show a complete deep learning solution for prediction of age from the brain connectivity in newborn babies.

10.1. Fully connected network architecture

In Chap. 9 we described in detail an artificial neuron (Sect. 9.1) and how multiple neurons can be organized in a single linear layer to produce multiple outputs, resulting in a **single-layer perceptron** model (Sect. 9.3). Multiple output features allow us to stack several layers of neurons, resulting in a **multilayer perceptron** model, as illustrated in Fig. 10.1. If we add nonlinear activation functions between the layers, we will be able to create flexible nonlinear models and overcome the in-built linearity of single-layer perceptrons. If the resulting network has at least three layers, we obtain a **fully connected deep neural network**.

10.1.1 Multilayer perceptron

A major limitation of the single-layer perceptron is that it is a linear model, and therefore not suitable for complex nonlinear machine-learning problems. In Fig. 10.2, left, we can see that the single-layer perceptron fails to separate co-centric circles, which requires a highly nonlinear boundary. We can obtain more complex models by **stacking** multiple linear layers, which means that the output of the previous layer is the input of the following layer. The resulting **multilayer perceptron** is shown in Fig. 10.1. Importantly, we can obtain nonlinear models only if we interleave the linear layers with nonlinear activation functions. This approach allows us to separate the co-centric circles, as seen in Fig. 10.2, middle and right.

10.1.2 Stacking layers of neurons

Single layer-perceptron models can be stacked one after another, to produce a more complex multilayer perceptron model. We will call the outputs of the layer l **activa-**

Machine Learning for Biomedical Applications
https://doi.org/10.1016/B978-0-12-822904-0.00015-7
Copyright © 2024 Elsevier Ltd.
All rights reserved.

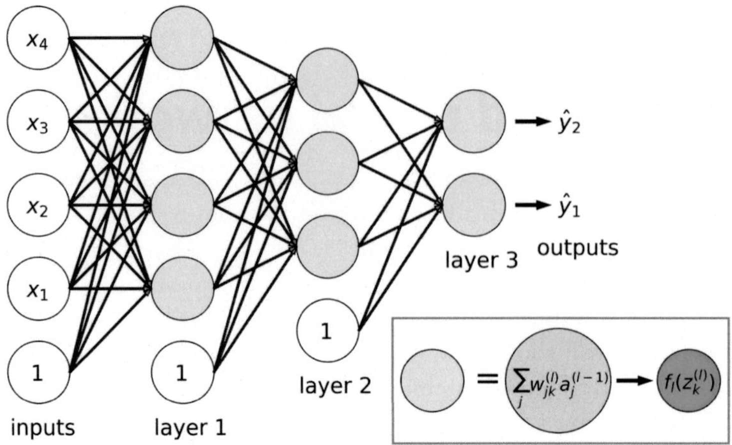

Figure 10.1 An example of a fully connected deep neural network, which is a multilayer perceptron with three layers. Yellow circles correspond to the individual artificial neurons (Fig. 9.1), and each layer of neurons corresponds to a single-layer perceptron (Fig. 9.5). For each layer l, the inputs $a_j^{(l-1)}$ are the outputs of the previous layer $l-1$. The outputs of the layer l are calculated as $a_k^{(l)} = f_l(z_k^{(l)})$, $z_k^{(l)} = \sum_j w_{jk}^{(l)} a_j^{(l-1)}$, where f_l is the activation function for layer l and the weights $w_{jk}^{(l)}$ are the learnable parameters of the layer l.

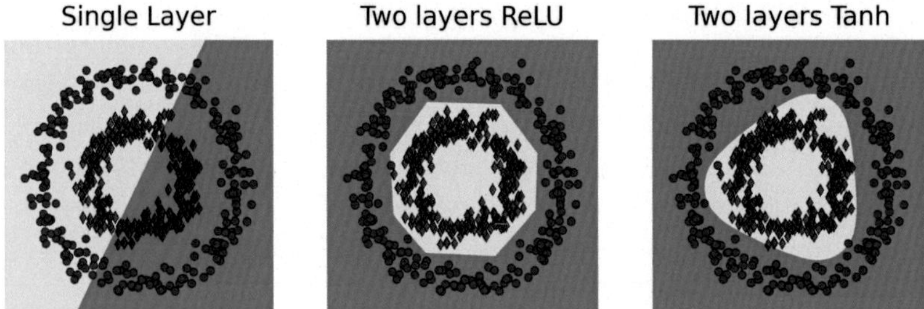

Figure 10.2 Comparison of single-layer and multilayer perceptrons for highly nonlinear binary classification. Left: Single-layer perceptron failed because it is only able to find a linear decision boundary. Middle: Multilayer perceptron with two layers and a nonlinear activation function (ReLU) successfully separated the circles with a nonlinear boundary. Right: Multilayer perceptron with two layers and Tanh activation also succeeded. Note that ReLU results in a piece-wise linear boundary, while Tanh produces a smooth boundary.

tions, and denote them $a_k^{(l)}$. The learnable weights of the layer l will be denoted $w_{jk}^{(l)}$. The mathematical equations for the layer l with D_l outputs can be derived directly from the equations for the single-layer perceptron (Eqs. (9.9) and (9.10)) as follows:

$$z_k^{(l)} = \sum_{j=0}^{D_{l-1}} w_{jk}^{(l)} a_j^{(l-1)} \tag{10.1}$$

$$a_k^{(l)} = f_l\left(z_k^{(l)}\right), \quad k = 1, ..., D_l. \tag{10.2}$$

Note that the layer l needs to have the same number of inputs D_{l-1} as the number of outputs of the layer $l-1$. Inputs of the first layer $l=1$ are the input features x_j. The outputs of the last layer will depend on the type of the neural network model. If it is a regressor, we will have an identity activation, and the outputs will be the predicted target values $\hat{y}_k$. If it is a classifier, we will have a sigmoid or softmax activation, and the outputs will be predicted probabilities $\hat{p}_k$ for each class k.

10.1.3 Activation functions

We have already introduced several activation functions (identity, Heaviside, sigmoid and softmax)—see Fig. 9.2. These functions are most useful after the final linear layer of the neural network to design regressors and classifiers.

The most common activation function placed between the successive layers of the neural network is a **Rectified Linear Unit (ReLU)**, shown in Fig. 10.3, left. Because this is a piece-wise linear function, the resulting function represented by the whole neural network will also be piece-wice linear, as shown in Fig. 10.2, middle. While this function is very simple, combining multiple layers of neurons allows modeling of very complex piece-wise linear functions that can approximate a function of any complexity, given a large enough number of artificial neurons.

The popularity of ReLU is partly due to its efficient computation. However, it can introduce a **vanishing gradient problem**, because, once the value $z_k^{(l)}$ turns negative, the gradient will become zero and the neuron will stop being active. This problem has been addressed by introducing a **Leaky ReLU** (Fig. 10.3, middle), which has a small gradient for the negative values and therefore neurons will not die.

An alternative nonlinear activation function is **Tanh** (Fig. 10.3, right), which produces nonlinear functions (see Fig. 10.2, right). Unlike Leaky ReLU, the Tanh activation function also suffers from vanishing gradients for large negative and positive values.

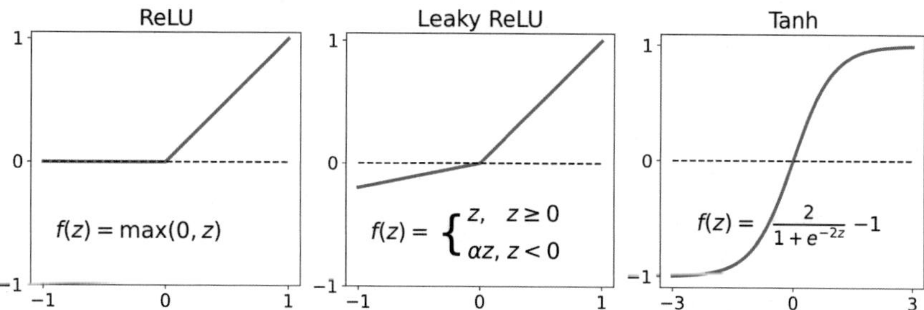

Figure 10.3 Activation functions $f(z)$. Left: Rectified linear unit (ReLU). Middle: Leaky ReLU. Right: Tanh.

10.1.4 Multilayer perceptron architecture in PyTorch

We will now show how we can create the multi-layer network architecture in PyTorch. To separate the circles in Fig. 10.1, we will create a multilayer perceptron classifier with two layers, implemented by the class `MLPClassifier`. The first layer has two inputs, defined by the dimension of the input data, and six outputs. The second layer has six inputs, which are the outputs of the first layer, and one output because this is a binary classifier. In between the two layers, we place a nonlinear activation function ReLU. The output of the second layer is passed through a sigmoid activation function to enable binary classification. Finally, we create an instance of the network `net`:

```
import torch.nn as nn
class MLPClassifier(nn.Module):
    def __init__(self):
        super(MLPClassifier, self).__init__()
        self.layer1 = nn.Linear(2, 6)
        self.relu = nn.ReLU()
        self.layer2 = nn.Linear(6, 1)
        self.sigmoid = nn.Sigmoid()

    def forward(self, x):
        x = self.layer1(x)
        x = self.relu(x)
        x = self.layer2(x)
        x = self.sigmoid(x)
        return x

net = MLPClassifier()
```

10.2. Training neural networks

10.2.1 Training a multilayer perceptron

To train the multilayer perceptron and also deep neural networks in general, we need to evaluate the gradients with respect to learnable weights $w_{jk}^{(l)}$ in all layers l, so that we can update them at each iteration or epoch, just as we have done with single-layer perceptron (Eq. (9.13)). We do that by calculating the gradients of the weights iteratively, starting from the final layer M and working our way towards the lower layers. This is called **backpropagation** [40]. We will give the mathematical details of backpropagation in Sect. 10.2.3. In practice, the backpropagation is performed in PyTorch automatically by Autograd (see Sect. 9.2.3).

One of the common ways to optimize neural networks is using **Stochastic Gradient Descent**, described in Sect. 3.1.2. In fact, the training is performed in **mini-batches**, which are randomly selected subsets of training samples. If a batch gradient was used (e.g., we would use all samples at each iteration), this would result in unacceptable computational burden because of large number of samples needed for the training of deep neural networks. Additionally, stochasticity can help the algorithm escape from suboptimal local minima. The training can be further sped up by adding **momentum**, which is composed of gradients collected from the past iterations, to stabilize the gradient descent path, and thus enable a higher learning rate. One of the popular variants of the optimizers that use momentum is **Adaptive Moment Estimation (Adam)**.

10.2.2 Training a multilayer perceptron in PyTorch

We will now show how we can fit the multilayer perceptron model that we constructed in Sect. 10.1.4 to separate co-centric circles, as shown in Fig. 10.2, middle. First, we generate the dataset in scikit-learn:

```
from sklearn.datasets import make_circles
X,y = make_circles(n_samples=500,factor=0.5,noise=0.08)
```

Next, we prepare the data for training by converting them to PyTorch tensors of type `float` and reshaping `y` into 2D:

```
import torch
X = torch.from_numpy(X).float()
y = torch.from_numpy(y.reshape(-1,1)).float()
```

To perform training, we create a function `train`. First, we define the binary cross-entropy loss and stochastic gradient-descent optimizer. Note that we use momentum, which allows us to increase the learning rate and train the network in as little as 100 epochs. The remainder of the training follows the same steps as previously shown for a single-layer perceptron. Finally, we call the function `train` to fit the network to the dataset `X,y`:

```
def train(net, X, y):
    loss_function = nn.BCELoss()
    optimizer = torch.optim.SGD(net.parameters(),
                                lr=2,
                                momentum=0.75)
    epochs = 100
    for i in range(epochs):
        optimizer.zero_grad()
        prediction = net(X)
        loss = loss_function(prediction, y)
```

```
        loss.backward()
        optimizer.step()
    return net

train(net,X,y)
```

To visualize the results of the trained network, we predict the labels on the training data, so that we can see whether the network managed to separate the circles. The network predicts the probabilities $\hat{p}_i$ for the positive class:

```
p=net(X)
```

We obtain the labels by thresholding the probabilities at 0.5, converting them to integer values of type `long` and reshaping to 1D vector using `view`:

```
y_pred=(p>0.5).long().view(-1)
```

We can visualize the samples by different colors and markers based on the class of the predicted labels as follows:

```
import matplotlib.pyplot as plt
plt.plot(X[y_pred==0,0],X[y_pred==0,1],'bo')
plt.plot(X[y_pred==1,0],X[y_pred==1,1],'rd')
```

10.2.3 Backpropagation

In this section we provide an in-depth mathematical explanation of the backpropagation algorithm. In Sects. 9.1.2 and 9.3.1, we have shown how the single-layer neural network can be trained in two steps—by first predicting the network outputs using the current estimate of the weights in the forward pass (Eq. (9.5)) and then updating the weights of the network (Eq. (9.6)) based on the errors between the predicted and desired outputs (Eqs. (9.7) and (9.8)) in the backward pass. While expanding the forward pass to multiple layers is straightforward (Eqs. (10.1) and (10.2)), the backward pass is slightly more complicated because the loss L is directly calculated only from the errors in outputs $a_k^{(M)}$ of the final layer M. In order to calculate the gradients of the weights in all the different layers, we will backpropagate the output errors from the final layer M to the lower layers.

How backpropagation works

To calculate how the network weights need to be updated to decrease the loss L_i for a training sample i, we will keep track of the quantities $\delta_{ik}^{(l)}$ defined as the gradient of the loss L_i with respect to the *total input* $z_{ik}^{(l)} = \sum_{j=0}^{D_{l-1}} w_{jk}^{(l)} a_{ij}^{(l-1)}$ of the neuron k in the layer l

(Eq. (10.1)):

$$\delta_{ik}^{(l)} = \frac{\partial L_i}{\partial z_{ik}^{(l)}}.$$

The derivatives with respect to the weights $w_{jk}^{(l)}$ can be easily calculated from $\delta_{ik}^{(l)}$ using the chain rule:

$$\frac{\partial L_i}{\partial w_{jk}^{(l)}} = \frac{\partial L_i}{\partial z_{ik}^{(l)}} \cdot \frac{\partial z_k^{(l)}}{\partial w_{jk}^{(l)}} = \delta_{ik}^{(l)} . a_{ij}^{(l-1)}.$$

Once we have the weight gradients, we can update the weights using classical gradient descent (Eq. (10.7)) or another numerical technique, such as momentum.

We will start the backpropagation by evaluating $\delta_{ik}^{(M)}$ for the last layer M:

$$\delta_{ik}^{(M)} = \frac{\partial L_i}{\partial z_{ik}^{(M)}} = \frac{\partial L_i}{\partial a_{ik}^{(M)}} \frac{\partial f_M}{\partial z_{ik}^{(M)}}.$$

The value of $\delta_{ik}^{(M)}$ will depend on the particular choice of the loss function L and the activation function f_M. For example, for the regression with the sum of squared-errors loss and the identity activation, we simply obtain *errors in the predicted outputs* $\hat{y}_{ik} = a_{ik}^{(M)}$ compared to the expected outputs y_i:

$$\delta_{ik}^{(M)} = a_{ik}^{(M)} - y_{ik}.$$

Interestingly, the same result is obtained for the binary cross-entropy loss and the sigmoid activation function. For more details of how to calculate these derivatives, refer to Sect. 9.1.2.

We will now show how we can backpropagate the output errors $\delta_{ik}^{(M)}$ into the other layers. We will use the chain rule to express $\delta_{ij}^{(l)}$ using $\delta_{ik}^{(l+1)}$:

$$\delta_{ij}^{(l)} = \frac{\partial L_i}{\partial z_{ij}^{(l)}} = \sum_{k=1}^{D_{l+1}} \frac{\partial L_i}{\partial z_{ik}^{(l+1)}} \cdot \frac{\partial z_{ik}^{(l+1)}}{\partial z_{ij}^{(l)}} = \sum_{k=1}^{D_{l+1}} \delta_{ik}^{(l+1)} . f'_{l+1} . w_{jk}^{(l+1)},$$

where $f'_{l+1} = \frac{\partial f_{l+1}}{\partial z_j^{(l+1)}}$. We can therefore calculate the output errors $\delta_{ij}^{(l)}$ propagated to layer l by summing up the output errors $\delta_{ik}^{(l+1)}$ weighted by the weights and the derivative of the activation function for the layer $l+1$.

The training algorithm

Training of the neural network can be summarized as follows:
For each iteration n and for each sample i:

1. **Forward pass:** Using current estimated weights $w_{jk}^{(l,n)}$, predict the activations $a_{ik}^{(l,n)}$ for sample i, starting from the first layer

$$a_{ik}^{(1,n)} = f_1\left(\sum_{j=0}^{D_1} w_{jk}^{(1,n)} x_{ij}\right) \tag{10.3}$$

and iteratively moving through the layers $l = 2, .., M$

$$a_{ik}^{(l,n)} = f_l\left(\sum_{j=0}^{D_l} w_{jk}^{(l,n)} a_{ij}^{(l-1,n)}\right). \tag{10.4}$$

2. **Output errors:** Calculate the output errors $\delta_{ik}^{(M,n)}$

$$\delta_{ik}^{(M,n)} = \frac{\partial L_i}{\partial z_{ik}^{(M,n)}},$$

where $\delta_{ik}^{(M,n)} = a_{ik}^{(M)} - y_{ik}$ for standard regression and binary classification.

3. **Backward pass:** Moving backwards from layer M towards layer 1,
   - calculate the propagated output errors $\delta_{ij}^{(l,n)}$

$$\delta_{ij}^{(l,n)} = \sum_{k=1}^{D_{l+1}} \delta_{ik}^{(l+1,n)} . f'_{l+1} . w_{jk}^{(l+1,n)} \quad l = M-1, ..., 1; \tag{10.5}$$

   - calculate the derivatives with respect to the weights $w_{jk}^{(l,n)}$

$$\frac{\partial L_i}{\partial w_{jk}^{(l,n)}} = \delta_{ik}^{(l,n)} . a_{ij}^{(l-1,n)} \quad l = M, ..., 1. \tag{10.6}$$

4. **Update network weights** using the gradient-descent equation (Eq. (3.8)) (or similar):

$$w_{jk}^{(l,n+1)} = w_{jk}^{(l,n)} - \eta \frac{\partial L_i}{\partial w_{jk}^{(l,n)}}. \tag{10.7}$$

The weights of the network $w_{jk}^{(l,0)}$ are initialized to small random values to make sure that different neurons in each layer learn different information.

10.2.4 Exercises

1. Define the Rectified Linear Unit (ReLU) activation function. What is the problem with this activation function and how can it be addressed?

2. Describe the purpose and the properties of a loss function in neural networks. Give the most common loss function for a multilayer perceptron classifier and multilayer perceptron regressor.
3. Which version of gradient descent is most commonly used to train a neural network? What is momentum and how can it improve training?
4. Create the co-centric circle dataset shown in Fig. 10.2. Follow the code from Sect. 10.1 to train a neural network with two layers to separate the circles. Try both ReLU and Tanh activation functions. Play with the value of `lr` and `momentum` parameters, as well as the number of epochs, to investigate the convergence properties.[1]

10.3. Predicting age from brain connectivity using deep learning

In this section we will show, using a real-world example, how we can use a fully connected deep neural network to predict the age of a newborn baby from structural brain connectivity.[2] Magnetic resonance imaging can reveal white matter tracts in the brain, by measuring how the water diffuses in the brain. The water molecules are able to travel along the white matter fibers, but not across them. We can measure the direction of the water diffusion and then track its path along the white matter tracts, as shown in Fig. 10.4.[3] We can also track the fibers between two particular regions of the brain and calculate how strongly they are connected. This gives rise to the structural connectivity matrices[4] shown in Fig. 10.5 [45].

10.3.1 Neonatal structural connectivity dataset

Structural connectivity matrices contain a measure of connectivity between pairs of brain regions. There is 90 regions and matrices have 90×90 values. They are symmetric and have zeros on the diagonal (the connectivity of a region which itself is not meaningful). Our dataset consists of *a connectivity matrix for each baby*, together with information about their *age at scan*. We will predict age at scan from the matrices using a *fully connected deep neural network*.

The dataset is provided in these files:

- `matrices_train.p`—the connectivity matrices of the training set;
- `subject_info_train.csv`—age at scan for the training set;
- `matrices_test.p`—the connectivity matrices of the test set;
- `subject_info_test.csv`—age at scan for the test set.

[1] The skeleton code is available from github.com/MachineLearningBiomedicalApplications/notebooks.
[2] Data from Developing Human Connectome project (developingconnectome.org).
[3] The image was created in MRtrix (mrtrix.org) by Dr Maximilian Pietch.
[4] The connectivity matrices were calculated by Dr Dafnis Batalle.

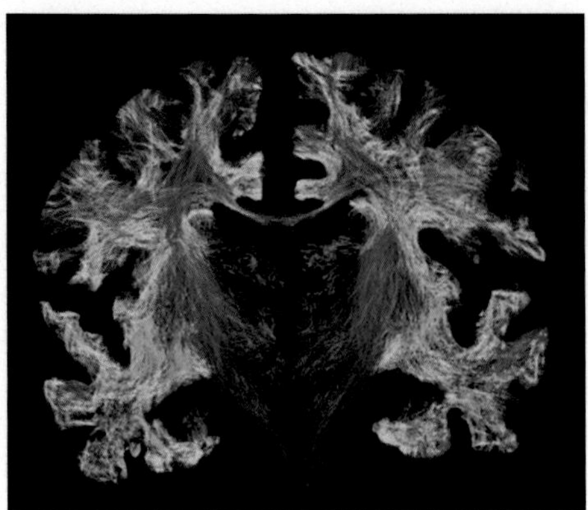

Figure 10.4 White-matter tracts in neonatal brain revealed by diffusion magnetic resonance imaging.

Figure 10.5 A connectivity matrix showing the strength of connections between pairs of regions in a neonatal brain.

The dataset has been split into training and test sets manually, by making sure that age at scan and age at birth are proportionally distributed in both sets. This gives us a representative test set to evaluate the performance of the network.

Load the training data

We will first load the connectivity matrices for training. An example connectivity matrix is shown in Fig. 10.5. We can see that we have 341 babies and the matrices are of size 90×90.

```
import pickle
matrices = pickle.load(open('matrices_train.p','rb'))
print(matrices.shape)
>>> (341, 90, 90)
```

Next, we load the information sheet about each baby. It contains the age at scan that we would like to predict:

```
import pandas as pd
subject_info = pd.read_csv('subject_info_train.csv')
subject_info.keys()
>>> Index(['age', 'prematurity'], dtype='object')
```

Preprocess the training data

First, we need to preprocess the connectivity matrices to reshape them into a feature matrix. To do that, we need to extract the upper triangle from each connectivity matrix and convert it into a feature vector. The function to create a feature matrix is provided next. We can see that we have 4,005 features after processing.

```
import numpy as np

def ConvertMatrices(matrices):
    # dimensions
    n = matrices.shape[0]
    m = matrices.shape[1]
    D = round(m*(m-1)/2)

    # create feature matrix
    X=np.zeros([n,D])
    for i in range(n):
        index=0
        for j in range(m):
            for k in range(j):
                X[i,index]=matrices[i,j,k]
                index=index+1
    return X

X = ConvertMatrices(matrices)
print('Feature matrix: ', X.shape)
>>> Feature matrix:  (341, 4005)
```

We would like to predict the age at scan, so we need to extract it from the information sheet:

```
y = subject_info['age'].to_numpy()
```

The final preprocessing steps are scaling and converting the data into PyTorch tensors. We will scale both the feature matrix `X` and target vector `y` to make the convergence easier for the stochastic gradient-descent optimizer. The PyTorch tensors need to be 2D and of type `float`.

```
from sklearn.preprocessing import StandardScaler
import torch

# Scale the features
scaler = StandardScaler()
X = scaler.fit_transform(X)

# Scale the targets
```

```
target_scaler = StandardScaler()
y = target_scaler.fit_transform(y.reshape(-1,1))

# Convert to tensors
X = torch.from_numpy(X).float()
y = torch.from_numpy(y).float()
```

Training and validation sets

In deep learning applications, the training data is often split into training and validation sets. We fit the neural network model to the training data and use the validation data to monitor the performance of the network. We select 15% of the training samples for validation and stratify them by age at scan:

```
from sklearn.model_selection import train_test_split

# extract validation set
groups = np.round(y/3)
X_train, X_val, y_train, y_val = \
train_test_split(X,y,test_size=0.15,stratify=groups)

# display info
print('Training samples: ', y_train.shape[0])
print('Validation samples: ', y_val.shape[0])
>>> Training samples:  289
>>> Validation samples:  52
```

10.3.2 Design a deep neural network model

Network architecture

We create a deep fully connected network `FCNRegressor` with *five linear layers* and *ReLU* activations after each of the first four layers. Because this is a regressor, we do not need any activation after the final layer. We choose the number of outputs of the layers 1–4 as 512, 128, 64, and 32. The final layer has to have one output, the predicted age at scan. The number of inputs of the first layer is determined by the number of features (4,005 connections). For all other layers the number of inputs needs to be equal to the number of outputs of the previous layer. Based on this, the network architecture is implemented as follows:

```
import torch.nn as nn

class FCNRegressor(nn.Module):
```

```
    def __init__(self):
        super(FCNRegressor, self).__init__()
        self.layer1 = nn.Linear(4005, 512)
        self.layer2 = nn.Linear(512, 128)
        self.layer3 = nn.Linear(128, 64)
        self.layer4 = nn.Linear(64, 32)
        self.layer5 = nn.Linear(32, 1)
        self.relu = nn.ReLU()

    def forward(self, x):
        x = self.relu(self.layer1(x))
        x = self.relu(self.layer2(x))
        x = self.relu(self.layer3(x))
        x = self.relu(self.layer4(x))
        x = self.layer5(x)
        return x
```

Finally, we create an instance of the network `net` to be ready for the training:

```
net = FCNRegressor()
```

Loss and optimizer

Our network is in fact a nonlinear regression, and therefore we need a mean-squared-error-loss function to fit the network parameters to our dataset:

```
loss_function = nn.MSELoss()
```

We will use stochastic gradient-descent optimizer as before, but this time we will add *momentum*. Momentum speeds up the training and helps to converge complex networks to a good solution:

```
optimizer = torch.optim.SGD(net.parameters(),
                            lr=0.001, momentum=0.7)
```

10.3.3 Train a deep neural network

The deep neural network will be trained similarly to our previous example in Sect. 10.2.2. Again, we will fit the network to the training set, however, we will also monitor training by calculating the loss on the validation set during epochs. If the validation loss increases, we will stop the training to minimize overfitting. This is called **early stopping,** and it is a type of regularization technique.

Training iteration

To simplify the code, we will create a function `train` that will perform one training iteration and return the latest training loss. This function takes the instance of the network as an input, together with the training dataset. It performs the usual five steps that we need to train a network in PyTorch. It returns the loss without gradients, which is extracted as `loss.data`.

```
# performs one training iteration
def train(net,X,y):
    # training iteration
    optimizer.zero_grad()
    prediction = net(X)
    loss = loss_function(prediction, y)
    loss.backward()
    optimizer.step()
    # return loss without gradients
    return loss.data
```

Validation

We also create a function `validate` that calculates the loss for a given dataset without performing any training. This function will be used to calculate the loss on the validation set during each epoch to monitor the training:

```
# calculates the loss without any training
def validate(net,X,y):
    # do not calculate gradients
    with torch.no_grad():
        # forward pass
        prediction = net(X)
        # calculate loss
        loss = loss_function(prediction, y)
        # return loss
        return loss
```

Training loop

We are ready to train our first deep neural network! We will train for a maximum of 1000 epochs. In each epoch we perform a training iteration using the function `train`, calculate the validation loss using the function `validate`, and save the training and validation losses. In each epoch we also check whether validation loss has increased. If that happens, we stop the training because this is a sign that it has started overfitting to the training data:

```
# to save the losses
train_losses=[]
val_losses=[]
# training loop 1000 epochs
for i in range(1000):
    # training iteration
    loss = train(net, X_train, y_train)
    # save training loss
    train_losses.append(loss)
    # calculate and save validation loss
    val_losses.append(validate(net,X_val,y_val))

    # stop training if validation loss increases
    if(i>0):
        if val_losses[i]>val_losses[i-1]:
            print('Final iteration: ', i)
            break
>>> Final iteration:  873
```

And we are done! Let's now check how our losses behaved during training. We simply plot the train and validation losses as a curve:

```
import matplotlib.pyplot as plt
plt.plot(train_losses,label='training loss')
plt.plot(val_losses,label='validation loss')
plt.legend()
```

The result is shown in Fig. 10.6. We can see that both losses nicely decreased, however, the training loss decreased significantly more than the validation loss. This means that we are overfitting to the data. This is not surprising, however, because we have very large number of parameters to fit.

10.3.4 Evaluate the trained network

Root-mean-squared error

Our network is a nonlinear regression, and therefore it can be quantitatively evaluated using a root-mean-squared error (RMSE). RMSE is easily derived from MSE loss by calculating its square root. However, we need to remember that we scaled the target values (age of the baby), so we need to adjust the error to account for the scaling. We can do that by multiplying the MSE by variance of the fitted standard scaler `target_scaler.var_`. To avoid repetitive coding, we write a function `RMSE` that can be applied to all the different sets:

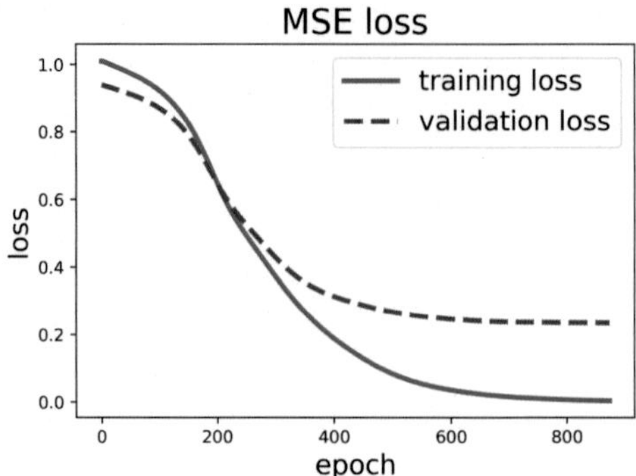

Figure 10.6 The graph shows the training and validation loss evolving over training epochs when fitting a fully connected deep neural network to predict the age of a baby from structural connectivity matrices.

```
# Calculates RMSE in weeks
def RMSE(net,X,y):
    # calculate MSE loss
    loss = validate(net,X,y).numpy()
    # Convert to RMSE in weeks
    rmse = np.sqrt(loss*target_scaler.var_[0])
    # Return RMSE
    return np.round(rmse,2)
```

Training and validation error

First, we will have a look how the network performed on training and validation sets. To do that, we will calculate the root-mean-squared error using function `RMSE`.

```
rmse_train = RMSE(net,X_train,y_train)
print('Training RMSE:', rmse_train)
rmse_val = RMSE(net,X_val,y_val)
print('Validation RMSE: ', rmse_val)
>>> Training RMSE: 0.12
>>> Validation RMSE:  0.86
```

The validation error of only 0.86 weeks is excellent, though the very low training error 0.12 weeks tells us that we have overfitted to the training dataset. But, in spite of that, it seems that the network generalizes well. We need to confirm that on the test set, though.

Load the test set

We will now load the test set to check how the network generalizes to the unseen data. Before we can predict the age of the baby using the test set, we need to perform the same preprocessing steps as for the training set. The only difference is that we will not fit the `StadardScaler` again but instead scale the test data the same way as the training data with the fitted scaler using the function `transform`:

```
# load and process connectivity matrices
matrices_test=pickle.load(open('matrices_test.p','rb'))
X_test=ConvertMatrices(matrices_test)
X_test=scaler.transform(X_test)

# load and process age at scan
subject_info_test=pd.read_csv('subject_info_test.csv')
y_test=subject_info_test['age'].to_numpy()
y_test=target_scaler.transform(y_test.reshape(-1,1))

# convert to Pytorch tensors
X_test = torch.from_numpy(X_test).float()
y_test = torch.from_numpy(y_test).float()
```

Test error

Now we are ready to calculate the error on the test set. As we already prepared the dataset and the evaluation function, this is very simple:

```
rmse_test = RMSE(net,X_test,y_test)
print('Test RMSE: ', rmse_test)
>>> Test RMSE:  0.74
```

The error 0.74 weeks (5 days) on the test set is even lower than the validation error (6 days), which is a good sign. We can conclude that, in spite of overfitting, the network still generalizes well to the unseen data and can predict the age of the baby with an error of less than one week.

Visualize the results

Finally, we will visualize how the model performed on training, validation, and the test set. To do that, we will create a scatter plot predicting the target values (ages) against the expected target values. We implement a function `PlotTargets` to do that:

```
# Plots predicted against expected targets
def PlotTargets(y_pred,y, label = 'Target values'):
```

```
    plt.plot([-3,3],[-3,3],'r', label = '$y=\hat{y}$')
    plt.plot(y,y_pred,'o', label = label)

    plt.xlabel('Expected target values')
    plt.ylabel('Predicted target values')
    plt.legend()
```

We will now create a figure with three subplots, one for each of the sets:

```
# display results
plt.figure(figsize=(14,4))

# plot training set predictions
plt.subplot(131)
PlotTargets(net(X_train).data,y_train)
plt.title('Training set')

# plot validation and test set predictions
plt.subplot(132)
PlotTargets(net(X_val).data, y_val)
plt.title('Validation set')

# plot training and validation loss
plt.subplot(133)
PlotTargets(net(X_test).data,y_test)
plt.title('Test set')
```

The resulting plot is shown in Fig. 10.7. We can see that the training targets are very tight around the red line, while this is not the case in validation and test sets. The plot thus shows the overfitting to the training set that we already identified using RMSE. On the other hand, the fits on the validation and test sets are still good, and we do not see any obvious bias, so we can say that we successfully trained our deep neural network for our task.

10.3.5 Exercises

1. Follow the code from this section to implement prediction of the age of the baby from structural connectivity matrices.[5]
2. Amend the code from this section to predict prematurity from structural connectivity matrices. The prematurity is a binary value (1=premature) given in the

[5] We provide the datasets for exercises 1–3 at github.com/MachineLearningBiomedicalApplications/notebooks. The skeleton code and solution is provided only for the exercise 3.

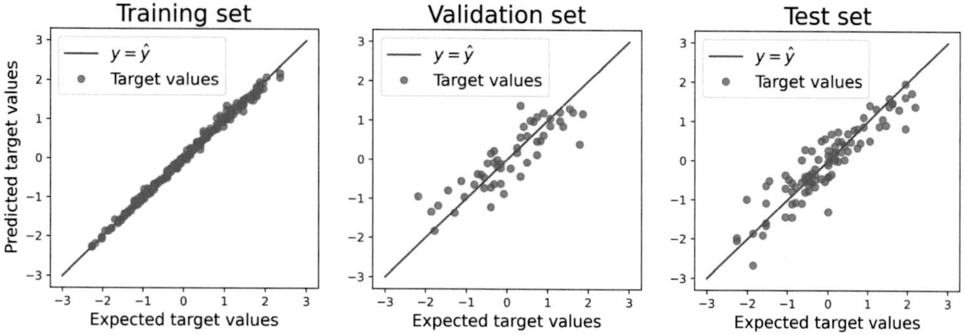

Figure 10.7 Scatter plots showing predicted against expected target values for training, validation, and test sets.

files `subject_info_train.csv` and `subject_info_test.csv`. Implement a deep neural network classifier to solve this task. Evaluate accuracy, sensitivity, and specificity.

3. Amend the code from this section to predict age of the baby from volumes of 86 brain structures given in the file `GA-brain-volumes-86-features.csv`.

10.4. Conclusions

We have now seen the full design, training, and evaluation process for fully connected deep neural network. We have seen that one of the primary advantages of fully connected neural networks is their flexibility to adapt to complex patterns in the data, demonstrated in Sect. 10.1. However, their disadvantage is a large number of parameters and resulting overfitting, as we have seen in Sect. 10.3. In fact, the fully connected networks are not very different from classical machine learning models presented in earlier chapters of this book and may not perform any better. The true power of neural networks can be seen once the convolutional layers are introduced and more complex tasks, such as image segmentation, are attempted. We will demonstrate this in Chapter 11.

Once we start working with large databases of images, rather than relatively compact feature matrices, we will also need to start paying attention to computational resources, such as the training time and amount of memory. The problems with training time are addressed by using a GPU to train networks and predict the outputs. The problems with memory can be addressed by training in smaller batches, rather than using the whole training dataset, and loading these batches directly from the disk, rather than run-time memory. Training in batches also decreases the training time, as we explained in Sect. 3.1.2.

These advanced concepts and techniques are the topic of the final chapter of this book.

CHAPTER 11

Convolutional neural networks

We have seen in Chap. 10 that neural networks are very versatile and flexible machine learning models. However, a downside of fully connected networks is that their linear layers have large numbers of parameters. Let's take an example of typical image, with 300×200 pixels and 3 channels (red, green and blue). This image has $300 \times 200 \times 3 = 180{,}000$ features. If we want to implement a neural network with second layer of size $150 \times 100 \times 6$, which has 90,000 features, our linear layer would have $180{,}000 \times 90{,}000 = 16.2$ billion parameters. A network with such a number of parameters would be computationally very expensive to store and optimize and would certainly result in overfitting. Medical images tend to be even larger and 3D, for example, a modern MRI of the brain can have dimensions of $300 \times 200 \times 200$ voxels.

A solution to this problem arrived in computer vision in the form of *convolutional layers* [28]. In a convolutional layer, the weights are shared between different features, which significantly reduces the number of parameters. At the same time, the convolutional neural networks are inspired by how the mammalian visual system works and, therefore, are well adapted for visual tasks, such as object recognition. In this chapter we will explain these concepts and show how to implement a simple convolutional neural network to classify brain MR images of term and preterm babies. We will conclude the chapter by implementing a convolutional neural network for segmentation of brain structures in neonatal MRI.

11.1. Why convolution?

11.1.1 Convolution operation

Convolutions are often used for *filtering* of images, e.g., to smooth or denoise images or detect the edges. The desired effect is achieved by hand-engineering a *filter*, also called a convolution kernel, that is repeatedly applied to all locations of the image to produce a new filtered image. Fig. 11.1 shows examples of the resulting filtered images and the corresponding filters. Vertical and horizontal edges are obtained using a Sobel filter and the blurred image by a Gaussian filter.

So, how does the convolution or filtering work? Let's denote the image pixels x_{ij} and elements of a filter w_{kl}. In our case, the values of k and l are $-1, 0$ and 1, because we have 3×3 convolution kernels (Fig. 11.1, bottom row). The convolution can be

Machine Learning for Biomedical Applications
https://doi.org/10.1016/B978-0-12-822904-0.00016-9
Copyright © 2024 Elsevier Ltd.
All rights reserved.

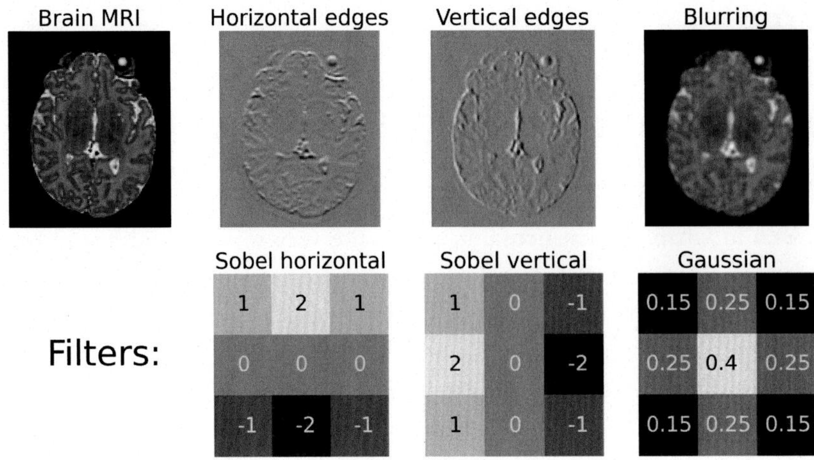

Figure 11.1 Top row: the neonatal brain MRI and the filtered images. Bottom row: the corresponding filters.

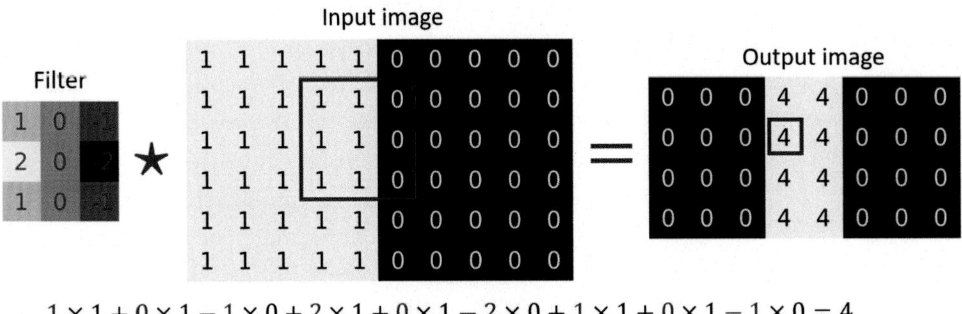

Figure 11.2 Filtering using convolution. The filter is applied to all the locations in the image, and the output intensity is calculated by weighted averaging using the weights from the filter. The red square in the input image shows the position of the filter over location (3,5). The resulting value in the same location in the output image is shown also by a red square. Calculation of the output value is given.

mathematically written as

$$(w \star x)_{ij} = \sum_{k=-s}^{s} \sum_{l=-s}^{s} w_{kl} x_{i+k,j+l}, \tag{11.1}$$

where s means that the size of the kernel is $2s + 1 \times 2s + 1$. From this equation, we can see that for each location (i, j) we overlay the kernel $\mathbf{w}$ over the image $\mathbf{x}$ and perform weighted averaging of the pixel intensities using the weights in the kernel. This process is illustrated in Fig. 11.2.

Note that the output image is smaller in size than the input image because we cannot place the filter over the locations on the boundaries of the image. This is called a *valid* convolution. If we would like the output image to have the same size, we can pad the input image with zeros and calculate convolution at all locations. This is called *padded* convolution.

We have illustrated how convolution works in two dimensions. In three or more dimensions, the convolution works exactly the same way. For example, in three dimensions, the filter, the input image and output image will all have three dimensions.

Finally, we should note that Eq. (11.1) is slightly different from the traditional definition of convolution. The convolution operation flips the filter before applying it to the image. This difference is of no consequence for deep learning, where the filters are learned during training, and therefore this simplified equation is preferred.

11.1.2 Convolutional neural networks

Convolutional neural networks (CNNs) are designed to mimic the mammalian visual system. They learn spatial filters of increasing complexity, from edge filters to object detectors. The architecture of CNNs combines three ideas [28]:

- *Local receptive fields*: Features are extracted only from local neighborhoods, rather than from the whole image. Convolution achieves that by applying a small filter to the image. In Fig. 11.2, the size of the filter (and therefore the local neighborhood) is 3×3 pixels. Local receptive fields support extraction of low-level features, such as edges and corners, as we illustrated in Fig. 11.1.
- *Shared weights*: The features should be extracted the same way, independent of their location. This is called *translation invariance*. The convolution applies the same filter to all locations of the image.
- *Subsampling*: The feature maps extracted by convolutions are subsampled and subsequently fed to the next convolutional layer to be combined into higher-level features. As the size of the feature maps reduces, the exact positions of extracted features become irrelevant, and only the patterns of salient features and their relative positions remain.

Fig. 11.3 shows an example CNN architecture diagram in LeNet style.[1] The network input is one grey-scale image of size 64×64 (shown as 1@64x64). The first *convolutional layer* applies 8 different filters to extract 8 feature maps of the same size as the image (shown as 8@64x64). These feature maps are then downsampled by a factor of two using the *max-pooling* operation, which simply selects a maximum feature value from each 2×2 image patch (resulting feature maps shown as 8@32x32). The second convolutional layer applies 16 filters, resulting in 16 feature maps (shown as 16@32x32). The second max-pooling layer reduces the feature maps to size 16×16 (shown as 16@16x16).

[1] Created using the NN SVG online tool: alexlenail.me/NN-SVG/LeNet.html.

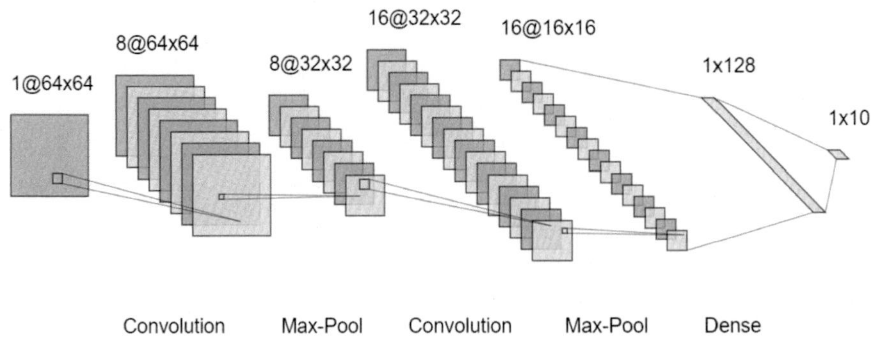

Figure 11.3 Diagram of an example CNN in LeNet style.

At this point a fully-connected layer (also called a *dense* layer) is applied to produce a vector of 128 features. A second fully connected layer produces 10 outputs, which could correspond to 10 output classes of objects, such as digits.

The key strength of CNNs compared to the classical filtering techniques is that they *learn the filters* to extract the most salient features. This is achieved by fitting the CNN model to the data where learnable parameters are the filters. The fitting is performed using *backpropagation*, similarly to the fully connected networks, as we have seen in Sect. 10.2.3.

11.1.3 Exercises

1. Describe the concept of translation invariance in convolutional layers.
2. Explain why convolutional layers have fewer parameters than fully connected layers.
3. What is the difference between convolutional neural networks and traditional filtering techniques?

11.2. Building blocks of convolutional neural networks

In this section we will describe the essential components of a CNN, namely,

- the *convolutional layers* for feature extraction;
- the *activations* to support learning of non-linear interactions;
- the downsampling operations (*pooling* or *striding*).

Optional components of CNNs are *batch normalization* to speed up training and *dropout* to prevent overfitting. Additionally, CNNs often contain fully connected layers to transform the network output to the required shape (Fig. 11.3).

Fig. 11.4 shows a typical *convolutional block*, composed of a convolutional layer, batch normalization, activation (in this case ReLU) and pooling.

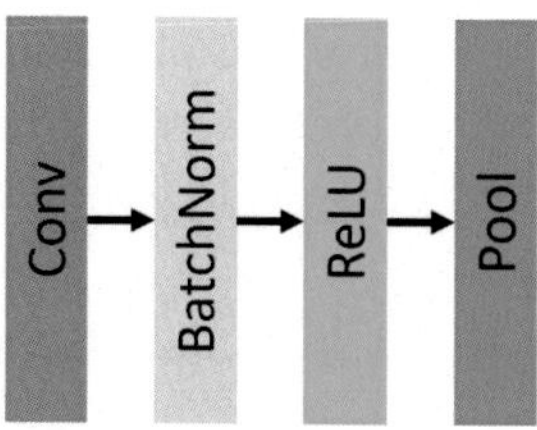

Figure 11.4 A typical convolutional block.

11.2.1 Convolutional layers

In Sect. 11.1.2 we have learned that CNNs are characterized by *local receptive fields* and *weight sharing*, which results in a decrease in the number of learnable parameters and translation invariance, meaning that the same features are learned independent of their location. These characteristics are achieved thanks to the *convolutional layers*, which implement convolutions (Fig. 11.2, Eq. (11.1)) to model relationships between successive layers of the network. This is in contrast to fully connected (linear) layers, which learn independent parameters to connect each incoming feature to each neuron in the layer.

Definition of a convolutional layer

A 2D convolutional layer performs convolutions of multichannel input feature maps with multichannel convolutional kernels. For a feature map $\mathbf{x}$ with C channels, a convolution operation is defined as

$$z_{ij} = \sum_{c=1}^{C} \sum_{k=-s}^{s} \sum_{l=-s}^{s} w_{kl}^{c} x_{i+k,j+l}^{c} + b,$$

where $\mathbf{w}$ is a convolutional kernel of size $C \times f \times f$, $f = 2s + 1$ represents the height and width of the kernel, b is a bias term and $\mathbf{z}$ is the 2D output of the convolution operation. Each 2D convolutional layer performs several such convolutions, and their number is defined by the number of the output channels.

Due to this design, each neuron in a convolutional layer has a restricted receptive field, constrained to the dimension f of the filter kernel. This means that the output of each neuron is calculated only from a small neighborhood in the incoming feature maps, centered around the location this neuron (denoted (i, j)).

Parameters of a convolutional layer

The learnable parameters of a convolutional layer are the filters $\mathbf{w}$ and biases $\mathbf{b}$. The number of the learnable parameters depends on the receptive field f and the number of input and output channels (but not on the spatial dimensions of the image).

The receptive field f can vary (typically, odd numbers, e.g., 3×3, 5×5, 7×7); however, the number of input channels must be equal the number of the output channels from the previous layer. The input layers might have 3 channels for a RGB image or 1 channel for a grey-scale image.

In the example CNN shown in Fig. 11.3, the first convolutional layer learns filters with dimension $1 \times f \times f$ since the input image has one channel (we have not specified the receptive field f). It will learn 8 such filters, corresponding to the number of the output feature maps, together with 8 bias parameters. The second convolutional layer has 8 input channels and 16 output channels, so it will learn 16 filters of size $8 \times f \times f$ and 16 bias parameters.

This design results in a significant reduction of number of parameters compared to the fully connected layer. For example, assuming a receptive field 5 and excluding the bias parameters for simplicity, the first convolutional layer in Fig. 11.3 learns 8 filters of size $1 \times 5 \times 5$, resulting in $8 \times 1 \times 5 \times 5 = 200$ parameters. Fully connected layers, however, would learn $1 \times 64 \times 64 \times 8 \times 64 \times 64$ parameters (approximately 1.4 million) to connect all the pixels in the input and output feature maps.

Convolutional layers in Pytorch

In Pytorch a 2D convolutional layer is implemented as

```
import torch
conv = torch.nn.Conv2d(in_channels = 1,
                       out_channels = 8,
                       kernel_size = 5)
```

We set the parameters to implement the first layer of Fig. 11.3, with one input channel, 8 output channels and a kernel size of 5×5. This can be written in a shorter form as

```
conv = torch.nn.Conv2d(1,8,5)
```

We can now print the convolution layer that we defined as

```
print(conv)
>>> Conv2d(1, 8, kernel_size=(5, 5), stride=(1, 1))
```

We see that there is 1 input channel, 8 output channels and the kernel is 5×5. Stride 1×1 means that convolution will be applied to every pixel in the image, without skipping any. By default, the convolution filters also have a bias term and do not use any padding.

We will now create a random input image to pass through the convolutional layer with

```
input_image = torch.randint(0, 255, (1, 1, 64, 64))
```

Note that the inputs of the 2D convolutional layers must have a shape $N \times C \times H \times W$, where N is the number of images in a batch, C is the number of channels, H is the image height and W is the image width. Because we have one gray-scale image, the first two dimensions are both equal to one. Additionally, the convolutional layers take values of type `float`, so we need to convert the image before passing is through the layer:

```
input_image=input_image.float()
```

Now we can pass the image through the convolutional layer and check the size of the output with

```
output = conv(input_image)
print(output.shape)
>>> torch.Size([1, 8, 60, 60])
```

We have one image with 8 channels and size 60×60. This is because by default we have a *valid* convolution that applies no padding. If we wish to obtain output of the same size, we can pad the image with zeros. For convolution kernel of size 5, this can be done by adding two columns/rows of zeros on each side of the image (setting `padding` to 2) with

```
conv = torch.nn.Conv2d(1,8,5,padding=2)
output = conv(input_image)
print(output.shape)
>>> torch.Size([1, 8, 64, 64])
```

To further inspect the parameters of the convolutional layer, we can print them out

```
for name, param in conv.named_parameters():
    print(name, param.data.shape)
>>> weight torch.Size([8, 1, 5, 5])
>>> bias torch.Size([8])
```

We can see that we have 8 convolutional kernels as expected. In addition we have 8 bias values, one for each filter.

Finally, 1×1 convolutions are used to reduce the number of channels of the feature maps. In the next example we combine 8 channels of the `output` into a single channel of the same spatial dimension using a 1×1 convolution.

```
conv1 = torch.nn.Conv2d(8,1,1)
output1=conv1(output)
print(output1.shape)
>>> torch.Size([1, 1, 64, 64])
```

11.2.2 Activations

Convolutional networks require activation layers in order to learn nonlinear mappings of the data, similarly to the fully connected networks. In CNNs it is typical to implement activations as ReLU functions. Because activation functions operate element-wise, they are used the same way for the convolutional layers as for the linear layers.

In this example, we apply the ReLU activation to the output of the convolutional layer

```
relu = torch.nn.ReLU()
output_activations = relu(output)
print(output_activations.shape)
>>> torch.Size([1, 8, 64, 64])
```

We see that activation functions do not change the shape of the output feature maps.

11.2.3 Downsampling

An important feature of convolutional networks is that they use downsampling to increase the receptive field of filter kernels to be able to learn to recognize objects across a hierarchy of scales. While early layers recognize low-level features, such as sharp edges, middle layers can then learn more complex textures and shapes, building towards the deep layers recognizing the whole objects. There are two different mechanisms for downsampling in CNNs: pooling and striding.

Pooling

Pooling works by applying a pooling kernel typically to nonoverlapping patches of an image. Pooling kernels perform maximum or averaging operations to produce downsampled outputs.

Fig. 11.5 shows and example of max pooling, implemented by a pooling filter shape 2×2 and a stride of 2. In this example, the image is split into 2×2 nonoverlapping blocks shown by different colors. The max-pooling filter takes the maximum of each block as an output. Because there is only one output value for each 2×2 block, the image is downsampled by a factor of 2.

1	9	2	7
4	3	6	2
1	1	4	8
0	3	7	9

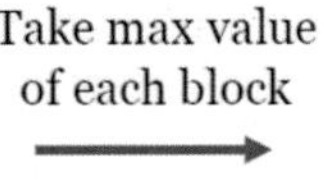

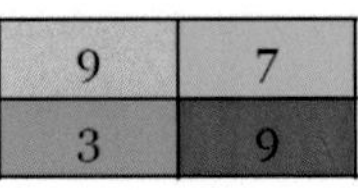

Figure 11.5 Max pooling.

Let's now apply max-pooling to the `output` that we created by passing the `input_image` through a convolutional layer in the previous section. First, let's print out its shape with

```
print(output.shape)
>> torch.Size([1, 8, 64, 64])
```

Now we define the max-pooling operation with kernel size 2 and stride 2 to downsample the output by factor two with

```
maxpool = torch.nn.MaxPool2d(kernel_size=2,stride=2)
downsampled = maxpool(output)
print(downsampled.shape)
>>> torch.Size([1, 8, 32, 32])
```

The alternative commonly used pooling operation is average pooling, where, instead of taking the maximum of the block, the average value is calculated. In Pytorch this is implemented by the function

```
torch.nn.AvgPool2d(2,2)
```

Striding

Striding can be used to downsample the image while performing the convolution operation. For example, when applying convolution with a stride 2, we skip every second pixel in the image, as illustrated in Fig. 11.6.

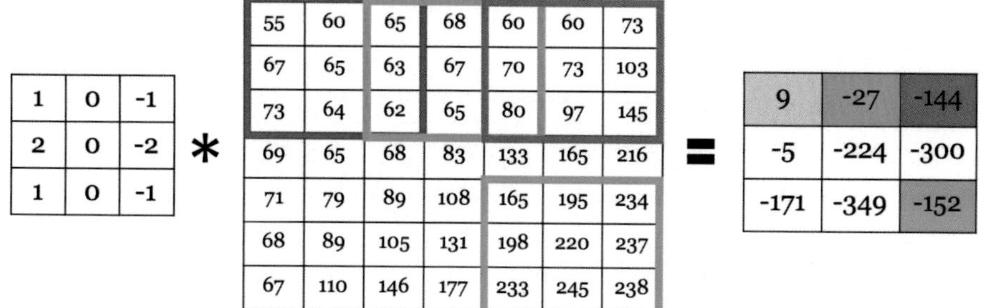

Figure 11.6 Strided convolution.

The following code illustrates how we can perform *strided* convolutions of the `input_image` to reduce its spatial dimension two-fold, by setting the `stride` to 2:

```
print(input_image.shape)
>>> torch.Size([1, 1, 64, 64])
```

```
conv = torch.nn.Conv2d(1,8,5,padding=2,stride=2)
downsampled = conv(input_image)
print(downsampled.shape)
>>> torch.Size([1, 8, 32, 32])
```

11.2.4 Batch normalization

Deep neural networks are typically trained with variants of stochastic gradient descent, which sample batches from the data sets and estimate average loss for each batch rather than estimating it across all examples. This can lead to noisy gradient updates since the composition of each batch is subject to change. *Batch normalization* [22] seeks to address this by normalizing and rescaling the features in each batch, at every layer throughout the network. By doing so, it can considerably speed up training. Commonly, the batch norm is placed between convolutional layer and activation, or after the activation.

The batch normalization layer rescales its inputs to zero mean and unit variance. This is done by substracting the mean and dividing by variance calculated from the data. The normalization is done across the batch and spatial dimensions, but separately for each output channel. Because means and variances vary across the batches, the batch-norm layer keeps track of them through the iterations and calculates moving averages.

The batch-norm layer also learns a linear transformation (parameterized by two parameters, i.e., the slope and bias) for each channel, which is applied to the features after the normalizations.

In the following example, we would like to apply batch-norm to the output of the convolutional layer:

```
print(output.shape)
>>> torch.Size([1, 8, 64, 64])
```

Because we have 8 channels, we apply batch-norm as follows:

```
bn = torch.nn.BatchNorm2d(8)
normalized=bn(output)
```

11.2.5 Dropout

Dropout [43] is a technique that can be used to perform network regularization. It works by randomly dropping activations (setting them to zero) during training, in other words, by applying a randomized masking operation on the output of each layer. In doing so, the approach prevents individual network components from memorizing the inputs, which would lead to overfitting. There is a trade-off, however, because dropping out too many weights will prevent the network from learning well enough and will cause underfitting.

If the dropout operator is applied to the output of the convolutional layer, it will zero entire channels with probability set by the parameter p.

```
d = torch.nn.Dropout2d(p=0.5)
d(output)
```

11.2.6 Convolutional blocks

Convolutional blocks implement several operations in one object using torch.nn.sequential. We will now create the block, shown in Fig. 11.4, that implements the first convolutional layer and the first pooling layer of the network shown in Fig. 11.3.

```
import torch.nn as nn

conv_block = nn.Sequential(
             nn.Conv2d(1,8,5,padding=2),
             nn.BatchNorm2d(8),
             nn.ReLU(),
             nn.MaxPool2d(kernel_size=2,stride=2))
```

This block can now be applied to the input image as a single operation with

```
output = conv_block(input_image)
print(output.shape)
>>> torch.Size([1, 8, 32, 32])
```

The second convolutional block will implement the second convolutional layer and the second pooling layer with

```
conv_block2 = nn.Sequential(
              nn.Conv2d(8,16,5,padding=2),
              nn.BatchNorm2d(16),
              nn.ReLU(),
              nn.MaxPool2d(kernel_size=2,stride=2))
output2 = conv_block2(output)
print(output2.shape)
>>> torch.Size([1, 16, 16, 16])
```

Next, we need to apply the fully connected layers. We need to calculate the number of inputs of the first fully connected layer as $16 \times 16 \times 16$ and reshape into a 1D vector. Then, we can apply linear layers and activations with

```
n=16*16*16
fc_block = nn.Sequential(
```

```
            nn.Linear(n, 128),
            nn.ReLU(),
            nn.Linear(128,10),
            nn.ReLU())
output3=fc_block(output2.view(-1,n))
print(output3.shape)
>>> torch.Size([1, 10])
```

11.2.7 CNN model

Finally, we are ready to implement the whole network in Fig. 11.3.

```
class CNNModel(nn.Module):
    def __init__(self):
        super(CNNModel, self).__init__()

        self.conv_block1 = nn.Sequential(
            nn.Conv2d(1,8,5,padding=2),
            nn.BatchNorm2d(8),
            nn.ReLU(),
            nn.MaxPool2d(kernel_size=2,stride=2))
        self.conv_block2 = nn.Sequential(
            nn.Conv2d(8,16,5,padding=2),
            nn.BatchNorm2d(16),
            nn.ReLU(),
            nn.MaxPool2d(kernel_size=2,stride=2))
        self.fc_block = nn.Sequential(
            nn.Linear(16*16*16, 128),
            nn.ReLU(),
            nn.Linear(128,10),
            nn.ReLU())

    def forward(self, x):
        x = self.conv_block1(x)
        x = self.conv_block2(x)
        x = x.view(-1, 16*16*16)
        x = self.fc_block(x)
        return x
```

We can now create an instance of this network and perform the forward pass:

```
net = CNNModel()
```

```
o = net(input_image)
print(o.shape)
>>> torch.Size([1, 10])
```

We can see that the network returned 10 outputs as expected.

The convolutional neural networks are trained the same way as fully connected networks presented in Chap. 10. For example, to classify digits with this network, we could optimize a cross entropy loss using a stochastic gradient descent optimizer.

11.2.8 Exercises

1. Implement a convolutional layer as follows[2]:
   a. Create a random image with spatial dimensions 100×100 and 3 channels;
   b. Implement a convolutional layer that outputs 5 channels and has a kernel size of 3×3. Pass the image through it. Print out the dimensions of the results;
   c. Change the convolutional layer so that its output has spatial dimensions 100×100;
   d. Change the stride of the convolutional layer, so that the output has spatial dimensions 20×20;
   e. Instead of changing the stride, implement a max-pooling operation to reduce the dimension of the output of the convolutional layer with stride 1 to 20×20.
2. Calculate the number of learnable parameters of the convolutional layer in Exercise 1.
3. Modify the `CNNmodel` by changing each of the following:
   a. the name of the model to `CNNmodel2`;
   b. the number of output channels of the first and second convolutional layer to 4 and 6 respectively;
   c. the number of outputs of the first and second fully connected layer to 32 and 2, respectively

   Create an instance `net2` of the new model. Perform forward pass with `input_image`. Check that you have 2 outputs.

11.3. Predicting prematurity from neonatal brain MRI

In this section we will design and train a *CNN classifier* to predict prematurity status directly from neonatal MR images [13,18]. We will use 2D slices rather than whole 3D images to reduce the need for GPU memory and to speed up training. The 2D brain MR images and the prematurity status of 157 babies are given in the file

[2] Skeleton code and solutions for exercises 1 and 3 are available from github.com/MachineLearning-BiomedicalApplications/notebooks.

`neonatal_mri.npz`,[3] which contains compressed numpy arrays with this data. Before we can start on this example, we have to make sure that we have access to GPU.

11.3.1 Accessing GPU

Your local GPU card

If you have an NVIDIA GPU with at least 4 GB memory and CUDA installed, you can implement the example in this section locally on your computer. If you do not have these resources, you can use Google Colab.

To check whether CUDA is available, run the following code:

```
torch.cuda.is_available()
>>> True
```

If the answer is true, Pytorch is able to access your GPU. You can also check properties of your GPU as follows:

```
print(torch.cuda.get_device_properties('cuda:0'))
>>> _CudaDeviceProperties(name='Quadro M2000',
    major=5, minor=2, total_memory=4096MB,
    multi_processor_count=6)
```

We can see that the GPU card used here has 4096 MB of memory, which is approximately 4 GB.

Google Colab

Google Colab offers limited access to GPU free of charge, and this resource is ample for implementing the example in this section. To use Google Colab, you will need a google account. Once you are signed in go to

colab.research.google.com

You will see a screen where you have several options, including opening existing notebooks. If you already created your notebook, click on the tab *upload* and drag the file there. Alternatively, if you plan to type the code into a new notebook, click *New notebook*. You can change the name of this notebook by clicking on it in the top right corner.

By default Google Colab runs on CPU. To access the GPU, click *Runtime* in the top menu, then click *Change runtime type*. From the *Hardware Accelerator* drop-down menu choose *GPU* and click *Save*.

Finally you need to upload the data set. To do that, type the following code to an empty cell and run the cell (by clicking on the arrow):

[3] Available from github.com/MachineLearningBiomedicalApplications/notebooks.

```
from google.colab import files
files.upload()
```

After a while, a button will appear that is called *Choose files*. Click on this button and upload the file `neonatal_mri.npz`. It will take a minute or so for the file to upload. Now, you are ready to proceed with the code given in the rest of this chapter.

To add a new cell to your notebook, click on *+Code* if you would like to write code, or on *+Text* if you would like to write some comments.

11.3.2 Load and prepare the data

Load the data

First we use numpy package to load the compressed data set with

```
import numpy as np
data = np.load('neonatal_data.npz')
data.files
>>> ['MR_images', 'prematurity']
```

We see that the file contains two numpy arrays named `'MR_images'` and `'prematurity'`. We will now extract these arrays. The first array contains 157 MR images, with 1 channel (gray-scale) and size 64 × 64.

```
mri = data['MR_images']
print(mri.shape)
>>> (157, 1, 64, 64)
```

The second array contains prematurity status, a binary label where 1 means 'preterm' and 0 means 'term'.

```
prem = data['prematurity']
print(prem.shape)
>>> (157,)
```

We also find that there is 41% preterm babies in the data set

```
np.around(np.sum(prem)/np.size(prem),2)
>>> 0.41
```

Plot the data

We will now plot the first 8 images with prematurity status in the titles. The plot resulting from the code below is presented in Fig. 11.7.

```
from matplotlib import pyplot as plt
plt.figure(figsize=(12,6))
```

```
for i in range(8):
    plt.subplot(2,4,i+1)
    plt.imshow(mri[i,0,:,:],cmap='gray')
    if prem[i]:
        plt.title('Preterm')
    else:
        plt.title('Term')
    plt.axis('off')
```

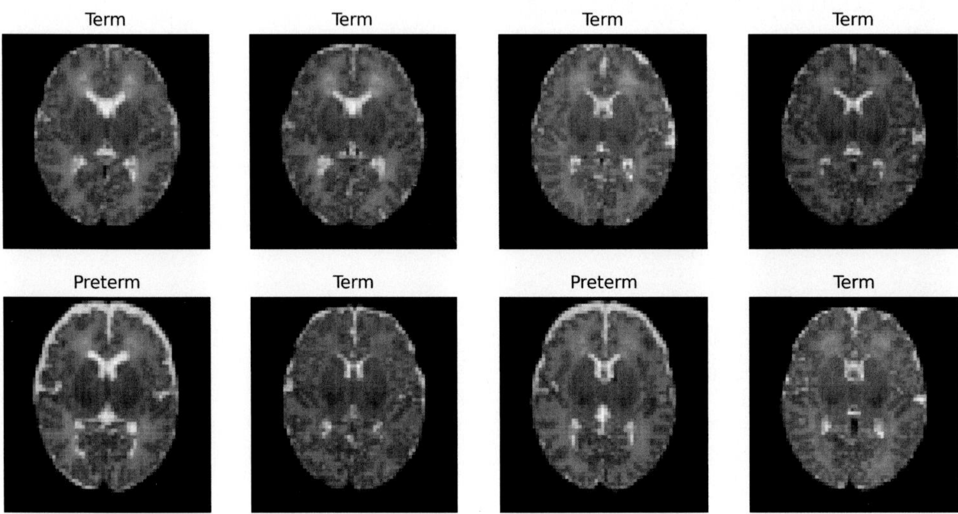

Figure 11.7 Example images from the neonatal MRI dataset.

Convert to Pytorch tensors

Note that data has been already prepared in the shapes required by Pytorch. We still need to convert it to Pytorch tensors of a correct type, namely, `float` for the images and `long` for the labels with

```
import torch
X = torch.tensor(mri).float()
y = torch.tensor(prem).long()
```

Training, validation and test sets

Next, we need to split the data for training, validation and testing. We will remove 20% of the data for testing, and another 10% for validation. We will perform stratified split to ensure that there is the same proportion of preterm babies in all sets with

```
from sklearn.model_selection import train_test_split
X_train, X_test, y_train, y_test = \
    train_test_split(X, y, test_size=0.2, stratify=y)
X_train, X_val, y_train, y_val = \
    train_test_split(X_train, y_train, test_size=0.1,
                     stratify=y_train)
print('Training samples: ', y_train.size())
print('Validation samples: ', y_val.size())
print('Test samples: ', y_test.size())
>>> Training samples:  torch.Size([112])
>>> Validation samples:  torch.Size([13])
>>> Test samples:  torch.Size([32])
```

We have 112 subjects for training, 13 for validation and 32 for testing. We are ready to implement and train our CNN.

11.3.3 CNN classifier

Model architecture

The network architecture will be similar to the one that we have seen in Sect. 11.2, with some small differences. We will have three convolutional blocks, and one fully connected blocks. These will be implemented as follows:

- `conv_block1`: 2D convolutional layer with 8 filters and kernel size 3, followed by batch-norm, ReLU and max-pooling;
- `conv_block2`: 2D convolutional layer with 16 filters and kernel size 3, followed by batch-norm, ReLU and max-pooling;
- `conv_block3`: 2D convolutional layer with 32 filters and kernel size 3, followed by batch-norm, ReLU and max-pooling;
- `fc_block`: Linear layer with 32 outputs followed by ReLU and second linear layer with 2 outputs followed by ReLU.

The implementation of this network architecture done with

```
import torch.nn as nn

class CNNclf(nn.Module):
    def __init__(self):
        super(CNNclf, self).__init__()

        self.conv_block1 = nn.Sequential(
            nn.Conv2d(1,8,3,padding=1),
            nn.BatchNorm2d(8),
            nn.ReLU(),
```

```
            nn.MaxPool2d(kernel_size=2,stride=2))
        self.conv_block2 = nn.Sequential(
            nn.Conv2d(8,16,3,padding=1),
            nn.BatchNorm2d(16),
            nn.ReLU(),
            nn.MaxPool2d(kernel_size=2,stride=2))
        self.conv_block3 = nn.Sequential(
            nn.Conv2d(16,32,3,padding=1),
            nn.BatchNorm2d(32),
            nn.ReLU(),
            nn.MaxPool2d(kernel_size=2,stride=2))
        self.fc_block = fc_block = nn.Sequential(
           nn.Linear(32*8*8, 32),
           nn.ReLU(),
           nn.Linear(32,2),
           nn.ReLU())

    def forward(self, x):
        x = self.conv_block1(x)
        x = self.conv_block2(x)
        x = self.conv_block3(x)
        x = x.view(-1, 32*8*8)
        x = self.fc_block(x)
        return x
```

Set up the model on CUDA device

We start by setting up our cuda device with

```
if torch.cuda.is_available():
    device = torch.device("cuda")
else: device = torch.device("cpu")
print(device)
>>> cuda
```

Next, we create an instance of the CNN classifier and send it to the GPU with

```
net = CNNclf().to(device)
```

We are building a CNN classifier, so we choose a cross-entropy loss, which we also send to GPU, with

```
loss = nn.CrossEntropyLoss().to(device)
```

Finally, we also create the optimizer. It is important to send the model to GPU before creating the optimizer.

```
import torch.optim as optim
optimizer = optim.SGD(net.parameters(), lr=0.001,
                      momentum=0.5)
```

11.3.4 Training

Now we are ready to start training. We will train for a maximum 2,000 epochs (iterations). We choose to stop training after at least 100 epochs have passed (to let network find an initial solution) and until the validation loss stops decreasing.

Note that we are using all data for training at every iteration, so each iteration is an epoch. This is generally not possible with larger data sets, and training is performed with mini-batches as we will show in the next section.

Note that training and validation data need to be sent to GPU before performing a forward pass. We save both training and validation losses to plot after the training has finished. We also print these losses every 100 iterations to be able to monitor the training. Here is how we implement this in Pytorch:

```
epochs = 2000
train_losses=[]
val_losses=[]

for epoch in range(epochs):

    #training mode
    net.train()
    # send training data to GPU
    data = X_train.to(device)
    labels = y_train.to(device)
    # training
    optimizer.zero_grad()
    pred = net(data)
    ce = loss(pred, labels)
    ce.backward()
    optimizer.step()
    # save training loss
    train_losses.append(ce.item())

    # validation mode
    with torch.no_grad():
```

```
        net.eval()
        # send validation data to GPU
        data_val = X_val.to(device)
        labels_val = y_val.to(device)
        # calculate validation loss
        pred_val = net(data_val)
        ce_val = loss(pred_val, labels_val)
        # save validation loss
        val_losses.append(ce_val.item())

    # Print loss every 100 iterations
    if epoch % 100==0:
        s='Iter: {}, Train loss: {:.4f}, Val Loss: {:.4f}'
        print(s.format(epoch, ce, ce_val))

    # After 100 iterations stop if validation loss
    # stops decreasing
    if(epoch>100):
        if val_losses[epoch-1]>=val_losses[epoch-2]:
            print('Final iteration: ', epoch)
            break

>>> Iter: 0, Train loss : 0.7511, Val Loss: 0.7157
>>> Iter: 100, Train loss: 0.5358, Val Loss: 0.5591
>>> Iter: 200, Train loss: 0.4114, Val Loss: 0.4871
>>> Iter: 300, Train loss: 0.3190, Val Loss: 0.4471
>>> Iter: 400, Train loss: 0.2494, Val Loss: 0.4280
>>> Iter: 500, Train loss: 0.1937, Val Loss: 0.4192
>>> Final iteration:  560
```

Evolution of the losses over epochs is plotted using code below and shown in Fig. 11.8.

```
plt.plot(train_losses,'b',label='train')
plt.plot(val_losses,'r',label='validation')
plt.legend(fontsize=14)
plt.xlabel('epochs',fontsize=14)
plt.ylabel('CE loss',fontsize=14)
```

11.3.5 Evaluation

Finally, we will evaluate the prediction accuracy on all three sets. To do that, we need to send the data (images) to the GPU, perform the forward pass to obtain predictions, send

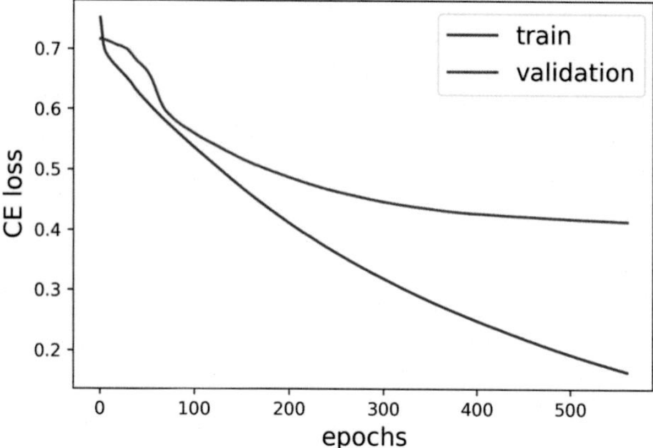

Figure 11.8 Evolution of the training and validation losses over epochs.

the predictions to the CPU, and take the maximum of the predicted logits to calculate the label (for details on classification in Pytorch, see Sect. 9.3.3). This is implemented as follows in the function `acc`:

```
from sklearn.metrics import accuracy_score

def acc(net,X,y,text='Accuracy: '):
    net.eval()
    X=X.to(device)
    pred=net(X).cpu()
    y_pred = torch.argmax(pred, dim=1)
    print(text, round(accuracy_score(y, y_pred),2))

acc(net,X_train,y_train,'Train accuracy: ')
acc(net,X_val,y_val,'Validation accuracy: ')
acc(net,X_test,y_test,'Test accuracy: ')
>>> Train accuracy:  0.96
>>> Validation accuracy:  0.85
>>> Test accuracy:  0.91
```

In this particular run, the network achieved high accuracy in correctly predicting preterm babies from the 2D brain MRI. However, when you run this code yourself, you can observe that this is not always the case. The network can easily get stuck in local minima and not converge to a good solution. This is partly because the weights of the network are initialized randomly, and, consequently, it will not converge to the same solution every time. The common local minima is assigning all the subjects to the term class and thus obtaining 59% accuracy. Rerun the training if that occurs. If the training stopped because the validation loss increased a bit, but performance is not yet good, you can try to train for more iterations by running the training cell again. Note that the network parameters will only be reset if you create a new instance of the object `net`.

11.3.6 Exercises

1. Implement the prediction of prematurity by following code in this section. Rerun the training several times and see how the performance changes.[4]
2. Implement prediction of malignant tissue using CNN using the histology data set provided in Chap. 8.[5]

11.4. CNN segmentation for medical images

Segmentation is a very important task for processing of medical images. It enables extraction of quantitative measures, such as volumes of brain structures or indices of cardiac function, including ejection fraction and global longitudinal strain, which we have used in the previous chapters. Training convolutional neural networks for medical image segmentation, however, comprises unique challenges. Medical images are often 3D, with hundreds of thousands or even millions of voxels. On the other hand, training data is very difficult to obtain because manual segmentations of these large 3D images are time-consuming. Therefore, the segmentation networks most often need to be trained with a small number of segmented images, with data sets including hundreds or sometimes even tens of samples.

Is spite of these challenges, CNN segmentation has been extremely successful in medical imaging, due to specific approaches to deal with smaller datasets. These include:

- using smaller networks with fewer layers and weights;
- *data augmentation*, where the dataset is enlarged by random spatial and intensity transformations [35,38];
- employing *encoder-decoder* architectures, that reduce network overfitting [38].

In this final section of the book, we will implement a CNN to segment cortex in neonatal MRI. This example demonstrates a binary segmentation, but extension to multi-label segmentation is straightforward. The solution is based on encoder-decoder network called *UNet* [38], called after its U-shape architecture (Fig. 11.9). Its configurable version called *no-new-UNet*, or shortly *nnUNet*,[6] consistently outperforms most alternative architectures for medical image segmentation [23].

[4] Skeleton code and solutions for exercise 1 is available from github.com/MachineLearningBiomedicalApplications/notebooks.

[5] The dataset is available from gin.g-node.org/MachineLearningBiomedApplications/data. Code to load this dataset was provided in Chap. 8.

[6] Code available from github.com/MIC-DKFZ/nnUNet.

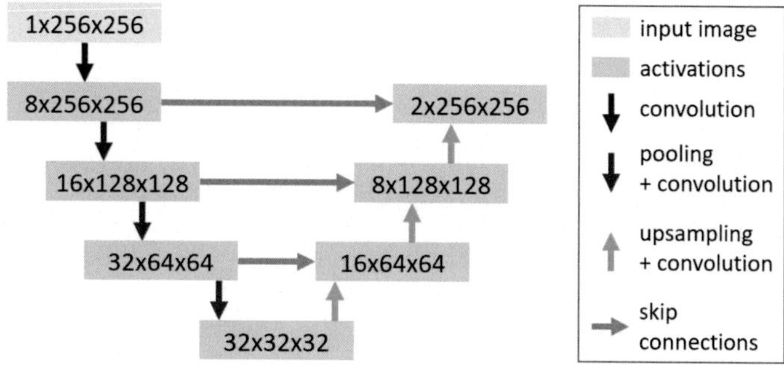

Figure 11.9 A UNet-style architecture.

11.4.1 UNet architecture

We will implement the UNet-style architecture shown in Fig. 11.9, which has fewer layers and weights compared to the original UNet implementation [38].

UNet architecture is composed of *encoder* and *decoder* branches with *skip connections*. The encoder branch increases number of features in each layer, while reducing spatial resolution. In the decoder branch, the number of feature maps is reduced, while spatial resolution is increased. The loss of spatial resolution in the encoder branch is addressed by inputting activations from the encoder layers to the decoder layers of the same spatial resolution, to ensure that fine detail is not lost in the final segmentation.

Note that Fig. 11.9 shows the outputs of various layers for input images with a spatial resolution of 256×256, however, UNet architecture can be applied to images of various sizes because it is composed of only the convolutional (and no fully connected) layers. This type of architecture is called a *fully convolutional network*.

We will now go through the UNet architecture shown in Fig. 11.9 in detail. We will start by generating a random image to demonstrate how we use different layers with

```
import torch
im = torch.randint(0,255,(1,1,256,256)).float()
im.shape
>>> torch.Size([1, 1, 256, 256])
```

Encoder

The first convolutional block of the encoder (blue arrow) extracts 8 low-level feature maps from the input image and uses ReLU activation function to produce activation maps `enc1`. This is implemented with

```
import torch.nn as nn
conv1_down = nn.Conv2d(1,8,3,padding=1)
ReLU = nn.ReLU()
```

```
enc1 = ReLU(conv1_down(im))
enc1.shape
>>> torch.Size([1, 8, 256, 256])
```

The encoder activations in the following blocks are obtained by downsampling using average pooling, followed by a convolution to further increase the number of features (red arrows). The second level activation maps `enc2`, obtained using the following code, have 16 channels and reduced spatial resolution 128 × 128:

```
down = nn.AvgPool2d(kernel_size=2)
conv2_down = nn.Conv2d(8,16,3,padding=1)
enc2=down(enc1)
enc2=ReLU(conv2_down(enc2))
enc2.shape
>>> torch.Size([1, 16, 128, 128])
```

Obtaining the third-level encoder activation maps `enc3` is analogous to the second level, resulting in 32 channels and resolution 64 × 64:

```
conv3_down = nn.Conv2d(16,32,3,padding=1)
enc3=down(enc2)
enc3=ReLU(conv3_down(enc3))
enc3.shape
>>> torch.Size([1, 32, 64, 64])
```

For the fourth-level encoder activation maps, we opt not to increase the number of channels any more to keep the network small, resulting `enc4` with 32 channels with spatial resolutions 32 × 32:

```
conv4 = nn.Conv2d(32,32,3,padding=1)
enc4=down(enc3)
enc4=ReLU(conv4(enc4))
enc4.shape
>>> torch.Size([1, 32, 32, 32])
```

Decoder

The decoder block (green arrow) consists of three steps: upsampling the activation maps using bilinear interpolation; concatenating the encoder activation maps from the same resolution level (skip connection, grey arrow); and convolution that decreases the number of feature maps:

```
up = nn.UpsamplingBilinear2d(scale_factor=2)
conv3_up = nn.Conv2d(32+32,16,3,padding=1)
```

```
dec3=up(enc4)
dec3=torch.cat([dec3, enc3], dim=1)
dec3=ReLU(conv3_up(dec3))
dec3.shape
>>> torch.Size([1, 16, 64, 64])
```

Bilinear upsampling increases the spatial dimension to 64 × 64, which allows concatenation with enc3 of the same spatial dimension. Since upsampled enc4 and enc3 both have 32 channels, after the concatenation, there will be 64 channels. The convolution will reduce the channels for 64 to 16, resulting in a third-level decoder activation maps enc3. The final two decoder levels are analogous:

```
conv2_up = nn.Conv2d(16+16,8,3,padding=1)
dec2=up(dec3)
dec2=torch.cat([dec2, enc2], dim=1)
dec2=ReLU(conv2_up(dec2))
dec2.shape
>>> torch.Size([1, 8, 128, 128])

conv1_up = nn.Conv2d(8+8,2,3,padding=1)
dec1=up(dec2)
dec1=torch.cat([dec1, enc1], dim=1)
dec1=ReLU(conv1_up(dec1))
dec1.shape
>>> torch.Size([1, 2, 256, 256])
```

UNet model

We can now join all these building blocks to create a UNet model. Note that it is possible to create blocks using nn.sequential, but we opted to keep it simple here for clarity with

```
class UNet(nn.Module):
    def __init__(self):
        super(UNet, self).__init__()

        self.conv1_down = nn.Conv2d(1,8,3,padding=1)
        self.conv2_down = nn.Conv2d(8,16,3,padding=1)
        self.conv3_down = nn.Conv2d(16,32,3,padding=1)
        self.conv4 = nn.Conv2d(32,32,3,padding=1)
        self.conv3_up = nn.Conv2d(32+32,16,3,padding=1)
        self.conv2_up = nn.Conv2d(16+16,8,3,padding=1)
```

```
        self.conv1_up = nn.Conv2d(8+8,2,3,padding=1)

        self.down = nn.AvgPool2d(kernel_size=2)
        self.up = nn.UpsamplingBilinear2d(scale_factor=2)

        self.ReLU = nn.ReLU()

    def forward(self, x):
        #encoder
        enc1=self.ReLU(self.conv1_down(x))
        enc2=self.down(enc1)
        enc2=self.ReLU(self.conv2_down(enc2))
        enc3=self.down(enc2)
        enc3=self.ReLU(self.conv3_down(enc3))
        enc4=self.down(enc3)
        enc4=self.ReLU(self.conv4(enc4))
        #decoder
        dec3=self.up(enc4)
        dec3=torch.cat([dec3, enc3], dim=1)
        dec3=self.ReLU(self.conv3_up(dec3))
        dec2=self.up(dec3)
        dec2=torch.cat([dec2, enc2], dim=1)
        dec2=self.ReLU(self.conv2_up(dec2))
        dec1=self.up(dec2)
        dec1=torch.cat([dec1, enc1], dim=1)
        dec1=self.ReLU(self.conv1_up(dec1))

        return dec1
```

To test our network, we can create an instance `net` and pass the image `im` through it with

```
net=UNet()
o=net(im)
o.shape
>>> torch.Size([1, 2, 256, 256])
```

We see that the output has two channels and a spatial resolution of 256×256, the same as the input.

Loss function

Since segmentation is a multi-output classification task, cross-entropy loss can be used. We aim to build a binary segmentation, and for that we will use cross-entropy loss with two classes, defined as

```
nn.CrossEntropyLoss()
```

There are many other losses popular for image segmentation, including dice loss and generalized dice loss [44], however, for our example classical cross-entropy loss performs well.

11.4.2 Neonatal MRI dataset

Exploring the data set

The neonatal MRI data set is available as a zip-file named *'mridata.zip'*.[7] It consists of 396 2D neonatal brain MRI images [13] in jpeg format, together with segmentations of brain structures [29].

We will start by unzipping the file with

```
from zipfile import ZipFile
with ZipFile('mridata.zip', 'r') as zipObj:
    zipObj.extractall()
```

We load the MRI image and segmentation for subject i as follows:

```
import matplotlib.pyplot as plt
import numpy as np

i = 100
image_name = "mridata/{}_t2w.jpg".format(i)
im = plt.imread(image_name)
label_name = "mridata/{}_lab.jpg".format(i)
lab = plt.imread(label_name)
```

and view them in a Matplotlib figure shown in Fig. 11.10 with

```
plt.figure(figsize=(12,4))
plt.subplot(131)
plt.imshow(im,cmap='gray')
plt.title('Neonatal MRI')
plt.subplot(132)
plt.imshow(lab, cmap='jet')
```

[7] Available from github.com/MachineLearningBiomedicalApplications/notebooks.

```
plt.title('Segmentation')
plt.subplot(133)
cortex = np.logical_and(lab>=100,lab<=150)
plt.imshow(cortex,cmap='gray')
plt.title('Cortex')
```

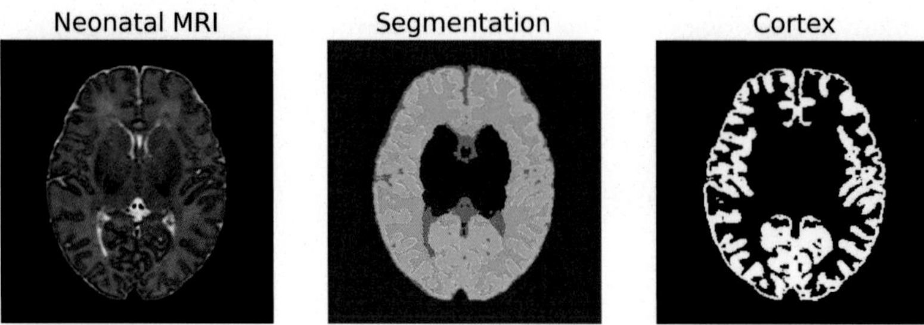

Figure 11.10 A neonatal MRI image (left), multi-label segmentation of brain structures (middle) and extracted cortical label (right).

Note that we extracted the cortical label by taking all pixels with intesities within range [100, 150]. This is because the segmentation image has been stored in jpeg format, and therefore it is rescaled and contains compression artefacts. You can change the index `i` to visualize data for different babies.

Dataset class

Previously, we have stored our datasets as numpy arrays, which we loaded into memory. We also passed the whole dataset to the stochastic gradient descent optimizer during training at each iteration. However, this is not possible in many practical situation, where the dataset is stored as individual images on the disk, and it does not fit to CPU and GPU memory because it is too large. For this reason, Pytorch offers a class `Dataset` that provides an interface to facilitate training using a custom dataset:

```
from torch.utils.data import Dataset
```

The `Dataset` provides three mandatory member functions that have to be implemented:

- `__init__` takes input parameters and initializes member variables
- `__len__` returns the length of the dataset
- `__get_item__` returns one sample from the dataset for a given index `idx`

For our neonatal MRI dataset, we have these requirements: First, we need to split it into training, validation and test set. To do that, we simply assign the first 320 (81%) subjects for training, the next 32 (8%) for validation and the remaining 44 (11%) for testing. We will aim at using batches of 16 for training and validation so we make sure that the numbers in these two sets are divisible by 16 (though this is not necessarily required).

Additionally, for each index, the image and segmentation need to be loaded from the disk and converted to Pytorch tensors of the correct shape and type. The following is the implementation that performs these tasks:

```
import numpy as np
class NeonatalDataset(Dataset):

    def __init__(self, set_type='train'):
        # split dataset into train/val/test
        nTrain=320
        nVal=32
        nTest=44
        if set_type=='train':
            self.start_idx=0
            self.len=nTrain
        if set_type=='val':
            self.start_idx=nTrain
            self.len=nVal
        if set_type=='test':
            self.start_idx=nTrain+nVal
            self.len=nTest

    def __len__(self):
        # return length of the dataset
        return self.len

    def __getitem__(self, idx):
        # load MR image
        image_name="mridata/{}_t2w.jpg".format(idx)
        image=plt.imread(image_name)
        image=image/255
        # load label
        label_name="mridata/{}_lab.jpg".format(idx)
        labels=plt.imread(label_name)
        cortex=np.logical_and(labels>=100,labels<=150)
        # convert to tensor float and shape 1x256x256
        image=torch.Tensor(image).float().unsqueeze(0)
        # convert to tensor long and shape 256x256
        cortex=torch.Tensor(cortex).long()
        # return prepared data
        data=[image, cortex]
```

```
        return data
```

Let's describe in detail what each member function does:

- `__init__` takes an input parameter `set_type` with values `'train'`, `'val'` or `'test'`, and, depending on which set we want to create, it will assign a start index `self.start_idx` and the number of samples `self.len` for this particular set;
- `__len__` returns length of the data set saved in `self.len`;
- `__get_item__` loads the image and the segmentation for the subject `idx` from the disk, processes them and converts them to a required format. The images is normalized to the range [0, 1], and the cortex label is extracted from the segmentation image.

Our training, validation and test data sets can now be created by calling

```
data_train = NeonatalDataset('train')
data_val = NeonatalDataset('val')
data_test = NeonatalDataset('test')
```

Dataloader class

The `Dataset` objects can be manipulated using the `Dataloader` class also provided by Pytorch. The `Dataloader` will create a list of batches of data samples as follows:

```
from torch.utils.data import DataLoader
data_train_loader=DataLoader(data_train,batch_size=16)
data_val_loader=DataLoader(data_val,batch_size=16)
data_test_loader=DataLoader(data_test,batch_size=16)
```

The batches can be accessed in a for loop as follows:

```
for i, (data, labels) in enumerate(data_val_loader):
    print(i)
    print(data.shape)
    print(labels.shape)
>>> 0
>>> torch.Size([16, 1, 256, 256])
>>> torch.Size([16, 256, 256])
>>> 1
>>> torch.Size([16, 1, 256, 256])
>>> torch.Size([16, 256, 256])
```

We show the example of the validation set because it contains only 32 samples and, therefore, only two batches were created. You can see that each batch contains a Pytorch tensor of 16 images with size $16 \times 1 \times 256 \times 256$, and another pytorch tensor of

16 segmentations with size $16 \times 256 \times 256$. Segmentations do not have the channel dimension since the cross-entropy loss function requires labels to be coded by integers of type `long`, with no channels needed. Similarly, the object `data_train_loader` contains 20 batches of data with size 16, and the test object `data_test_loader` contains 3 batches. You can verify that by changing the data loader object in the `for` loop above.

11.4.3 Training the segmentation model

Now, we are ready to train our model. In fact, training a UNet segmentation network is not any different from training a classifier in Sect. 11.3, except that we need to incorporate data loaders into the training loop to be able to train in batches.

Create the UNet model and the loss

We start as usual by creating the GPU device for fast training with

```
if torch.cuda.is_available():
    device = torch.device("cuda")
else: device = torch.device("cpu")
print(device)
>>> cuda
```

Next, we create the instance of a UNet network and the cross-entropy loss. Both are sent to the GPU with

```
net = UNet().to(device)
loss = nn.CrossEntropyLoss().to(device)
```

Optimizer

We could use a standard Stochastic Gradient Descent (SGD) optimizer as usual, however this time we will choose the *Adam* optimizer [25]. The Adam (Adaptive Moment Estimation) optimizer takes advantage of second-order information to improve convergence and speed up training. In our example we can observe significant improvement compared to SGD. To create the Adam optimizer, we call the Pytorch object `torch.optim.Adam` and set learning rate to 0.005 with

```
import torch.optim as optim
optimizer = optim.Adam(net.parameters(), lr=0.005)
```

Training

The training loop is very similar to what we implemented in Sect. 11.3.4. The training loop over the epochs now also contains an inner loop over the batches of the training and validation data loaders:

```
epochs = 50
train_losses=[]
val_losses=[]

for epoch in range(epochs):

    # training mode
    net.train()

    # to collect loss over the batches
    mean_ce = 0.0
    # loop over training batches
    for i, (data, label) in enumerate(data_train_loader):
        # send training data to GPU
        data = data.to(device)
        labels = label.to(device)
        # training
        optimizer.zero_grad()
        pred = net(data)
        ce = loss(pred, labels)
        ce.backward()
        optimizer.step()
        # add loss
        mean_ce += ce.item()

    # save training loss
    # divided by number of batches
    mean_ce /= 20
    train_losses.append(mean_ce)

    # validation mode
    with torch.no_grad():
        net.eval()

        # to collect loss over the batches
        mean_ce_val=0.0
        # loop over validation batches
        for i, (data, label) in enumerate(data_val_loader):
            # send validation data to GPU
            data_val = data.to(device)
```

```
            labels_val = label.to(device)
            # calculate validation loss
            pred_val = net(data_val)
            ce_val = loss(pred_val, labels_val)
            # add validation loss
            mean_ce_val += ce_val.item()

        # save validation loss
        # divided by number of batches
        mean_ce_val /= 2
        val_losses.append(mean_ce_val)

    # Print loss every 10 epochs
    if epoch % 10==0:
        s='Epoch: {}, Train loss: {:.4f}, Val Loss: {:.4f}'
        print(s.format(epoch, mean_ce, mean_ce_val))

>>> Epoch: 0, Train loss: 0.4929, Val Loss: 0.3287
>>> Epoch: 10, Train loss: 0.1993, Val Loss: 0.1888
>>> Epoch: 20, Train loss: 0.1762, Val Loss: 0.1682
>>> Epoch: 30, Train loss: 0.1683, Val Loss: 0.1621
>>> Epoch: 40, Train loss: 0.1612, Val Loss: 0.1546
```

Note that we did not use early stopping but trained for a fixed number of epochs. This is because validation loss sometimes increases a bit, but then the algorithm continues to converge. If you test different numbers of epochs, you can observe that you can get a decent result quickly, e.g., after 10–15 epochs, but the segmentation will be more accurate if training is longer. We can observe that in the plot of training and validation losses in Fig. 11.11. The plot was created using the following code:

```
plt.plot(train_losses,'b',label='train')
plt.plot(val_losses,'r',label='validation')
plt.legend(fontsize=14)
plt.xlabel('epochs',fontsize=14)
plt.ylabel('CE loss',fontsize=14)
```

11.4.4 Evaluation

Visual inspection

To check whether our network converged to a good solution, we need to visualize the results. We will now show how to predict and plot the segmentations on the test

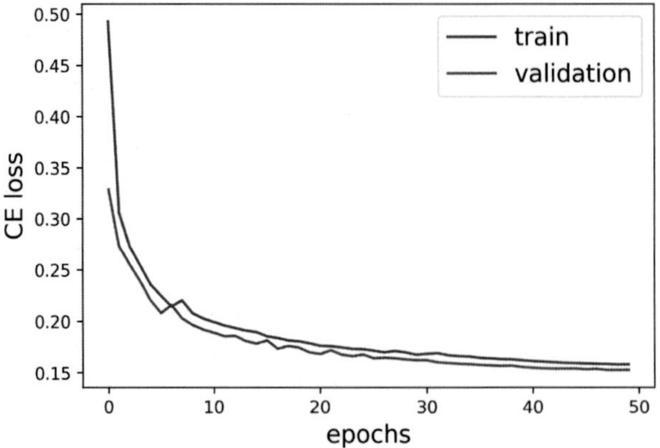

Figure 11.11 Training UNet segmentation: training and validation losses over epochs.

set. We have previously created a data loader `data_test_loader` that we will now use. We need to loop over test batches, predict the output for each batch of test data and then combine the two output maps into a label image by assigning label according to a maximum value. This is identical to a classification, but it is done on multiple output values (pixels). We will plot the predicted segmentation and the ground truth segmentation for first image in each test batch with

```
plt.figure(figsize=(9,6))
for i, (data, labels) in enumerate(data_test_loader):
    # predict the labels
    data = data.to(device)
    pred = net(data).detach().cpu()
    l_pred = torch.argmax(pred, dim=1)
    # plot first subject from each batch
    plt.subplot(2,3,i+1)
    plt.title('Predicted: batch {}'.format(i))
    plt.imshow(l_pred[0,:,:],cmap='gray')
    plt.subplot(2,3,i+1+3)
    plt.title('Ground truth: batch {}'.format(i))
    plt.imshow(labels[0,:,:],cmap='gray')
```

From this plot, shown in Fig. 11.12, we can see that the network works very well and generalized well on the test set.

Precision and recall

We have already said that binary segmentation is in fact a multi-output binary classification. The most common measure to evaluate classification is accuracy, together with

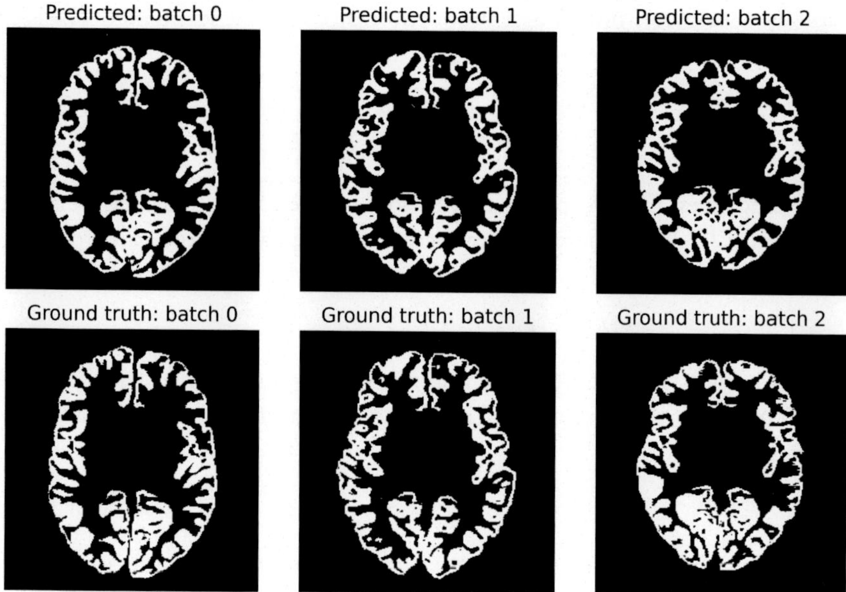

Figure 11.12 Predicted and ground-truth segmentations on the test set.

sensitivity and specificity (see Sect. 4.1.5). However, accuracy is not a very good measure to evaluate binary segmentation because a correctly classified background class is not very important to us. Note that we have quite a lot of empty space around the brain in our MR images, which is easy to segment correctly as background. This will artificially increase accuracy compared to the situation in which we cropped the images around the brain more tightly. A much more meaningful way to evaluate segmentation is to look at *precision* and *recall* because these measures always look at the foreground class, in our case, the cortical segmentation.

Precision (or positive predictive value) measures a proportion of correctly segmented voxels in the predicted segmentation. It can be numerically expressed as

$$\text{precision} = \frac{TP}{TP + FP},$$

where true positives TP are pixels of the foreground label (cortex) classified correctly and false positives FP are pixels of the background incorrectly classified as the foreground label. $TP + FP$ therefore comprises all the pixels that are predicted as a foreground label. To evaluate this measure we can use the scikit-learn object

```
sklearn.metrics.precision_score
```

Recall (or sensitivity) measures a proportion of correctly segmented pixels in the ground-truth segmentation. It can be numerically expressed as

$$\text{recall} = \frac{TP}{TP + FN},$$

where false negatives FN are pixels of the foreground class incorrectly classified as the background. $TP + FN$ therefore comprises all the pixels of the foreground in the ground-truth segmentation. To evaluate this measure, we can use scikit-learn object

```
sklearn.metrics.recall_score
```

Note that neither of these measures considers correctly classified background (true negatives). Therefore, the amount of backround surrounding the image will have no effect on these measures.

Dice score

In machine learning it is common to create a composite score from precision and recall that is called **F1 score** and is defined as

$$\text{F1} = \frac{2 \times \text{precision} \times \text{recall}}{\text{precision} + \text{recall}}.$$

This measure is known in medical image segmentation as **dice score**, and it represents the number of correctly segmented pixels of the foreground label, over the average number of foreground label pixels in the predicted and ground-truth segmentations. In fact, this score is often used as a segmentation loss instead of the cross-entropy. To evaluate dice score, we can use the scikit-learn object

```
sklearn.metrics.f1_score
```

Quantitative evaluation of the segmentation performance

We will now evaluate F1 score, precision and recall on the test set. We will calculate the scores for all individual test images and then average them. To do that we need to loop over all test batches and then over all the images in each batch:

```
from sklearn.metrics import f1_score, \
    precision_score, recall_score

# scores to calculate
f1_scores=[]
prec_scores=[]
recall_scores=[]
```

```
# loop over batches
for i, (data, labels) in enumerate(data_test_loader):
    # predict the labels for the batch
    data = data.to(device)
    pred = net(data).detach().cpu()
    l_pred = torch.argmax(pred, dim=1)
    #loop over images in the batch
    for j in range(pred.shape[0]):
        # flatten to vectors
        y=labels[j,:,:].flatten()
        y_pred=l_pred[j,:,:].flatten()
        # calculate and save the scores
        f1_scores.append(f1_score(y,y_pred))
        prec_scores.append(precision_score(y,y_pred))
        recall_scores.append(recall_score(y,y_pred))

# print out scores averaged over test images
print('f1 score:',round(np.mean(f1_scores),2))
print('precision:',round(np.mean(prec_scores),2))
print('recall:',round(np.mean(recall_scores),2))
>>> f1 score: 0.9
>>> precision: 0.94
>>> recall: 0.87
```

The performance of the segmentation network is good. Dice score (F1 score) 0.9 for the complicated structure such as cortex is quite high. Precision is higher than recall, so we can say that the network is better at not making a mistake with a positive prediction (a pixel belongs to the cortex) than with correctly identifying all the pixels that belong to the cortex in the ground truth. In other words, the network is slightly more likely to miss some cortical pixels than to assign the background pixels to the cortex.

11.4.5 Exercises

1. Implement the segmentation of cortex in 2D Neonatal MRI by following the code in this section.[8]
2. Modify the `NeonatalDataset` class to predict white matter, instead of cortex, by taking pixel values in interval $[165, 215]$ as the white matter label.

[8] Dataset, skeleton code and solution is available from github.com/MachineLearningBiomedicalApplications/notebooks.

3. Modify the code to perform multi-label segmentation of 5 classes: background (0), CSF (1), cortex (2), white matter (3), deep grey matter (4). To obtain the labels, you can process the segmentations in the `NeonatalDataset` object with

```
seg = np.around(labels/62.5,0)
```

Note that you also need to change the number of outputs of the `UNet` object to five. Evaluation also needs to be performed for each label separately. For details of how to evaluate performance of multi-label segmentation, see Sect. 4.1.5. Hint: You will need to increase the number of feature maps in the lowest-level encoder convolution and the decoder convolutions.

11.5. Conclusion

Congratulations! You have just trained and evaluated your first advanced neural network for image segmentation. And this is where the learning objectives of this book have been fully achieved. Of course, there is so much more to learn: Machine learning and deep learning, in particular, are very fast evolving fields, with new ideas, algorithms and concepts being generated every year. There are many more architectures to learn, such as attention mechanisms, visual transformers and generative adversarial networks, which are all widely used in biomedical applications. We hope that the strong foundation that you gained while studying the material in this book will motivate you to confidently explore these advanced concepts. And, as importantly, we hope that you enjoyed learning with us!

References

[1] C. Bass, M. Silva, C. Sudre, P. Tudosiu, S. Smith, E. Robinson, ICAM: interpretable classification via disentangled representations and feature attribution mapping, in: NeurIPS 2020, 2020.

[2] M. Belkin, P. Niyogi, Laplacian eigenmaps for dimensionality reduction and data representation, Neural Computation 15 (6) (2003) 1373–1396.

[3] I. Borg, P.J. Groenen, Modern Multidimensional Scaling: Theory and Applications, Springer Science & Business Media, 2005.

[4] L. Breiman, Bagging predictors, Machine Learning 24 (2) (1996) 123–140.

[5] L. Breiman, Random forests, Machine Learning 45 (1) (2001) 5–32.

[6] L. Buitinck, G. Louppe, M. Blondel, F. Pedregosa, A. Mueller, O. Grisel, V. Niculae, P. Prettenhofer, A. Gramfort, J. Grobler, R. Layton, J. VanderPlas, A. Joly, B. Holt, G. Varoquaux, API design for machine learning software: experiences from the scikit-learn project, in: ECML PKDD Workshop: Languages for Data Mining and Machine Learning, 2013, pp. 108–122.

[7] C.-C. Chang, C.-J. Lin, Libsvm: a library for support vector machines, ACM Transactions on Intelligent Systems and Technology 2 (3) (2011) 1–27.

[8] J.R. Clough, D.R. Balfour, P.K. Marsden, C. Prieto, A.J. Reader, A.P. King, MRI slice stacking using manifold alignment and wave kernel signatures, in: 2018 IEEE 15th International Symposium on Biomedical Imaging (ISBI 2018), IEEE, 2018, pp. 319–323.

[9] T.M. Cover, J.A. Thomas, et al., Entropy, relative entropy and mutual information, Elements of Information Theory 2 (1) (1991) 12–13.

[10] Antonio Criminisi, Jamie Shotton, Ender Konukoglu, Decision forests: a unified framework for classification, regression, density estimation, manifold learning and semi-supervised learning, Foundations and Trends® in Computer Graphics and Vision 7 (2–3) (2012) 81–227.

[11] D.L. Donoho, C. Grimes, Hessian eigenmaps: locally linear embedding techniques for high-dimensional data, Proceedings of the National Academy of Sciences 100 (10) (2003) 5591–5596.

[12] H. Drucker, Improving regressors using boosting techniques, in: ICML, in: Citeseer, vol. 97, 1997, pp. 107–115.

[13] A.D. Edwards, D. Rueckert, S.M. Smith, S. Abo Seada, A. Alansary, J. Almalbis, J. Allsop, J. Andersson, T. Arichi, S. Arulkumaran, M. Bastiani, D. Batalle, L. Baxter, J. Bozek, E. Braithwaite, J. Brandon, O. Carney, A. Chew, D. Christiaens, R. Chung, K. Colford, L. Cordero-Grande, S.J. Counsell, H. Cullen, J. Cupitt, C. Curtis, A. Davidson, M. Deprez, L. Dillon, K. Dimitrakopoulou, R. Dimitrova, E. Duff, S. Falconer, S.-R. Farahibozorg, S.P. Fitzgibbon, J. Gao, A. Gaspar, N. Harper, S.J. Harrison, E.J. Hughes, J. Hutter, M. Jenkinson, S. Jbabdi, E. Jones, V. Karolis, V. Kyriakopoulou, G. Lenz, A. Makropoulos, S. Malik, L. Mason, F. Mortari, C. Nosarti, R.G. Nunes, C. O'Keeffe, J. O'Muircheartaigh, H. Patel, J. Passerat-Palmbach, M. Pietsch, A.N. Price, E.C. Robinson, M.A. Rutherford, A. Schuh, S. Sotiropoulos, J. Steinweg, R.P.A.G. Teixeira, T. Tenev, J.-D. Tourier, N. Tusor, A. Uus, K. Vecchiato, L.Z.J. Williams, R. Wright, J. Wurie, J.V. Hajnal, The developing human connectome project neonatal data release, Frontiers in Neuroscience 16 (2022).

[14] B. Ehteshami Bejnordi, M. Veta, P. Johannes van Diest, B. van Ginneken, N. Karssemeijer, G. Litjens, J.A.W.M. van der Laak, CAMELYON16 consortium, Diagnostic assessment of deep learning algorithms for detection of lymph node metastases in women with breast cancer, JAMA 318 (22) (2017) 2199–2210.

[15] Y. Freund, R.E. Schapire, A decision-theoretic generalization of on-line learning and an application to boosting, Journal of Computer and System Sciences 55 (1) (1997) 119–139.

[16] J.H. Friedman, Greedy function approximation: a gradient boosting machine, The Annals of Statistics (2001) 1189–1232.

[17] K.E. Garcia, E.C. Robinson, D. Alexopoulos, D.L. Dierker, M.F. Glasser, T.S. Coalson, C.M. Ortinau, D. Rueckert, L.A. Taber, D.C. Van Essen, et al., Dynamic patterns of cortical expansion during folding of the preterm human brain, Proceedings of the National Academy of Sciences 115 (12) (2018) 3156–3161.

[18] I. Grigorescu, L. Cordero-Grande, A.D. Edwards, J. Hajnal, M. Modat, M. Deprez, Interpretable convolutional neural networks for preterm birth classification, in: Medical Imaging in Deep Learning – MIDL 2019, 2019.

[19] C.R. Harris, K.J. Millman, S.J. van der Walt, R. Gommers, P. Virtanen, D. Cournapeau, E. Wieser, J. Taylor, S. Berg, N.J. Smith, R. Kern, M. Picus, S. Hoyer, M.H. van Kerkwijk, M. Brett, A. Haldane, J.F. del Río, M. Wiebe, P. Peterson, P. Gérard-Marchant, K. Sheppard, T. Reddy, W. Weckesser, H. Abbasi, C. Gohlke, T.E. Oliphant, Array programming with NumPy, Nature 585 (7825) (Sept. 2020) 357–362.

[20] J.D. Hunter, Matplotlib: a 2D graphics environment, Computing in Science & Engineering 9 (3) (2007) 90–95.

[21] A. Hyvärinen, E. Oja, Independent component analysis: algorithms and applications, Neural Networks 13 (4–5) (2000) 411–430.

[22] S. Ioffe, C.Szegedy, Batch normalization: accelerating deep network training by reducing internal covariate shift, arXiv:1502.03167, 2015.

[23] F. Isensee, P.F. Jaeger, S.A. Kohl, J. Petersen, K.H. Maier-Hein, nnU-Net: a self-configuring method for deep learning-based biomedical image segmentation, Nature Methods 18 (2021) 203–211.

[24] K. Kamnitsas, W. Bai, E. Ferrante, S. McDonagh, M. Sinclair, N. Pawlowski, M. Rajchl, M. Lee, B. Kainz, D. Rueckert, et al., Ensembles of multiple models and architectures for robust brain tumour segmentation, in: International MICCAI Brain Lesion Workshop, Springer, 2017, pp. 450–462.

[25] Diederik P. Kingma, Jimmy Ba, Adam: A Method for Stochastic Optimization, arXiv:1412.6980, 2017.

[26] A. Kulesa, M. Krzywinski, P. Blainey, N. Altman, Sampling distributions and the bootstrap, Nature Methods 12 (2015) 477–478.

[27] B. Lakshminarayanan, A. Pritzel, C. Blundell, Simple and scalable predictive uncertainty estimation using deep ensembles, in: NeurIPS 2017, 2017.

[28] Y. LeCun, P. Haffner, L. Bottou, Y. Bengio, Object recognition with gradient-based learning, in: Shape, Contour and Grouping in Computer Vision, Springer, Berlin, Heidelberg, 1999, pp. 319–345.

[29] A. Makropoulos, I.S. Gousias, C. Ledig, P. Aljabar, A. Serag, J.V. Hajnal, A.D. Edwards, S.J. Counsell, D. Rueckert, Automatic whole brain MRI segmentation of the developing neonatal brain, IEEE Transactions on Medical Imaging 33 (9) (2014) 1818–1831.

[30] The MathWorks Inc., MATLAB version: 9.13.0 (R2022b) Natick, Massachusetts, 2022.

[31] J. O'Muircheartaigh, E.C. Robinson, M. Pietsch, T. Wolfers, P. Aljabar, L.C. Grande, R.P.A.G. Teixeira, J. Bozek, A. Schuh, A. Makropoulos, D. Batalle, J. Hutter, K. Vecchiato, J.K. Steinweg, S. Fitzgibbon, E. Hughes, A.N. Price, A. Marquand, D. Reuckert, M. Rutherford, J.V. Hajnal, S.J. Counsell, A.D. Edwards, Modelling brain development to detect white matter injury in term and preterm born neonates, Brain 143 (2) (2020) 467–479.

[32] Travis E. Oliphant, A Guide to NumPy, vol. 1, Trelgol Publishing, USA, 2006.

[33] A. Paszke, S. Gross, F. Massa, A. Lerer, J. Bradbury, G. Chanan, T. Killeen, Z. Lin, N. Gimelshein, L. Antiga, A. Desmaison, A. Kopf, E. Yang, Z. DeVito, M. Raison, A. Tejani, S. Chilamkurthy, B. Steiner, L. Fang, J. Bai, S. Chintala, Pytorch: an imperative style, high-performance deep learning library, in: H. Wallach, H. Larochelle, A. Beygelzimer, F. d'Alché-Buc, E. Fox, R. Garnett (Eds.), Advances in Neural Information Processing Systems, vol. 32, Curran Associates, Inc, 2019.

[34] F. Pedregosa, G. Varoquaux, A. Gramfort, V. Michel, B. Thirion, O. Grisel, M. Blondel, A. Müller, J. Nothman, G. Louppe, P. Prettenhofer, R. Weiss, V. Dubourg, J. Vanderplas, A. Passos, D. Cournapeau, M. Brucher, M. Perrot, E.Duchesnay, Scikit-learn: machine learning in Python, Journal of Machine Learning Research 12 (2011) 2825–2830.

[35] F. Pérez-García, R. Sparks, S. Ourselin, TorchIO: a python library for efficient loading, preprocessing, augmentation and patch-based sampling of medical images in deep learning, Computer Methods and Programs in Biomedicine (2021) 106–236.

[36] E. Puyol-Antón, B. Ruijsink, B. Gerber, M.S. Amzulescu, H. Langet, M. De Craene, J.A. Schnabel, P. Piro, A.P. King, Regional multi-view learning for cardiac motion analysis: application to identification of dilated cardiomyopathy patients, IEEE Transactions on Biomedical Engineering 66 (4) (2019) 956–966.

[37] J. Rasero, A.I. Sentis, F.-C. Yeh, T. Verstynen, Integrating across neuroimaging modalities boosts prediction accuracy of cognitive ability, PLoS Computational Biology 17 (3) (2021) e1008347.
[38] O. Ronneberger, P. Fischer, T. Brox, U-net: convolutional networks for biomedical image segmentation, in: N. Navab, J. Hornegger, W.M. Wells, A.F. Frangi (Eds.), Medical Image Computing and Computer-Assisted Intervention – MICCAI 2015 (Cham, 2015), Springer International Publishing, 2015, pp. 234–241.
[39] S.T. Roweis, L.K. Saul, Nonlinear dimensionality reduction by locally linear embedding, Science 290 (5500) (2000) 2323–2326.
[40] D.E. Rumelhart, G.E. Hinton, R.J. Williams, Learning representations by back-propagating errors, Nature 323 (6088) (1986) 533–536.
[41] G. Salimi-Khorshidi, G. Douaud, C.F. Beckmann, M.F. Glasser, L. Griffanti, S.M. Smith, Automatic denoising of functional mri data: combining independent component analysis and hierarchical fusion of classifiers, NeuroImage 90 (2014) 449–468.
[42] R.E. Schapire, Explaining adaboost, in: Empirical Inference, Springer, 2013, pp. 37–52.
[43] N. Srivastava, G. Hinton, A. Krizhevsky, I. Sutskever, R. Salakhutdinov, Dropout: a simple way to prevent neural networks from overfitting, Journal of Machine Learning Research 15 (56) (2014) 1929–1958.
[44] Carole H. Sudre, Wenqi Li, Tom Vercauteren, Sebastien Ourselin, Cardoso M. Jorge, Generalised dice overlap as a deep learning loss function for highly unbalanced segmentations, in: Lu Zhi, Cardoso M. Jorge, Tal Arbel, Gustavo Carneiro, Tanveer Syeda-Mahmood, João Manuel R.S. Tavares, Mehdi Moradi, Andrew Bradley, Hayit Greenspan, João Paulo Papa, Anant Madabhushi, Jacinto C. Nascimento, Jaime S. Cardoso, Vasileios Belagiannis (Eds.), Deep Learning in Medical Image Analysis and Multimodal Learning for Clinical Decision Support, Springer International Publishing, Cham, 2017, pp. 240–248.
[45] Y. Taoudi-Benchekroun, D. Christiaens, I. Grigorescu, O. Gale-Grant, A. Schuh, M. Pietsch, A. Chew, N. Harper, S. Falconer, T. Poppe, E. Hughes, J. Hutter, A.N. Price, J.-D. Tournier, L. Cordero-Grande, S.J. Counsell, D. Rueckert, T. Arichi, J.V. Hajnal, A.D. Edwards, M. Deprez, D. Batalle, Predicting age and clinical risk from the neonatal connectome, NeuroImage 257 (2022) 119319.
[46] J.B. Tenenbaum, V.d. Silva, J.C. Langford, A global geometric framework for nonlinear dimensionality reduction, Science 290 (5500) (2000) 2319–2323.
[47] L. Van der Maaten, G. Hinton, Visualizing data using t-sne, Journal of Machine Learning Research 9 (2008) 11.
[48] B.S. Veeling, J. Linmans, J. Winkens, T. Cohen, M. Welling, Rotation equivariant CNNs for digital pathology, in: A.F. Frangi, J.A. Schnabel, C. Davatzikos, C. Alberola-López, G. Fichtinger (Eds.), Medical Image Computing and Computer Assisted Intervention – MICCAI 2018 (Cham, 2018), Springer International Publishing, 2018, pp. 210–218.
[49] U. von Luxburg, A tutorial on spectral clustering, Statistics and Computing 17 (4) (2007) 395–416.
[50] Wes McKinney, Data structures for statistical computing in Python, in: Stéfan van der Walt, Jarrod Millman (Eds.), Proceedings of the 9th Python in Science Conference, 2010, pp. 56–61.
[51] Z. Zhang, J. Wang, Mlle: modified locally linear embedding using multiple weights, Advances in Neural Information Processing Systems 19 (2006).

Index

D

E

F

N

O

P

Q

R

Printed in the United States
by Baker & Taylor Publisher Services